James Bond
FAQ

Series Editor: Robert Rodriguez

James Bond FAQ

All That's Left to Know About Everyone's Favorite Superspy

Tom DeMichael

APPLAUSE
THEATRE & CINEMA BOOKS
An Imprint of Hal Leonard Corporation

Published in 2013 by Applause Theatre & Cinema Books
An Imprint of Hal Leonard Corporation
7777 West Bluemound Road
Milwaukee, WI 53213

Trade Book Division Editorial Offices
33 Plymouth St., Montclair, NJ 07042

All photos are from the personal collection of the author.

The FAQ series was conceived by Robert Rodriguez and developed with Stuart Shea.

Printed in the United States of America

Book design by Snow Creative Services

Library of Congress Cataloging-in-Publication Data

DeMichael, Tom.
   James Bond FAQ : all that's left to know about everyone's favorite superspy /
Tom DeMichael.
      pages cm
   Includes bibliographical references and index.
   ISBN 978-1-55783-856-8
   1. James Bond films—Miscellanea. 2. Bond, James (Fictitious character)—
Miscellanea. I. Title.
   PN1995.9.J3D47 2013
   791.43'651—dc23

                                                                    2012039417

www.applausebooks.com

To Sean, George, Roger, Timothy, Pierce, Daniel,
and all the rest who kept us entertained for a couple of hours

Contents

Foreword

I was delighted to be asked to pen a few words to open Tom's book on all things 007, and even more so when I read the opening page and saw that my character Sylvia Trench was mentioned! But then again, it seems quite fitting she should be mentioned first, as she was the very first Bond girl.

Although my fifty-odd-year career has encompassed scores of films, TV series, and many theater roles, it is for James Bond that I am primarily remembered; not that I mind, of course, as to be associated with anything successful is an actor's joy. But it's made me realize the power of James Bond.

The popularity of the films, in this the series' fiftieth-anniversary year, is greater than ever, and people's thirst for knowledge about all things 007 is equally great . . . and Tom will certainly help quench it with this fact-filled tome. Having just penned my own autobiography, *The First Lady of Bond*, I know too well the research and work involved in compiling a book, and I take my hat off to Tom for bringing together the facts, figures, and personalities in a very interesting, immensely readable, and delightfully pleasing format.

What else is there to say, aside from:

"I admire your writing, Mr. . . . ?"

Eunice Gayson
July 2012

Acknowledgments

When assembling a book, it's impossible to write in a vacuum. (Let's face it, you'd hardly last past the first page without any air.) Seriously, putting together a book like this is the result of many, many people who donate their time, knowledge, experience, and resources to the cause.

I am eternally grateful and offer thanks to the following folks:

Adam Savage and Dan Tapster from *MythBusters*
Cathy Hoyle from Beyond International Limited
Doug Redenius from the Ian Fleming Foundation
Terry Reed from Otter FX
Marybeth Keating, Jessica Burr, Gary Morris, Jaime Nelson, and John Cerullo from Applause Books for their direction and backing along the way
Rob Rodriguez for his guidance and trust

and for who they are and what they make me:

Wife Paula (my personal M)
Sons Anthony and Alex (my Q and R)
Dad (who dressed in a white dinner jacket at my wedding so he looked like Blofeld)
Daughter-in-law Ian and grandson Charlie
Mark Poncer for his assistance, his deep interest in 007, and access to his vast body of knowledge and unique references
Tom Edinger for his encouragement and never-ending friendship

and to all the Bond fans in the world, who have made this the greatest fifty years in film.

Introduction

Dr. Know (a Lot)

Bond. James Bond.

Why, nearly fifty years after that simple response to Sylvia Trench's query of who her casino opponent was in *Dr. No*, does the film franchise of James Bond continue to raise the pulses of pop culture fans around the world?

Why does a film that opens with the sight of a rifled gun barrel following an unsuspecting man walking in its crosshairs, accompanied by staccato brassy horn stabs, cause followers to perk up like hungry children hearing the bells of an ice cream truck coming down the street?

What is it about the film character of James Bond that tricks us to believe that we are driving along the expressway in a sleek, silver, gadget-filled Aston Martin DB5 instead of the rusting old hulk of our SUV, while dressed in a crisp white formal dinner jacket and black bow tie instead of khaki shorts and a faded blue golf shirt with a tattered armpit?

Put simply—why is the world so in love with James Bond?

While psychologists may have the correct answers, laymen can only guess what is so captivating about the life and loves of Commander Bond. It might be the time of his birth, the world in which he lives, the brand of his vodka, or an amalgam of all those things.

Writer Ian Fleming created the fictional character of James Bond in the mid-1950s, a time of escalating Cold War fears and swiftly developing technology. Bond was an elite member of the British Secret Service, known as MI6—an agency committed to international intelligence and espionage. As an agent who was "licensed to kill," Bond held the assigned serial number 007. His world was populated with a host of memorable characters, including Bond's boss, known simply as M; Miss Moneypenny, M's secretary; Q, the source of Bond's many ingenious gadgets; scheming villains such as Auric Goldfinger and Ernst Stavro Blofeld; and a bevy of attractive women, like the suggestively named Pussy Galore.

By the time Fleming's sixth novel, *Dr. No*, became the first feature film, premiering in England in October 1962 (although it would be a full seven months before the film reached American screens), global technology and world politics had continued to grow at a dizzying rate. The radio, once a fine piece of furniture that occupied a prominent place in the living room, now fit in the palm of one's hand. People talked of computers that could store millions of bits of data and perform thousands of computations in the blink of an eye. Communications that once traveled by coaxial cable now bounced off satellites that orbited thousands of miles around the Earth. America had its first president *not* born in the nineteenth century, Russia had placed the first man into space, and ideology around the world seemed divided between democracy and Communism. Khrushchev threatened to bury Americans, conceptually if not physically. Russia was placing offensive missiles a mere ninety miles from American shores on a little island called Cuba. Who could possibly save the free world from such impending doom?

James Bond.

Life in America, and in much of the free world, was defined by where you lived, what you drove, what you ate, and what you did. Americans, who for decades had tilled the soil, grown the grains, slaughtered the hogs, collected the eggs, and brought them all to market, had moved to the city. There, they lived in a world of asphalt and concrete, a world of skyscraping office buildings and spaghetti-bowl expressways. For many, it was called "the rat race."

In and around those cities, mass transit had given way to one- and two-car families. Many drove quaint four-door sedans and eight-seat station wagons, some with a busted tailgate. Madison Avenue, recognizing the drabness of it all, encouraged everyone to let a rental car company put them "in the driver's seat" and to let a gasoline company "put a tiger in their tank."

As life continued this humdrum yet hectic pace, fast-food emporiums dotted the landscape like weeds. Wholesome, home-cooked meals turned into hamburgers, fried chicken, and pizza—all in a moment's notice. If that wasn't appealing, there were always TV dinners. Soft drinks came in every flavor and color. The alternate choice to a cola was the "uncola," and every one of them had a diet counterpart.

After a hard day at the office, the breadwinner drove home, ate the fast food, sipped the soft drink or brewed beverage of choice, plopped down on the couch, and clicked on the boob tube. Here was the never-ending selection of Westerns, sitcoms, variety shows, sporting events, and news programs to while away the hours until it was bedtime. The next day, it all started again.

Bear in mind, there was absolutely nothing wrong with this type of lifestyle. Many considered it "the American dream." But if it all seemed a bit too mundane, why wouldn't someone want to escape to a world wholly unlike this one? A world where martinis were shaken, not stirred, while nibbling on caviar and foie gras; a world where its people drove a Bentley, a Rolls-Royce Phantom III, or Aston Martin DB5; a world where its characters traveled to exotic and famous locations like London, Jamaica, Istanbul, Japan, and Miami. Not to mention, a world where one got the chance to save millions of lives, billions of dollars, and make love to the most beautiful women imaginable. Who lived in a world like that?

James Bond.

The attraction of James Bond is simple. He gets to do things that most of the world doesn't do. Or can't do. Or chooses not to do. So, as is so often the case, the moviegoing public takes about two hours out of their everyday lives to don the tuxedo (including the shoulder holster that holds the Beretta or Walther PPK) and walk in the patent leather Savile Row shoes of James Bond. Essentially, men want to *be* him and women want to be *with* him.

There must be an awful lot of these folks. The twenty-three "official" James Bond theatrical releases have grossed nearly $6 billion worldwide since that fateful day in 1962 (more on what "official" and "unofficial" mean later on, so sit tight). The latest three films alone accounted for more than half a billion dollars *each* (enough to make Blofeld's mouth water). And those figures don't include video rentals, tape and DVD sales, not to mention untold billions of dollars in James Bond merchandising.

This book that you hold in your hands can only hope to scratch the surface of the cinematic legend of James Bond. Yes, the focus will be films, although there will be references along the way to Ian Fleming and the others who penned the novels and short stories. (Although their relevance to the films ended after the first four or five flicks, save for borrowing a title for title's sake. At least until the refreshing reboot of the Bond film series in 2006 that featured Daniel Craig came along.) The literary trip contained within will travel through the gadgets, girls, guns, gangsters, and goings-on of our favorite secret agent.

As 007 himself might offer, "Cheers!"

The Word Is Not Enough

James Bond in the Books of Ian Fleming

Before he graced the screen, James Bond was a product of words. For author and creator Ian Fleming, those words were his Bond. His detailed descriptions placed pictures in the reader's mind, painting vivid images of the British secret agent and his adventures. Much of Bond and his escapades were drawn from the author's life experiences. Yet Fleming maintained a clear distance between the world in which he and his readers lived, and the world of James Bond.

Ian Fleming

Born on May 28, 1908, Ian Lancaster Fleming was the second of four boys born to Valentine and Eve Fleming in London. The family was very well off, as father Valentine became a Conservative member of Parliament. When he was killed in a World War I battle in France, the obituary was penned by a good friend and comrade-in-arms named Winston Churchill.

Ian attended the prestigious Eton College as a teen, where a combination of skill, strength, and perseverance gained him recognition as an outstanding athlete. His track and field skills twice found him named the Victor Ludorum—Champion of the Games—a rare accomplishment. Fleming's academics, however, were not of the same high standards, and he moved on shortly to the Royal Military Academy at Sandhurst, then to schools of higher education in Austria, Germany, and Switzerland.

Never finishing his school endeavors, Fleming wound up as a journalist for the Reuters news service in 1931. His time spent with the service included a stint in Moscow, where he improved his already ample talent for languages. By 1933, the Fleming family decided the banking world would better suit Ian. He tried wearing the hat of a banker, then a stockbroker,

Fleming. Ian Fleming.

both of which did nothing for him except keep him connected with an array of lady friends in affluent clubs.

In early 1939, certain agencies began vetting Fleming for a position with British Naval Intelligence. His diverse background served as a perfect foundation for what he would need to address as the Second World War opened in Europe. Ian Fleming found himself commissioned as a lieutenant commander in the Royal Naval Volunteer Reserves, centered in the highest of secret affairs for the war effort.

He traveled Europe and North Africa during those years, forging a plan to repel the Germans from Gibraltar if they tried to invade through Spain. The plan's name? Operation Golden Eye (sounds familiar). He also developed hundreds of intelligence specialists into a group called 30 Assault Unit, who moved quietly to collect foreign weapons, cyphers, and other vital military artifacts. A naval conference in 1942 brought him to Jamaica—a land that grabbed him and would become his vacation home after the war. All his activities were performed as the assistant to the Director of Naval Intelligence, Admiral John Godfrey.

Fleming left the admiral and the war in 1945, joining the London *Times* newspaper as its Foreign Manager. As part of the deal, he negotiated a two-month vacation during the winter every year. On those holidays, he would stay in the home he built in Jamaica—he called it Goldeneye (still sounds familiar). Always the ladies' man, Fleming often spent his time there with Anne Charteris, who was Lady O'Neill when he first met her and started keeping time in the 1930s, was Lady Rothermere in the 1940s as they continued to keep time, and finally became Anne Fleming when they married in March 1952.

Bond Is Born

Another important event in March 1952—about a week before the wedding—was Ian Fleming's completion of his first novel. Its title was *Casino Royale,* and it was forged in the mold of adventure stories penned by Raymond Chandler and Dashiell Hammett. Instead of alliterative and catchy names like Sam Spade, Nick and Nora Charles, and Philip Marlowe, Fleming named his hero James Bond. He felt the name was "suitably flat and colourless," as he said in a 1964 interview with *Playboy.* Fleming noted the name of James Bond was that of a famous ornithologist, who had published a book on birds of the West Indies.

Curiously, Fleming had also been close to a well-known Bond family while at prep school. They owned a large estate next to it and—not so coincidentally—had an ancestor named John from the late 1500s who spied on behalf of the Queen of England. John Bond, according to a journal kept by his son, adopted a motto for his family—*Orbis Non Sufficit.* What's that mean? The World Is Not Enough. Fleming never saw the journal, but it's believed he heard the tales of Bond from family members while he was in school and felt the maxim was appropriate for his Bond family.

The apple of James Bond did not fall far from the tree of Ian Fleming. The author easily incorporated much of his own experiences, likes, dislikes, and persona into the character of 007. Fleming shared these traits with his fictitious secret agent: an affinity for gambling and golf, a favorite breakfast of scrambled eggs, attendance at Eton College, being ruggedly handsome, a pushed-in nose, overt sexuality, and a taste for exotic cars, among others. They all created a rich, three-dimensional individual that readers took to heart with the very first Fleming novel.

British publishing house Jonathan Cape Ltd. published Fleming's *Casino Royale* in 1953, and it was an immediate hit. The print run of nearly five thousand copies sold out in a month's time, and two more printings were ordered within a year's time. First editions of the hardcover are now priced at $40,000 and up. American publisher Macmillan released the book the following year, following rejection from three other publishers. The American market was much slower to jump on the Bond bandwagon, and when *Casino Royale* was released as an American paperback in 1955, it was retitled *You Asked for It* (sales were still lackluster).

However, readers in the UK couldn't get enough of 007, and Fleming proceeded to publish a Bond book every year through 1966 (the last two posthumously). Here's the complete Bond book breakdown:

Title	UK Release Date
Casino Royale	1953
Live and Let Die	1954
Moonraker	1955
Diamonds Are Forever	1956
From Russia with Love	1957
Doctor No	1958
Goldfinger	1959
For Your Eyes Only (short stories)	1960

    "From a View to a Kill"

    "For Your Eyes Only"

    "Quantum of Solace"

    "Risico"

    "The Hildebrand Rarity"

Thunderball	1961
The Spy Who Loved Me	1962
On Her Majesty's Secret Service	1963
You Only Live Twice	1964
The Man with the Golden Gun	1965
Octopussy & The Living Daylights (short stories)	1966

    "Octopussy"

    "The Living Daylights"

    "The Property of a Lady"

    "007 in New York"

America and the Rest of the World Discover Bond

The American market finally perked up in the early 1960s. In a March 1961 *Life* magazine article, President Kennedy mentioned that *From Russia with Love* was one of his favorite books. America was thoroughly impressed—and influenced by the popular politician's choice of reading material. Then the first 007 film, *Dr. No*, hit the screens the following year. After that, the entire world was hooked. Novel after novel sold thousands of copies.

The author's enjoyment of that adulation was short-lived. Among the traits he shared with Bond were the self-destructive attraction to heavy smoking, heavy drinking, and womanizing. As a young student at Sandhurst, he contracted gonorrhea from a London tart. He admitted to smoking three to three-and-a-half packs of gold-ringed cigarettes from Morland's of Grosvenor Street. In his mid-fifties, Fleming still drank four or more gin drinks every day.

The abuse led to a heart attack in 1962, although doctors had diagnosed heart disease when he was only thirty-eight. Unable to work at a typewriter,

Fleming handwrote a story for his ten-year-old son, Caspar. It was all about a flying car called Chitty Chitty Bang Bang.

As his convalescence progressed, the author saw the first two 007 films and he was able to visit the shooting sets of the first three films. His film deal earned $100,000 per picture, plus 5 percent of the profits. Fleming did have the chance to meet Sean Connery once *Dr. No* started shooting and really wasn't impressed. The author called him "an overgrown stuntman," although their relationship was cordial. As Fleming saw more of Connery as 007, he accepted him and, in a nod to Connery, even gave his secret agent a Scotch heritage in the last few novels.

The manuscript for *The Man with the Golden Gun,* not at all to Fleming's liking, was finished at the beginning of 1964. *Goldfinger* had just wrapped principal photography when Ian Fleming suffered another major heart

Bond-like pose by Fleming.

attack in August 1964—this time fatal. It was son Caspar's twelfth birthday. Fleming was only fifty-six years old.

At the time of Fleming's death, his twelve Bond books had totaled thirty million copies sold around the globe. The last two were released in 1965 and 1966, making a total of fourteen James Bond books. Since then, the 007 books penned by Ian Fleming have sold an amazing one hundred million copies worldwide, making him one of the world's best-selling authors.

2

Live and Let's Spy

The Men Playing James Bond

History has recorded some of man's greatest questions—all seemingly without answers: Which came first—the chicken or the egg? What is the meaning of life? Is there really a God? Is there life after death? Are we alone in the universe? And, of course . . .

Who is the best James Bond?

Connery. Sean Connery. (OK, let's put that whole thing away right now.)

Sean Connery

Of course, there are those who will disagree and cast their vote for men named Moore, Brosnan, Craig, and more. (No, we didn't mention him twice.) Everyone is entitled to their own opinion—after all, this *is* America. While all six actors who have officially portrayed James Bond have done creditable jobs of varying value, one could argue that Connery's interpretation of 007 has been the best of the bunch. Like the others, his Bond was appropriately suave, civil, cruel, fearless, anxious, amusing, charming, clever, and any other demeanor the situation required. But his was just a bit more so.

And he was the first.

Born on August 25, 1930, in Edinburgh, Scotland, Thomas Sean Connery was the elder of two sons born to Effie and Joseph Connery, a working-class family. The young lad slept in the bottom drawer of his family's dresser until he was eight and started working a year later, delivering milk and assisting the local butcher. He quit school at thirteen and continued a series of menial jobs, including polishing coffins, posing near-nude for artists, and working day labor. He joined the Royal Navy at age sixteen, but had to leave three years later due to a painful ulcer. His hobby of bodybuilding led to him placing third in the 1950 Mr. Universe competition.

Connery's rough good looks and imposing physique led to bit parts in theater, including a road production of *South Pacific*. Bitten by the acting bug, he turned down an offer to play pro football (soccer) for the

Sean Connery.

Manchester United club, figuring his athletic career would be over by the time he reached the age of thirty. He continued with roles onstage and British television, including the lead in BBC's *Requiem for a Heavyweight*. His first film role was uncredited, as he appeared with Errol Flynn in *Lilacs in the Spring* in 1954. By 1957, Connery had graduated to American television, where he appeared as a luggage-toting Italian porter on an episode of the *Jack Benny Show*. The actor continued to appear in minor, go-nowhere roles, until Walt Disney cast him as the romantic lead in the 1959 fantasy film *Darby O'Gill and the Little People* (perhaps fittingly, the very first film I had the chance to see in a movie theater, as my mom sought to escape the heat of the sweltering Chicago suburbs that summer).

It would appear that I was not the only one that saw the Disney film that summer. According to some published accounts, movie producer Albert R. Broccoli (or his wife, say some) took note of the young and handsome Connery in *Darby O'Gill and the Little People*. Following a failed contest in search of cinema's first James Bond, the producers selected the sexy Scot to introduce 007 to the world. (While the contest had been won by a print model named Peter Anthony, it was quickly established that he was not up to the iconic part by any means. There is no word as to what became of Anthony or his consolation prize, a supposed on-screen appearance in *Dr. No.*)

Yet, perhaps understandably so, Connery was reluctant to accept the role at first. Interviewed for the November 1965 issue of *Playboy* magazine, he stated, "I didn't want to do it, because I could see that properly made, it would have to be the first of a series and I wasn't sure I wanted to get involved in that and the contract that would go with it. Contracts choke you, and I wanted to be free." That aside, Connery would go on to make the first five Bond films across the next five years. While his first, *Dr. No*, paid him a salary of $16,500, he was making three-quarters of a million dollars (plus a major percentage of the merchandising take) by the time his contract apparently choked him with *You Only Live Twice*. He'd had enough and left the franchise, making a few films that didn't exactly set box-office records. (For example, he starred with Richard Harris in *The Molly Maguires* in 1970, a film budgeted at $11 million. It brought in slightly above $1 million in US theaters.)

The Bonds That Followed

It is without question that Sean Connery had set the pace in the relay race of the James Bond film series. Having left his acting style and physical presence stamped all over the character, it would have been difficult for anyone to follow up with a performance that would be equal or better than his. That is not to say that those who followed provided an inferior interpretation of Bond. It's just that their performances were not the same as Connery's, and that's what the moviegoers of the world had seen. Quoting the age-old song: "How you going to keep them down on the farm, after they've seen Par-ee?" (Not quite the same as: "Rah-rah, oh-mah-mah . . .")

No actor, regardless of acting talent, physical presence, sexual magnetism, and awards on the shelf, could have properly filled the vacant role in Saltzman and Broccoli's *On Her Majesty's Secret Service*. As the producers had done ten years before, a search had been started for James Bond. Another unknown would become the next 007. From hundreds of candidates, five finalists remained.

- Robert Campbell—New to the film world in 1969, he would show up in a few action films in the 1980s.
- Hans de Vries—A bit-part player, he appeared as an extra in Blofeld's control room in *You Only Live Twice.*
- George Lazenby—Featured in British print and television ads, including the role of "Big Fry," hawking Fry's Turkish Delight chocolate bar.
- John Richardson—Previously starred in Hammer's *One Million Years B.C.*, opposite Raquel Welch, in 1966.
- Anthony Rogers—Played the part of Sir Dinadan in the musical *Camelot,* one of 1967's biggest cinema hits.

George Lazenby

George Lazenby might as well have been named "Laurence Olivier" when he accepted the thankless task of taking the Bond baton from Connery in 1969. Lazenby is often handed the dirty end of the stick when his portrayal of Bond is examined. But look at it this way—when the producers were first looking to fill the role in 1960, no one had seen or heard the character of James Bond on the big screen. But now the decade had made Bond (and Connery) one of the world's most recognizable visages. Who could match that?

Lazenby was born George Robert on September 5, 1939, in New South Wales, Australia. The only child of George Edward and Sheila Lazenby, George grew up in a rural area known as Goulburn. He liked to ride bikes, was known as a bit of an upstart, and, not surprisingly, liked to play with guns and knives. Lazenby enlisted in the Australian army after high school, where he earned the rank of sergeant and became skilled in martial arts like judo.

Following his discharge, he moved to England, settling in London in 1964 and taking various jobs while seeking to become a male model. His break came when photographer Chard Jenkins saw him working at a car dealership and suggested he use his rugged good looks to pose for the print medium. Lazenby was soon appearing in cigarette ads and became known as the "European Marlboro Man." A chance meeting with a talent agent led to an opportunity to audition for the open role of James Bond.

The brash Australian was only twenty-nine and showed up at the London casting office one day sans appointment, sporting a Rolex watch as well as a haircut from Sean Connery's barber and a suit from Sean Connery's tailor. Turned away, he showed up again some days later and finally connected with producer Harry Saltzman. But, for some reason, Lazenby fed him a load of baloney, claiming to be an expert skier, an expert motorsports driver, an experienced actor in European and Asian films. When Saltzman asked

the actor to meet *On Her Majesty's Secret Service* director Peter Hunt, Lazenby got cold feet and—fibbing some more—excused himself for a nonexistent modeling job in France. But Saltzman was hooked and wrote Lazenby a check for £500 to stick around. When he finally did meet with Hunt, Lazenby had

George Lazenby.

to come clean and admit that he was no actor. Hunt believed the opposite, considering Lazenby had gotten this far on a ruse—of course, he was an actor!

Screen testing got underway, with Lazenby getting £150 a week to work with other performers. The resulting rushes were somewhat painful, especially for former British pro wrestler Yuri Borienko, who was working as a stuntman during the process. During one take, Lazenby accidentally popped the grappler in the nose, breaking it. Folks on the film were summarily impressed (Borienko got to stick around, appearing in *On Her Majesty's Secret Service* as one of archvillain Blofeld's henchmen). After four months of grueling work, the fun would now begin, as George Lazenby was officially announced as the new James Bond for *On Her Majesty's Secret Service*.

Just as Lazenby's aggressive arrogance had served him well in getting the part of 007, it would lead to the shortest tenure as the film world's biggest secret agent. In a 2011 television interview on BBC4, costar Diana Rigg says Lazenby thought he was "a film star, immediately . . . he was really difficult. He definitely was the architect of his demise as a film star." But to set one thing straight—a legendary tale has Rigg deliberately eating garlic prior to lovemaking scenes with Lazenby, in order to make the situations as uncomfortable as possible for the new Bond. Both actors agree this is nothing but a typical exaggeration by the press. The actual story: The actress ate some liver pate that contained garlic in the Pinewood commissary one day, then stood up and kiddingly yelled to George across the room, "I've just eaten garlic; I hope you have, too." Both claim to have, at the very least, a civil respect and liking for each other to this day.

By his own admission, Lazenby was looking forward to the 007 role, largely for the perks of money and women that obviously went along with it. Yet despite rumors to the contrary, the producers were willing to offer the nascent thespian a long-term seven-film contract. Lazenby, however, backed out on his own choice, for several reasons. One, he received (and heeded) some bad advice from close friend and "advisor" Ronin O'Rahilly (well known as the father of pirate radio, starting the British broadcast vessel *Radio Caroline* in 1964). O'Rahilly suggested that rough-and-tumble movie characters like James Bond were definitely on the way out. In a world torn between "peace and love" and the horrors of the Vietnam War, there would seemingly be no place for 007. Secondly, Lazenby himself felt out of place among the bellbottoms and shaggy hair of the world as the swinging 1970s were beginning. He didn't enjoy going into bars and public places with short hair and straight-legged pants, standing out in the crowd—in the wrong way, he felt.

For the most part, the initial reaction to George Lazenby was not very kind, with some British reviews stating Lazenby was "not a good actor," and "looks . . . like a size four foot in a size ten gumboot." Others sided with him, if weakly, lauding him with adjectives like "casual, pleasant, satisfactory" and "handsome." Time has healed some of the viewing wounds, as many now realize how difficult the task at hand must have been.

Sean Connery Returns

Sean Connery's absence from the 007 role lasted exactly one film. After *On Her Majesty's Secret Service,* producers Saltzman and Broccoli signed handsome American actor John Gavin to play 007, but then dangled a carrot in front of the original actor's nose that few could have refused: Return as 007 in *Diamonds Are Forever* for a salary of more than $1 million (plus, once again, a major cut of the profit pie). What's more, film distribution company United Artists agreed to back two of Connery's future film production projects. Gavin, his contract paid in full by the producers, dropped out and Connery dropped in.

This is not to say that Connery was greedy. In fact, he donated his salary for *Diamonds Are Forever* to founding the Scottish International Educational Trust, a charity that would provide academic scholarships to deserving Scot students. The organization continues to this day, with Connery annually contributing a significant amount to the fund. His work led to the honor of knighthood, as Connery added "Sir" to the front of his name in July 2000.

Having played the British agent six times and reaching forty-one years of age, Sean Connery finally said "Never again" in 1971.

(Until opportunity knocked once again, twelve years later—and outside the official franchise—with *Never Say Never Again.* More about that in chapter 9.)

No matter, the juggernaut known as James Bond continued, with Saltzman and Broccoli remaining at the helm. And, finally, third time would be the charm for actor Roger Moore.

Roger Moore

When Saltzman and Broccoli were getting the Bond franchise underway in 1961, the fair and dapper Moore was heavily considered (supposedly given the OK by Ian Fleming himself). But the actor was already attached to the television series *The Saint,* which would soon become his trademark. Again, when Connery said "Never again" (for the first time) in 1967, Moore was all set to make the next Bond entry, which was to be *The Man with the*

Golden Gun. Scheduled to shoot in Cambodia, political turmoil in the area created numerous delays. When the coast was clear, the role of 007 went to Lazenby, as Moore was now attached to other projects.

Roger George Moore was born in London on October 14, 1927. His dad, George, was a cop; his mom, Lily, stayed at home, as Roger was their only offspring. Growing up, young Roger enjoyed art and worked for a short while in a London animation studio. The eighteen-year-old got a small uncredited part as a Roman soldier in *Caesar and Cleopatra,* starring Claude Rains and Vivien Leigh. Moore was spotted by assistant director Brian Desmond Hurst, who offered to send the young man to the prestigious Royal Academy

Roger Moore.

of Dramatic Arts (referred to as RADA). While there, he studied with other promising performers like Lois Maxwell (the future Miss Moneypenny). As World War II ended, Moore was drafted into the Royal Army, where he became an officer and part of the entertainment unit. When his service was finished, Moore took another small part in a film called *Trottie True* (also known as *The Gay Lady,* and directed by—no surprise—Brian Desmond Hurst). The 1949 film paired Moore with a man who would someday have a golden gun, Scaramanga—Christopher Lee, who also had a small role in the flick.

Into the 1950s, Moore's success grew, slowly but steadily, as he split his work between stage, film, and television. In 1957, he gained the title role in the worldwide syndicated TV show *Ivanhoe*—the first of several heroic roles in his career. Two years later, Moore would costar with Jack Kelly and James Garner in the hit American TV western *Maverick,* playing their English dandy cousin, Beauregarde Maverick. He left the show to star in the British ITC Productions syndicated series *The Saint* as debonair do-gooder Simon Templar. It was a role that would keep him busy throughout the 1960s.

Roger Moore kicked off the 1970s by teaming with superstar Tony Curtis for one season of another ITC show, *The Persuaders.* The two were British and American playboys, teamed up to solve cold cases for the police. Not surprisingly, Moore's character drove an Aston Martin. The driving experience would pay off, as Saltzman and Broccoli finally got Moore into the 007 role once Connery was done in *Diamonds Are Forever*.

Say what you will, Roger Moore was determined to make the role of 007 his own (hairless chest notwithstanding). In a 2008 issue of the British edition of *Gentlemen's Quarterly*, Moore admitted, "I played James Bond in a certain way because I found the character unbelievable." The result was, to many, a tongue-in-cheek Bond; it was a Bond that constantly winked at the audience. Many moviegoers didn't like it one bit. But Moore was fully aware of that. In a 2008 edition of the London newspaper *The Telegraph*, Moore stated, "I'm the worst Bond, according to the Internet. Generally hated! I was too funny, too light. Didn't take it seriously enough." Like it or not, Roger Moore would be James Bond for the next seven films, starting with *Live and Let Die* in 1973.

Moore's last stint as 007, perhaps a bit out of breath, was *A View to a Kill* in 1985. At age fifty-eight, he had left a clear stamp on the character of James Bond (like it or not). Never one to take himself too seriously, he continued to appear in forgettable films like *Fire, Ice and Dynamite* in 1990 and *Spice World* in 1997. But, like Connery before him, playing the iconic role of James Bond gave Roger Moore the leverage to make a difference in the world. At the urging of friend and actress Audrey Hepburn, Moore became deeply involved in UNICEF, a charity devoted to helping children around the world. His fund-raising efforts raised millions of dollars in relief, and Moore was knighted for his work in June 2003.

The Bond film franchise was now nearly twenty-five years old, and the world had changed quite a bit in that period of time. The Berlin Wall, a solemn symbol of communism and the Cold War, was barely one year old when *Dr. No* was released in Britain in 1962. Now, as the late 1980s approached, the Wall and the ideology along with it were ready to crumble. Free love and sex without guilt in the 1960s and 1970s had earned a serious rethinking following the plague of AIDS that engulfed the world in the decade. If 007 never worried about unprotected sex in the 1960s, it sure gave him pause to consider safe sex now. America had elected a Harvard scholar, Pulitzer Prize winner, and World War II hero as president to start the 1960s. By the 1980s, the country was now being run by a former Hollywood actor who once costarred with a chimpanzee. Yes, the world had certainly changed.

It was decided that Bond, too, should change—or at least change back to what he had once been. Gone would be the self-deprecating, fourth-wall-busting Bond that Moore had championed. The next Bond would be dark and brooding, with a streak of sadism lurking beneath his marching orders. Enter, stage left: Timothy Dalton.

Timothy Dalton

Born Timothy Peter Dalton on March 21, 1946 (although there is some question about the year), this Bond-to-be was the oldest of five children to an English father and American mother (with Italian and Irish roots). Born in Wales, he and the family moved to Derbyshire, England, when Dalton was young. At sixteen, he saw a stage performance of *Macbeth* and, following the tracks of his vaudevillian grandfathers, decided to become an actor. He joined the Royal Youth Theater and eventually enrolled in the illustrious RADA. At age twenty, Dalton joined the Birmingham Repertory Theater, whose former members included Laurence Olivier, Albert Finney, Julie Christie, and Paul Scofield. The experience allowed Dalton to perform many Shakespearean roles, leading to his first serious film performance in 1968, playing King Philip II of France in the multiple-Oscar-winning *The Lion in Winter.*

Yet when Sean Connery decided to leave the Bond films after *You Only Live Twice* that same year, producers offered the opportunity of becoming 007 to the twenty-two-year-old Dalton. Wisely, he declined for two main reasons: (1) he did not want to be the actor attempting to follow up Sean Connery's well-known performance; and (2) he felt, at only twenty-two years of age, that he was too young to effectively play the mature and experienced secret agent.

Dalton would be approached once more, in 1980, when Roger Moore was ready to leave *For Your Eyes Only* to another able actor. Again, Dalton turned the chance down, as he had just finished the role of Prince Barin in the big-screen version of *Flash Gordon,* and several stage commitments remained to be filled.

As it was, Dalton would actually end up replacing Pierce Brosnan, rather than Roger Moore, as the next Bond (yes, yes—we'll get to that very soon). Preparations began in 1985 to more or less "reboot" the Bond series (an overused term, to be sure, in the cinema world) with *The Living Daylights.* With Dalton finishing a main role on the long-delayed and long-forgotten *Brenda Starr,* the track would finally be cleared for the Welsh actor to assume the throne of 007. (He actually finished shooting *Starr* on a Saturday in America, traveled on Sunday, and was Bond in Gibraltar by Monday.)

Timothy Dalton had a clear vision of how Bond should be portrayed. Although very aware of the character as others had played him, Dalton wanted the secret agent to be well grounded, a professional at his job,

Timothy Dalton.

and a bit vulnerable. In the MGM Home Entertainment documentary "Inside *The Living Daylights*," the actor explained, "[Bond] is not a superman; you can't identify with a superman." Yet Dalton would prove himself to be somewhat a "man of steel," performing many of the strenuous and dangerous stunts himself, such as hanging off the roof of the speeding Land Rover in the exciting opening scenes. Dalton also proved to be a bit elusive, insisting on no personal questions during the rare interviews he chose to sit for. Nevertheless, he made the requisite junkets to properly promote the film.

The relative success of *The Living Daylights* proved that Bond would live to see another day, and Dalton would return in *Licence to Kill*, released in 1989. The film would perhaps be the darkest of all Bond films to date. The actor was ready to take on a third Bond film, but a nasty lawsuit between the producers and film distributors MGM/UA put the series in limbo for nearly five years. When the smoke cleared, Dalton was out and Brosnan was in.

Pierce Brosnan

Pierce Brosnan was well known as the title character of private investigator Remington Steele, from the NBC-TV show of the same name. But that notoriety nearly cost him the role of James Bond.

Pierce Brendan Brosnan was born in Ireland on May 16, 1953. He was an only child to mother May and dad Thomas, a carpenter who walked out on the family after only a few years. May moved to London to seek work as a nurse, leaving Pierce to move among relatives, friends, and even a Christian Brothers mission. In a 1997 interview in *Cigar Aficionado* magazine, Brosnan admitted, "It wasn't all bleak . . . you learn how to create your own happiness." When May remarried, eleven-year-old Pierce joined the couple in London. One day, stepdad William took the boy to the cinema to see a film called *Goldfinger*. Young Pierce was very impressed, realizing "James Bond was very cool."

Brosnan attended school to be a commercial artist and landed an apprentice job in a small South London studio at the age of eighteen. But he had become enamored with movies and, at the urging of a coworker, joined up with a local theater workshop. Soon, they had formed the Oval House Theater Company, and Pierce quit his art job. He waited tables, cleaned houses, anything that allowed him to be free to act in the evenings. Brosnan attended drama school, acting in repertory theater and London West End productions like *The Red Devil Battery Sign* by Tennessee Williams. The playwright had personally selected Brosnan for the lead role.

British theater led to appearances on British TV by 1980. His wife, actress Cassandra Harris, landed a supporting role in the 1981 Bond flick *For Your Eyes Only*. Brosnan would amuse Harris by offering his impression of 007 when he would drive her home from the studio. (Perhaps a view of things to come for Brosnan. Tragically, Harris would succumb to ovarian cancer in 1991.) A successful 1981 ABC-TV miniseries, *The Manions of America*, led to Brosnan's casting in NBC-TVs *Remington Steele* in 1982. The detective show ended up being in the top twenty-five TV ratings, but was canceled after four seasons as those numbers waned. Broccoli recalled Brosnan from the *For Your Eyes Only* days, and he tested for the role of Bond for the upcoming *The Living Daylights*. Pleased with the results, producers named Pierce Brosnan as the new James Bond.

Apparently, NBC read the trade papers that day, and, realizing the ratings boost having the "next James Bond" would give the network, they immediately renewed Brosnan's contract as Remington Steele—effectively blocking his chances to play Bond. Ironically, the series would only air six episodes before getting the ax once more, but the damage was done. *The Living Daylights* would shoot with Timothy Dalton as 007.

Brosnan was understandably upset, but continued to work on TV and in films, including hits like *Lawnmower Man* in 1992 and *Mrs. Doubtfire* in 1993. When the 007 legal snafus were cleared up in 1994, it became apparent that Pierce Brosnan would be Bond in *GoldenEye* (over suggestions that included Mel Gibson and Ralph Fiennes), and it wouldn't be enough to rescue the world—this time, he was expected to rescue the character from oblivion.   Pierce Brosnan.

So, with that small task at hand, it was Pierce Brosnan who brought Bond into the twenty-first century. It was Pierce Brosnan who had to come to terms with a new boss—still M, but this time, a female (gasp!). It was Pierce Brosnan who, with his four Bond films, brought nearly $1.5 *billion* to box offices worldwide. In his four turns as James Bond, Pierce Brosnan brought the suave and calm demeanor to the character that one would expect from an experienced performer. In 1995, he told *Big Screen* magazine, "The way I see James Bond is as a man with a passion to get the job done . . . This film is . . . not a cure for cancer, it's supposed to be fantasy." Film critics like Roger Ebert praised his portrayal of 007, offering that Brosnan was "somehow more sensitive, more vulnerable, more psychologically complete, than the [other] Bonds." High praise indeed.

No matter, producers Barbara Broccoli and Michael G. Wilson decided to (get ready, here it comes . . .) "reboot" the role of Bond once more in 2005, just as Brosnan was in negotiations for a fifth whirl as 007. In a 2005 interview for *Premiere* magazine, he said, "It would have been sweet to go back for a fifth . . . It would have been wonderful to go out there for one last game and pass the baton." Less poetically, he added, "it f . . . ing sucks."

Indeed. But bad luck for Brosnan meant good fortune for the next actor to don the shoulder holster and cock the Walther PPK (or Walther P99, as the case may have been). Once again, Broccoli and Wilson considered hundreds of actors to play 007 (the list this time around included Hugh Jackman, Jude Law, Ewan McGregor, Jason Statham, Gerard Butler, Colin Firth, Colin Farrell, Clive Owen, Colin Clive . . . no, wait—he played Dr. Frankenstein years ago). After a search that took most of the remaining months in 2005, the winner was: Blond, James Blond.

Daniel Craig

The sixth official 007 would be flaxen-haired Daniel Craig. As usual, the public reaction was less than supportive, saying he was too short, too blond, or too pug-faced. The vitriol included hate mail to Sony Pictures and Eon Productions, as well as the establishment of an Internet site called "www. danielcraigisnotbond.com." And Daniel Craig had yet to even order his first martini.

Daniel Wroughton Craig was born on March 2, 1968, in Chester, Cheshire, England. His dad, Tim, was a merchant seaman and eventually ran a pub called Ring O'Bells. Mom's name was Carol—an art teacher—and the Craigs divorced when Daniel was four. Carol took Daniel and older sister Lia to the working-class city of Liverpool, where Daniel appeared in school plays like *Oliver!* Craig did find time to rough it up on the rugby fields, but was not the scholarly type, dropping out at age sixteen and joining the NYT—National Youth Theater, with alums that included Dame Helen Mirren, Sir Derek Jacobi, Daniel Day-Lewis, and Colin Firth. Craig toured Europe, while seeking admittance to the celebrated Guildhall School of Music and Drama. His auditions were repeatedly refused, and he waited tables in the meantime (poorly, by his own admission). But Craig was persistent and finally entered Guildhall in 1988 at the age of twenty. With three years of classical training in performance, he graduated in 1991 and was ready to leave the world of table-waiting.

Daniel Craig.

Craig's first film role came the next year, as he played a soldier in the John Avildsen–directed *Power of One*, which starred Morgan Freeman, Sir John Gielgud, and Stephen Dorff. His next ten years were steadily spent on British television shows and miniseries, as well as feature films.

Daniel Craig's first prominent role came in 2001, teaming up with Angelina Jolie as they searched for lost treasure in *Lara Croft: Tomb Raider*. He followed that up by playing Paul Newman's crooked son in 2002's *Road to Perdition*. Craig played poet Ted Hughes to Gwyneth Paltrow's poet Sylvia Plath in the 2003 biopic *Sylvia*. His roles as XXXX, the anonymous drug dealer, in 2004's *Layer Cake,* and an assassin in Steven Spielberg's *Munich* in 2005, filled Craig's résumé with enough firepower to justify his appointment as James Bond in 2006's *Casino Royale*.

Justly, Craig's take on JB changed a lot of opinions from negative to positive. Fans and critics alike appreciated his vicious physicality, his "rough-around-the-edges" charm, and straight-out acting talent. Dame Judi Dench—Bond's boss, M, in the latest films—called Craig "a cracking good actor." His performance in *Casino Royale* garnered something no other Bond actor had achieved—a nomination as Best Actor by BAFTA, the British Academy of Film and Television Arts (the equivalent of the American Academy of Motion Picture Arts and Sciences, which gives out America's Academy Awards). Former Bonds, including Brosnan and Connery, gave their approval of the actor. Sir Sean Connery himself, appearing in the 2008

"James Bond Special" on the British TV program *The South Bank Show*, said Craig was "fantastic, marvelous in the part."

No doubt, Daniel Craig had done his homework in tackling the role. He knew the physical part would be key, working out with a personal trainer. He told an interviewer in a 2008 interview in *Playboy*, "I got big because I wanted Bond to look like a guy who could kill." Craig also gave much thought to what this Bond would be. In another interview, this time in a 2008 *Parade* magazine, he wondered about 007, "Am I the good guy or just a bad guy who works for the good side?"

The actor took his rough-and-tumble Bond into *Quantum of Solace* in 2008. When he accidentally cut the pad of his finger off during a fight scene, Craig made light of the incident. "There's nothing to tell about it," he told an interviewer in a 2008 British edition of *GQ*, joking, "I lost my fingerprint so I can now commit all sorts of crimes with that finger. I look forward to that."

Craig was also able to look forward to a third Bond film, following a two-year delay due to bankruptcy issues with MGM. Production of *Skyfall*, the twenty-third official film in the James Bond franchise, began in November 2011, with release scheduled to coincide with the fiftieth anniversary of the UK release of *Dr. No* in November 2012. Furthermore, producer Michael C. Wilson announced plans for Craig to be 007 for five more films (up through Bond 28). At the rate of a Bond film every two years, that would make Daniel Craig fifty-four years old (four years younger than Moore when he abdicated the throne) when that last film is released in 2022. Not at all an unreasonable expectation, but time will tell.

Ranking the Bonds

Considering the six actors who donned the crown of Bond, here is one person's opinion of how they rate, worst to first. Of course, you may believe differently (as is well your prerogative). Guaranteed to be a hot topic of conversation around the watercooler, but remember—this is not a competition so, please, no wagering.

6. George Lazenby. Not necessarily for the reason you may think. At only one appearance as 007, he hardly had the chance to develop any sense of character or continuity. Of course, his limited acting skills certainly factor in, as well.
5. Roger Moore. Although he gains points for longevity, he loses even more for his lack of chest hair. Not just by his own doing, Moore took a dark

and thrilling character and, in terms of sincerity, left him just short of Shemp Howard.

4. Pierce Brosnan. Not bad, not bad at all—but he looks too skinny to peel a banana, let alone save the world. Still, he gave Bond a sense of urgency and worked very hard to make the character his own. Bravo, Brosnan.

3. Timothy Dalton. (Yes, yes—I can hear you already. But, this is *my* list— when you write *your* Bond book, you can do it your way.) Dalton had the difficult task of breaking the paradigm long established by Moore, but clearly made Bond a brooding and stern spy in a nasty business. Dalton certainly read what Fleming had written.

2. Daniel Craig. Great, smoldering screen presence; built like a tank. Understood the challenge of remaking Bond in his own image and got it done. Also proved that blond Bonds *do* have more fun.

1. And the number one 007—Sean Connery. Pioneered the part, going where no one had gone before. Debonair when he needed to be. Ruthless when he needed to be. Witty when he needed to be. Animalistic when he needed to be. Pure Bond, all the time.

And to place a period on the entire argument, Connery is the only actor of the six to win an Academy Award (albeit not for Bond), and the three top-grossing 007 films (adjusted for ticket price inflation) all featured Connery as Bond.

Go ahead—discuss.

3

From Russia (and Elsewhere) with Love (Not!)

The Vilest of Bond Villains

F act: Good stories need conflict. Good movies need conflict. Consider the lack of excitement in a Bond film, if the only conflict 007 encountered was what color of socks to wear under his Savile Row shoes. If Bond lost the keys to his Aston Martin, how much conflict would be in the resulting two-hour film? Agreed then, the 007 films needed real conflict, among other things, to be successful.

Most of the conflicts and tensions in the Bond franchise came courtesy of a villain (or villains) of some sort. They may have been members of SMERSH, SPECTRE, the Quantum organization, or some other amalgam of criminals and lowlifes. Or they might have been independent workers-for-hire (oh, for a really good medical plan) available to the highest bidder. Or even worse, the lone megalomaniac, godlike in his or her plot to remake the world in their own image. Regardless of the criminal type, Bond had his hands full in eliminating some of the following baddies over the last half-century.

Doctor Julius No: The Character

Ian Fleming had created many villains in his five novels before *Doctor No*. But this villain came from an amazingly creative mind; perhaps Fleming had outdone himself with this one. The physicality, the backstory, everything added up to one crazy bad dude.

Fleming described the doctor as seemingly ageless and incredibly tall—maybe six foot, six inches or more. His bald head was much broader than the chin, looking much like an inverted raindrop. Yellow skin, black eyes, thin mouth, all making for a strange visage. And where hands should be—steel pincers.

No was born in Peking, the son of a German Methodist missionary and a well-to-do Chinese girl. His mother's aunt raised the boy, until he was old enough to join the Chinese underworld known as the Tongs. Sent to America, No wound up with a Tong faction in New York, where he stole $1 million from them. When the Tongs caught up to No, they tortured him for the location on the money—even cutting off his hands—but he wouldn't talk.

No escaped to Milwaukee, where he studied medicine. Afterward, he traveled the world before buying Crab Key, where he ran a successful (get ready for this) bird dung business (really!). Selling the guano at fifty dollars a ton, he was rolling in it—money, that is. Ultimately, the nasty stuff was his downfall, as Bond stabbed Doctor No and dumped him into a mountain of guano.

The movie version strayed a bit from the novel, both in appearance and story. In *Dr. No,* he was the former treasurer of the Chinese Tong Society, embezzling $10 million in gold and fleeing to America. Going for something a little cleaner, No operated a bauxite plant, instead of processing bird dung. While his efforts at space sabotage were for the Soviets' benefit in the novel, he worked for SPECTRE in the film.

Physically, Dr. No was handsome and dark-haired, with bionic hands rather than pincers. But he still showed little patience for Bond, calling him "a stupid policeman."

Doctor No: The Portrayal

When first casting the film, Ian Fleming himself suggested the worldly playwright and actor Noel Coward for the role of Doctor No, but he quickly refused. Producers set their sights on Canadian-born actor Joseph Wiseman.

Born in 1918, he came to New York in the late 1940s and quickly established himself on the stage as a versatile actor. He split his time between Broadway, television, and film roles before landing the part of Doctor No.

Wearing latex eyelids to create an Oriental appearance was not very comfortable for the actor. Ursula Andress remembered her costar was nervous about the part. Wiseman recalled his doubts, once saying, "I had no idea it would achieve the success it did . . . I thought it might be just another grade-B Charlie Chan mystery." Yet the actor played the villain with an icy calm and quiet demeanor.

Wiseman continued in films, showing up in titles like *The Night They Raided Minsky's* and *The Valachi Papers,* as well as episodic TV like NBC's

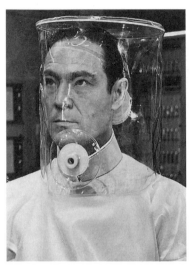

Joseph Wiseman as Dr. No.

Crime Story. He also stayed with his roots on Broadway, acting well into his eighties in the 2001 stage production of *Judgment at Nuremberg.*

Wiseman passed away in 2009 at the age of ninety-one.

Donovan/Donald "Red" Grant: The Character

Fleming's novel of *From Russia with Love* spent a great deal of time detailing Donovan Grant, the Chief Assassin of the Russian counterintelligence agency called SMERSH. In reality, started during World War II by Josef Stalin, SMERSH was an acronym of SMERt SHpionam—"Death to Spies."

The author described Grant as immensely strong and muscled, handsome with red-gold curly hair. His father was a German weightlifter in the circus, his mother was an Irish waitress—it was a brief tryst. Grant was born at a hefty twelve pounds, and his mother died shortly thereafter. Raised by an aunt, Grant soon discovered he shared a trait with the mythological werewolf—when a full moon rose, Grant had to kill. Quite simply, it made him feel better.

As he grew up, he became a champion boxer and joined the Royal Army after the war. But he defected to the Soviets—he wanted to kill. Donovan Grant was a psychopath.

Known as Granitsky, he is assigned to kill Bond by SMERSH. Together on the Orient Express, and with Romanova drugged and asleep, Grant reveals the blackmail plot to Bond. He's carrying a copy of *War and Peace,* but it's not for reading—it has a ten-shot gun inside its pages. Grant fires, but Bond has hidden his metal cigarette case inside his own book, so the bullet aimed at his heart never makes it there. Bond fakes death, and as Grant steps over him, he topples the assassin and shoots him with the assassin's gun-book.

Red Grant really did exist in Ian Fleming's life. The name of the SMERSH assassin was taken from a river guide the writer had known and used in Jamaica.

The film version of Grant is pretty close, changing his first name from Donovan to Donald. He even carries over the annoying habit of referring to Bond as "old man."

Robert Shaw as Red Grant in *From Russia with Love.*

Donald "Red" Grant: The Portrayal

Spot-on was actor Robert Shaw as "Red" Grant. Physically, he fit the role to a tee (with his dark brown straight hair dyed blond but not curled). Big, broad, and mean—Shaw was Grant, all the way.

Robert Shaw was born in 1927, the son of a nurse and a physician. He studied theater at the RADA and, like most grads, performed in Shakespeare while landing small parts in British films and TV. He also enjoyed a successful career as a novelist and playwright.

His portrayal of Red Grant in *From Russia with Love* was his first major role, followed by films like *The Battle of the Bulge,* an Oscar nomination in *A Man for All Seasons, Young Winston, The Sting,* and *Jaws,* among many others. Shaw showed his versatility in the role of Grant, assuming a formal Brit accent when pretending to be Captain Nash, then roughing it up when revealing himself to be Grant.

Plagued by alcoholism most of his adult life, Shaw suffered a heart attack and died in 1978, only fifty-one years of age.

Colonel Rosa Klebb: The Character

As the head of SMERSH Operations and Executions, Colonel Rosa Klebb proved that women certainly could rise to prominence. But, male or female, she was cold, mean, and ruthless.

Fleming painted a not-too-rosy picture of Rosa in his novel. She was in her late forties, short and squat, actually toad-like. Klebb had thin orange hair, tied back in a tight bun. Her eyes were yellow behind square, rimless glasses, and she had a noticeable mustache. Even though Fleming called her "sexually neutral," Klebb made obvious romantic advances toward Romanova. The opinion was offered that the colonel was personally lazy and lacking in hygiene. Sounds like she was perfect for the SMERSH job.

In the novel's conclusion, Bond tracks Klebb down in Paris, with the help of Rene Mathis. Disguised as an old woman, she assaults Bond with poisoned knitting needles, as well as the dagger-tipped shoe. She actually does get 007 in the shin with the toe-knife, and as the French Secret Service take her away, Bond passes out. (Fleming had gotten bored with the five novels he'd written up to that point and left himself the option of letting the secret agent die after *From Russia with Love*.)

Colonel Rosa Klebb: The Portrayal

Lotte Lenya was an international star, born in Austria in 1898. After classical training as a dancer, she met and married German composer Kurt Weill, singing and performing in many of his shows in Berlin.

Leaving Germany as the Nazis took power, Lenya and Weill came to America, where Lenya began a successful run of appearances onstage and in nightclubs. Winning a Tony Award in 1954 for *The Threepenny Opera* (written by Weill and Bertolt Brecht), Lotte Lenya continued her work on Broadway and took a role in the 1961 film adaptation of the Tennessee Williams novel *The Roman Spring of Mrs. Stone*. The performance earned her an Academy Award nomination.

An interesting sidenote about Ms. Lenya comes from the popular song "Mack the Knife." An enormous hit for Bobby Darin in 1959, it was originally written by (no surprise) Kurt Weill for *The Threepenny Opera*. Many fans wondered why "Look out, Miss Lotte Lenya!" appeared in the midst of the lyric's list of victims. Even though Lenya was married to the composer and had appeared in the production many times, her name was not part of the original lyrics. When jazz singer and trumpeter Louis Armstrong recorded a well-known version of the song in 1956, Lenya happened to be in the studio watching the session. Armstrong spontaneously added her name to the victims' list as a "tip of the hat," and the change stuck ever since.

Cast as Rosa Klebb, Lenya wore eyeglasses with lenses so thick they would have made Percy Dovetonsils envious. Diminutive and pleasant in real life, Lenya surprised her fellow actors with her cold and sometimes violent performance. She admitted that after becoming known for the villainous character, people always looked at her shoes when meeting her.

Auric Goldfinger: The Character

The name in Fleming's novel came from his next-door neighbor, famed architect Erno Goldfinger. When he heard the title, Goldfinger threatened to sue Fleming. In turn, Fleming threatened to change the book's title to *Goldprick*—and tell everyone why. The parties settled out of court, for costs and six copies of the novel.

Ian Fleming's character Auric Goldfinger was something to behold. A Latvian expatriate living in England and the Bahamas in his early forties. Short, maybe only five feet tall. A large, perfectly round head, topped with flaming red hair. Light blue eyes and thin lips. As Bond observed, Goldfinger looked as if he "had been put together with bits of other people's bodies."

Goldfinger was also a cheat, evidenced by his behavior while playing canasta and on the golf course. As treasurer of SMERSH, Goldfinger could be close to the thing he loved most—gold. As England's richest man, he had bullion (the ingots, not the soup) spread out across the world. He also fancied himself as a scientist of sorts, displaying a solid knowledge of chemistry.

With Operation Grand Slam, he planned to steal $15 billion in gold from Fort Knox by blowing open the vault with an atomic bomb, then escaping to Russia. (In the movie, the absurd concept of physically moving that much gold prompted the filmmakers to change the scheme to exploding the bomb at Fort Knox, making the gold radioactive and unusable. Then the value of Goldfinger's gold would make him infinitely richer.)

In the novel, Bond strangles Goldfinger in a fit of rage, unlike the film's demise of being sucked into space when the airplane in which they are riding has its window broken with a gunshot. Actually, that fate belonged to Oddjob, as 007 broke the plane's window with his knife.

Auric Goldfinger: The Portrayal

As the film was only the third of the series, much of the novel's characterization was transferred to the screen, largely due to the actor chosen to portray Goldfinger.

Gert Fröbe was a well-known German actor, born in 1913. He studied to be a classical violinist until acting attracted him to Berlin in the 1930s. Even though Fröbe was a member of the Nazi Party, he actually used his position in the party to hide two Jewish friends until after the war.

Gert Fröbe as Goldfinger struggles with 007 (Sean Connery).

His first film appearance, in 1948's *Berlin Ballads*, led reviewers to proclaim Gert Fröbe as Germany's "new Danny Kaye." His career continued into the 1950s as he appeared in German and French films. In 1962, he turned up in Darryl F. Zanuck's international epic *The Longest Day*.

Although Theodore Bikel had tested for the part of Goldfinger, producers saw Fröbe in a German film where he played a serial killer and felt he was their man. While Fröbe worked hard to phonetically learn his lines in English, his voice was replaced by that of actor Michael Collins.

Even though he was mean on the screen, fellow performers noted that Fröbe was kind and funny. Fröbe himself admitted to being a "big man and I have a laugh to match my size."

Following *Goldfinger*, Fröbe appeared in lighthearted films like *Those Magnificent Men in Their Flying Machines* and *Chitty Chitty Bang Bang*, as well as more serious films like *Is Paris Burning?*, and many German films and TV shows.

Passing away in 1988, Fröbe would forever be remembered as what most folks believe was the greatest Bond villain—Goldfinger.

Oddjob: The Character

A character as unique as Goldfinger clearly needed a manservant that was equally unique. One "Oddjob," coming right up.

Bond comes upon the mute Korean (a cleft palate) when visiting Goldfinger at his home in Reculver. As Goldfinger employed Koreans, he chose Oddjob to be his "handyman" (his joke, not mine). Neatly dressed in a black suit and shiny black shoes, Oddjob did whatever his boss asked—including the driving and acting as bodyguard.

He demonstrates his enormous strength and talents in martial arts by smashing a staircase banister and fireplace mantle with his hands and feet. (There is no mention if Oddjob was any good at carpentry.) He also acquired a taste for cats—as dinner, not pets—based on his impoverished upbringing in Korea.

Bond can only shake Oddjob's hand—lightly—out of amazement and respect, realizing he would have no chance in a one-on-one confrontation with this man. That idea translated to the film, where Bond had to resort to electrocution in order to put his foe down in the depths of Fort Knox.

Oddjob: The Portrayal

In the novel, Bond noted that Oddjob "looked rather like a Japanese wrestler." He couldn't have been more correct. Harold Sakata was born to play the role of Goldfinger's manservant.

Hailing from Hawaii, Toshiyuki Sakata was born in 1920 and worked as a youth on his family's coffee farm. At age eighteen, he was unhappy to be five feet eight and weigh only 113 pounds. He started lifting weights at the local YMCA, with impressive results.

Growing to more than 180 pounds, Sakata started winning state and national weightlifting competitions. He became quite good, in fact, winning a silver medal for the United States in the light-heavyweight division in the 1948 Olympics in London.

Like many weightlifters, Sakata made the natural transition into the world of professional wrestling. Taking the ring name of Tosh Togo, he wrestled around the world in the 1950s and early 1960s. It was in England that Harry Saltzman and Cubby Broccoli saw Sakata wrestling on television. Here was their Oddjob.

As the massive manservant, Sakata took pride in developing great skill in throwing his famous bowler hat. But he didn't want to kill a pretty girl like Tania Mallet, asking producers if he couldn't "kill an ugly one." Sakata also showed his devotion—and tolerance for pain—when his hand was severely burned during his electrocution scene. Despite the injury, he refused to release his hat until director Guy Hamilton yelled "Cut!"

After the film's phenomenal success, Sakata made a living by basically being Oddjob—in films, on TV, and in commercials. One memorable spot for Vicks 44 cough syrup had him walking through a suburban neighborhood, with a bad cough that caused him to violently flinch and destroy

Sean Connery as Bond with Harold Sakata as Oddjob in *Goldfinger.*

practically everything in his path. Only a soothing spoonful of syrup from his wife brought relief—and a smile . . . the same smile that put chills into 007's spine.

A victim of liver cancer, Sakata was only sixty-two when he died in 1982.

Emilio Largo: The Character

From Fleming's fertile imagination came Emilio Largo, the number two man at SPECTRE in *Thunderball.* According to the author, he was broad and handsome, about forty years of age. A Roman by heritage, Largo was deeply tanned, had wavy black hair, and enormous, hirsute hands. Extremely athletic, he had represented Italy in the Olympics as a fencer and was a natural swimmer and water-skier.

His past included running the black market in Naples, smuggling in Tangiers, and pulling off big-time jewelry heists on the French Riviera. It all added up to a strong résumé for his position with SPECTRE. Largo was also cold and ruthless—just listen to the theme song.

The film version of Largo resembled the book, although he was silver-haired and wore an eye patch on the screen. In both versions, Domino has the ultimate revenge—shooting a spear into Largo from behind. In the book, it's underwater, and in the film, it's on the *Disco Volante*—but dead is dead.

Emilio Largo: The Portrayal

Sicilian Adolfo Celi was born in 1922. Starting his acting career in South America, he owned a small actors' company. By the 1950s, Celi was directing films in Brazil. He returned to Europe, where he continued acting in many Italian films in the 1960s.

Celi became known to American and British audiences, appearing with Frank Sinatra and Trevor Howard in *Von Ryan's Express,* followed by *The Agony and the Ecstasy,* both in 1965.

Having read *Thunderball* while traveling to Spain in 1965, Celi thought it would make a great film, but felt there was little chance to be part of it. Producer Harry Saltzman met with the actor in Paris, where he was offered the role.

On set, Celi admitted to being nervous about his baccarat game with Bond—he had no idea how to play card games of any sort. He also had some difficulties remembering over which eye he wore his patch (it was the left). And while Celi was fluent in several languages—including English—his Largo was dubbed by voice actor Robert Rietty.

After *Thunderball,* Celi appeared in films and TV all over the world, including *Grand Prix* with James Garner, *Hitler: The Last Ten Days* with Sir Alec Guinness, and *The Borgias.*

He died in 1986 after suffering a heart attack.

Ernst Stavro Blofeld: The Character

The underworld has a phrase—*capo di tutti capi*—Italian for "boss of bosses." In the world of James Bond, that person is Ernst Stavro Blofeld. Fleming developed a strong backstory for the villain, and the movies used him often as the icon of everything evil.

Fleming took the villain's name from a member of his private club, Boodles, in London. John Blofeld, also an author, spent time at the club—his father's name was Ernst Blofeld. The middle name of Stavro is common in Greek culture, as Blofeld had a Polish father and Greek mother. Fleming also gave his own birthdate to Blofeld—May 8, 1908—in Poland.

Blofeld had a noble beginning, studying economics and political history, later engineering and radionics (radio and communications technology, not the unscientific belief that a person's "unique energy" can be used to heal). He became a communications expert for the Polish government, then made a large amount of money as a stockbroker.

During World War II, Blofeld stole and sold secrets to both the Allies and the Nazis, then sided with the winners. He was decorated as a hero, with awards and citations from the Allies. Taking the name of Serge Angstrom, he relocated to South America for nearly ten years. In the mid-1950s, he moved to Paris and formed SPECTRE as "a private enterprise for private profit."

First showing up in Fleming's ninth novel, *Thunderball*, Blofeld was described as an enormous man of 280 pounds—a former weightlifter gone south—with a black crew cut and black eyes. When Bond came face-to-face with him in *On Her Majesty's Secret Service*, Blofeld had morphed into someone tall and thin, having lost more than 100 pounds. (Quick, Ernst—How'd you do it?) With long silver hair, he hardly resembled his former self. By *You Only Live Twice*, Blofeld had bulked up once more, this time with muscle. Hiding in Japan as Doctor Shatterhand, he had a gold-capped tooth and a droopy mustache. In revenge for killing his wife in *On Her Majesty's Secret Service*, Bond strangled Blofeld to death at the end of *You Only Live Twice*.

The filmmakers obviously didn't care for any of those versions, hiding Blofeld in *From Russia with Love* and *Thunderball* behind a desk or a set of blinds and giving him a cat to caress. When finally revealed in *You Only Live Twice*, he was bald, with a large scar across the right side of his face (the cat was still around). In the next film, *On Her Majesty's Secret Service*, Blofeld showed his chameleon-like ways by losing his earlobes (and facial scar). In *Diamonds Are Forever*, his appearance is changed in a more drastic fashion— he had a full head of silver hair and looked a lot like Dikko Henderson from *You Only Live Twice*.

Blofeld's final scenes happened ten years later, in *For Your Eyes Only*. Bond took great pleasure in giving the wheelchair-bound villain a new job as a chimney sweep, dropping him down a smokestack to his death (cat included—call the SPCA!).

Ernst Stavro Blofeld: The Portrayals

The first two appearances of Blofeld were not challenging for Anthony Dawson (seen in *Dr. No* as the slimy Professor Dent) as an actor—unless he didn't like cats. The man behind the desk and blinds was voiced by German actor Eric Pohlmann (although some erroneously believed it was Dr. No himself, Joseph Wiseman).

When producers decided it was time to actually show Blofeld in *You Only Live Twice*, their first choice didn't pan out. Czech actor Jan Werich—known in his native country as "the Wise Clown"—was hired and shot scenes as Blofeld for about a week. Some publicity pics were taken. But director Lewis Gilbert realized the actor was not at all right for the part—think "Santa

Claus" and you get the idea. Claiming the actor was ill, producers moved quickly and brought in Donald Pleasence as a replacement.

Born in England in 1919, Pleasence took up acting at an early age, after a brief stint managing a railway station. As a member of the RAF during the war, his plane was shot down and he became a prisoner of war in a Nazi camp. Ironically, one of his best-known roles was as Blyth the forger in the 1963 prison-camp epic *The Great Escape.*

Starting with English TV and films in the 1950s, Pleasence expanded to American television in the sixties, appearing in *The Twilight Zone, The Outer Limits,* and others. After playing Blofeld, his résumé continued to grow, most notably as Dr. Loomis in John Carpenter's *Halloween* and many of the sequels.

In a 1995 issue of *Starlog* magazine, Pleasence recalled his role of Blofeld as not very "rewarding or fulfilling." Since he came in after Werich had started shooting, Pleasence performed many of his scenes to an unblinking camera lens instead of Sean Connery. The star had already shot his reactions to Werich. Plus, the ever-present cat (actually, three felines) was green when it came to movie explosions and gunfire—reacting by emptying its bladder on Blofeld. Every take required another cat—and another costume.

Pleasence claimed to have developed the facial scar with producers, as his slight stature seemed to make him less intimidating as the world's greatest bad guy. In some shots from behind, the actor didn't even need to be on-set—a stand-in wore his costume.

With a career of more than two hundred film and TV appearances, Pleasence died in 1995 following cardiac valve surgery.

Telly Savalas was a New York native, born to Greek immigrants in 1922. After the war, he studied at Columbia University and became a radio announcer and television producer. Moving to the other side of the camera in 1960, Savalas began making TV appearances.

Donald Pleasence as Blofeld in *You Only Live Twice.*

He then made a big impact with a supporting role in 1962's *Birdman of Alcatraz*, earning an Oscar nomination.

Shaving his head for the role of Pontius Pilate in *The Greatest Story Ever Told* gave Savalas the inside track to playing heavies in films like *The Dirty Dozen*. The bald pate also left the actor tailor-made (or barber-made) for the part of Blofeld in *On Her Majesty's Secret Service*.

Despite being a night owl and having a penchant for poker, Savalas was a pro on the set, coming in on time and prepared. Savalas—perhaps wisely—made no attempt at any type of European accent in his performance, yet played the role with intelligence and conceit. And there was no report of incontinent cats giving Telly any problems.

After *On Her Majesty's Secret Service*, Savalas became a television mega-star with the detective series *Kojak*, making lollipops and the phrase "Who loves ya, baby?" part of American pop culture. A longtime smoker, Savalas died from cancer in 1996.

Charles Gray (profiled in the Thunderpals chapter) played Blofeld in *Diamonds Are Forever* with arrogance and a touch of upper crust—despite trading his former Eastern European accent for a British twang. While many fans have questioned the casting of Gray (no bald head, different accent, etc.), it actually was consistent with the concept of Blofeld's chameleon ways.

Charles Gray as Blofeld in *Diamonds Are Forever*.

Gray took to the part with relish, camping it up by dressing in feminine makeup and a dress at one point (more of Blofeld's chameleon ways?). Plus, as the villain was attempting to build multiple versions of himself through plastic surgery, Gray had the chance to play several Blofelds at once.

Bond seemed to have fun with the villain, slamming him into the oil-rig control room repeatedly while he tried to escape in his bathosub. While his fate seemed to be sealed, filmmakers left a crack open for any future appearances.

Ten years later, with the legal matters between Broccoli and Kevin McClory still swirling around, the crack opened up a tiny bit. An unnamed bald-headed master criminal with a white cat made a final appearance in the opening of *For Your Eyes Only*. British actor John Norris, seen in many British television series during the 1960s and 1970s, as well as films like *The Dirty Dozen* and *Superman*, played the Blofeld-esque character. His voice was supplied by British voice talent and actor Robert Rietty.

Mr. Wint and Mr. Kidd: The Characters

History's greatest writers have given inseparable teams to the world—Shakespeare gave us Romeo and Juliet; Dickens gave us Fagin and the Artful Dodger; Fleming gave us Wint and Kidd.

The author's fourth Bond novel, *Diamonds Are Forever,* featured a gang of diamond smugglers known as the Spangled Mob. Two of its members were Wint and Kidd, who pose as American businessmen when doing their dirty work. Wint is heavy-set, with glasses and a terrible fear of traveling. Kidd, although thirty years old, has white hair and is considered a "pretty boy." During a discussion with Bond, Felix Leiter suggests the two thugs are gay, but nothing is ever described beyond that.

Fleming made these men very sadistic in their work. In one case, a crooked racehorse jockey is buried under searing mud by Wint and Kidd. In another, they put on football spikes and viciously assault Bond with what's called "the Brooklyn stomp." Onboard the Queen Elizabeth ocean liner, Bond shoots and kills them both near the end of the story.

The movie versions of Wint and Kidd take these extravagant characters and blow them up even more. They use a scorpion for murder, they drown a little old lady (even though she's part of a smuggling scheme), they hold hands, and finish each other's proverbs and puns. While they pose as cruise ship servers, Bond eliminates them in the end by setting Kidd on fire before he jumps over the railing, then placing a bomb between Wint's legs and blowing him up before he flips overboard.

Mr. Wint and Mr. Kidd: The Portrayals

Producers first cast diminutive songwriter Paul Williams ("We've Only Just Begun," "Rainy Days and Mondays," "Evergreen") as Mr. Wint, but when money couldn't be agreed upon, Bruce Glover was hired. Born in Chicago in 1932, Glover conducted acting classes and played his assortment of television roles in the 1960s before *Diamonds Are Forever.*

As the possessive Mr. Wint, Glover brought a real sense of psychosis—using a smooth, soothing voice and constantly spritzing himself with a perfume atomizer, but willing to bump anyone off at the drop of a hat. The filmmakers had been hesitant at first to hire the handsome Glover, originally wanting an unusual-looking performer in the Peter Lorre mold.

The father of eccentric but talented actor Crispin Glover (*Back to the Future, River's Edge*), Bruce Glover continued to make character appearances on TV and in films into the 2000s, as well as teach acting in Los Angeles.

The casting of Wint's partner, Mr. Kidd, was inspired. *Diamonds Are Forever* director Guy Hamilton sat in the audience of Shelly's Manne-Hole, a famous jazz club in Los Angeles, watching bebop great Thelonious Monk. But it was the bass player, Putter Smith, who caught Hamilton's eye. Quiet, balding, but with long hair, sideburns, and a drooping mustache, Smith was exactly what the director had in mind for Mr. Kidd.

A veteran of recording sessions with the Beach Boys, Sonny and Cher, the Righteous Brothers, Burt Bacharach, and many more, Smith was born

in LA in 1941. Although he had never acted before, the musician fit naturally into the film, offering a most memorable nervous laugh to the character. Putter Smith continues to play and teach music in the LA area, often accompanying his wife, singer VR Smith.

When Mr. Wint and Mr. Kidd are first introduced to the audience, they are in South Africa, picking up diamonds from the dentist. When Kidd feigns a toothache, Wint drops a scorpion down the back of

Putter Smith (left) as Mr. Kidd and Bruce Glover as Mr. Wint in *Diamonds Are Forever.*

the dentist's shirt, killing him in a sadistic way. Even more sadistic was a different version—shot but not used—where the dentist opens his mouth to get Mr. Kidd to do the same. When the dentist does, Mr. Wint shoves the scorpion into his mouth. Wisely, producers felt the scene was too grisly and opted for the first.

Peter Franks: The Character

Fleming used the name of Peter Franks as an identity for Bond to assume when arranging the smuggling of diamonds in *Diamonds Are Forever.* To make the connection with Tiffany Case, Bond looked enough like Franks to match his description. As the novel went, that was about it.

The movie decided to add some good ol' mayhem to the mix by fleshing out the character to allow Bond to take Franks' name—and life—in an expanded role. Here, Franks was big and blond, so there was no way his description matched that of 007. But since Case had never seen Franks—and she had a wardrobe-sized device to match fingerprints (Q set Bond up with a set of false Franks fingers, just in case)—there was no need for Bond to look like the criminal.

MI6 uses Moneypenny in the field for once, as she acts as a customs agent at the Dover Ferry Terminal. Telling the arriving Franks he has a message in their office, he exits and Bond enters with his credentials. Later, Q informs 007 that Franks has escaped. Heading Franks off before he can blow his cover to Case, Bond struggles with Franks in the quaint glass-lined elevator of Tiffany's apartment building. Blinding the brute with a foam fire extinguisher, Bond flips Franks over the railing and down six floors to his death.

Peter Franks: The Portrayal

Joe Robinson, born in 1927 in England, came from a long line of wrestlers. His dad and granddad were both World Champions, and, appropriately, Joe won the European World Wrestling Championship in 1952. But a back injury forced Joe to consider acting on the screen rather than in the ring.

After studying at the RADA, Robinson's six-foot-two-inch, 220-pound physique made him a perfect fit for many of the sword-and-sandal sagas coming out of Italy. Moving on to appearances in films like 1962's *Barabbas* with Anthony Quinn and Jack Palance and *The Loneliness of the Long Distance Runner* in the same year, Robinson picked up work in TV on shows like *The Avengers,* where he also tutored Honor Blackman in judo (Joe holds advanced degrees of black belts in judo and karate).

Losing the role of Red Grant in *From Russia with Love* to Robert Shaw, Robinson focused on teaching martial arts and running a London gym. But the idea of stuffing two large men into a tiny elevator amused director Guy Hamilton, and Robinson—who had also trained Sean Connery for previous Bond films—got the part of Peter Franks.

Retiring from TV and films in the early 1980s, Robinson made news in 1998. Visiting Cape Town, South Africa, he was getting off a bus when eight toughs attacked him with baseball bats and a knife. After drop-kicking two assailants, sharply chopping another in the chest, and breaking the arm of a fourth, the rest suddenly got smart and ran for their lives.

Not bad for a seventy-year-old man.

Bambi and Thumper: The Characters

Created strictly for the film version of *Diamonds Are Forever,* Bambi and Thumper were two attractive, scantily clad bodyguards assigned to guard the body of reclusive billionaire Willard Whyte. When 007 showed up at his place, the girls did their job and beat the snot out of Bond, until he could get the upper hand and dunk them in the pool.

They were sexy, but dangerous—lithe, high-flying, and tough on Bond's tailor. Named after the young deer and rabbit characters from the 1942 Disney animated film *Bambi,* the pair in the Bond flick were hardly innocent like the cartoon characters.

Bambi and Thumper: The Portrayals

Wearing a yellow bikini and her hair in a tight nap (during the days of enormous Afros), Trina Parks used her dance background to land the part of Thumper.

The Brooklyn, New York, native was born in 1947 and studied modern dance at the New York High of Performing Arts. Her dad played sax with the Cab Calloway Orchestra and Duke Ellington, so performing was in her blood. After high school, Parks danced and modeled in New York City.

Moving west, she had her own dance revue in Los Angeles in the early 1970s. When Bond producers were looking for a dancer who also knew karate, Parks answered the call. Winning the part, she choreographed her own moves and helped to create a memorable two-and-a-half-minute scene in the film. The experience opened new doors for Parks, as she appeared in TV shows like *Night Gallery,* movies like *The Blues Brothers,* and many Broadway shows.

Very little information is available concerning Lola Larson as Bambi. Although stuntwoman Donna Garrett was originally signed to play the part—and shot some footage for it—gymnast Lola Larson wound up in the final film. Despite reports that she was an Olympian, rosters for US, UK, and Canadian athletes from the 1964, 1968, and 1972 Summer Games do not list her as a participant.

Mr. Big/Dr. Kananga: The Character

While *Live and Let Die* was the eighth Bond film, it was only Ian Fleming's second novel. As such, he was still developing his characters, including his main protagonist. Mr. Big, then, was the first of several similar villains that would pop up in his books.

The novel made Mr. Big half Haitian, half French, describing him as the "most powerful negro [*sic*] criminal in the world." The initials of his full name—Buonaparte Ignace Gallia—spelled B-I-G, so became the source of his name, Mr. Big. It was also fitting, as Fleming created another physically impressive villain—six feet six and weighing 280 pounds. Mr. Big was a gangster smuggling drugs in America, a leader of a large voodoo cult, and trained by the Russian agency SMERSH. He was quite a handful.

The movie tapped into some of the story from the book, but deviated and varied much of it. Mr. Big is still an American drug king, but the alter ego of Dr. Kananga, the cultured leader of the Caribbean island country of San Monique, was created to handle the voodoo side of the tale. What's more, Kananga is the real criminal; Mr. Big is only a front.

Part of the reason can be attributed to 007 producers wanting to cash in on the success of "blaxploitation" films that were popular in the early 1970s. Targeted to primarily black filmgoers, films like *Blacula, Shaft, Cotton Comes to Harlem,* and *Foxy Brown* made stars of performers like Richard Roundtree and Pam Grier.

In Fleming's 1954 novel, Mr. Big reached his first success in Harlem. Twenty years later, the movie also presented Mr. Big as a rough-talking, dressed-like-a-pimp street thug. If he had been the only character, Bond producers might have been accused of stereotyping blacks. Certainly, Kananga (invented for the film and named for the owner of the alligator farm seen in the movie) was a criminal, but not a street thug. He was refined, cultured, the head of a country (albeit drenched in voodoo culture).

The book finished off Mr. Big by having him become lunch for sharks and barracudas in Jamaica. The film gave him a more spectacular ending, as Bond stuffed a compressed gas pellet in Kananga's mouth. He blew up like a holiday balloon—and then some.

Mr. Big/Dr. Kananga: The Portrayal

Being the first African American villain in a James Bond film was a very big deal for actor Yaphet Kotto. Yet producers were so afraid of how filmgoers would react to a black Bond villain, they simply kept the actor from doing any promotion for the film when it was released. In fact, he wasn't even invited to the premiere.

Born in New York City in (your guess is as good as anyone's—various sources list his birth year as 1937, 1939, and 1944. Pick one and go with it), Yaphet Kotto had an epiphany in Times Square as a teen. He saw Marlon Brando in *On the Waterfront* and decided at that moment he would be an actor.

Kotto studied at the Actors Studio, eventually playing Othello and other roles on stage, off Broadway, and 1960s television. Moving to the big screen, he costarred with Lee J. Cobb in *The Liberation of L. B. Jones* and Anthony Quinn in *Across 110th Street*, among other films, before landing the Bond picture.

His memories of *Live and Let Die* were poignant; he felt he had to work against the script to avoid stereotyping his character. If he hadn't, Kotto feared his role would come off like the 1940s black comic Mantan Moreland. While the experience was not as satisfying as Kotto would have liked, he was still proud of his work on the film. The challenge of playing two different sides of the same person suited Kotto, as he brought a clear distinction between Mr. Big and Kananga.

Kotto's career continued with hits like *Alien, Brubaker, The Running Man,* and *Midnight Run,* as well as six years on NBC-TV's *Homicide: Life on the Street.*

Tee Hee Johnson and Baron Samedi: The Characters

Tee Hee Johnson appears in the Fleming novel, described as "paunchy" but still a very strong person (there is no mention of him having a mechanical arm or a pincer for a hand—those were cinematic license). He's one of Mr. Big's henchmen and has a hilarious time in breaking the little finger of 007 at the request of Mr. Big. At least Tee Hee must have found it funny, as he giggled wildly when he did it. Bond got his revenge, wrestling the thug over a staircase railing to his death.

Baron Samedi, although discussed and referred to in the book, never appears. Mr. Big has a scarecrow-like figure in his office that is decked out to resemble the Baron, and many people in Harlem know there's some sort of connection between Baron Samedi and Mr. Big. Fleming drew the character from a Haitian voodoo spirit with the same name.

The movie characters, as one might expect, differ greatly from their novel namesakes. Like Oddjob and his hat or Jaws with his teeth, Tee Hee has the aforementioned mechanical arm and hook hand in the film. The device is used to threaten the severing of 007's little finger, perhaps a tip of the hat (or finger) to the scene from the novel. And while he never reaches full giggledom, he does appear with a smile for most of the picture.

The good Baron does appear and may actually be some sort of spirit, zombie, or other-world being (in fact, this Baron has an infectious laugh that would better suit Tee Hee). First seen as a dancing entertainer, he has definite ties with Kananga. Although he seems to be killed in a coffin of poisonous snakes during the climax, he appears—once again, laughing—riding the cowcatcher of the train at the film's close.

Tee Hee Johnson and Baron Samedi: The Portrayals

Julius W. Harris was born in Philadelphia in 1923. An Army medic during World War II, he continued in civilian life as an orderly and nurse. Hanging out in a Greenwich Village tavern, Harris became friends with out-of-work actors like James Earl Jones, Yaphet Kotto, and Louis Gossett Jr.

He debuted in a 1964 film about life in black America called *Nothing but a Man*. His performance was well acclaimed, which led to film and TV roles. Harris appeared in several blaxploitation films, such as *Shaft's Big Score*, *Super Fly*, and *Black Caesar*.

For the role of the menacing Tee Hee, Harris himself suggested the mechanical arm and hook, figuring the previous villains had guns and knives ad nauseam and something unusual would be a good idea.

Harris moved on after Bond, appearing in films like *The Taking of Pelham One Two Three, King Kong, Looking for Mr. Goodbar*, and *Harley Davidson and the Marlboro Man*. He died from a heart attack in 2004.

Geoffrey Holder's face—and voice—were well known before he appeared as Baron Samedi. The Trinidad-born (in 1930) dancer, artist, and actor had been seen hawking 7-Up—the uncola—in TV commercials for several years.

His visibility in the media, along with his six-foot, six-inch frame and bold, bass voice, made him the only logical choice for the voodoo spirit in *Live and Let Die*. But even spirits had fears. Holder apparently had a dislike for snakes and wasn't too keen on diving into a coffin of them, as called for in the script. Being told the snakes were "not biters, but crushers" did little to assuage his anxiety.

As a young man in the 1950s, Holder quickly hit Broadway, respected as a skilled and creative dancer. He continued with a varied career, finding

Geoffrey Holder as Baron Samedi and Jane Seymour as Solitaire in a posed shot for *Live and Let Die*.

success as a choreographer (including the steps seen in *Live and Let Die*), painter, costume designer, writer, and voice artist.

Francisco Scaramanga: The Character

In Fleming's last novel, *The Man with the Golden Gun*—published nearly a year after his death—the villain was the wildly eccentric Francisco Scaramanga. The name originally belonged to an unpleasant fellow the author knew while he was at Eton.

A well-paid assassin and considered to be one of the world's best pistol shooters in the novel, he used a six-shot, gold-plated Colt .45 with silver-coated golden bullets. Physically, the man was young (thirty-five years of age), tall, with a red-haired crew cut. Scaramanga also had a third nipple, a real medical condition known as polythelia that occurs in 1 to 5 percent of the world's population. The killer was a voracious womanizer, often engaging in sex just before an assassination assignment, believing it improved his aim (at least that's what he told his partners).

He came from a circus upbringing, eventually becoming a hitman for the Spangled Mob—a group largely featured in Fleming's novels but never exploited in the film series. Scaramanga spent time as an enforcer for Castro's regime in Cuba, as well as working for the Russian KGB. Bond was assigned to eliminate him, and in a final gun battle, Scaramanga was killed with a bullet through the heart and Bond was seriously wounded.

The film version borrowed much of the novel's lore about Scaramanga and, of course, expanded on it. Here, he was a complete gun-for-hire, earning $1 million per job, although it was clear that he had ties with the Red Chinese. His shootout with Bond started on the beach of his private island, then moved into his funhouse, where Bond killed him.

Francisco Scaramanga: The Portrayal

Forever associated with the sinister character of Count Dracula in the Hammer film series, Christopher Lee jumped at the chance to trade in his cape for a golden gun. For once, he would be able to show his face in the light of day.

Born in London in 1922, Lee attended Eton and Wellington Colleges, then joined the RAF during the war. He began his film career with the British Rank Organization in 1947, continuing into British television in the 1950s. By the late 1950s, he joined Peter Cushing (later his best friend) and Hammer Films to bring shocking new Technicolor versions of horror classics like *The Curse of Frankenstein, Horror of Dracula,* and *The Mummy,* among many others.

The step-cousin of Ian Fleming, his first brush with Bond was being named by the author as the choice to play Dr. No in the 1962 film. As producers had already cast Joseph Wiseman in the part, Lee was passed over. Finally emerging from the Dracula cape, Lee played Sherlock Holmes' brother, Mycroft, in Billy Wilder's *The Private Life of Sherlock Holmes* in 1970, as well as other roles in popular films like *The Three Musketeers* and *The Wicker Man.*

As Scaramanga (a role first refused by Jack Palance), Lee brought a sense of charm and elegance, playing the killer—as Lee once said—"like the dark side of Bond." He also recalled having difficulties in assembling his golden gun, especially while having to look up at his fellow actor in the scene, Richard Loo, rather than down at the prop.

Lee's career—he was recognized by the *Guinness Book of World Records* as having the most screen appearances of any actor—continued to soar, with parts in two *Star Wars* films, the *Lord of the Rings* trilogy, and many, many others. Nearing the age of ninety, the actor showed no signs of slowing down, appearing in the three-dimensional fantasy *Hugo* and J. R. R. Tolkien's *The Hobbit.*

Nick Nack: The Character

Exclusive to the film, Scaramanga's manservant, the diminutive Nick Nack, disproved the saying that "good things come in small packages." He may have been small in stature, but Nick Nack proved to be a big headache for 007.

Splendidly dressed as a gentleman's gentleman, Nick Nack acted as butler, housekeeper, gourmet cook, and sommelier for Scaramanga on his private island. His minute height was very useful in his role as lookout and snoop for the killer when on the streets.

The pair had an interesting employer-employee relationship. It's hard to tell how much was a game and how much was deadly serious, but Scaramanga had promised his servant if he could find someone who could assassinate the assassin, then Nick Nack would get all of the villain's wealth and property.

Hence his anger and desire for revenge when Bond killed Scaramanga, but they also destroyed the island and everything on it. Nick Nack hid away on the Chinese junk that Bond and Goodnight escaped on, attempting to kill Bond with a knife. Bond subdued the character with relative ease and trapped him in a wooden cage high on a mast, apparently saving him for justice.

Nick Nack: The Portrayal

Showing great talent as an artist in his native country of France, Herve Villechaize became one of the more unique performers in Hollywood. First appearing with Jerry Orbach and Robert De Niro in *The Gang That Couldn't Shoot Straight,* the actor got his first major role in *The Man with the Golden Gun.*

Born in 1943, Villechaize was afflicted with dwarfism, which led to his being bullied at school. He escaped into the world of art and painting, studying at Ecole des Beaux-Arts in Paris. Coming to New York in 1964, Villechaize aimed his interests at acting on the stage.

Opportunities for film jobs were limited for Villechaize, so when Cubby Broccoli contacted him for *The Man with the Golden Gun,* he was living out of his car. The role was life-changing for the actor. Costar Christopher Lee recalled that working with Villechaize was "very fun," while Roger Moore noted that the three-foot, eleven-inch actor was fearless around women, even propositioning costar Maud Adams one evening.

Villechaize moved to American TV, playing the assistant (again) to Ricardo Montalban on ABC-TV's *Fantasy Island.* As the comical Tattoo,

Villechaize brought the phrase "de plane, de plane" to the pop culture lexicon. But when the actor asked for the same money that his costar was getting, producers fired him (perhaps fittingly, the show was cancelled the next year).

From there, work was very sparse for the actor, and he drank heavily, many times to dull the physical torture of normal-sized vital organs that were crowded into his small body. In 1994, no longer able to bear the pain, Villechaize took his life at the age of fifty.

Jaws: The Character

Showing the widespread impact of the Bond films, the character of Jaws—introduced in *The Spy Who Loved Me*—became an icon almost as recognizable and popular as Bond himself. Granted, his physical form resembled many of the oversized villains that came from Fleming's books, but like much of the cinema Bond in the 1970s, he was supersized, with a major dose of humor.

Jaws was the juggernaut, unable to be stopped, whether buried under ancient rubble, sent crashing through the roof of a house, thrown from a speeding train, or left to face off against a man-eating shark. (The result? A man, eating shark.) Equipped with super-strength (a baddie requisite of Bond henchmen) and a set of chrome-plated teeth, Jaws was clearly a force to be avoided.

The basic character of Jaws did originate from Fleming's novel *The Spy Who Loved Me*. A rough thug named Sol "Horror" Horowitz, his steel-capped teeth were obvious when he opened his mouth. But other than the metal mouthful and being on the wrong side of the law, there's little to connect Fleming's Horror with the movie's Jaws.

Borrowing a trick from the playbook of Count Dracula, Jaws used his metal teeth to bite the necks of his victims. Of course, with his enormous hands and brute strength, Jaws was certain to be more than just a pain in the neck.

Although the film's original script called for him to lose his match against the shark, his apparent popularity led to letting him swim his way free and into the next Bond film, *Moonraker*. Although assumed to be mute, Jaws did speak (and got a sweetie . . . and became a good guy—there's nothing like the love of a good woman) in the film. With Bond escaping Drax's space station, Jaws toasted his blonde babe, Dolly, with champagne and, "Well, here's to us."

Jaws: The Portrayal

Being seven feet two certainly didn't hurt Richard Kiel's chances of getting into the movies. As a leading man, not so much, but as a character actor—almost entirely roles as aliens or villains—you bet. Add to it the fact that he really could act, and you've got your perfect Jaws for Bond films.

Born in Detroit in 1939, Kiel grew fast—by age twelve, he was already six feet two. Planning to be a lawyer, he changed directions at age nineteen and made his way to Hollywood, hoping to cash his unique height into an acting career. Working as a bouncer in a nightclub, Kiel eventually got into TV westerns playing bad guys and monster movies playing the you-know-what.

Appearing in high-profile films like 1974's *The Longest Yard* and 1976's *Silver Streak* gave the big man plenty of visibility when Cubby Broccoli called. Over lunch, he described the character of Jaws and mentioned that actor David Prowse (a former British weightlifter, later inside the dark uniform of *Star Wars*' Darth Vader) had already been considered. Kiel first thought the role was another monster, and he'd had enough of that. He convinced the producer that, to offset the near-invincible strength and menacing teeth, Jaws should have human attributes like perseverance and frustration. Broccoli took the bait and Jaws was cast.

Richard Kiel as Jaws and Blanche Ravalec as Dolly in *Moonraker*.

The custom-formed chromium steel teeth were incredibly uncomfortable, and Kiel could only wear them for thirty-second increments. But Kiel relied on more than just metal teeth to create his character. As director Lewis Gilbert said, Kiel was able to improvise and ad-lib (much like Roger Moore was prone to do), giving Jaws the chance to lighten up a tense scene. For example, when Jaws raised an enormous boulder in an attempt to crush Bond and Agent XXX, he dropped it on his foot with a comedic reaction. Or, when thrown off the train, he tumbled down a ravine, picked himself up, brushed off his jacket, and headed toward his next meeting with 007. While many fans didn't care for the humorous direction the films were taking, producers felt Kiel was right in line with what they wanted.

It was also Kiel's suggestion to have a diminutive Dolly, his girlfriend in *Moonraker*. The production team had originally lined up a seven-foot, four-inch woman—even taller than Kiel—for the part, but the actor felt it would result in a one-note joke. When producer Broccoli offered his doubts that people would accept a tiny woman with such a huge man, Kiel noted his own wife was only five-feet, one-inch tall. Everyone bought it and French actress Blanche Ravalec was cast as Dolly.

After Bond, Kiel was cast in the title role for TV's *Incredible Hulk,* but was considered too tall and not brawny enough (just as well, as the special contact lenses and green body makeup didn't agree with the actor). He continued to show up in films, including Clint Eastwood's *Pale Rider* and the Adam Sandler movie *Happy Gilmore.*

Kiel semiretired from performing, often making appearances at film collectibles and autograph shows, where he always drew long lines of fans who just wanted to spend a few minutes with Jaws.

Karl Stromberg: The Character

Created strictly for the film version of *The Spy Who Loved Me,* Karl Stromberg—like many Bond villains—had his own idea of what the world should be like. And like most, his plan involved shaping the world into his vision.

In the case of Stromberg, his ideal world was under the seas, where everything was quiet, peaceful—and wet. As a wealthy, self-made industrialist, Stromberg put some of his money into the development of a sub tracking system. With it—and his supertanker *Liparus*—his plan was to capture submarines belonging to the superpowers of the world. Using their nuclear missiles, he would attack major cities, prompting a lot of finger-pointing, name-calling, and world anarchy. With the world above the water destroyed, Stromberg's undersea kingdom would rule.

Stromberg's character and motives were cut from the same cloth as villains like Dr. No, Goldfinger, and Blofeld—if you've seen one megalomaniac, you've seen them all.

Karl Stromberg: The Portrayal

Bavarian-born in 1915, Curt Jurgens entered the world of journalism before becoming a stage and film actor in Austria in the late 1930s. Although a

German, he opposed the Nazi credo and was sent to a concentration camp in 1944 as an enemy of the Third Reich.

In the mid-1950s, he scored a major role opposite Brigitte Bardot in Roger Vadim's . . . *And God Created Woman*. Coming to America, he became the iconic German soldier in films like *The Longest Day* and *Battle of Britain*.

Jurgens was an international star when cast as Karl Stromberg in *The Spy Who Loved Me*. His portrayal was underplayed, a decision that some fans approved and some disdained. The actor does seem somewhat aloof and distracted, but no one ever said a self-absorbed egomaniac had to run around yelling and waving his arms about frantically.

Curt Jurgens developed heart disease and died in 1982.

Hugo Drax: The Character

Fleming's third novel, *Moonraker*, introduced a hero-turned-villain named Hugo Drax. The author had an acquaintance by the name of Sir Reginald Drax, an admiral in the Royal Navy, and as he liked to do, Fleming assigned the admiral's surname to the character in the book.

Hugo Drax was a hero of World War II, afterward becoming the head of Drax Metals Ltd. Cornering the market on an ore called columbite, Drax became a multimillionaire. He donated 10 million pounds (money, not rocks) to the development of a British defense project called Moonraker— an atomic rocket (bear in mind, the book was first published in 1955, when the mere mention of a rocket was amazing stuff).

As the story continued, Drax was revealed to really be a former Nazi named Drache who actually planned to point and launch the Moonraker missile directly at London. Drax would cash in on the stock market just before the disaster. The man is also in cahoots with the KGB and escapes in a Russian submarine. As fate would have it, Bond reprograms the Moonraker to land in the ocean—and it lands just when Drax's sub passes by.

The movie version of Drax borrowed the Nazi undertone of the novel, but made him the dreamer of a master race—much like another Nazi of years ago. But that's basically where the connection to the novel ended.

Hugo Drax: The Portrayal

Michael Lonsdale, a product of a French-Irish mother and English father, was born in Paris in 1931, but raised in Jersey (a small British island off the coast of France), London, and Morocco. First attracted to painting as a teen, he shifted his interest to acting and studied with some of France's finest drama teachers.

Being bilingual in French and English, Lonsdale worked in movies and TV made in France or England during the 1950s and 1960s, also working with directors like Orson Welles in 1962's *The Trial* and François Truffaut in 1968's *Stolen Kisses*. He continued with films like 1973's *Day of the Jackal* before taking the role of Hugo Drax.

Lonsdale approached the character with thought, giving him a clear sense of intelligence and upper-class arrogance. In a 2011 interview, Lonsdale said being part of the Bond franchise was an "enjoyable and entertaining experience." Sir Laurence Olivier noted that Lonsdale was "one of the best bad characters in James Bond"—high praise indeed.

Post-Bond, Lonsdale appeared in award-winning films like *Chariots of Fire, The Remains of the Day,* and *Munich*. Nearing eighty years of age, he continued to work in films, like the 2010 Cannes Grand Prize winner *Of Gods and Men.*

Aris Kristatos: The Character

Ian Fleming's eighth book was not a James Bond novel, but a collection of short stories called *For Your Eyes Only*. One of the stories, "Risico," introduced the shape-shifting villain called Kristatos (no first name given).

The written story of "Risico," is basically told in the *For Your Eyes Only* film as the scene where Bond meets Kristatos for the first time, Bond's meeting with Columbo, and the raid on the Kristatos drug warehouse—although it is Bond and not Columbo that kills Kristatos in the book.

The movie version of Kristatos fleshes out the character—he has a first name (Aris, short for Aristotle); he is the sponsor of a world-class ice skater Bibi Dahl (although his intentions are clearly not honorable); he is a war hero (even though he was—and still is—a double agent for Britain and the Soviets).

Aris Kristatos: The Portrayal

Julian Glover was born in London in 1935, studying for a while at RADA before taking the stage with small parts in Shakespeare. Glover began to appear in British television in the 1960s, continuing into the 1970s, showing up in favorites like *The Saint, The Avengers,* and *Doctor Who*. Around that time, he was also considered for the role of James Bond, replacing Sean Connery.

With occasional movie parts in films like *Five Million Years to Earth* (known in England as *Quatermass and the Pit*), Glover became part of the *Star Wars* series in *Episode V: The Empire Strikes Back*. Then came the Bond experience.

Getting the role of Kristatos was good fortune for the actor, as he had been out of work for six months and forced to sell his home. When he arrived on set for the first day of shooting, he received his cash stipend—the first real money he'd seen in two years. Glover has noted his work on *For Your Eyes Only* was "wonderful . . . a good time." The actor's take on Kristatos was that, as a part of the world of espionage, the character wasn't really bad. His world was doing just fine, until Bond showed up.

Glover scored a "hat trick" in pop culture films, costarring with Harrison Ford and Sean Connery in *Indiana Jones and the Last Crusade* in 1989. The prolific actor showed no signs of slowing down in the twenty-first century, including voicing a character in *Harry Potter and the Chamber of Secrets* in 2002 and holding a major part in the HBO series *Game of Thrones*.

Emile Locque: The Character

Strictly a character in the film version of *For Your Eyes Only,* assassin and professional killer Emile Locque was bad—all bad. "Silent but deadly" fit the man perfectly.

A member of the Brussels underworld, he was imprisoned in Belgium and broke free after choking his shrink. As a freelancer, Locque joined with Kristatos to assist with the Havelock murders and the framing of Columbo. The latter was accomplished by leaving a Dove pin with his victims, falsely associating him with the killings.

Locque was creepy, never speaking (but certainly capable of speech), seemingly appearing wherever Bond or death lurked. His unique appearance was easily recreated by Q, using a computer device called the Identigraph—a technology that really exists for law enforcement agencies today.

Bond took great relish in doing Locque in by kicking his car off a cliff, since the bad guy had just murdered the likable Ferrara.

Emile Locque: The Portrayal

Michael Gothard was born in London in 1939. While many performers claim they always knew they wanted to be in films or on the stage, such was not the case for Gothard.

He quit school as a teen, scuffling around in jobs as a dishwasher and construction laborer. Gothard tried modeling (which he didn't enjoy at all), then became a scenery mover at the New Arts Theatre in London's West End. He attended an acting workshop and finally started getting small parts in British television and film in the late 1960s.

Director Ken Russell cast Gothard in 1971 as the witch-hunting priest in *The Devils*. Curtis Harrington directed Gothard in *Who Slew Auntie Roo?* in 1971 and called Gothard "one of the most neurotic actors" he had ever worked with. He also appeared in Richard Lester's *Three Musketeers* in 1973 and its sequel the next year.

After his disturbing performance as Locque in *For Your Eyes Only*, Gothard played small roles in films like 1985's *Lifeforce* and 1992's *Christopher Columbus: The Discovery* (directed by Bond director John Glen).

Troubled by depression most of his life, Michael Gothard took his own life in 1992, at age fifty-three.

Kamal Khan: The Character

Purely a figment of Bond filmmakers, Kamal Khan slithered his way through *Octopussy*. An Afghan prince living exiled in India (for what—who knows?), Khan, like many wealthy folks, desired even more money and didn't care if he got it legally or not.

He formed a business relationship with Russian General Orlov, exchanging bogus Soviet treasures for the real ones. With the real merchandise, he was able to deal with a lovely jewelry smuggler called Octopussy. The resulting money allowed Khan to live in the lap of luxury at the Monsoon Palace in India.

Khan had unusual tastes, serving stuffed sheep head (not the fish, the real thing) to Bond at a formal dinner (hopefully, 007 filled up on the soufflé). He dressed in fine clothes, spoke in a calm and civilized manner, and kept his hands clean—leaving the dirty work to Gobinda or hired thugs.

Which may have been his downfall. If Khan had climbed atop the circus train or gone outside the twin-prop plane, maybe the job of killing 007 would have gotten done right. But then, who would have piloted the plane? No matter, as Khan wound up flying the aircraft smack into a mountainside and perished.

Kamal Khan: The Portrayal

Although Frenchman Louis Jourdan earned his reputation as a suave ladies' man, he preferred—by his own admission—to be considered a character actor rather than a star. The role of Kamala Khan, then, suited him well.

Born in Paris in 1921 (or 1919, or 1920) as Louis Gendre, he lived with his parents in London and Istanbul as a young boy before returning to France. Always wanting to be an actor, Jourdan enrolled in Paris' prestigious Ecole Dramatique. As a teen, he was befriended by French superstar Charles Boyer, who worked with him on his first film in 1939.

As the war escalated in Europe and France came under German control, Jourdan found himself expected to appear in Nazi propaganda films. He refused and was sent to a labor camp. He escaped and worked for the French resistance as a messenger.

After the war, Jourdan came to America to appear in Alfred Hitchcock's *The Paradine Case*. Typecast as a foreign romantic lead, he starred in films like *Three Coins in the Fountain,* the Oscar-winning *Gigi,* and *Can-Can*. He continued to appear in films and television, in France and America, through the 1970s.

Close friend Cubby Broccoli was instrumental in securing Jourdan for *Octopussy*. As Kamal Khan, Jourdan was able to tap all of his performing resources—he could be suave and sophisticated, but also be the main villain for Bond at the same time. His coworkers remember him as a gentleman and a real pleasure to be around.

Jourdan's last film was a small comedy called *Year of the Comet* in 1992. Retired in Los Angeles, he was awarded the National Order of the Legion of Honor in 2010, the highest decoration in France.

General Orlov: The Character

As one of the antagonists in *Octopussy,* Russian General Orlov represented one of the last relics of the Cold War, which was rapidly drawing to a "no contest" decision. Still intent on burying the rest of the world in Soviet ideology, Orlov had no stomach for peaceniks like General Gogol.

Very little was revealed about Orlov, other than the fact that he would stop at nothing to achieve his goal. By exploding the nuclear bomb at the US Air Force base in West Germany, America would be blamed for the incident, placing pressure on them to stand all nuclear weapons in Europe down. Then Orlov would be able to march his divisions across the land untouched.

The general is also involved in smuggling priceless state heirlooms through Kamal Khan, replacing them with counterfeits while being paid big money for his effort. But justice catches up with the general, as he is gunned down by his own troops when he attempts to catch the circus train traveling across the border between East and West Germany. Dying, he tells an unsympathetic Gogol that he'll be a hero after the bomb goes off—only in his mind.

General Orlov: The Portrayal

English-born Steven Berkoff is one of those actors that would be a pleasure to watch even without his interesting appearance. His intensity has made him a favorite for directors looking for a grade-A villain. And if acting weren't enough, Berkoff is a renowned playwright and author.

Born in 1937, Berkoff studied acting and mime in London and Paris. He started the London Theater Group in 1968, focusing on profound productions of the works of Kafka, Poe, and others. Like many British actors, he made the rounds on television, showing up on *The Avengers* and *The Saint,* among others. In the early 1970s, Berkoff worked with director Stanley Kubrick, playing a sadistic cop in *A Clockwork Orange* and Lord Ludd in *Barry Lyndon.*

In the 1980s, the actor landed in three box-office hits—*Octopussy, Beverly Hills Cop,* and *Rambo: First Blood Part II.* His angular looks made Berkoff an easy choice for Russian and other European villains.

In 1982, Berkoff had been spotted in a play he'd written and was performing in at a Los Angeles theater. When Bond casting director Debbie McWilliams called him in for an audition, Berkoff wowed everyone by showing up in a full samurai outfit. The man obviously knew how to make an impression. As Orlov, the actor made him big, blustery, and intense.

As an active playwright and director, Berkoff has taken acting and voiceover jobs in order to finance his works. His heart belongs to the stage, where he has delivered one-man performances of his works, like *Requiem for Ground Zero.*

Steven Berkoff as General Orlov in *Octopussy.*

Steven Berkoff was respected by his Bond coworkers as a flamboyant, talented actor. His role as General Orlov proved that.

Gobinda: The Character

Goldfinger had Oddjob, Blofeld had Hans, Stromberg and Drax had Jaws. The enormous, brutally strong henchman was a staple in many Bond films, so Khan had Gobinda in *Octopussy*.

As Khan's bodyguard, Gobinda spoke softly, but was a big stick himself. When Bond beat Khan with his own crooked dice in backgammon, he gave the ivory cubes to Gobinda. He must have seen *Goldfinger*, where Oddjob crushed a golf ball with his bare hand—the tall Sikh did the same with the dice, turning them to powder.

Although fiercely devoted to Khan, Gobinda had second thoughts when his boss ordered him to climb out onto the roof of a soaring airplane to vanquish 007. Bond cleverly slapped the big man in the face with a radio antenna and sent him tumbling to his death.

Gobinda: The Portrayal

Born in 1946 in Mumbai (then Bombay), Kabir Bedi used his piercing eyes, manicured beard, and dark good looks to conquer the media worlds of Bollywood, Hollywood, and Europe. As Gobinda in *Octopussy*, he proved to be a formidable opponent for James Bond.

Bedi began his acting career in Indian theater in the late 1960s, moving to Hindi films in the early 1970s. The rich and vigorous Indian film industry—known as Bollywood—embraced Bedi and his acting skills. He made his first major impact, starring in the title role of the European TV miniseries *Sandokan* in 1976.

As Gobinda, Bedi was happy to be shooting an international film in his home country of India, although the throngs of locals made things awkward at times. In the midst of the taxi chase scene between Gobinda and 007 in the busy streets of Udaipur, a bicyclist decided to ride right between the two vehicles—oblivious to the camera crews. The incident remained in the final cut.

Although stunt doubles performed the dangerous scenes on top of the airplane, Bedi and Moore did their own stunts on the train rooftop scenes. Even in the safety of a Pinewood Studios soundstage, Bedi admitted that a fall was still painful. Yet the actor was proud to be part of the Bond franchise.

His role as Gobinda earned Bedi international status, as he began to appear in American television shows like *General Hospital, Dynasty,* and *The Bold and the Beautiful,* among others. At the same time, he began a long relationship with Italian film and TV, leading to being awarded Knighthood of the Italian Republic in 2010.

Kabir Bedi as Gobinda in *Octopussy*.

Max Zorin: The Character

For your one-stop villain shopping, go no further than Max Zorin. The bad guy from *A View to a Kill* had it all—Former KGB agent? You bet. Failed Nazi experiment? Yup. Maniacal mass killer? He's the one. Greedy and insatiable opportunist? That's Max.

The product of steroid experiments by Nazi doctor Carl Mortner (known back in the days as Hans Gloub), Zorin became his surrogate son when the Soviet Union came to call. The backstory continued with Zorin joining the KGB before making his fortunes in France.

Zorin—with his microchip manufacturing company—seeks to corner the processor market by destroying Silicon Valley. The move would leave him as the only microchip maker around (Zorin must have watched *Goldfinger* more than once).

To accomplish this, Max will flood the San Andreas Fault and the Silicon Valley, despite murdering millions of people—including his lover, May Day, and hundreds of Zorin Industries employees (tough way to receive a pink slip). Bond finds a way to foil his plot, save Stacey Sutton, and dunk Zorin into the San Francisco Bay.

Max Zorin: The Portrayal

By general definition, an actor is a person who pretends to be something else. For Christopher Walken, it means he is a quiet, former child performer and song-and-dance man who pretends to be a psycho, a killer, a generally mean guy.

Born in Queens, New York, in 1943, Walken was attending his first dance class by age ten. During the 1950s, he made numerous appearances on live TV in skits with Dean Martin and Jerry Lewis, Ernie Kovacs, Sid Caesar, and others, while attending the Professional Children's School. One summer in the late fifties, Walken joined a traveling circus as an assistant lion tamer (even though the cat was old, toothless, and friendly like a dog).

Enrolling in Hofstra University, he quickly headed for the stage as a dancer in musical theater. Shifting to acting in the mid-1960s, he studied at the Actors Studio while appearing in plays like *The Lion in Winter* and *The Rose Tattoo.*

By the 1970s, Walken hit the movies, appearing with Sean Connery in *The Anderson Tapes.* A quirky role in Woody Allen's *Annie Hall* led to the part of the troubled Vietnam vet in *The Deer Hunter,* earning Walken an Academy Award for Best Supporting Actor—as well as the knack for playing unusual and offbeat characters. Films like *Pennies from Heaven, Brainstorm,* and *The Dead Zone* followed before his Bond encounter.

As Max Zorin, Walken embraced the cartoon aspects of the villain. As motivation, the actor would do his scenes focusing on the unreal yellow color of his hair—dyed for the film. He told a writer in a September 1997 *Playboy* interview, "Next time you see the movie, every time I torture somebody, I'm really thinking, 'You see what they did to me with this hair?'" But handling guns was not his forte; he told an *Entertainment Weekly* writer in March 2000, "I don't even like holding them. Whenever I hold a gun, I want to get it out of my hand as quick as possible."

Walken continued his roles of intensity with films like *At Close Range, The Milagro Beanfield War,* and *King of New York.* Yet, he was also able to offer more lighthearted—but

Christopher Walken as Max Zorin and Grace Jones as May Day in *A View to a Kill.*

still dark—performances in *Batman Returns, Wayne's World 2*, and *Pulp Fiction.* Television and music videos allowed Walken to show off his comedic abilities and his dancing, as well. His seven guest-hosting appearances on *Saturday Night Live* put him in rare company for multiple hosting honors, and his dancing in electronic music artist Fatboy Slim's video of "Weapon of Choice" showed new audiences what Christopher Walken could do—along with being a creepy guy when he wanted to.

General Georgi Koskov: The Character

Devious, scheming, a liar—Georgi Koskov needed the sleeves on his military coat to be ten feet long in order to hide all his sneaky plans. As one of two main villains in *The Living Daylights,* Koskov was very easy to dislike.

Koskov's "touchy-feely" ways (at one point hugging and kissing 007 for helping to "save" him from assassination) seemed to make him a warm character. Cellist Kara Milovy was certainly bowled over by his charm, but Koskov was just as happy to coldly send his girlfriend to Siberia as an easy way to get her out of the picture.

A general in the KGB, Koskov had been stealing money from the Russian state coffers, and it appeared that his superior—General Pushkin—had discovered this. Koskov then faked his defection to the West, with his girlfriend as a naive part of the plot.

With MI6 leading the debriefing, Koskov fingered Pushkin, claiming he had reinstated an old Soviet covert program called Smiert Spionom. Hailing back to the days of Stalin, the phrase meant "Death to spies," and in eliminating British and American agents, it would increase tensions between East and West. With the target placed on Pushkin, he would be killed by Western agents, and—hopefully—Koskov would ascend to replace him as head of KGB.

Koskov also rubbed shoulders with crafty arms dealer and wannabe military leader Brad Whitaker. His vast financial resources helped to purchase a rare cello for Koskov's girlfriend, further endearing him to her. Also, a three-way deal would give Whitaker an enormous shipment of opium, the Mujahideen a load of diamonds, and Koskov a cache of weapons—to use in Afghanistan against the Mujahideen.

When his plans fall to pieces—thanks to Bond—Koskov's fate is unknown. Still, Pushkin makes it clear that Georgi will probably be rendered small enough to fit into a diplomatic bag—normally the size of a small briefcase.

General Georgi Koskov: The Portrayal

Since he was a teen, Dutch actor Jeroen Krabbé dreamt of being in a James Bond film. He just had to wait until he was forty-two for his dream to come true.

Born in 1944 in Amsterdam, Krabbé became the youngest student accepted to the Academy of Performing Arts. Focusing on art, and coming from a family of painters, Krabbé showed great talent as a master of the brush. But he changed direction and attended drama school, finishing in 1965 and becoming a recognized actor on Dutch stages and television. He also formed a touring company and translated plays into Dutch for performance.

He first came to international prominence in 1977, appearing in *Soldier of Orange,* by Dutch director Paul Verhoeven (who also directed *RoboCop, Total Recall, Starship Troopers,* among others). He continued with Dutch and American TV and movies before The *Living Daylights* in 1987.

Krabbé was thrilled to be the villain in the newest Bond film and brought his family along with him to enjoy the production. His first day of shooting found him at Stonor Park, in Oxfordshire, England, strapped to a gurney and taken away in a medical helicopter. As the shoot progressed, Krabbé found himself in Austria and Morocco.

Following Bond, Krabbé appeared in films like *The Prince of Tides, The Fugitive,* and *Ocean's Twelve,* while never straying far from his talent as a painter. As an abstract artist, Krabbé has staged many one-man exhibitions of his works in oil and watercolor. In 2010, he was awarded Holland's highest honor, receiving the title of Commander in the Order of the Dutch Lion from Queen Beatrix of the Netherlands.

Necros: The Character

The evil character of Necros in *The Living Daylights* came from the mold of former villains like Red Grant, Hans, and even Jaws. Tall, muscular (but not possessed with super strength), Necros was a freelance mercenary at the will of Brad Whitaker.

He was clever, slipping into the highly guarded Bladen safe house by posing as a milkman (after strangling the real driver with his Walkman headphones) and disrupting the activities with bombs disguised as pints of milk.

He was mean, grappling in the kitchen with an able servant and burning his face on a flaming grill. Necros also whacked the man in the head with a griddle, giving a new meaning to "pancake."

He was persistent, wrestling with 007 as the pair clung to a cargo net full of opium, dragged thousands of feet in the air behind the transport plane. But in the end, like nearly everyone, he feared death. Holding on to Bond's boot for dear life, he begged the agent for mercy as the bootlaces were being cut—he even said, "Please"—before falling to his death.

Necros: The Portrayal

Andreas Wisniewski was born in Berlin in 1959 to a Polish father and a German mother. Tall, blond, and strikingly handsome, he trained and performed as a ballet dancer. Wisniewski moved into dance theater and slowly made the transition to film, with *The Living Daylights* being his first major film and role.

Perhaps by fate, Wisniewski earned the part of Necros by looking exactly like the villain's description in the script. His background as a dancer served him well in his first fight scenes with stuntman Bill Weston, as the body control needed came easily to him. Unfortunately, Wisniewski's inexperience as an actor led to a broken finger for Weston, as well as getting knocked out at one point.

After aerial shots of the fight between Bond and Necros had been done with stuntmen B. J. Worth and Jake Lombard over the Mojave Desert, the close-up scenes with Timothy Dalton and Wisniewski had to be set up in Pinewood Studios. With a full re-creation of the plane's cargo hold, huge fans tossed the actors around for three days. After the first hour, Dalton admitted to Wisniewski, "I'm knackered [pooped] already!"

After Bond, Wisniewski played a henchman to Alan Rickman's villain in 1988's *Die Hard*. He also appeared in German, British, and American TV shows, as well as two of the *Mission: Impossible* films with Tom Cruise.

Brad Whitaker: The Character

Sneaky and conniving, Brad Whitaker was one of several villains to come up against Bond in *The Living Daylights*. Unable to play nice with the United States Army and their rules, he simply chose to build his own army.

Whitaker was thrown out of the West Point Academy for cheating, then engaged in mercenary activities in the Belgian Congo, then worked with underworld criminals to gain enough money to start making his own deals for illegal weapons. With these actions, Whitaker developed his own renegade army (fighting who?), making himself the general, based out of his own stronghold in Tangiers, Morocco.

Joe Don Baker as Brad Whitaker in *The Living Daylights.*

The general fancied himself a student of military history, engaging in his hobby of restaging great battles in wartime history in miniature. Believing his military mind to be superior to the best of history's leaders, Whitaker often fought the battles as he would have strategized against the enemy. Filling a hall with busts and wax figures of these great (and despicable) generals and leaders, he indulged his ego by casting each in his own image.

The general pursued Bond throughout this museum with the newest of high-tech weapons. Bond finally brought Whitaker down for good by planting a small explosive behind a bust of Wellington, who defeated France during the Napoleonic Wars in the early 1800s. Triggering the explosion with a wolf whistle, the bust fell onto Whitaker, killing him.

Brad Whitaker: The Portrayal

Joe Don Baker's place in Bond history is a rare one—shared only by actors Charles Gray and Walter Gotell—being the same actor to play a Bond villain and appearing in another film as a Bond ally. Baker would later play a Felix Leiter–type of CIA agent, Jack Wade, in *GoldenEye* and *Tomorrow Never Dies.*

Baker puffed plenty of hot air into the windbag of Brad Whitaker, playing the general with lots of arrogance and ego. The actor took an interesting approach to the character, noting once in an interview that, "Bad guys don't think they're bad . . . I'm sure Al Capone thought he was a helluva fella." Even though Whitaker knew he was breaking laws, Baker still played him as if he were on the side of right—with the knowledge that his character was "a nut."

Franz Sanchez: The Character

Seeking to get away from the plethora of Soviet generals and despotic maniacs, the villain of *Licence to Kill* was a rich South American drug lord. Franz Sanchez, by name, was a Jekyll-and-Hyde type, who could hug you warmly while sticking a knife in your back.

Fitting the stereotypical "tall, dark, and handsome," the character could have been taken from the news of the day, as drug trafficking in South America was rampant in the 1980s. The biggest of the cocaine drug lords from that period, Colombian Pablo Escobar, resembled Sanchez in many ways.

Ruthless, the villain caught his fearful girlfriend, Lupe, in bed with another guy. Stating he would give Lupe her lover's heart as he must have promised, it's clear he had the hapless fellow taken away and relieved of his blood-pumping organ. Calmly, he sat and cradled Lupe, while extracting a stingray-tail whip from his coat and sadistically thrashing her for the indiscretion. Sanchez also thought nothing of having his men break into Felix Leiter's home on the evening following his marriage to Della Churchill, to rape and murder the woman. Then, kidnapping Leiter, Sanchez had the CIA agent eaten alive by sharks (taking part of his leg and arm in the process).

Prone to carrying an iguana wearing a diamond bracelet around its neck on his shoulder, Sanchez offered Lupe a kiss, then kissed the iguana with equal affection. The man seemed to abhor disloyalty and embraced those around him who were loyal. His closest aides called him "padrone," slang based on "padre" or father (although usually Italian and not South American in origin).

Thanks to a serious error in character judgment, Sanchez allowed Bond to infiltrate his crew and toss multiple monkey wrenches into his illegal organization. In the end, Bond got the revenge he sought for the attacks on Felix and Della and put an enormous drug operation out of business.

Franz Sanchez: The Portrayal

Robert Davi as Franz Sanchez in *Licence to Kill*.

Robert Davi was born into a large Italian American family based in Queens, New York, in 1953. Attending parochial high school, Davi had a taste of acting before being plunged into the world of opera. Gifted with a fine voice, he studied and performed while still engaging in sports like football and baseball. A serious illness at age sixteen took much of his operatic power away, but still left him with a strong voice for acting and singing popular music.

With a drama scholarship to Hofstra University, Davi quickly lost his feel for college and sought dramatic training through classes at Juilliard, as well as working with Stella Adler and Lee Strasberg at the Actors Studio. At age twenty-four, he auditioned for, and won, a small part in a police drama for NBC starring Frank Sinatra, *Contract on Cherry Street.*

Moving to Los Angeles, Davi found his dark looks suited him for "bad guy" roles. He appeared in many television series and made-for-TV movies, including *Dynasty, Hill Street Blues,* and *T. J. Hooker.* In 1988, he appeared in the blockbuster hit *Die Hard* as FBI agent Big Johnson. Also in the same year, Davi played the role of a Middle Eastern terrorist in the CBS television movie *Terrorist on Trial: The United States vs. Salim Ajami.*

It was that last performance that drew the attention of *Licence to Kill* producers Michael Wilson and Cubby Broccoli. Even better, Broccoli's daughter Tina was acquainted with Davi and suggested him for the role of Sanchez to her father. The actor was quickly signed to the part.

Robert Davi dove right into the character, enhancing his research with Colombian music and culture and meeting with the architect who designed Pablo Escobar's mansion. He also took the role to heart, expecting the best table and the finest service when frequenting the local bars on location, just as Sanchez would have. Davi's performance walked a fine line, making Sanchez a callous and brutal drug dealer and killer while giving him a genuine (albeit warped) sense of warmth and affection for those close and loyal to him.

The actor also showed his grand sense of humor by assuming a fake English accent, calling fellow actor Benicio Del Toro, and immediately ordering him downstairs from the hotel for a wardrobe fitting. When Del Toro quickly and breathlessly arrived at the appropriate room, all he found was Davi and fellow actor Don Stroud falling about the place with laughter.

Robert Davi continued a very busy schedule, appearing in movies of all genres and landing a starring role for four seasons in the NBC crime drama *Profiler.* Davi also showed up for an extended part in *Stargate: Atlantis* on the SciFi Channel in the mid-2000s. Returning to his love of music, Davi recorded and released an album of Frank Sinatra tunes in 2011.

Milton Krest: The Character

The character named Milton Krest, and his boat the *Wavekrest,* first appeared in Ian Fleming's short story "The Hildebrand Rarity" as part of the collection *For Your Eyes Only.* Krest was a rough American who beat his wife with a stingray-tailed whip (a trait assigned to Sanchez in *Licence to Kill*). Bond joined Krest and others on the *Wavekrest* to fish for a unique species known as the Hildebrand Rarity (hence the title). After Krest caught the fish—by crudely poisoning the waters—Bond found him murdered, choked with the fish he killed.

The movie version of Krest was similar in name only, although he was given a rough and crude demeanor similar to the character in the short story. Running a marine research facility in the Florida Keys, Krest actually used it as a front for drug smuggler and partner Franz Sanchez.

In revenge for the attack on Felix Leiter and his newlywed bride Della, Bond made Krest a patsy in a supposed assassination plot against Sanchez. When the drug lord found the apparent payoff money—planted by Bond— in a decompression chamber aboard the *Wavekrest,* he threw Krest into the chamber and tweaked the pressure up and down. The result was perhaps the grossest and most unpleasant scene in Bond film history (excluding Denise Richards' portrayal of a nuclear scientist in *The World Is Not Enough*).

Milton Krest: The Portrayal

One of the world's most recognizable character actors (yet few can name him), Anthony Zerbe was born in Southern California in 1936. He attended Pomona College, then joined the US Air Force. With his discharge, he made his way to New York to pursue an acting career. Like many aspiring to the stage, he enrolled in the Actors Theater to study with Stella Adler. Zerbe spent much of the early to mid-1960s performing with repertory theater companies across America.

After a number of small roles on television series like *Route 66* and *12 O'Clock High,* Zerbe landed a solid role as Dog Boy in 1967's *Cool Hand Luke,* starring Paul Newman and George Kennedy. He continued in TV, showing up in shows like *Gunsmoke, Cannon,* and *Mission: Impossible,* among others. Zerbe also appeared in films like *The Omega Man, Papillon,* and *Rooster Cogburn,* starring John Wayne.

As Lt. Trench in the TV drama *Harry O,* starring David Janssen, Zerbe won an Emmy in 1976 for supporting actor. He found himself in recurring roles in other TV series like *The Red Hand Gang, Centennial,* and *Little House on the Prairie,* and appearing in films like *Who'll Stop the Rain, The Dead Zone,* and *See No Evil, Hear No Evil* with Richard Pryor and Gene Wilder.

As Milton Krest, Zerbe embraced a basic tenet of his acting philosophy: Give the audience someone they've never seen before and, in doing so, own that character—even if he's a leering, devious, murdering aide to a drug smuggler who winds up with, literally, a very over-inflated opinion of himself.

Post-Bond, the actor played Teaspoon Hunter for three seasons on ABC's *The Young Riders*. Zerbe continued to pick up plum character parts in films like *Star Trek: Insurrection, True Crime*—directed by and starring Clint Eastwood—and the two sequels to *The Matrix*.

Refusing to sit still after retiring from TV and films in the mid-2000s, Zerbe returned to the stage, as well as taking the opportunity to give his talent back to up-and-coming actors. He toured college campuses across the country, conducting hands-on workshops with, as well as performing for, young students who aim to be the next Anthony Zerbe.

Alec Trevelyan/006: The Character

Seldom seen in the Bond films were any of his double-oh associates, at least in any real detail. Alec Trevelyan in *GoldenEye* started out as 006, but turned out to be the villain behind the film's plot to ruin England's economy.

Standard skills for MI6 field agents would usually include weapons knowledge and marksmanship, interview and intelligence gathering, physical fitness and stamina, among others. To that list, James Bond added abilities in female seduction, fine dining gourmandy and spirits appreciation, and snappy patter and rapid-fire retorts. Trevelyan very likely held many of those same talents, as he seemed to be cut from the same cloth as Bond.

Famke Janssen as Xenia Onatopp and Sean Bean as Alex Trevelyan in *GoldenEye*.

It was obvious that Bond and Trevelyan had a certain friendship and rapport, kidding about drinking together "after closing time." Joining James on a mission to demolish a Soviet plant that made chemical weapons, 006 was caught and apparently shot dead by Colonel Ourumov. Nine years passed and Bond still felt somewhat sad and guilty about losing his friend and coworker. Tracking down a Russian crime syndicate run by a man named Janus, 007 was stunned to find that the crime lord was Trevelyan, who had faked his death. A descendant of Russian Cossacks who tried to defect to Britain after the war, only to be sent back and considered traitors, Trevelyan had a vengeful plan.

Using the GoldenEye satellite weapon system, he would send an electromagnetic pulse crashing into Great Britain, after first making massive money transfers from the Bank of England. The interruption of electronic devices and computers would erase data and disrupt operations across the country. The result would be total chaos and a dismantled economy that the country would be hard pressed to rebuild.

Bond prevented Trevelyan from achieving his goal and fought with his ex-associate on the GoldenEye antenna dish. The villain ultimately wound up losing the match, and when Bond had the chance to save him, he decided not to.

Alec Trevelyan/006: The Portrayal

Another actor to show up in both a Bond film and the Harry Potter series, Sean Bean was born in South Yorkshire, England, in 1959. Running their own welding business, Sean's parents thought their son might join in. But he wanted to play soccer for a living.

A leg injury ended that dream, but Bean discovered his interest in drama while attending Rotherham College of Arts and Technology. He received a scholarship to the RADA—in a class that included Kenneth Branagh—and upon completion, joined the Royal Shakespeare Company, as well as doing small parts on English television.

Various roles in British and American films followed, including the IRA terrorist in *Patriot Games* in 1992, facing off against Harrison Ford (who left Bean with a permanent souvenir from the film—a scar over his eye after being accidentally struck by Ford in a fight scene). He also starred in a popular English series of TV movies called *Sharpe,* surrounding the exploits of Richard Sharpe, a soldier in the Peninsular Wars in the early 1800s.

Approaching his role of Alec Trevelyan, Bean understood that 006 and 007 had a good working relationship, being the professionals they had to be to get their jobs done. He also had great fun doing his own stunts, knowing the audience can usually tell the difference. The actor was able to tap into his school days when he boxed. Bean knew that as a Bond villain, he would get the chance to "beat someone up during the course of the film."

Following *GoldenEye,* Bean appeared with Robert De Niro in *Ronin,* then as the noble Boromir in Peter Jackson's *Lord of the Rings* trilogy in the early 2000s. He starred as the pilot with Jodie Foster in *Flightplan,* then returned to several additional *Sharpe* TV movies. Bean had a recurring role in the first season of the popular HBO series *Game of Thrones.* He also played the murdered CIA agent Paul Winstone in ABC-TV's *Missing,* continuing a diverse career of movie and TV roles.

Boris Grishenko: The Character

Most Bond villains are evil and despicable, but Boris Grishenko is just plain unlikeable—self-absorbed, boastful, a sexual harasser of females, unkempt—actually, a lot like Bond, except for the unkempt part. Of course, they work the opposite sides of honor.

An icon of ultra-geekdom, Grishenko was a brilliant but intolerable computer programmer for the Soviet GoldenEye satellite system. Greasy-haired, with glasses that never stayed on his nose, Boris spent most of his time sending lewd computer drawings to coworker Natalya Simonova. He also found time to hack into the US Justice Department's computer system.

Although his contempt for the Western world of capitalists was well stated, he also had no problem becoming part of Janus' plan to rob the Bank of England. If successful, Boris' technical expertise would earn him millions of dollars. But a nervous tic of playing with pens while working proved to be his downfall.

As Bond attempted to stop the GoldenEye plot, his grenade pen ended up in Boris' hand. When the programmer unknowingly activated it, 007 slapped it away, only to explode and start a massive fire in the control center. Bond and Simonova went free as the building crashed down around Grishenko. In the aftermath, his recurring claim of invincibility proved to be inaccurate when Boris was doused with thousands of gallons of liquid nitrogen, freezing him solid. Good riddance.

Boris Grishenko: The Portrayal

It took a great performer to create the vile and unpleasant character of Grishenko in *GoldenEye.* Bond producers found that actor in Scotland native Alan Cumming.

Cumming was born in 1965, destined to be a man of many talents. Finishing high school, Cumming wrote and edited for the pop music magazine *Tops* before training as an actor for three years at the Royal Scottish Academy of Music and Drama. After graduation, he formed a successful comedy duet with Forbes Masson, Victor and Barry, becoming a hit onstage, in recordings, and on British television. Like many actors, Cumming worked in Shakespeare productions as well.

A series of theater, TV, and film performances earned the performer a variety of awards and nominations in the early 1990s. One British TV series, *The High Life,* allowed Cumming to show his skill as a songwriter as well as acting, leading up to his casting as Boris Grishenko in *GoldenEye* in 1995.

Cumming took on the role of Boris partly because the script described exotic locations like Siberia and the Bahamas. The actor was a bit disappointed when all of his scenes were shot in a London studio. Despite that, his performance was spot-on, one of the film's many highlights.

Cumming continued appearing in a wide selection of film roles, acting in features like *Romy and Michele's High School Reunion, Spice World,* and Stanley Kubrick's *Eyes Wide Shut.* He also showed up in films like the *Spy Kids* series, *Josie and the Pussycats,* and *Get Carter* with Sylvester Stallone.

At the same time, Cumming performed in London's West End and on Broadway, winning a Tony Award for the 1998 revival of *Cabaret.* He also penned a novel, *Tommy's Tale,* in 2002 before taking a villainous role as the blue-skinned mutant Nightcrawler in the X-Men sequel, *X2: X-Men United.* Among his many continuing projects, Alan Cumming held a recurring role in CBS-TV's hit drama *The Good Wife,* with Julianna Margulies.

Elliot Carver: The Character

Just as bloodthirsty as any of the Bond villains, *Tomorrow Never Dies*' Elliot Carver followed the path once noted by British playwright Edward Bulwer-Lytton—the pen is mightier than the sword. As the czar of a multifaceted media empire, Carver sought ratings like Goldfinger sought ingots.

As head of the Carver Media Group Network, Carver held worldwide outlets of radio stations, television stations, newspapers, magazines, and his newly formed satellite cable network. Like many proponents of the nasty world of yellow journalism, Carver found more satisfaction in creating the news than just reporting it. He was not afraid to quote media baron of the nineteenth and twentieth centuries William Randolph Hearst, who allegedly told artist Frederic Remington, "You supply the pictures, I'll supply the war," when the famous artist had been sent to Cuba to cover the Spanish-American War in 1898.

In search of bigger headlines, more readers, and increased viewership, Carver's plan involved using his secret stealth ship to sink a British Naval vessel, put the blame on the Chinese, and wait until the fur started flying. He also had a deal in place with rogue Chinese General Chang: Once the war was under way and Beijing was destroyed, Chang would take command, fashion a quick truce, and become a heroic world leader. Carver's cut included the exclusive broadcast rights to the media-tight country of China.

Carver showed a jealous streak when he discovered his beautiful wife, Paris, had been in a previous romantic relationship with James Bond, originally introduced to the mogul as an investment banker. He was, perhaps, insanely jealous, as his reaction was to send the sadistic Dr. Kaufman to kill the woman—not something a husband usually does.

Elliot Carver also disliked getting his hands dirty, so much of his mayhem and murder was carried out by his associate, Stamper. In the mold of many Bond henchmen, Stamper was big, brawny, blond, and belligerent—think Red Grant, Hans, Necros, etc.

As always, Bond brought the plot down, along with the creator. As Carver's ship exploded around him, 007 broke away from the villain's pistol sights, activated the spinning metal jaws of the sea drill, and held Carver in place while it advanced on—and through—him.

Elliot Carver: The Portrayal

A great actor on the stage and silver screen, Jonathan Pryce was known to most Americans for hawking Infinity autos in television commercials before playing Elliot Carver in *Tomorrow Never Dies*.

Pryce was born in Wales in 1947 and fancied becoming a teacher, until a drama class piqued his interest. Obtaining a scholarship to RADA, he found that some of his instructors felt he should have stayed with teaching. But Pryce stuck with it, graduating and performing with the Royal Shakespeare Company and the Everyman Theatre in Liverpool.

Winning a Tony Award in 1977, Pryce began his film career in the early 1980s, appearing in dark roles in films like *Something Wicked This Way Comes* (where he really did play a character named Mr. Dark), Terry Gilliam's future fantasy *Brazil,* and the black comedy *Consuming Passions.*

Back on the stage, Pryce won a second Tony for his role in the musical *Miss Saigon* in 1991. He also played Fagin in a revival of *Oliver!,* among other shows. Pryce played husband Juan Peron to wife *Evita* in the 1995 film musical of the same name, starring with Madonna and Antonio Banderas. Then came Bond.

Fans and critics have likened Pryce's performance to echoing the stories of media publishers Robert Maxwell and Rupert Murdoch. The actor enjoyed showing the audience the public and private sides of the same character—in public, enigmatic, and in private, evil. Pryce chose to play the role big and theatrical, knowing the character of Carver possessed an enormous ego. Like many actors playing Bond villains, Pryce just found playing the bad guy was fun.

Following the success of Bond, Pryce showed up in films like *Ronin, Stigmata,* and *The Suicide Club.* In the 2000s, he became part of the wildly successful *Pirates of the Caribbean* film series, appearing in three of the flicks as the governor of Jamaica, while continuing his involvement with stage roles as well.

Renard: The Character

His real name was Viktor Zokas, although he preferred Renard the Anarchist. As one of two main villains in *The World Is Not Enough,* he teamed with the beautiful Elektra King (profiled in Chapter 4) to in a plot based on anarchy and greed.

Originally an assassin for the Russian KGB, Renard found himself a free agent as the Cold War warmed up in the late 1980s. With the fall of communism, the Russians cut him from the crew, considering him to be a loose cannon. As such, he embraced terrorism in all forms, seeking to spread lawlessness around the world.

MI6 targeted Renard for assassination in Syria, with agent 009 putting a bullet through his right temple. Surprisingly, he survived the attack, with the slug left in his brain. With it moving slowly toward his cerebral cortex, the villain was living on borrowed time—the bullet would eventually kill him. A side effect of the injury stole Renard's senses, especially touch and the ability to feel pain (and pleasure). In his clandestine meeting with Davidov, Renard held a searing-hot stone with no reaction at all.

At first, it seems Renard kidnapped Elektra King to collect a handsome ransom. But the plot thickens, as King turns out to be an ally and lover of the dying villain, seeking to kill her father for refusing to pay the demanded money. As the heir to his oil empire, Elektra conspired with Renard to steal plutonium and a Russian submarine, triggering a deadly nuclear explosion in Istanbul. As a result, Russian oil pipelines would be useless, shipping oil would be impossible, and King's new pipeline would make her richer than she already was.

Bond spoiled the party, shooting King dead and cornering Renard as he attempted to load the dangerous plutonium rod into the sub's reactor. The quick-thinking agent replaced a broken pressure line leading to the nuclear core, blasting the rod out and into Renard's chest, killing him.

Renard: The Portrayal

Born in Scotland in 1961, Robert Carlyle survived a poor childhood in the east end of Glasgow. Supported only by the love and perseverance of his father, he fought to become a respected actor and the villain in *The World Is Not Enough.* Quitting school at age sixteen, Carlyle seemed destined to work with his father as a house painter and decorator.

But a gift card for a bookstore at age twenty-one led him to find Arthur Miller's play *The Crucible,* and Carlyle's eyes were opened. He attended Glasgow Arts Centre and entered the Royal Scottish Academy of Music and Drama. By 1990, he had formed the Rain Dog Theater Company and caught the attention of English film director Ken Loach. Carlyle starred in the director's highly acclaimed dramedy *Riff-Raff* in 1991.

The actor appeared in British TV series and movies like *Priest, Cracker,* and *Go Now.* His role as the psychotic Begbie in the cult favorite *Trainspotting* in 1996 stood out in a cast that included Ewan McGregor. At the same time, Carlyle starred as the title Scottish police constable in the popular British TV show *Hamish Macbeth.*

In 1997, Carlyle appeared in the Oscar-nominated English comedy *The Full Monty* as one of six unemployed men who decide to bare their butts to earn money. The part won Carlyle a BAFTA Film Award for Best Actor in a Leading Role and opened the opportunity to play Renard in *The World Is Not Enough.*

Losing his thick Scottish brogue for a slight Russian accent, Carlyle took the role partly for the chance to work with respected director Michael Apted. The actor also remembered his dad taking him to see Sean Connery's Bond films as a boy, which thrilled him because Connery's Scot accent sounded just like his. While Carlyle thoroughly enjoyed his Bond experience, he learned that films with big budgets led to hours of waiting while effects techs got explosions and gadgets rigged to go.

Following *The World Is Not Enough,* Carlyle chose roles in independent films that usually were very well received, including *Angela's Ashes* in 1999, *To End All Wars* and *Formula 51* in 2001, and *Black and White* in 2002. He tackled the demanding role of Adolf Hitler in the CBS-TV miniseries *Hitler: The Rise of Evil* in 2003.

Carlyle also appeared in the fantasy film *Eragon* in 2006, among others, as well as the horror sequel to *28 Days Later, 28 Weeks Later,* in 2007. He showed up in the Fox-TV movie of *24* in 2008, as well as starring in the SyFy Channel series *SGU Stargate Universe* for three seasons.

His role in the low-budgeted *California Solo* was a hit at the 2012 Sundance Film Festival, and Carlyle took the dual roles of Rumpelstiltskin and Mr. Gold in the popular ABC-TV fantasy series *Once Upon a Time*.

Zao: The Character

While he wasn't a member of the North Korean military, Zao still took his orders from the evil Colonel Moon in *Die Another Day*. When Bond posed as an arms dealer at Moon's camp, he blew up a briefcase full of diamonds. Zao's face received a handful of the diamonds, embedding themselves and permanently scarring him.

With Bond captured, Zao remained a free agent. But he was caught by Allied forces when he tried to violently disrupt a meeting between the Chinese and South Koreans, killing three Chinese agents in the process. More than a year later, a deal was struck, trading Bond for Zao and a terrorist to be named later. Despite the months of agonizing torture, Bond was angered at the exchange, upset that Zao was free again.

Bond almost caught Zao in Cuba, but the villain escaped by helicopter. Relocated with Gustav Graves in Iceland, Zao faced off against Bond in a car chase, driving his green convertible Jaguar XKR, complete with mini-gun, rockets, and mortars. When the race moved into the ice palace, Bond used the invisibility feature of his Aston Martin to trick Zao into driving into a pool. With the bad guy splashing about in the cold water, Bond shot a sharp-tipped chandelier from the ceiling down into the pool, killing Zao.

Zao: The Portrayal

Rick Yune was born in Washington, D.C., in 1971, attending parochial and military schools. His interest in martial arts led to reaching Olympic-qualifying skill in taekwondo at age nineteen. Putting himself through graduate school at the Wharton School of Business, University of Pennsylvania, for an MBA, Yune

Rick Yune as Zao in *Die Another Day*.

became a Wall Street trader and print model. He was honored to be the first Asian male to model for Versace and Polo.

The print work led to a few television commercials, acting classes, and endless auditions, until he gained the part of Kazuo, a man accused of murder in *Snow Falling on Cedars* in 1999. TV appearances followed, and Yune faced off as street racer Johnny Tran against Vin Diesel in *The Fast and the Furious* in 2001.

Taking the role of Zao, Yune lived a dream he'd had since he watched Bond films with his father as a young boy. Yet he was somewhat scared of turning in a performance that would destroy forty years of Bond history. Still, Yune went all in, shaving his head and eyebrows, sitting for three to four hours daily to endure Paul England's makeup application. The resulting character of Zao was the first Bond villain of the twenty-first century.

Yune's career moved forward, as he guested on TV series like *Alias, Boston Legal,* and *CSI.* In 2008, he wrote, produced, and starred in *The Fifth Commandment* as an Asian assassin. He continued in films like *Ninja Assassin* in 2009 and *Man with the Iron Fists,* starring Russell Crowe and Lucy Liu, in 2012.

Gustav Graves: The Character

A true chameleon of a villain in *Die Another Day,* Graves began his life as the son of North Korean General Moon. The general saw his son as the potential link between the North and South, as the young man attended Oxford and Harvard universities. But the young Moon became arrogant, mean-spirited, and a despot, seeking to finance his plot with a diamonds-for-weapons deal. But 007 broke the plan up and, seemingly, sent Moon to his death over a waterfall in a hovercraft.

Exit Moon and enter Graves. The general's son survived the fall, ending up in Cuba, where genetic therapy drastically changed his appearance and allowed him to become the wealthy British rogue Gustav Graves. With riches gained from South American diamond mines, as well as a lode in Iceland, Graves had the world on a silver string. Actually, the mine in Iceland was a ruse, as Graves really dealt in African war-zone diamonds to finance his evil plans.

But Graves was regarded as a hero, receiving knighthood from Her Majesty. He boldly arrived for the honor by parachuting into the courtyard of Buckingham Palace with a Union Jack on his silks. The billionaire built and launched Icarus, a solar-powered satellite intended to curb world hunger and improve agriculture. Behind it all was Graves' plan to use the powerful solar beam of Icarus to burn a safe path through the

DMZ that separates the Koreas. Once done, Graves could lead an attack on the south, into Japan and who-knows where else.

Bond discovered Graves' former identity and broke up the plot, but not before Graves killed his father, General Moon, aboard a cargo plane. The general, realizing Graves was his offspring, was appalled at the plan and tried to kill him. But Graves took control of the gun and shot the general instead. Bond's gunshot blew out a window in the plane, and he wrestled with Graves. The villain met his end when 007 released Graves' parachute, pulling him out the broken window and into one of the jet's engines—one death for two men.

Gustav Graves: The Portrayals

If Moon and Graves were really two characters, then two actors had to play them.

Will Yun Lee was born in Arlington, Virginia, in 1971. With a father who was a taekwondo grandmaster, it was inevitable for Lee to become part of the martial arts world. After teaching at his father's studios and competing for years, he needed something else.

The "something else" was acting, so Lee came to the West Coast at the age of twenty-six. He worked with a local theater company, absorbing everything he could about acting. He quickly landed parts in TV shows like *Nash Bridges, Profiler,* and *VIP*.

Films followed, with titles like *What's Cooking,* with Joan Chen, Julianna Margulies, and Mercedes Ruehl; and *Face* in 2002. His role as the brash Colonel Moon in *Die Another Day* led to recurring parts in shows like the FX Network miniseries *Thief,* the ABC-TV miniseries *Fallen,* and *The Bionic Woman* in 2007.

Lee appeared in more films in the late 2000s, as well as the villain Sang Min in the CBS-TV reboot of *Hawaii Five-0*. He also showed up in 2012 in the big-screen remakes of *Red Dawn* and *Total Recall.*

Born in London in 1969, Toby Stephens may have had a bit of a head start in his acting career. His mother was double Oscar-winning actress Dame Maggie Smith and his father was famed Shakespearean actor Sir Robert Stephens. The rest of his success has been up to him.

Attending the public school Seaford College, Stephens gained his acting training at the London Academy of Music and Dramatic Art. His first real acting part came while he was a stagehand; then he appeared in the TV miniseries *Camomile Lawn* in 1992.

Tapping into his Shakespearean background, Stephens joined Ben Kingsley and Helena Bonham Carter in the 1996 film version of *Twelfth*

Night. He starred with Ralph Fiennes and Liv Tyler in *Onegin* in 1999 and landed the title role in the 2000 television version of F. Scott Fitzgerald's *The Great Gatsby*. Playing the part of a young Clint Eastwood in the popular *Space Cowboys* set Stephens up for the role of Gustav Graves.

Interviewing with the producers and director, Stephens was taken aback at the premise of a Korean-turned-Caucasian. He left the interview, thinking it was the last he'd hear of it. It wasn't, and Stephens recognized the challenge of bringing something new to a film series that was forty years old. He chose to play Graves as slightly unhinged, as scary as any makeup could make an actor.

Die Another Day was a schoolboy fantasy for Stephens, right down to the grueling fencing duel with Pierce Brosnan. Passing on using stuntmen, for the most part, Stephens and Brosnan rehearsed for weeks. They worked with swordmaster Bob Anderson to get every move precise and, more importantly, real-looking. The results are, perhaps, the best scenes in the film.

While Stephens has largely opted to stay with theater and live stage since Bond, he still has kept a connection with 007. In 2008, Stephens took the role of James Bond on a BBC Radio 4 broadcast in a dramatization of *Dr. No,* as a nod to Ian Fleming's one-hundredth birthday. He reprised the role of 007 in a 2010 BBC radio broadcast of *Goldfinger*.

Le Chiffre: The Character

Ian Fleming's first villain in his first James Bond novel, Le Chiffre literally translated as "the number" or "the cypher." As the head of payroll for SMERSH, he considered himself "only a number on a passport."

Physically, the man was short and stocky, weighing more than 250 pounds. Aged around forty-five, Le Chiffre had a pale complexion and reddish-brown hair. A sharp dresser and chain-smoker, Le Chiffre was also known as a gambler. Perhaps too much of one, as he embezzled a huge amount of money from his own organization to invest in a chain of French brothels. When a government law banned prostitution, Le Chiffre was on the hook for the money he stole.

Figuring to make the money back playing baccarat at the Casino Royale-Les-Eaux, Le Chiffre was beaten by Bond. He tortured Bond with a carpet beater to retrieve his money, only to be shot and killed by a SMERSH agent for his crime.

The 2006 film version of Le Chiffre followed some of the book's lines, but they were enhanced for a modern-day villain. Described as a private banker for the world's terrorists, Le Chiffre knew numbers, was quick with odds, and had asthma, controlling it with an inhaler. He also had a rare affliction that caused his eyes to occasionally shed tears of blood.

The film made Le Chiffre an expert in Texas Hold'em, a poker game much more popular and well known than baccarat. His choice of torture weapons changed to a knotted rope, as finding a carpet beater in the hold of a cargo ship was highly unlikely, Still, Le Chiffre met his demise with a bullet between his eyes, at the hands of the mysterious Mr. White.

Le Chiffre: The Portrayal

Mads Mikkelsen was born in Copenhagen, Denmark, in 1965, excelling as a gymnast in his youth. He transitioned into professional dancing for a number of years before attending the School of Theater in Aarhus, Denmark.

Mikkelsen broke into the world of cinema as the misfit Tonny in the 1996 Danish film *Pusher.* He also reprised the role in the 2004 sequel, *Pusher II.* He also appeared in Danish films like *Bleeder* and *Flickering Lights.* Mikkelsen starred for four seasons in the Danish TV police drama *Unit 1.*

His first Hollywood film was 2004's *King Arthur,* with Clive Owen and Keira Knightley. Mikkelsen continued to star in Danish films, with his work in *Pusher* and 2002's *Open Hearts* coming to the attention of Bond casting folks and producers. He was cast as Le Chiffre in very little time.

Unlike many Bond performers who read some or all of the Fleming novels in preparation for their role, Mikkelsen had not and did not read *Casino Royale* before making the film. He relied on the script, making suggestions along the way. He also avoided the Le Chiffre performances of Peter Lorre in the 1954 TV version and Orson Welles in the 1967 farce.

The actor recognized that, unlike many Bond villains who dreamed of taking

Mads Mikkelsen as Le Chiffre in *Casino Royale* (2006).

over the world, Le Chiffre was only interested in the money—wherever it came from. Making money at the poker tables was nothing new for Mikkelsen, as he had enjoyed playing cards long before *Casino Royale*. During breaks in shooting, games on the set broke out all the time, with Mikkelsen and producer Michael Wilson considered the best of the card sharps.

The success of the Bond experience led to bigger films for Mads Mikkelsen, including the 2010 remake of *Clash of the Titans* and the 2011 version of *The Three Musketeers*. He continued to work in Danish films and received the honor of knighthood from the Queen of Denmark in 2010.

Mikkelsen won the Best Actor award at the 2012 Cannes Film Festival for his role as a teacher falsely accused of abuse in *The Hunt*. He also was cast as the clever but gruesome Hannibal Lecter in NBC-TV's *Hannibal* and gained a villainous role against Chris Hemsworth in the 2013 sequel to *Thor*.

Mr. White: The Character

As a member of the evil Quantum organization, Mr. White was someone who put people together. He brokered the meeting between terrorist Obanno and Le Chiffre. He somehow connected Vesper Lynd and Yusef Kabira and probably had something to do with Kabira and Canadian agent Corrine, as well.

Not much is really known about White, although he carried a lot of pull with Quantum. When Le Chiffre lost the money he planned on paying to Quantum, White eliminated his gang and Le Chiffre as well. Later, when Bond chased Vesper Lynd and the money, White was able to retrieve the briefcase full of loot from a sinking building in Venice.

Full of rage over Lynd's death, Bond tracked White down and shot him in the leg. When 007 delivered White to MI6 for a grilling, Quantum showed its reach by having a rogue agent shoot up the interrogation. In Austria, Bond was able to flush out many of Quantum's members during the opera, but White was smart enough to stay seated.

In a sequence shot but not used for the end of *Quantum of Solace*, the advisor to the British prime minister turned out to be Mr. White's superior in Quantum. Bond caught up with White, killed him, and questioned the advisor about the sinister organization.

Mr. White: The Portrayal

Born in Denmark in 1948, Jesper Christensen began his extensive performance career in 1972 on the Copenhagen stage. Moving to film in 1975, he appeared in many European films and television series, winning several Danish awards for acting.

In 2005, Christensen made his first American film, *The Interpreter,* with Nicole Kidman and Sean Penn, directed by Sydney Pollack. He also appeared in the NBC-TV miniseries *Revelations,* with Bill Pullman.

Playing the mysterious Mr. White in *Casino Royale* and *Quantum of Solace* apparently was enough Bond for Christensen. In 2010, he admitted that he was happy that his role as a Bond villain was over, adding that he regarded the two pictures as "really [excrement]."

Too bad he didn't say what he *really* thought.

Dominic Greene: The Character

Another member of the Quantum organization and the main villain in *Quantum of Solace,* Dominic Greene used a false sense of concern for the environment, heading an eco-friendly company called Greene Planet to finance his plot to squeeze Bolivia dry of water.

Callously, he hired a hit man to kill his former lover, Camille Montes, after they split up in Haiti. James Bond foiled that idea, then saved Camille when Greene gave her to the wicked Bolivian general Medrano. Greene's deal with Medrano involved supporting the general in his efforts to take control of his country. In return, Medrano would give Greene a seemingly worthless parcel of desert property.

No doubt, Greene was a horse trader, as he also wheeled and dealed with Gregg Beam of the CIA. The agency would support Medrano's rise to power, in exchange for any oil rights in the country. Of course, there was no oil; Quantum's plot was to control the water supply to Bolivia, gouging them with exorbitant prices.

Bond and Camille gummed up the works for Quantum, leaving Medrano dead and Greene alone in the desert with only a can of motor oil for thirst. Later, he was found dead with two bullets in his skull—courtesy of Quantum, no doubt—and motor oil in his tummy.

Dominic Greene: The Portrayal

As the Bond baddie in *Quantum of Solace,* Mathieu Amalric continued the long-standing tradition of casting international stars in the role of the key villain. The French-born Amalric has amassed a long list of acting and directing credits in a relatively short period of time.

Born in 1965, Amalric was only twenty-two when famed French director Louis Malle used him as an assistant director on *Au Revoir Les Enfants* in

1987. Acting still held his interest as well, and he appeared in French films like *My Sex Life . . . or How I Got into an Argument* in 1996. The role won Amalric a César Award, the national film award in France. He won a second award for *Kings and Queen* in 2004.

His first American feature was no small effort; he appeared in Steven Spielberg's *Munich* (along with future Bond costar Daniel Craig) in 2005. He followed up with Sofia Coppola's *Marie Antoinette* and another César Award–winning performance in *The Diving Bell and the Butterfly* in 2007.

Cast as Dominic Greene, Amalric had no scars, metal hands, or white cat to hide behind, relying on his face and eyes to present the crazy world of the villain. As the craziness spilled into the final fight scenes with Daniel Craig, Amalric worked to precisely know how hard to hit his costar. But they knew they couldn't really hold back, wanting a very savage and wild climactic battle.

Working the promotional trail after completing *Quantum of Solace* was a tedious but necessary task for Amalric, knowing that he could never face his kids with the fact that he had turned down the role of a James Bond villain.

Returning behind the camera to direct, Amalric won the Cannes Film Festival's Best Director award for *On Tour* in 2010.

Raoul Silva: The Character

Blond-haired Raoul Silva started out on the side of the "good guys" as Tiago Rodriguez, an agent for MI6. But an assignment in the Far East turned out to be too dangerous, and M was forced to abandon the field operative. In the hands of his captors, he was tortured. Refusing to talk, Silva took a cyanide capsule, but he didn't die. Instead, he was left disfigured—a frightening sight of missing teeth and puckered facial flesh. While a prosthetic appliance may have covered the injury, nothing could ease the pain of the betrayal.

The pain and bitterness led to his life as a criminal, a computer expert capable of terrorizing entire countries by remote control through the Internet. Silva masterminded the theft of a hard drive that contained data on every NATO agent tracking terrorists. The crime brought James Bond onto the trail of the villain.

Holding M personally responsible for his plight, Silva targeted her and all of MI6 for elimination. While he was able to blow up M's office in the MI6 building, the agency remained active and moved underground. Later, he tracked M and Bond to Scotland. Although M was fatally wounded, 007 killed Silva with a knife in the back.

Silva kept a frightened mistress named Séverine, but he flirted with Bond as well, implying a preference for men. Considering his crazed mental state, the act may have been merely a perverse tease, but nothing was certain.

Bond films are not foreign to featuring gay characters, obvious or otherwise—witness Rosa Klebb in *From Russia With Love*, Pussy Galore in *Goldfinger*, Misters Wint and Kidd in *Diamonds Are Forever*—but Raoul Silva was the first to come on to 007. (Remember, Bond supposedly and miraculously transformed Galore in the barn.)

Raoul Silva: The Portrayal

Joining Christopher Walken and Benicio Del Toro as Oscar winners to play Bond villains (although Del Toro earned his after his work in *Licence to Kill*), Javier Bardem wowed critics and fans alike in *Skyfall*. As Raoul Silva, ex-MI6-agent-turned-cyberterrorist, Bardem delivered a wicked and memorable performance not seen since the days of *Goldfinger* and Gert Fröbe.

Born in Spain's Canary Islands in 1969, Bardem came from a performing arts family—his mother was an actress; his brother, an actor; his sister, a former actress; his grandparents, early performers in Spanish cinema; and his uncle, a film writer and director. Even though he made his first film appearance at age six, he found himself more interested in painting.

Bardem attended art school for four years, taking acting jobs to support his education. He listened to the rock band AC/DC while he studied—satisfying his love for heavy metal music, with the side benefit of learning the English language. But acting was in his blood and he left art for the film world at age twenty. Bardem gained much of his performance skills from Madrid acting coach Juan Carlos Corazza, a mentor whom the actor still sees periodically to refresh and expand his abilities as a performer.

Instead of seeking fame and fortune in Hollywood, Bardem remained in Spain, where he made his name in television and film. He figured if he was good enough, Hollywood would come eventually. He was right.

His first major American film, *Before Night Falls* in 2000, earned the actor his first nomination for an Academy Award. He continued to appear in both Spanish and American features, as in the role of Felix, the drug dealer in the Tom Cruise–Jamie Foxx thriller *Collateral* in 2004. Cast in the Coen Brothers' 2007 drama *No Country for Old Men*, Bardem won the Oscar for Best Supporting Actor. With a haircut that looked like it was done by Floyd the Barber on LSD, Bardem's take as psycho-killer Anton Chigurh was clearly memorable.

Parts in films like Woody Allen's *Vicky Cristina Barcelona* in 2008, 2010's *Biutiful*—resulting in another nomination for an Oscar—and the 2010 romance *Eat Pray Love* with Julia Roberts, led up to *Skyfall*.

Director Sam Mendes lobbied hard for Bardem as his archvillain in *Skyfall*, knowing he had the flamboyant yet frightening ability to make Silva a true Bond bad guy. Bardem found himself impressed with Craig's ability to handle the physicality of the film, although he was uncomfortable sharing the rough aspects of Silva's character with fellow Oscar winner Judi Dench. No matter, as both were strictly pros shooting the scenes, bringing a tremendous performance to the screen.

Bardem's portrayal in *Skyfall* led to films like Spain's *Alacrán Enamorado* (Scorpion in Love), appearing with his brother Carlos, and director Ridley Scott's *The Counselor*, alongside his wife, Penélope Cruz, plus Brad Pitt and Cameron Diaz.

4

The Spy Who Loved Us

The Girls of James Bond

Years ago, someone once said, "Behind every great man is a great woman." Feminists may think the opposite (and may be right—remember, I'm married and she's gonna read this), but in the case of James Bond, the quote usually applies. In written form, and for the first decade or so of the films, 007 was a product of sexist, but never misogynist, male writers and producers. It's just the way the world was in the 1950s and 1960s.

Consider *From Russia with Love:* Tatiana was beautiful, desirable, and helpless, while Klebb was deadly, mannish, and unattractive—pretty much black and white. But across the years, women in the world of Bond—on-screen and behind-the-cameras—made their marks and helped to mold the greatest and longest-running character in film history.

In most cases, Bond had the charisma (and chutzpah) to sweep any woman he desired off her feet, romance her, and, often, lose her phone number quicker than a hobo eating a ham sandwich. His style and demeanor rose above mere mortals, with the power to change a woman's sexual orientation. (See Pussy Galore and her apparent lesbian lifestyle, which she obviously was happy with until Bond ambled into Goldfinger's stables one day.)

As stated previously, part of Bond's appeal to men has been the ability to attract women that the majority of male audience members would never have an iota of a chance to romance. That's why we embrace the fantasy of the James Bond world. Bond has more women than you can shake a stick at (if that's your idea of a good time). He does what men can only dream of doing. The following is a selection of women that 007 did.

Miss Moneypenny: The Character

Secretary to M at MI6, Moneypenny played a much larger role in the film series than she did in Ian Fleming's novels. The writer revealed little about the woman, other than that she didn't smoke and owned a poodle. The paucity of backstory in the books left the territory wide open for the films.

Fleming's inspiration for Moneypenny can be traced to several real-life possible choices. One is Kathleen Pettigrew, who was the personal assistant to Stewart Menzies, the head of MI6 during World War II. In fact, Fleming's first draft of *Casino Royale* called M's secretary "Miss Pettavel," but he decided to further distance the character from reality in the final draft. Other potential influences included MI6 secretary Victoire "Paddy" Bennett and French intelligence officer Vera Atkins.

The author took the name of "Moneypenny" from an unfinished novel written by his brother, Peter. Fleming never gave her a first name, although a trio of novels written in the 2000s, *The Moneypenny Diaries*, bestowed the first name of "Jane."

The films followed the basic premise of the books, creating a sexual tension between the secretary and the secret agent. Their romance was always teased and never consummated, although *Die Another Day* allowed Moneypenny the chance to enjoy Bond, albeit through the technology of Q Branch's virtual simulator. For the most part, Moneypenny was a steadying force whenever 007 came to the offices of Universal Exports. She understood Bond (even when M didn't) and kept hope that someday, her prince—007—would come.

Still, Moneypenny was a presence throughout the Bond films, failing to appear only in the rebooted *Casino Royale* and *Quantum of Solace*, although M had a male assistant named Villiers in *Casino Royale*. After

Lois Maxwell as Miss Moneypenny in *Goldfinger.*

a stint as a field agent in *Skyfall*, Moneypenny took the role of executive assistant to M, and she finally had a first name—Eve.

Miss Moneypenny: The Portrayals

Although four women played the part of Moneypenny, the role will always belong to Lois Maxwell. A veteran of the first fourteen James Bond films, she brought class, beauty, and a fine sense of humor to the character.

Born in Canada in 1927, Maxwell began as a radio actress in her teens. She moved to England and attended the RADA, where she studied with future Bond Roger Moore. She had a fast start in the movie business, winning a Golden Globe in 1947 at age twenty, as Best Newcomer in a Shirley Temple and Ronald Reagan comedy called *That Hagen Girl*. After appearing in a photo layout for *Life* magazine with another newcomer—named Marilyn Monroe—Maxwell showed up in films like *The Big Punch* in 1948 and *The Crime Doctor's Diary* in 1949.

Disillusioned by Hollywood, Maxwell moved to Italy in 1950, where she starred in the award-winning *Tomorrow Is Too Late* and drove race cars when not making films. She came to England in the early 1950s, where she appeared in a variety of movies and television series.

In 1962, Maxwell appeared as a nurse in Stanley Kubrick's *Lolita*. But her husband had fallen ill and the family needed money, so Maxwell called director Terence Young, with whom she'd worked on several films. He offered her one of two roles in his newest film, *Dr. No*: the sexy Sylvia Trench or down-to-earth Miss Moneypenny. The rest, as they say, is history.

In fourteen appearances in the Bond films, Maxwell was on-screen for less than one hour's time and had less than two hundred words of dialogue. She was never paid more than $250 a day for her work. Yet, she was loyal to the character, feeling the audience wanted Bond to end up with Moneypenny because she was real and the other women were two-dimensional.

Along with the Bond films, Maxwell appeared in films like director Robert Wise's *The Haunting* in 1963, as well as television shows like *The Avengers* and providing voices for Gerry Anderson's Supermarionation program *Stingray*. The actress also starred as the mother in the popular Canadian show *Adventures in Rainbow Country* in 1969. Like other Bond actors, she appeared as a Moneypenny-like character in two foreign 007 send-up films: *Operation Kid Brother* and *From Hong Kong with Love*.

When Roger Moore retired after *A View to a Kill* in 1985, Maxwell decided to retire from the Bond films as well. Moore thought Maxwell should have been promoted to the role of M. She was fifty-eight years old, having spent twenty-three of them waiting for Bond to call. Maxwell passed away in 2007, at the age of eighty.

Caroline Bliss, born in 1961, played Miss Moneypenny in the two Timothy Dalton Bond films, donning eyeglasses to distinguish herself from Maxwell.

Samantha Bond—appropriately named—picked up the role for the Pierce Brosnan Bond pictures. Even though she loved playing the part, Bond saw how Moneypenny had been the sum of Lois Maxwell's acting career. She resolved from the start to play M's secretary only for Brosnan's run.

Born in London in 1976, the daughter of TV writer Lisselle Kayla, Naomie Harris attended Cambridge University, receiving a degree in social and political science. She found the experience to be less than pleasant, however, never losing her love for performing. She moved on to spend two years studying at the Bristol Old Vic Theater School.

Her efforts were rewarded with roles on British television through the 1990s. Harris' first major film role came in 2002, showing up in the hit zombie thriller *28 Days Later*. The actress won a recurring role in the second and third *Pirates of the Caribbean* films: *Dead Man's Chest* in 2006 and *At World's End* in 2007. She continued to appear in action films, including *Street Kings* in 2008 and the bio-pic of punk-rocker Ian Dury, *Sex & Drugs & Rock & Roll*, in 2010.

Word of Harris being cast in *Skyfall* immediately led to rumors that she would play Miss Moneypenny. The actress spent months denying them, and she got physical in playing an MI6 field agent named Eve. The role called for extensive training, including flexibility, stunts and stunt driving, kickboxing, and weapons use. At the film's end, she turned up at MI6 as Moneypenny . . . Eve Moneypenny.

With her take in *Skyfall* behind her, Harris took the role of Winnie Mandela, wife of South African activist and politician Nelson Mandela, in the 2013 British production of *Mandela: Long Walk to Freedom*. However, chances are very good that she will be reprising the part of Moneypenny in future Bond films.

Sylvia Trench: The Character

Created with the intention of being a recurring character in the Bond series, Sylvia Trench was a woman who, frankly, was seldom seen in films up to that point in the 1960s. Appearing first in *Dr. No*, she was rich, independent, and a risk-taker.

Losing heavily at the chemin de fer table in a posh London club, Trench's beauty and courage attracted James Bond. It was the very first scene ever in which the agent was shown and set the definitive tone for the fifty-year series. Even though Bond was clearly a womanizer in the films, it was Trench who made the move on him when he got up to leave.

It is also interesting to note that 007's signature introduction of "Bond, James Bond" was actually a mimicry of Trench's initial introduction—"Trench, Sylvia Trench." The woman was aggressive and sure, making

Eunice Gayson as Sylvia Trench in *Dr. No.*

her way into Bond's apartment and practicing her golf stroke—after first finding and changing into one of Bond's shirts (her lovely long legs were bare, as it was obviously a "pants optional day"). She kissed him, and his departure suddenly wasn't so immediate.

In *From Russia with Love,* Bond and Trench enjoyed an afternoon tryst beside a river before a call from the office interrupted everything. (A clip-on beeper and a telephone in a car? What a futuristic concept for 1963.) Moneypenny ordered Bond to come in, and Trench showed her claws, cutting the call short and insisting that 007 take care of business before taking care of business.

Sylvia Trench: The Portrayal

Born in England in 1931, Eunice Gayson studied music and dance as a teen before going into repertory theater. At age seventeen, she earned her first film role in *My Brother Jonathan,* with more parts in British movies and television shows during the 1950s.

She joined the group of comics known for BBC Radio's *Goon Show* for a TV movie called *Goonreel* in 1952. The troupe included Peter Sellers, Spike Milligan, and Harry Seacombe. Gayson also joined the Goons for a follow-up film, *Down Among the Z Men.* In 1957, she starred with Peter Cushing in Hammer Films' *The Revenge of Frankenstein.*

Having worked with director Terence Young in the 1950s, Gayson was easily cast in *Dr. No,* with Young's intention of bringing Gayson and the character of Trench back in every subsequent film. Every time, the romance between Bond and Trench would be cut short just when things would get interesting. The idea died when Guy Hamilton came in for *Goldfinger.*

Gayson continued to appear on British television through the 1960s and early 1970s, including *The Saint, The Avengers,* and *Secret Agent,* starring Patrick McGoohan. Retiring afterward, she returned to the London stage in 1990 to play Little Red Riding Hood's granny in the musical *Into the Woods.*

Honey Ryder: The Character

Known as Honeychile Rider in the *Doctor No* novel, the lovely lady was presented as a loner, an orphan, a victim of assault as a young girl, a vengeful person (she later killed her attacker), and a collector of shells on Crab Key when Bond spies her naked form one morning on the island.

Bond's first sight of Rider reminded him of the classic statue of Venus— she was beautiful, despite a broken nose (a souvenir from the assault). He gained her trust, and they hid from No's men by ducking underwater with bamboo reeds for breathing. But they were eventually captured, and No attempted to kill her by feeding her to crabs, but she escaped and took an injured Bond to Jamaica. The book ended with the couple making love at Rider's home.

The film's introduction of Honey Ryder became legendary, although a

nude woman on the silver screen in 1962 was not possible. Instead, the image of a gorgeous blonde rising out of the water in a white bikini was iconic, a scene twice echoed in later Bond films (Halle Berry in an orange suit in *Die Another Day* and Daniel Craig in blue trunks in *Casino Royale*). The bikini worn by actress Ursula Andress sold for nearly $60,000 in a 2001 auction at Christie's of London.

Although the book had Honey whistling a calypso tune called "Marion" to which Bond joined in, the film used a song Monty Norman had written specifically for the scene, "Underneath the Mango Tree."

The film's ending featured a relatively healthy Bond engaging Ryder in romance in a boat being towed by Felix Leiter and the Coast Guard.

Ursula Andress as Honey Ryder in *Dr. No.*

Honey Ryder: The Portrayal

Swiss-born Ursula Andress was close to being unknown when cast as Honey Ryder. Born in 1936, she ran away at age seventeen and found her way into small roles in several Italian films. She met and married handsome American actor and photographer John Derek in 1957, and she dropped out of films at that point, having had bad experiences with various studio contracts.

In 1962, producer Cubby Broccoli, seeking his Honey Ryder, came across a photo of a beautiful blonde with dripping wet hair. It was Andress, and the producer had found what he was looking for. But her heavy Swiss accent was difficult to understand, so actress Nikki Van Der Zyl would replace Andress' voice, although Monty Norman's wife, Diana Coupland, recorded the singing of "Underneath the Mango Tree" for the soundtrack LP.

As shooting first started with the final love scene in the boat, the actress became fast friends with costar Sean Connery. But there was a problem with Andress: Ryder was supposed to be a beach girl, heavily tanned, and Ursula was pale. With a makeup artist applying a dark pancake from head-to-toe to her nude form, Andress noticed a large number of men were finding reasons to knock on the door and check the progress of the application.

The role of Honey Ryder confirmed Andress' status as a bona fide sex symbol, although she would receive recognition as a legitimate actress. She won a Golden Globe award in 1963 as the Most Promising Newcomer—Female, as well as being noted as a Star of Tomorrow. Within a year of *Dr. No,* Andress was costarring with performers like Frank Sinatra and Dean Martin in *Four for Texas* and Elvis Presley in *Fun in Acapulco.*

Her international film career continued, as she starred in Hammer Films' *She* in 1965, *What's New Pussycat?* with Peter Sellers in the same year, and *The 10th Victim* with Marcello Mastroianni. Andress played the role of Vesper Lynd in the farcical 1967 version of *Casino Royale.*

Taking a number of questionable parts in low-budget films in the 1970s, Andress recharged her career as the beautiful Aphrodite in the 1981 fantasy film *Clash of the Titans.* She continued through the 1980s and 1990s in films and occasional TV shows like *Falcon Crest.* Nearly seventy, she appeared in *The Bird Preachers* in 2005, still as beautiful as the day she stepped out of the water in Jamaica.

Tatiana Romanova: The Character

Fleming's fifth novel, *From Russia with Love,* presented Tatiana Romanova as Bond's love interest. Originally planning a career as a ballerina, Romanova abandoned that after growing an inch over regulation height. She became a clerk for Russian intelligence, working in the Soviet Embassy in Istanbul, Turkey. Romanova became a chess piece for both the Russians and Brits. The communists used her to lure James Bond (supposedly to his death at the hands of Romanova's boss, Rosa Klebb), while MI6 planned to have her smuggle a Spektor code machine into their hands.

Traveling on the Orient Express train from Istanbul to London, Bond fell in love with Tatiana, but villain Red Grant drugged her and planned to kill the couple. Bond gained the upper hand in a fight with Grant and killed him, although Tatiana's fate was somewhat blurry. In the novel, Bond pulled the groggy girl from the train, and that's the last mention of her.

In the film, Romanova was crucial to the climax, as Bond tussled with Klebb in their hotel room. As the evil woman attempted to stab 007 with her poisoned shoe-knife, Romanova shot Klebb dead with a pistol she recovered from the floor.

Much like the ending of *Dr. No*, Bond reclined with Romanova in a boat, although it was a gondola on a Venice canal. As they embraced, Bond tossed an incriminating film into the drink, saving the reputations of the girl and himself.

Tatiana Romanova: The Portrayal

As they would do several times, producers Broccoli and Saltzman tapped the beauty pageants of the world to find their Bond girl for *From Russia with Love*. They found their Romanova in the ravishing Daniela Bianchi, an Italian who had been the first runner-up in the 1960 Miss Universe pageant in Miami.

Born in 1942, Bianchi's early career mirrored that of Tatiana Romanova: ballet dancing. Modeling followed, with small parts in several Italian and French films as well. Bond director Terence Young came to Rome, saw Bianchi, and brought her (along with dozens of other actresses) to London for a screen test.

The scene for the audition would become a standard for future Bond girls: the bedroom sequence with 007 in *From Russia with Love*. Interestingly, Bianchi didn't play the test with Sean Connery, but with English actor Anthony Dawson, who had played Professor Dent in *Dr. No*. The actress waited several months before she was finally cast as Romanova.

As with Ursula Andress before her, Bianchi's heavy accent would have to be dubbed, with English actress Barbara Jefford brought in to voice Romanova. Bianchi was amazed at how different actress Lotte Lenya was from her character of Rosa Klebb. Off camera, Lenya was petite and very nice, and Bianchi found her portrayal of the cold and calculating Klebb an incredible transformation. She sympathized with Lenya having to wear the thick-lensed eyeglasses, since she was unable to see anything with them on.

Shooting the famous bedroom scene was a challenge for Bianchi. Although dressed in a flesh-colored body stocking, she feared revealing too much and worked hard to keep the bed covers in place. In an effort to keep the spirits light, Sean Connery complicated the shooting by constantly toying with the covers. Young's insistence that they shoot the scene multiple times also led to Bianchi's amused embarrassment.

Following Bond, the actress appeared in a handful of mostly Italian films, including an appearance in the 1967 Bond knockoff *Operation Kid Brother*, which starred—appropriately—Sean Connery's kid brother Neil.

Bianchi retired from show business in 1970 to start her family.

Pussy Galore: The Character

Among the colorful characters to come from Ian Fleming's novels, Pussy Galore was one of the best. Modeled after Fleming's late-in-life mistress, Blanche Blackwell, the character's name in *Goldfinger* was a childish sexual double-entendre, but certainly memorable.

The book gave her black hair, violet eyes (imagine Elizabeth Taylor), and the control of a crime organization from New York, made up of lesbian trapeze-artists-turned-cat-burglars (!) called the Cement Mixers. Although Galore's sexual orientation was played down in the film version, the book openly identified her as a lesbian.

Dressed as nurses, Galore and her group helped Goldfinger in his plan to rob Fort Knox of its gold bullion. When the plot was foiled, Bond wound up on a plane bound for Russia, with Galore posing as a stewardess. Oddjob and Goldfinger were killed by 007, and the plane crashed in the sea. Bond and Galore were rescued, and notwith-standing her previous preference,

Honor Blackman as Pussy Galore in *Goldfinger*.

Bond bedded her while they recovered, despite the indication that Pussy would end up in prison.

Of course, the film version took certain liberties with the character, for story and censorship reasons. The entire backstory of the Cement Mixers was dropped, with Galore's team becoming pilots in an acrobatic flight group called "Pussy Galore's Flying Circus" (several years before Monty Python took a crack at it).

Pussy became Goldfinger's personal pilot and succumbed to Bond's charms in Goldfinger's stables. In the film's climax, Galore was flying Bond and Goldfinger to escape, when Goldfinger got pulled through a broken window to his death (like Oddjob's demise in the book). The depressurization sent the plane into a dive, but 007 and Galore parachuted to safety. They ended the movie by romancing in some remote tropical area.

Pussy Galore: The Portrayal

Beautiful Honor Blackman was born in London in 1927. As a teen, her father offered her the choice of a bicycle or diction lessons for a birthday present. Surprisingly, she took the lessons.

Blackman then enrolled in the Guildhall School of Music and Drama. When she finished, she began her career in London's West End theater community. Her first film appearance, at age twenty, was in *Fame Is the Spur.* It was almost her last as well, as she barely avoided being trampled by a horse in her scene.

Blackman began a steady run of British movie roles in the 1950s, including the 1958 story of the Titanic, *A Night to Remember.* British television followed, guesting on shows like *Danger Man* with Patrick McGoohan (which would become *Secret Agent* after three seasons), and *The Saint.*

In 1963, Blackman appeared as Hera in the fantasy film *Jason and the Argonauts*, which featured the great stop-motion animation of Ray Harryhausen. She also joined Patrick Macnee in *The Avengers*, as the athletic Cathy Gale. The experience led to her cowriting *Honor Blackman's Book of Self-Defense* (collaborating with future Bond stuntman and *Diamonds Are Forever*'s Peter Franks, Joe Robinson).

Producer Cubby Broccoli cast Blackman as Pussy Galore in *Goldfinger* largely based on her success in *The Avengers.* At the time, the show was only aired in England, but Broccoli was sure the actress would be a hit worldwide. No matter, Blackman was a hot commodity and a natural for the role.

Her martial arts background had taught Blackman how to fall properly, which came in handy during the stable scenes with Sean Connery. Accustomed to landing hard on cement floors for *The Avengers,* the actress found the piles of straw in *Goldfinger* to be luxurious. She noted that her costar was fun and charismatic, "the sexiest thing on two legs."

Blackman's first scene with German actor Gert Fröbe was memorable, sitting on the porch of the Kentucky estate where Goldfinger raised horses and planned mayhem. As he started with his opening line, Blackman heard an unusual form of English come from his mouth, as he had learned his lines phonetically. Not understanding one thing he said, she waited until his mouth stopped moving and then said her line. The unorthodox process seemed to work just fine.

The strong character of Pussy Galore and Honor Blackman's athletic abilities led to an extremely unusual rumor in England at the time. A nervous television interviewer broached the subject, seriously asking the actress, "What is it like being half-male and half-female?" Blackman could only laugh out loud.

Having scored big with *Goldfinger*, Blackman maintained a solid mix of film and TV work, in England and America, for the next forty-plus years. She reteamed with Sean Connery in the 1968 western *Shalako*, appeared in the 1986 version of *Doctor Who*, starred in the popular 1990s British comedy series *The Upper Hand*, and showed up in 2001's *Bridget Jones's Diary*, among others.

Jill Masterton/Masterson: The Character

The character of Jill Masterton (changed to "Masterson" for the film) was merely an opportunist. She helped Goldfinger cheat at the game of canasta for £100 a week—a decent sum in 1959. When she had saved enough money, Masterton would leave her employer.

But Bond discovered the tall, beautiful blonde in the midst of the plot and convinced the reluctant accomplice to blackmail Goldfinger into admitting the cheat and paying $50,000 to his pigeon. As an additional tweak, Bond took Masterton with him on his train ride from Miami to New York. Later, he found that Goldfinger had his revenge by painting the woman in gold paint, killing her by skin suffocation (a process, by the way, proven to be completely false by the good television folks on Discovery Channel's *MythBusters*).

The film focused more directly and quickly on Masterson's death, eliminating the train trip and allowing Bond and the woman to enjoy a romance at the Miami hotel. Bond was knocked out by Oddjob when retrieving a bottle of champagne (and disparaging the Beatles at the same time). When he came to, Masterson was dead on the bed, covered in gold.

Jill Masterson: The Portrayal

Born in Middlesex, England, in 1937, Shirley Eaton attended the Royal Academy of Dancing as a child, progressing to an acting school called Aida Foster's. By age twelve, she was appearing on television and the stage.

After modeling as a teen, Eaton's first film experience was stunt riding a horse, doubling for Janet Leigh in *Prince Valiant*. She followed with comedies, musicals like *Charley Moon* (directed by future *Goldfinger* director Guy Hamilton), and dramas like *Date with Disaster* in 1957.

In the 1960s, Eaton starred with writer Mickey Spillane, who was playing his own fictional detective Mike Hammer, in *The Girl Hunters*. The pairing led to a lifelong friendship between the actress and the author.

Acting on a conversation at a party, producer Harry Saltzman interviewed Eaton for *Goldfinger*. Confident that she would have no problem being nude and painted in gold, Eaton accepted the offer to play Jill Masterson. In the makeup room, the actress wore a gold thong and large cone-shaped pasties while the makeup man painted her with a cream-based foundation, mixed with fine gold particles.

Eaton underwent the paint job two times—once for the shoot and once for a publicity photo shoot. With no real complaints about the application of the paint, Eaton found getting it off required a lot of scrubbing and a steamy Turkish bath.

After the release of *Goldfinger*, Eaton was forced to sue the Bond producers, as her contract indicated she would receive the same billing as Honor Blackman and Gert Fröbe. Instead, the opening credits placed her name after Blackman and Fröbe, in the list of supporting performers. The suit was settled out of court, and, fortunately, her relationship with the Bond franchise remained cordial.

Eaton continued to star in films for another five years after *Goldfinger*, including *The Naked Brigade* (no, she wasn't naked in it), *Agatha Christie's Ten Little Indians*, and *The Million Eyes of Su-Maru*, with Frankie Avalon and *Robot Monster*'s George Nader, among other films.

With films like those, there is little surprise in the fact that Shirley Eaton retired afterward, raising a family at age thirty-two.

Tilly Masterton/Masterson: The Character

With an expanded role in the *Goldfinger* novel, the sister of Jill Masterton sought revenge for her murder. Bond introduced himself to the beautiful, black-haired woman by backing his Aston Martin DBIII into the front of her Triumph two-seater.

The accident led to the lady taking a ride with Bond to Geneva, giving him the false name of "Tilly Soames" and claiming to be on her way to a golf tournament. Going their own ways, Bond later caught her attempting to shoot Goldfinger at his smelting plant. The two were taken prisoners and became aides for Goldfinger's plan to blow up Fort Knox.

Tilly refused Bond's romantic advances, preferring the company and protection of Pussy Galore. When Operation Grand Slam went down the drain, Tilly ran and was killed by Oddjob, her neck broken with his razor-edged hat.

The film basically shortened the part of Tilly Masterson to one of a car chase—where her Mustang convertible was customized by Bond's tire slashing blades—the failed assassination attempt on Goldfinger, and her elimination, still at the hands of Oddjob and his bowler hat.

Tilly Masterson: The Portrayal

Tania Mallet was born in Blackpool, England, in 1941, attending Lucy Clayton's School of Modeling. By age sixteen, she was appearing in print ads, becoming one of the most famous models of the 1960s.

Mallet was considered for the role of Tatiana Romanova in *From Russia with Love*. Having a mother of Russian heritage carried no weight, as she did not get the part. But Cubby Broccoli saw a picture of Mallet in a bikini and cast her as Tilly Masterson in *Goldfinger*. While she enjoyed her experience making the film, it couldn't compare with modeling. Offered £50 a week, Mallet negotiated the fee up to £150 a week, which was not even what she could earn in one day as a model.

As such, *Goldfinger* was the only film in which Mallet appeared, although she made a few television appearances as herself in the 1960s and 1970s.

Domino Vitali/Derval: The Character

Other than a change of surnames, Domino was a Bond girl whose movie character pretty much resembled her novel character in *Thunderball*. Fleming made her strong and independent, although she was largely what was known as "a kept woman."

Italian born, she was Dominetta Petachi, but everyone called her Domino. She was schooled in England, eventually attending the Royal Academy of Dramatic Art. With her parents killed in a train accident, she came back to Italy to act. Once there, she adopted the stage name of Vitali. She also hooked up with Emilio Largo romantically at that point, although she told Bond that he was "a close friend, a guardian."

Claudine Auger as Domino in *Thunderball*.

Bond and Domino first met in Nassau, where she often drove around when not on Largo's yacht, the *Disco Volante*. Tired of the romantic come-ons from the seemingly endless stream of old millionaires, Domino was intrigued to meet someone as handsome and virile as Bond. The spy was also intrigued, although he thought her to be a bit of a vixen after their first encounter.

Bond revealed that Largo killed her brother, pilot Giuseppe Petachi, and enlisted her to look for the hijacked atomic bombs onboard Largo's ship. When Largo found her Geiger counter, he bound and tortured her. She broke free, and just as Largo was about to kill Bond, Domino shot her former guardian dead with a speargun. The woman's strength and determination impressed Felix Leiter, as he related to Bond in the novel's conclusion.

Other than changing Domino from Italian to French, the 1965 film presented the lady just as Fleming saw her. The acting backstory was left out, along with the hospital epilogue with Leiter.

Domino Derval: The Portrayal

The role of Domino was, by offer or consideration, originally targeted for actresses like Julie Christie, Raquel Welch, Faye Dunaway, and several other international actresses. All fell through, leaving the door open for actress and former first runner-up in the 1958 Miss World competition, Claudine Auger.

Born in Paris in 1942, she received her acting education at the Paris Drama Conservatory. With the success of the beauty pageant, she began her film career with an uncredited role in French director Jean Cocteau's *Testament of Orpheus* in 1960. She continued in more than a dozen French and Italian films before grabbing the lead Bond girl role in *Thunderball* in 1965.

Film editor Peter Hunt found the actress' voice to be quite weak after shooting had completed, so he brought in Nikki Van Der Zyl—the same actress who had helped out in earlier Bond films—to dub Auger's lines. And, attending the Cannes Film Festival with her costar in 1965, Auger had a ringside seat to witness the frenzy that Connery and Bond had created.

The fame of being a Bond girl had its rewards, as Auger found herself guesting on NBC-TV's *A Bob Hope Comedy Special* in 1966, with other international stars like Michael Caine and Cantinflas. She also continued steady work in European cinema, with some questionable entries like *Black Belly of the Tarantula* in 1971. The Italian horror film was like a 007 All-Star show, with Auger appearing with past and future Bond stars Giancarlo Giannini (2006's *Casino Royale* and *Quantum of Solace*), Barbara Bouchet (1967's farce *Casino Royale*), and Barbara Bach (*The Spy Who Loved Me*).

Claudine Auger retired in 1997, having appeared in more than eighty films and television shows in a career that lasted nearly forty years.

Fiona Volpe: The Character

Created for the film version of *Thunderball*, the beautiful but deadly Fiona Volpe was a member of SPECTRE. She set up the murder of NATO pilot Francois Derval and his surgically altered double in order to hijack two atomic bombs.

She also took care of fellow SPECTRE agent Count Lippe, blowing up his car as he followed 007, with missiles fired from a snazzy BSA motorcycle. This scene in the film was adapted from Ian Fleming's novel, although Volpe was originally an anonymous SPECTRE No. 6, and the motorcycle missiles were merely a hand grenade tossed into Lippe's vehicle.

Volpe picked Bond up in Nassau, roaring along the darkened roads in a muscle-bound Mustang. Later, Volpe and Largo's men tried to interrogate field agent Paula Caplan, but she committed suicide.

Fiona decided to bathe in Bond's bathroom. When 007 found her naked in the tub, she asked for something to put on. Bond obliged by handing her a pair of sandals. After some wild romancing, Volpe was joined by Largo's men, who took Bond into the Junkanoo festival. He escaped, only to be caught by Volpe at the Kiss Kiss Club.

While dancing with Volpe, Bond noted Largo's men in the shadows, preparing to shoot him. Deftly, he made a quick turn and the bullet struck Volpe, killing her.

Fiona Volpe: The Portrayal

In the late 1940s, Italy gave the world the voluptuous allure of actress Gina Lollobrigida. As was often the case, the search was never-ending for the next great Italian beauty. Luciana Paluzzi was one of those.

Born in Rome in 1937, Paluzzi did some modeling and was only sixteen when she had a small role in the romance *Three Coins in the Fountain*. She continued in other European films in the 1950s, including *My Seven Little Sins* with Maurice Chevalier, *Tank Force* (directed by future *Thunderball* director Terence Young), and *Sea Fury*. She also costarred with future Felix Leiter David Hedison on NBC-TV's short-lived *Five Fingers* in 1959.

Paluzzi began popping up in many American TV shows in the 1960s, including *Bonanza, The Man from U.N.C.L.E.*, and *Burke's Law*. She also starred with Frankie Avalon and Annette Funicello in the cult fave *Muscle Beach Party* in 1964.

Like hundreds of other actresses, Paluzzi auditioned for the role of Domino in *Thunderball*. But she didn't mind being cast as the villainous Fiona Volpe, since she found roles like those were much more fun to play. The casting of the Italian-born actress led to changing the character from an Irish woman—Fiona Kelly—to Italian Fiona Volpe (appropriately, "volpe" is Italian for "fox").

Paluzzi had steady work after Bond, appearing in films like *The Venetian Affair* with Robert Vaughan, *Chuka* with Ernest Borgnine, and the campy sci-fi flicks *The Green Slime* in 1968 and *Captain Nemo and the Underwater City* the following year.

In the 1970s, the actress split her time between Italian films like *The Italian Connection* in 1972, teaming up once more with her *Thunderball* costar Adolfo Celi, American films like *Black Gunn* with Jim Brown and *The Greek Tycoon* with Anthony Quinn, and television shows like *Hawaii Five-0,* along with guest appearances on *The Tonight Show Starring Johnny Carson*.

Luciana Paluzzi retired from show business in 1980, living with her husband in California.

Kissy Suzuki: The Character

From the pages of *You Only Live Twice* came the character of Kissy Suzuki. In the story, she was a young Japanese woman who had gone to Hollywood to be an actress, preened as the "Japanese Greta Garbo." But she disliked the experience and returned to her family to dive for pearls.

Distantly related to Tiger Tanaka, the Suzuki family would provide cover for Bond in his search for Blofeld and his Japanese castle. When Bond located Blofeld and killed him, he escaped, suffering from amnesia. Believing himself to be a local fisherman, he lived with Kissy, and she became pregnant with Bond's child. Not aware of this, Bond had his memory jogged by his chance sighting of the word "Vladivostok," and he left for Russia to find who he was.

In the film, Kissy was a diver on the Japanese island where Bond was to train as a ninja fighter and blend in. A fake wedding between the two helped, although as an agent of Japanese SIS, Kissy made sure the marriage would remain unconsummated.

Mie Hama as Kissy Suzuki with Sean Connery as Bond in *You Only Live Twice*.

As Bond prepared to assault Blofeld's volcano fortress, Suzuki was sent to retrieve Tanaka and his ninjas. She spent the balance of the film running in a white bikini and avoiding gunfire. When Bond was triumphant, Kissy decided they could now start their honeymoon. The plan was foiled when their life raft wound up on the deck of a British submarine.

Kissy Suzuki: The Portrayal

Mie Hama, along with costar Akiko Wakabayashi and Kumi Mizuno, became known as the big three actresses in Japanese films of the 1960s. All three appeared together in 1963's *The Lost World of Sinbad,* Toho Studios' response to the success of the Ray Harryhausen fantasy films of the period.

Hama, born in Tokyo in 1943, was a bus fare collector in 1959 when a coworker entered her picture in a New Face Contest at Toho. Chosen as a new star in the making, she made only one picture before becoming unhappy with the film world. A chance meeting with Italian star Marcello Mastroianni convinced her to take another crack at acting. She returned to appear in a number of Japanese films, including *King Kong vs. Godzilla* in 1962.

With future Bond costar Akiko Wakabayashi, Hama appeared in a Japanese spy film called *Key of Keys* in 1965—a demonstration of how pervasive the Bond films had become around the world. The Japanese series, featuring handsome Tatsuya Mihashi as the Bond-like Jiro Kitami, would last for five films between 1963 and 1967. *Key of Keys* also had a rebirth as *What's Up Tiger Lily?* in 1966, with Woody Allen stripping the Japanese soundtrack and writing his own hilarious dubbed screenplay.

When producers for *You Only Live Twice* began their search for Japanese actresses, they were dismayed to find that none of those they tested could speak English. Choosing Akiko Wakabayashi and Hama, the producers decided to bring the pair back to England, where they could learn the language by complete immersion. Akiko did very well; Hama, not as well.

Director Lewis Gilbert asked Hama's costar Tetsuro Tamba—Tiger Tanaka—to tell the actress she would have to leave the picture and return to Japan. The next morning, Tamba reported to Gilbert that the discussion didn't go very well. In shame, Hama would commit suicide that night by jumping from her hotel room. Stunned, the director and producers agreed that Hama would work out just fine in *You Only Live Twice*. Still, they solved the language problem by switching the parts between the two Japanese actresses, and Hama's voice would be replaced by Nikki Van Der Zyl.

Hama would stay in the business for many years after her Bond days, including another monster film, *King Kong Escapes,* in 1967. But Hama wanted to make a bigger contribution to society, becoming a political and environmental activist.

Aki: The Character

As an example of how the Bond films began to stray from the Ian Fleming novels, the character of Aki in *You Only Live Twice* was nowhere to be found in the book, but played an important part of the 1967 picture.

A capable agent for Japanese SIS and Tiger Tanaka, Aki (no last name ever given) made the introduction between Bond and Henderson in Tokyo. When Henderson was murdered, Bond ended up at the offices of Osato Chemicals, where he stole some microfilm and Aki drove him away in a sharp Toyota 2000GT convertible. She then lured 007 to his initial meeting with Tanaka in Tokyo. Later, she took over Bond's massage, and they wound up spending the night.

Aki saved Bond's bacon once more when Osato's gunmen came after the spy. Driving him away once more from Osato's offices, she efficiently ordered a helicopter to pick up the bad guys' car and dump it into Tokyo Bay. Bond and Aki started to nose around the Kobe Docks, and when danger approached, Bond sent the Japanese agent away to safety, although she originally refused to leave 007 alone.

Bond had to be disguised as a Japanese fisherman to slip unnoticed into the local village, and Aki supervised the transformation. Later, as Bond and Aki lay sleeping, an assassin wrongly killed Aki with poison intended for 007.

Aki: The Portrayal

Akiko Wakabayashi, born in Japan in 1941 (although some sources state 1939), became known to Western film audiences in several monster and sci-fi films produced by Japan's Toho Studios in the 1960s.

Wakabayashi appeared in what may have been the fight of the century, *King Kong vs. Godzilla*, in 1962, as well as *Dagora the Space Monster* and *Ghidorah the Three-Headed Monster*, among other films. She also costarred with future *You Only Live Twice* actress Mie Hama in a Japanese Bond knockoff called *Key of Keys*.

The *You Only Live Twice* screenplay originally called for Wakabayashi's character to be named Suki, but the actress suggested the change to Aki.

In the scenes of Aki driving the Toyota 2000GT, the actress found herself being towed, or, in long shots, it wasn't even her—it was one of Japan's top race car drivers. Wakabayashi didn't know how to drive.

The actress' career came to an abrupt end after *You Only Live Twice*. Injured on the set of *Diamonds of the Andes* in 1968, Wakabayashi left the business.

Helga Brandt: The Character

Created for the film version of *You Only Live Twice*, the character of Helga

Sean Connery as Bond and Karin Dor as Helga Brandt in *You Only Live Twice*.

Brandt was another of the "beautiful but deadly" women that would cross James Bond's path in the flicks. Like Fiona Volpe and Elektra King, Brandt would just as soon kill 007 as kiss him—although not necessarily in that order.

Brandt was a German beauty, SPECTRE No. 11, the personal assistant and pilot—certified in helicopters and prop planes—to Mr. Osato. She welcomed Bond to his meeting with Osato, offering a morning sip of champagne and a "healthy chest" for Bond's entertainment.

When Bond was subdued at the Kobe Docks, he wound up bound to a chair in the vixen's stateroom on the *Ning Po*. He admitted to being a spy—for industrial secrets—and seduced Brandt. Agreeing to run away together, Bond and Brandt took off in a private plane, but the lady trapped him and jumped out with a chute. Bond was able to get the plane under control and land it safely.

Later, Osato and Brandt were called on the carpet by Blofeld. When quizzed as to why Bond hadn't been killed yet, Osato—like all good employers—threw Brandt under the bus, pinning the failure on her. As a result, she found herself dumped into a pond of deadly piranhas, with no chance of redemption.

Helga Brandt: The Portrayal

Born in 1938 in Wiesbaden, Germany, Karin Dor began her film career as a teen in West German productions in the early 1950s. Later, she starred in German films based on British crime novelist Edgar Wallace, among others. Many of her films paired her with one-time Tarzan Lex Barker. In the 1960s, she expanded into English films, like *The Face of Fu Manchu,* starring Christopher Lee, with most of her movies still produced in West Germany.

When Bond producers began their search for a tall, blonde German, Brandt—a short brunette—was preparing for a well-earned vacation in the Bahamas. Her agent convinced her to audition, and she got the role, with high heels and tinted hair.

Her first meeting with Connery was uneventful, as Dor found him very nice but nothing out of the ordinary. Dor had never seen any of the Bond pictures, so she wondered how women all over could be going crazy for Connery as Bond. When director Lewis Gilbert called for action, the actor seemed to come alive, and Dor immediately saw what the world had seen.

After *You Only Live Twice,* Dor starred in Alfred Hitchcock's spy thriller *Topaz* in 1969, then began appearing in American TV series like *It Takes a Thief, Ironside,* and *The F.B.I.,* among others. The actress also remained a standard in German films and television, although she began to make fewer appearances in the later years.

Teresa di Vicenzo/Tracy Bond: The Character

As one of the more complex and confusing characters Ian Fleming ever created, Teresa di Vicenzo—Tracy—was the woman James Bond would fall in love with and marry in *On Her Majesty's Secret Service.* Fleming based the character of Tracy on Muriel Wright, an early paramour of the author. The pair were deeply in love when Wright was killed during an air raid during the war. Fleming was left dazed and disconsolate.

Saving Tracy from committing suicide by drowning in the novel's opening, Bond discovered Tracy could be passionate one minute, then throw him out of her room the next. She was the only child of Marc-Ange Draco, the boss of a major crime ring in Corsica. The widow of an Italian count, she seemed to come to life when Bond was around.

Draco encouraged the relationship, and Bond stuck around, not only for Tracy but for her father's resources to track Blofeld. Bond broke up the villain's plan to send the UK into agricultural disaster, with Blofeld escaping with his aide, Irma Bunt. Meanwhile, Bond fell in love with Tracy and married her. But Blofeld and Bunt returned, killing the newlywed Tracy with machine-gun fire. Bond was left dazed and disconsolate.

The film did a fine job of staying with the novel; a rarity, as the success of the films had driven them further and further from Fleming's novels. One addition was having Blofeld kidnap Tracy and hold her for Bond's rescue. Tracy was portrayed as a free spirit; Draco would have preferred her to settle down a bit. With Bond, she finally did, at least for a short while.

Teresa di Vicenzo/Tracy Bond: The Portrayal

Faced with a new 007 in George Lazenby, who had no previous acting experience, Bond producers decided they needed a professional actress with a strong résumé to balance against the man. A brilliant but obvious choice, they cast Diana Rigg as Tracy in *On Her Majesty's Secret Service.*

Born in Yorkshire, England, in 1938, Rigg spent the first seven years of her life in India, where her father worked for the national railroad. She returned to England in 1945 to attend a small boarding school, away from her parents. It wasn't a happy time for the young girl.

At sixteen, Rigg auditioned for RADA in London. Enrolled and attending for three years, she graduated and began modeling, as well as joining the Royal Shakespeare Company. By the early 1960s, she was

George Lazenby as Bond and Diana Rigg as Tracy di Vicenzo Bond in *On Her Majesty's Secret Service.*

appearing onstage with fellow performers like Ian Holm, Judi Dench, and Paul Scofield.

When Honor Blackman left the *Avengers* TV show to appear in *Goldfinger* in 1965, the show's producers noticed a pretty brunette in a TV play called *The Hothouse*. It was Rigg, and she beat out hundreds of other actresses to take the part of Mrs. Emma Peel in the popular detective show.

Rigg left the series in 1968, starring with Oliver Reed and Telly Savalas— soon to be Blofeld to her Tracy—in *The Assassination Bureau*. She continued her work in live theater as well.

Taking the role of Tracy in *On Her Majesty's Secret Service*, the actress brought a sense of intelligence and independence to the part, hardly the bimbo that many people seem to think when considering "Bond girls." Rigg was not a skier, so her scenes on the snow were doubled. But she did her own driving sequences on the ice track, having a great time but leaving her cameraman a bit shaken. While she found costar George Lazenby to be difficult on the set, she still thought his performance was "quite good . . . attractive and sexy."

Rigg landed plum roles in 1970s films like Paddy Chayefsky's black comedy *The Hospital* and the campy horror flick with Vincent Price *Theater of Blood*. She also took a shot at an American sitcom, starring in NBC-TV's *Diana* for one season in 1973.

Not one to take herself too seriously, Rigg starred with Charles Grodin, John Cleese, and a bunch of felt-covered actors in *The Great Muppet Caper* in 1981. In the film, Rigg played the wealthy Lady Holiday, whose secretary is Miss Piggy. She also played the Evil Queen in the MGM musical version of *Snow White* in 1987, and had many British TV appearances.

Into the 2000s Rigg maintained a strong presence on the stage, and she was honored with the title of Dame of the British Empire.

Tiffany Case: The Character

From the pages of Fleming's fourth novel, *Diamonds Are Forever,* Tiffany Case was a pretty, blonde, blue-eyed San Franciscan in her late twenties. Felix Leiter—once CIA, then joining Pinkerton's detectives after being fed to the sharks in *Live and Let Die*—noted she never had much of a chance for a decent life, since her mother ran the best little whorehouse in Frisco. After being brutalized at sixteen by a gang of thugs, Tiffany Case had no use for men.

Her job in the story was to act as a go-between for Bond—posing as diamond smuggler Peter Franks—and the organized crime ring known as the Spangled Mob. Bond got his payoff in a blackjack game at a Las Vegas hotel, with Case as the dealer. When he took too much, Bond was grabbed by the gang. But Case helped him to get free, and on their way to London aboard the *Queen Elizabeth* ocean liner, the lady was kidnapped by killers Wint and Kidd. Bond saved her and sent her to live in a spare room at his place.

Fleming actually closed the story between Bond and Case in his next novel, *From Russia with Love*. In it, Tiffany had stayed with 007 for a few months then moved out, coming back to America.

Sean Connery as Bond and Jill St. John as Tiffany Case in *Diamonds Are Forever.*

The film version of Case made the lady cocky and extremely independent. The backstory also attributed her name to being born on the sales floor of Tiffany and Company jewelers while her mother shopped for a wedding ring.

Yet for someone so sure of herself, Case became a total klutz when trying to fire a machine gun in the film's climax. Pulling the trigger (after 007 had to tell her what to do with the gun), she found the weapon's recoil sufficient to send her tumbling off the oil platform.

Tiffany Case: The Portrayal

A razor-sharp woman like Tiffany Case needed an actress equal to the role. With an IQ reported in the 160s, Jill St. John certainly brought beauty and brains to the part.

Born in Los Angeles in 1940, St. John was an early starter, landing on the local stage at the age of five. By age ten, she was touring in *Annie Get Your Gun* with Martha Raye and taking ballet lessons with fellow classmates Natalie Wood and Stefanie Powers.

She made television appearances as Jill Oppenheim, showing up on *The George Burns and Gracie Allen Show* and *Sky King*, among others. St. John enrolled in UCLA at fifteen but eloped the next year, allowing her only two years of schooling. With amazing looks and a fabulous figure, St. John became one of America's answers to sexy European actresses like Brigitte Bardot and Sophia Loren.

As a young Hollywood starlet, St. John appeared in comedies like *The Remarkable Mr. Pennypacker, Holiday for Lovers,* and *Come Blow Your Horn* with Frank Sinatra (earning St. John a Golden Globe nomination), adventure films like *The Lost World* and *The Liquidator,* and big-time dramas like *The Oscar* and *Tony Rome*, again with Sinatra. She also made numerous TV appearances, guesting on everything from *The Red Skelton Hour* to *The Big Valley* to *Batman.*

In *Diamonds Are Forever*, St. John wisely recognized the "Bond girl" was someone larger-than-life, never symbolizing real women. When producer Cubby Broccoli offered the role to the actress, she jumped at the chance to become part of an elite group of performers. Little did she realize she'd find herself sitting next to a stunt driver in the scene where the red Mustang went up on two wheels in a Las Vegas alley. The experience was scary but thrilling at the same time.

The role of Tiffany Case was good for St. John's already successful career, as she received many movie and TV offers after *Diamonds Are Forever*. She starred in *Sitting Target* with Oliver Reed, along with various television appearances in shows like *Rowan and Martin's Laugh-In*, *The Love Boat*, *Magnum P.I.*, and *Fantasy Island*. She also had her own drama series, *Emerald Point N.A.S.*, with Dennis Weaver and fellow Bond girl Maud Adams, in 1984.

Additional TV and film appearances led into the early 2000s, when Jill St. John retired from show business to a quiet ranch in Aspen, Colorado.

Plenty O'Toole: The Character

As first runner-up for "The Most Obvious Double-Entendre Name in Bond History," Plenty O'Toole provided humor and drama to the film version of *Diamonds Are Forever*. The busty brunette added something special to the glitz and glamour of Las Vegas.

She might best have been described as a professional gold-digger, making her living off of the gambling winnings of gambling men. O'Toole knew the right things to say, even demonstrating the proper etiquette in how to drop a loser without making him feel like one.

First introduced as the escort of a plain-looking man at the craps table, she quickly lost him with a kind word once he lost his bundle of dough. Noting the successful gaming acumen of James Bond, she immediately shifted to his side. Bond tried to lose her with a tip of five grand after winning fifty grand, but O'Toole invited herself back to Bond's room for additional activities. Gangsters aligned with Morton Slumber tossed a close-to-nude O'Toole out the window. To their surprise, there was a life-saving pool below.

In a scene shot but not included in the final cut of the film, a water-logged Plenty returned to Bond's room, where he was now enjoying the company of Tiffany Case. O'Toole quietly rifled through Case's purse, finding her home address. In a scene written but never filmed, O'Toole paid a visit to the house, where she was surprised by Mr. Wint and Mr. Kidd, who mistook her for Case and killed her. When the film picked the story back up, O'Toole was found drowned in Case's pool by Bond and Tiffany.

Plenty O'Toole: The Portrayal

Despite being the younger sister of superstar actress Natalie Wood, Lana Wood found her own way into a long, albeit uneven, career in Hollywood.

Born in 1946 in California, Wood's first screen role was in the John Ford western *The Searchers*, with John Wayne, in 1956. She continued through the 1950s with guest appearances on TV shows like *Have Gun, Will Travel* and *The Real McCoys*.

The 1960s started with more television roles in programs like *Dr. Kildare* and *The Fugitive.* After the minor beach comedy *The Girls on the Beach* in 1965, Wood had regular parts in two prime-time TV soap operas—*The Long, Hot Summer* and *Peyton Place.* More guest appearances in the late 1960s and early 1970s—along with a spread in *Playboy* magazine—led to her part in *Diamonds Are Forever.*

Wood's scenes in the casino with Connery required a bit of screen magic. With the Bond actor at six feet two and Wood at five feet three, the actress—even in high heels—had to stand on a wooden crate when next to Connery.

Wood's exit through the hotel window involved another bit of cinematic sleight of hand. The actress was shot being actually tossed out a first-floor window into an offscreen mattress. Stunt woman Patty Elder then did the fall in a flesh-colored body stocking. Wood completed the landing into the pool by jumping from a scaffold at three in the morning.

Love scenes with Sean were particularly difficult, as the couple had begun seeing each other during the production. Kissing Bond felt somewhat like the crew was watching the pair on a date.

Wood continued on TV shows like *Rod Serling's Night Gallery, Mission: Impossible,* and *Baretta* in the 1970s. She made an appearance in *The New Mike Hammer* in 1985, then left the performing world for more than twenty years. In 2008, Wood returned to guest spots on TV shows and film roles, continuing a career of more than fifty years.

Solitaire: The Character

Ian Fleming's second novel, *Live and Let Die,* presented Solitaire. She was a young Frenchwoman, Haitian by birth, and gifted with telepathic skills. Bond thought she was one of the most beautiful women he'd ever seen. A lady kept by Mr. Big (remember, Kananga was a film development), Solitaire found Bond to be an ally and eventually escaped Mr. Big with the aid of 007.

Deep in the neighborhood of Harlem, in New York City, Bond met up with Mr. Big, and the villain suspected 007 was out to kill him. Bond lied, telling Mr. Big he was on the trail of missing English coins. Solitaire was summoned and, with her powers, asked if Bond was truthful. Seeing 007 as a way out, Solitaire lied as well, saying Bond was telling the truth.

Later, Solitaire convinced Bond to take her away, and the couple traveled by train to Florida. Big caught up with them, took Solitaire hostage, and headed for Jamaica. Bond was then captured, tied together with Solitaire, and the pair dragged over the coral reefs behind Mr. Big's yacht, the *Secatur* (a film scene saved for 007 and Melina Havelock in the film version of

For Your Eyes Only). A mine planted earlier by Bond blew up the boat, sending Mr. Big into the waters where he was eaten by sharks.

Bond and Solitaire were saved by old friend Quarrel. She stayed with 007 while he recuperated, and that's where Fleming ended his story.

Much of Solitaire's personality and character carried over to the film version, with some usual adjustments. As in the book, Solitaire was a virgin, but the movie tied her loss of virtue (to Bond, naturally) to a loss of her powers. To that end, Bond was responsible, loading her deck of tarots with nothing but "lovers" cards, leading her to sleep with him.

Jane Seymour as Solitaire and Roger Moore as Bond in *Live and Let Die.*

Solitaire: The Portrayal

British-born Jane Seymour was only twenty-two when she appeared as Solitaire in Roger Moore's initial film as James Bond in 1973's *Live and Let Die.* The movie was the first of a long performing career, mostly in television, for the actress.

Seymour originally aimed for a life in the world of dance, making her first appearance at age thirteen with the London Festival Ballet. But a knee injury brought her ballet career to an end and refocused the young girl toward acting.

She first made an uncredited appearance as a chorus girl in the 1969 film musical *Oh, What a Lovely War,* directed by Richard Attenborough. Only a few appearances in British movie and TV roles preceded her casting in *Live and Let Die.*

Although Diana Ross was originally considered for the role, producer Harry Saltzman took one look at Seymour and cast her as Solitaire. The inexperienced actress didn't ask for a stunt woman—even though Roger Moore had a stuntman driver—in the scenes with the double-decker bus. Every 180-degree spin and even the low viaduct that severed the upper deck from the bus featured Seymour being tossed around inside (a scene that no one was sure would even work).

Seymour did several television shows and miniseries in Britain before her first major American TV appearance in the popular 1976 miniseries *Captains and the Kings*. She then starred with Patrick Wayne and Ray Harryhausen's brilliantly animated creatures in *Sinbad and the Eye of the Tiger* in 1977.

She continued to split her time in the 1970s and 1980s among films, television, and miniseries in England and America, including *Battlestar Galactica, Somewhere in Time, Lassiter, Onassis*—where she starred as opera diva Maria Callas—and *War and Remembrance*.

Jane Seymour starred in her own successful TV series for six seasons in the 1990s, CBS's *Dr. Quinn, Medicine Woman*. The actress played a woman doctor practicing in the Rockies in the late 1800s. She won a Golden Globe for Best Actress in a TV Series for the role.

Along with writing several self-help and children's books, Seymour continued television and film appearances in the 2000s, including *Smallville, Modern Men, In Case of Emergency,* and a hilarious "older woman" scene with Owen Wilson in *Wedding Crashers*.

Rosie Carver: The Character

A landmark character in the film version of *Live and Let Die,* Rosie Carver was the first African American woman to share a bed with James Bond. It was groundbreaking, as America was still adjusting to the success of the civil right movements in the 1950s and 1960s.

Carver was an unproven agent with the CIA, assigned to help Bond for her second mission on the island of San Monique. Since her first mission resulted in the death of agent Baines, Bond hoped this one would be more of a success. She was the nervous sort, easily scared. When she was spooked by a voodoo sign in Bond's hotel room, Carver chose to spend the night in his company.

Unfortunately, Carver turned out to be a turncoat, working for Kananga. She was supposed to arrange for 007's death (a chance of redemption from Kananga for her first mission failure), but Bond got wise to her plans. She wound up running for her life through

Gloria Hendry as Rosie Carver in *Live and Let Die.*

the woods of the island and was shot dead with Kananga's remote-controlled voodoo heads.

Rosie Carver: The Portrayal

Born in 1949 in Florida, Gloria Hendry moved with her family to New Jersey as a child. With an interest in acting, she started taking lessons in drama, dancing, and singing. Hendry spent a short while as a Playboy Bunny in New York, then did some modeling.

She made her first film in 1968, a small role in *For Love of Ivy* with Sidney Poitier. Hendry appeared with future Bond costar Yaphet Kotto in 1972's *Across 110th Street,* followed by a major part in the urban drama *Black Caesar,* alongside Fred Williamson. That film was brought to the attention of Bond producers, who met Hendry in New York and immediately put her on a plane to New Orleans to meet with director Guy Hamilton and new Bond actor Roger Moore.

Shooting a scene on a fishing boat, Hendry got suddenly ill, and a crew member suggested she take a quick dip in the ocean to cool her off. Jumping in, she noticed a shark fin approaching—she exited the water in no time, feeling perfectly fine.

Interior scenes were shot at Pinewood Studios in London. The love scene between Bond and Carver was somewhat new territory, but Hendry had a situation that held a familiar ring. Just as Diana Rigg admitted to having something with garlic in it before one kissing scene with George Lazenby in *On Her Majesty's Secret Service,* Hendry began a scene with Moore realizing she'd eaten a meal with garlic the previous evening. Ever the gentleman, Moore put her at ease, reminding her that he was married to an Italian woman.

Hendry's role in the Bond film, coupled with her athletic abilities, landed the actress in a number of black action films in the 1970s, including *Slaughter's Big Rip-Off, Hell Up in Harlem, Black Belt Jones,* and *Savage Sisters.* She also made guest appearances in TV shows like *Falcon Crest, Hunter,* and *Doogie Howser, M.D.*

Mary Goodnight: The Character

Three of the Bond books featured Mary Goodnight as 007's personal secretary at MI6. She replaced his previous aide, Loelia Ponsonby, who left the service after getting married.

The character in the novels was attractive and had a nice figure. Although she joined Bond in the field in *The Man with the Golden Gun,*

Goodnight never slept with 007. The two, however, did show an attraction to each other.

The film version of Mary Goodnight was presented in *The Man with the Golden Gun* as an MI6 field agent, a bit of a newbie like Rosie Carver in the previous Bond flick. She introduced herself to 007 in Hong Kong, as he was on the trail of Scaramanga. By the time they had reached Bangkok, Bond and Goodnight were ready to have a good night. Interrupted by Scaramanga's mistress, Andrea Anders, Bond bedded her instead.

Later, Goodnight was kidnapped by Scaramanga and Nick Nack, locked in the trunk of the car that turned into a plane. Bond was able to track the group to Scaramanga's island. Goodnight helped Bond recover the Solex Agitator, and while the island exploded, the pair escaped in a Chinese junk.

Mary Goodnight: The Portrayal

Blonde Swedish beauty Britt Ekland was born in Stockholm in 1942. A stint in a drama school led to her joining a traveling theater group. Ekland also did some modeling jobs as a teen.

In the early 1960s, the actress made several uncredited film appearances, including *G.I. Blues* with Elvis Presley and *The Prize* with Paul Newman and Edward G. Robinson. After she met and married British funny man Peter Sellers in 1963, Ekland appeared with her husband in *Carol for Another Christmas, After the Fox,* and *The Bobo.*

By the late 1960s, the actress was starring in features like *The Double Man* with Yul Brynner and *Too Many Thieves* with Peter Falk. But her role as the Amish girl who danced in the burlesque theater in the 1968 comedy *The Night They Raided Minsky's* earned Ekland rave reviews.

The 1970s found the actress in films like *Get Carter* with Michael Caine and cult favorite *The Wicker Man* with future Bond costar Christopher Lee. When Ekland got word of a new Bond film coming up, it brought to her mind the scene from *Dr. No* where Ursula Andress made her legendary entrance from the ocean in a white bikini. Ever since seeing that, Ekland had dreamt of being a Bond girl.

So she dressed like a secretary and went to see Cubby Broccoli. She made her intentions very clear: She wanted to play Mary Goodnight. Ekland was crushed when the producer noted that they sometimes just used a character's name from the novels and nothing more. But a few months later, Broccoli handed her the script and welcomed her to the Bond family.

Being a Bond girl was not without its hazards. Roger Moore and Ekland were shooting the scene where they are running from Scaramanga's plant, which was blowing up around them. Clad only in a bikini, the actress wound up too close to one of the pyrotechnic charges as it went off. The flash burned her bottom, and her immediate reaction was to fall and cover up. Moore pulled Ekland to her feet, and they continued running.

While her Bond experience was great, it did nothing for Ekland's career, from her viewpoint. Apparently, many producers believed that type of role was all she could do. Still, *The Man with the Golden Gun* garnered a good deal of publicity for the actress.

Ekland made feature films and TV show appearances after Bond, including the comedy *Royal Flash,* starring Malcolm McDowell and directed by Richard Lester; *Battlestar Galactica; The Love Boat; Fantasy Island;* and *Scandal,* with John Hurt and Ian McKellen.

Britt Ekland retired from films in 2002, having developed osteoporosis. But she began appearing in live theater productions, including a one-woman show called *Britt on Britt.*

Andrea Anders: The Character

In many cases, the Bond films used a character that, for lack of a better term, could have been called "the villain's expendable lady." Think women like Jill Masterson, Helga Brandt, Rosie Carver, etc. They worked for the bad guy—sometimes against their will—slept with 007, then were killed at the hands of their boss. Andrea Anders was another one of those in *The Man with the Golden Gun.*

As the girlfriend of Francisco Scaramanga, she picked up his laundry and golden bullets, as well as looked real sharp in a bathing suit. Bond caught up with her in Hong Kong, where he slapped her around to find out why her boss sent a golden bullet to MI6. In reality, it was Anders who sent the shell, hoping Bond would respond. Scared of Scaramanga, Anders hoped 007 would make him go away—permanently. He agreed, in exchange for the Solex Agitator.

Having slept with Anders after stashing Mary Goodnight in the closet, Bond arranged to pick up the device the next day at a kickboxing match. When he got there, Anders had been shot dead by Scaramanga—left in her seat with no one noticing her.

Andrea Anders: The Portrayal

Two Swede beauties in one Bond film? Wow. Maud Adams, born in 1945, was a highly successful print model for years before her first appearance in a Bond film (there would be more).

As an eighteen-year-old, Adams was spotted shopping one day, and a photographer asked to snap her picture. It resulted in her entry for the Miss Sweden beauty contest, which she won. The success led to her modeling career, first in Paris, then in New York City, where she joined the well-known Eileen Ford Agency.

Her debut film appearance was 1970's *The Boys in the Band*, where she played—not surprisingly—a model. A few Canadian films followed, as well as a guest shot on ABC-TV's *Love, American Style*, leading up to *The Man with the Golden Gun*.

Bond producers knew of Maud Adams, and following a quick meeting in New York, they brought her on as Andrea Anders. But the actress soon experienced the highs and lows of making a Bond film.

In Hong Kong, the cast and crew entered the grand ballroom of their hotel and were surrounded by reporters and photographers eager for a quote or picture. However, when Adams and the group flew to the Thai province of Phuket, they were greeted by a tiny airstrip in the middle of the jungle, as well as seedy accommodations in what had once been a brothel.

Adams' role in *The Man with the Golden Gun* led to other substantial films, including playing James Caan's ex-wife in 1975's *Rollerball,* and the action-thriller *Killer Force,* featuring two ex-Bond villains—Telly Savalas and Christopher Lee. She also guested on TV shows like *Kojak, Hawaii Five-0,* and *Starsky and Hutch.* The actress also became the focus of tattoo artist Bruce Dern's desire in the creepy *Tattoo* in 1981.

After starring in the TV series *Chicago Story* in 1982, Adams scored the rare feat of being cast in a major role in her second Bond film, *Octopussy.* Another TV series, *Emerald Point N.A.S.,* followed, as well as an unprecedented—albeit uncredited—third appearance in a Bond film, *A View to a Kill,* in 1985.

Numerous film and TV appearances continued into the 1990s, including hosting and guesting on Swedish television. In 2000, Adams made a memorable guest shot on Fox-TV's *That '70s Show,* playing a bridesmaid—along with former Bond girls Barbara Carrera and Kristina Wayborn—to bride and former Bond girl Tanya Roberts.

Anya Amasova: The Character

Beautiful but deadly, Major Anya Amasova—aka Agent XXX—was an operative for the Russian KGB in *The Spy Who Loved Me.* Amasova was romantically involved with Sergei Barsov, another KGB agent. Bond killed Barsov in the film's opening scenes, not knowing the dead man's relationship to Anya.

Reporting to General Gogol in Moscow, Agent XXX was assigned to find a Russian submarine that had disappeared. Gogol also informed her of Barsov's demise. Bond was also investigating a similar disappearance of a British sub, so both agents arrived in Egypt to obtain microfilm valuable to their search. The pair subdued Jaws, got the film, and escaped. But Agent XXX knocked out 007 and grabbed the microfilm.

Bond caught up with Amasova, along with Gogol and M at the Abu Simbel Temple. Russia and Britain agreed to work together on the missing subs and identified Karl Stromberg as a possible villain. Bond and Amasova set out for Sardinia, courtesy of Q's underwater Lotus Esprit. Anya seemed to know the car's equipment as well as 007, having had complete access to the MI6 secret files years back. When Anya finally discovered that it was Bond who killed her lover, she vowed to kill 007 when their mission was complete.

The pair's investigation led to Stromberg's supertanker, the *Liparus*. Anya was taken prisoner by Stromberg in his underwater city, Atlantis, and saved by Bond when it was attacked by an American submarine. With the mission complete, Anya prepared to shoot 007, but realized she was in love with him and wound up under the covers with the British agent.

Anya Amasova: The Portrayal

Born in Queens, New York, in 1947, Barbara Bach left high school at age sixteen to become a model. Within a year, the beautiful brunette was working for the Eileen Ford Agency, attaining world fame as the cover girl of *Seventeen* magazine.

With modeling work in Italy, she was soon offered acting jobs, appearing in the Italian television miniseries of Homer's *Odyssey* in 1968. The actress appeared in comedies like *Mio Padre Monsignore* (*My Father, the Monsignor*), horror films like *Black Belly of the Tarantula,* crime dramas like *Stateline Hotel* with former Bond girl Ursula Andress, and sex romps like *The Sensuous Sicilian,* with future Bond ally Giancarlo Giannini.

Barbara Bach as Agent XXX/Anya Amasova in *The Spy Who Loved Me.*

When Cubby Broccoli saw a videotape of the actress in a screen test for an unproduced film, he realized he had found the Bond girl he always dreamed of. He contacted Bach and, along with director Lewis Gilbert, tested her for the role of Agent XXX. Soon after, she was cast in *The Spy Who Loved Me*, with only days before shooting started.

Bach had what Cubby Broccoli believed was essential for any Bond girl: acting talent, extreme beauty, and being unknown to most of the filmgoing world. Of course, the last point also assured the budget wouldn't be broken on the leading lady. As Bach was nearly twenty-eight years old at the time, her lack of cinematic notoriety was rare as well.

Barbara Bach was certainly known after *The Spy Who Loved Me*, landing major parts in *Force 10 from Navarone*, with former Bond villain Robert Shaw and former Bond costar Richard Kiel; *Humanoid*, again with Richard Kiel; and *Jaguar Lives!*, kind of a reunion of Bond villains with Christopher Lee, Donald Pleasence, and Joseph Wiseman.

The actress was cast in 1981 in the Stone Age comedy *Caveman*, costarring with future husband and former Beatle Ringo Starr. After her marriage, Bach wound her performing career down, with her last role in 1987 in a German TV movie. She returned to school, earning a master's degree in psychology and focusing on charity work in a variety of fields.

Holly Goodhead: The Character

With another trip to the "cabinet of risqué names," Bond producers and writers came up with Dr. Holly Goodhead as the Bond woman in 1979's *Moonraker*. No shrinking violet, she was smart as a whip and, like more and

more of the female allies, perfectly able to hold her own against the threats of the world. Goodhead's roots appeared to have come from the character of Gala Brand in Fleming's novel of *Moonraker*.

Bond was touring the Moonraker shuttle plant of Hugo Drax when he first met Goodhead. Showing no tolerance for Bond's surprise at finding a woman doctor, she had no problem

Roger Moore as Bond and Lois Chiles as Dr. Holly Goodhead in *Moonraker*.

responding in a sarcastic manner. Hair in a bun and holding a clipboard—Dr. Goodhead was a far cry from Honey Rider's emergence from the water in a white bikini.

The good doctor was also a good astronaut and a good CIA agent, working undercover in Drax's corporation. Bond discovered her true identity, and the pair seemed to seduce each other into bed, things being equal. Later, in Rio de Janeiro, as Drax's Moonraker shuttles were being launched, Bond and Goodhead found themselves trapped beneath the engine nozzles of one of the rockets. They escaped and made their way onto the last shuttle as it lifted off.

They arrived at Drax's space station, where Goodhead showed good aim with her laser gun, and after Drax had been sent into the vacuum of space, the doctor's experience as an astronaut came in handy. She took control of a Moonraker shuttle and, before landing, found time to cavort with Bond in the zero gravity of space.

Holly Goodhead: The Portrayal

Lois Chiles was born in Houston, Texas—appropriately the home of the Johnson Space Center—in 1947. First attending the University of Texas, she moved to New York to finish at Finch College in Manhattan. When *Glamour* magazine spotted her for their college issue, Chiles began a successful modeling career for the Wilhelmina Agency.

Acting classes followed, earning her parts in major feature films like *The Way We Were* with Robert Redford and Barbra Streisand; *The Great Gatsby,* again with Redford; and Michael Crichton's *Coma.* Major modeling jobs were pending when Chiles canceled them, forfeiting tens of thousands of dollars. She felt she needed to study acting on a more serious level and did just that.

Chiles turned down the role of Anya in *The Spy Who Loved Me* but, strictly by chance, found herself sitting next to director Lewis Gilbert on an airplane when casting was being held for Holly Goodhead in *Moonraker.* This time she took the part, seeing the role—despite its suggestive name—was that of a strong, independent woman, very equal to 007.

Life on the Bond set was always jovial, especially when Roger Moore was present. Chiles, growing up as a tomboy and with brothers, thought she had heard all the dirty jokes in the world, but Moore's were "absolutely filthy." Her final scene with Moore, simulating lovemaking in the weightlessness of space, was extremely uncomfortable. Suspended on wires, with little platforms underneath her back and legs, Chiles made the best of the situation.

With time off to tend to a dying brother, Chiles dug back into her work with a recurring role on the wildly popular prime-time TV drama *Dallas*. The actress also acted in films like *Creepshow 2*, *Broadcast News*, and *The Babysitter* with Alicia Silverstone, among others. She also has made various appearances in television shows over the years, like *L.A. Law*, *The Nanny*, and *CSI: Crime Scene Investigation*.

Chiles also taught acting at the University of Houston, in the hope of perhaps tutoring the next generation of Bond stars.

Corinne Dufour: The Character

Moonraker's disposable Bond ally was Drax's personal pilot (Helga Brandt, anyone?) Corinne Dufour.

She picked up Bond at LAX, brought him to Drax's plant, and slept with the spy. Tipping Bond to the location of Drax's safe and secret technical drawings, Dufour incurred the wrath of her boss. The billionaire released his hounds, they raced after the poor girl—and Dufour was no more.

Corinne Dufour: The Portrayal

Born in Paris in 1950, the beautiful Corinne Cléry began acting in French and Italian films as a teen. In 1975, she gained notoriety by starring with Udo Kier in the controversial X-rated film *The Story of O*.

She continued with Italian films like *Holiday Hookers*, *Stormtroopers*, *Hitch Hike*, *Covert Action*, and *The Humanoid* before being cast in *Moonraker*.

After her part in *Moonraker*, Cléry worked in more Italian films like *Yor, the Hunter from the Future* and *The Gamble*, with Matthew Modine and Faye Dunaway. The actress also maintained a steady line of work in Italian television well into the 2000s.

Judy/Melina Havelock: The Character

Ian Fleming's short story "For Your Eyes Only" offered the double murder of Colonel and Mrs. Havelock. They lived in Jamaica and were old friends of M. When they refused to sell their property to Herr von Hammerstein, he hired a man named Gonzales to kill them.

In a purely personal and vengeful reaction, M sent Bond to a retreat in Vermont where the killers were hiding out. His orders were to kill them. Once there, 007 found Judy Havelock, daughter of the murdered couple, armed with a bow and arrow. She had the same killing agenda as Bond.

Convincing her to work with him, Bond allowed Judy the first shot, and she killed von Hammerstein as he dove into a lake.

Judy Havelock was blonde, pretty, and athletic. Bond did get the chance to kiss her when the mayhem was over, offering to take her to a motel for comfort.

The film version of "For Your Eyes Only" took a number of plot points from the short story, with Judy Havelock becoming part-Greek and named Melina. Her blonde hair became brown, and her skill with a bow and arrow transferred to a high-powered crossbow. She used the weapon to kill a Cuban hitman named Gonzales, who had killed her marine archaeologist parents, while he was diving into a swimming pool.

Melina, a marine archaeologist like her folks, helped Bond find a sunken British ship and recover a portable submarine defense system. In a scene taken from Fleming's *Live and Let Die* novel, Melina and Bond were bound together by the villainous Kristatos and dragged behind a fishing boat. They broke free and escaped, defeating Kristatos at his monastery retreat. In the film's closing moments, the couple took a midnight swim.

Melina Havelock: The Portrayal

French beauty Carole Bouquet was born in 1957. A very shy girl, she aimed to study philosophy at the Sorbonne, but turned her attention to the Conservatoire d'Art Dramatique—France's version of RADA.

At twenty years of age, Bouquet was stopped on the street and offered a screen test in director Luis Buñuel's Oscar-nominated *That Obscure Object of Desire*. The role led to more European films, including the popular French comedy *Buffet Froid* (Cold Buffet) in 1979.

Originally considered for the part of Holly Goodhead in *Moonraker,* Bouquet got the role of Melina Havelock after the recommendation of her publicist. But the actress didn't embrace the publicity that usually accompanied Bond premieres, recalling the entire experience as "no fun."

One reason could have been the need to shoot a substantial amount of her scenes underwater. With a sinus condition, Bouquet couldn't spend any extended time in the water, so special effects helped to create the illusion. Her close-up scenes were shot in slow-motion, with fans softly blowing her gorgeous hair around. Postproduction overlaid air bubbles, completing the effect.

Bouquet, always a stunning beauty, modeled throughout her career. She became the "Face of Chanel" in 1986, appearing in print and television ads for the company's famous perfume No. 5. She appeared in Francis Ford Coppola's portion of the multidirector film *New York Stories* in 1989.

Still an amazing beauty past the age of fifty, Carole Bouquet continues her career in European films.

Bibi Dahl: The Character

Bibi Dahl, a somewhat humorous character in the film version of *For Your Eyes Only,* was pretty, talented, energetic. Perhaps too energetic—a cold shower might have helped to tone down the raging hormones of the fifteen-year-old pro ice skater.

A protégée of villain Aris Kristatos, Dahl worked with her stern and demanding trainer, Jakoba Brink, in the northern Italian town of Cortina d'Ampezzo. The young Dahl set her sights on Bond as soon as he showed up, stripped past her skivvies, and hopped into his hotel room bed. Knowing there could be laws against such things, Bond did the unthinkable and turned the offer down. No problem for Dahl, as she repositioned her libido toward the evil biathaloner Eric Kriegler.

Later, in the St. Cyril monastery, Dahl turned against Kristatos and helped Bond by stopping Kriegler from shooting him. With the bad guys out of the way, Bibi Dahl found a new sponsor in Milos Columbo.

Bibi Dahl: The Portrayal

Cute, bubbly, and blonde, professional ice skater Lynn-Holly Johnson was born in Chicago in 1958. She quit competitive skating to join the Ice Capades, then made a smooth transition to film with the lead role against Robby Benson in *Ice Castles* in 1978. Granted, her role was that of a competitive figure skater, but the performance was good enough to earn Johnson a Golden Globe nomination. More, Johnson had modeled in Chicago as a child, as well as appearing in more than one hundred TV spots before the age of ten.

She starred in the Disney film *The Watcher in the Woods* in 1980 before Cubby Broccoli called and offered the part of Bibi Dahl to Johnson, written specifically with her in mind. Along with her skating scenes, Johnson was able to exhibit her athletic skills in the snow skiing sequences with Roger Moore.

After *For Your Eyes Only,* Johnson made guest appearances on TV shows like *CHiPs* and *MacGyver,* as well as feature films like the sci-fi thrillers *The Sisterhood* and *Hyper Space,* and *The Criminal Mind.*

Octopussy: The Character

Filmmakers really took nothing other than the title from Ian Fleming's short story "Octopussy." There were no circuses, secret agents dressed as clowns, Fabergé eggs, nuclear bombs, or tennis-playing tuk-tuk drivers. There was an Octopussy, but it was the pet octopus of the story's villain. In reality, the name came from a small boat that the author owned in Jamaica.

The film's Octopussy was a beautiful jewel smuggler and successful businesswoman who had an island palace and a trained troupe of female acrobats as part of her traveling circus. The woman was in cahoots with Kamal Khan. When Bond showed up, she was grateful that the spy had allowed her father to choose an honorable way to die after stealing Chinese gold some years back.

When Khan tried to take Bond back into captivity, Octopussy stood up for him, which angered the already-fuming Khan. Following under-the-covers activities, Khan's assassins attacked Bond, but they were beaten by 007 and Octopussy. Later, when Octopussy attended a performance of her circus along with American military, Bond had to burst in and disarm a nuclear bomb planted by Khan.

Octopussy led her band of sisters as they made their way into Khan's palace. As they subdued Khan's men, Octopussy was taken hostage aboard Khan's plane by Gobinda. Bond saved Octopussy before the plane crashed, and the couple embraced in the woman's barge.

Octopussy: The Portrayal

Returning in her second Bond film—this time as the female lead—Maud Adams portrayed the tough, smart, and independent Octopussy. While the actress did have some reservations about her character's suggestive name, she accepted the fact that it was originally a title from Ian Fleming.

Adams also noted the difference between this character and Andrea Anders in *The Man with the Golden Gun*. While Anders was isolated, under the control of a mean man, and sought the help of Bond, Octopussy was a successful businessperson, surrounded by women, and able to help Bond in defeating Khan.

When it appeared Roger Moore would not return as 007, Maud Adams had been brought in to assist with auditions. As had become tradition, she played the role of Tatiana Romanova from the seduction scene in *From Russia with Love*, pairing up with potential Bonds.

The actress also found the circus scenes, shot at Pinewood Studios, to be great fun. Between genuine tent performers in front of eight hundred extras

Maud Adams (left) as Octopussy and Kristina Wayborn as Magda in *Octopussy*.

and Roger Moore's clowning in clown makeup, Adams was thoroughly entertained and impressed.

Magda: The Character

Unlike other secondary Bond girls, Magda actually made it to the final reel of *Octopussy*. Like most Bond girls, she was beautiful, sexy, and destined to eventually end up with the secret agent. As the sharp and trustworthy partner of Octopussy, Magda bedded Bond to get the valuable Fabergé egg. She then escaped over the balcony to a waiting car.

Later, she joined Octopussy at the circus. When Bond tried to convince everyone there was a bomb planted in a prop cannon, Magda refused to believe it. But Octopussy proved Bond right.

Magda: The Portrayal

Miss Sweden of 1970, Kristina Wayborn was cast as Magda after producers noted a poster of the woman, dressed in a brief khaki hunting outfit and posing next to a lion. As the role called for someone beautiful and athletic, Wayborn was perfect.

Born in 1950, Wayborn competed in several other beauty pageants, including Miss Universe and winning Miss Scandinavia of 1971. With a small role in the ABC-TV movie *Victory at Entebbe,* Wayborn kicked off her acting career. In 1980, she appeared as Greta Garbo in the NBC-TV movie *The Silent Lovers.*

As Magda, Wayborn was able to demonstrate her skills in horseback riding, as well as the acrobatic maneuver of tying her sari to a balcony post, rolling backward off it, and twisting down to a safe landing at street level—even though the takeoff was shot in India and the landing was shot in England.

The physicality of a Bond film can have its dangers, as Wayborn discovered. One scene required the actress to kick a bazooka out of the grip of a stuntman with her bare foot. Unfortunately, the real bazooka—sufficiently heavy—had not been replaced with the lightweight plastic one as intended. The kick resulted in several broken bones in Wayborn's foot.

Thrilled to be part of the Bond family, Wayborn did occasionally find herself lying when asked the title of the new Bond in which she appeared. She often replied—incorrectly—that it hadn't been named yet. Eventually, Wayborn got used to it.

Following *Octopussy,* Wayborn made guest appearances in TV shows like *The Love Boat, Dallas,* and *Baywatch,* as well as feature films like *Forbidden Warrior* and *The Frankenstein Syndrome.*

Stacey Sutton: The Character

As the main love interest in the 1985 film *A View to a Kill,* Stacey Sutton was a girl in trouble. As heir to the family oil business, she found herself in a hostile takeover by Max Zorin. Even with his check of $5 million in hand, Stacey needed help.

Of course, the help arrived in the guise of James Bond. Trapped in a burning San Francisco City Hall, Sutton was saved by 007—pulled from a falling elevator and driving her away in a fire engine. When Zorin's mines were about to explode, Bond got her to safety.

Taken hostage by Zorin in one of his airships, Sutton fought back as Bond wrestled with the villain on the Golden Gate Bridge. Bond defeated Zorin, Sutton regained control of the family business, and the couple enjoyed a well-earned steamy shower.

Stacey Sutton: The Portrayal

James Bond films have always required a certain level of suspension of disbelief, knowing that what was on the screen was make-believe. Believing Tanya Roberts was a geologist in *A View to a Kill* pushed that suspension level to the edge (but not as far as accepting Denise Richards as a nuclear scientist).

Tanya Roberts was born in the Bronx, New York, in 1955. She dropped out of high school to begin an acting career, studying with famed instructors Lee Strasberg and Uta Hagen. The beautiful blonde supported herself in a number of ways, including modeling, doing television commercials for Ultra-Brite toothpaste and Clairol hair products, and teaching at an Arthur Murray dance studio.

Tanya Roberts as Stacey Sutton in *A View to a Kill.*

Still in New York, Roberts made her film debut, starring in the low-budget horror thriller *Forced Entry*, in 1975, with Nancy Allen. She continued to work in feature and television films like *The Private Files of J. Edgar Hoover, Pleasure Cove,* and *Waikiki,* among others.

Moving to California, Roberts earned the distinction of becoming Julie Rogers, the last of Charlie's Angels, in the wildly popular ABC-TV show of the same name in 1981. Additional appearances in *The Love Boat* and *Fantasy Island* led up to her breakthrough role in the cult classic *The Beastmaster,* helmed by *Phantasm* director Don Coscarelli. Featured in a photo spread in *Playboy* magazine and starring in *Sheena: Queen of the Jungle,* Roberts became known around the world.

The exposure made the actress a perfect choice for the latest Bond film. Cubby Broccoli had seen Roberts in *Beastmaster* and offered her the role in *A View to a Kill.* She accepted, glad to be in good physical shape. Roberts found herself doing a fair amount of hanging by the arms—in the elevator shaft and on the replicated set of the Golden Gate Bridge.

Like many Bond girls, Roberts found the worldwide exposure of her performance didn't necessarily open any new or bigger doors in the industry for her. After *A View to a Kill,* Roberts starred in the wrestling comedy *Body Slam,* then appeared in a number of erotic thrillers like *Night Eyes, Inner Sanctum,* and *Sins of Desire.* The actress also teamed with Shannon Tweed to star in a Cinemax cable series called *Hot Line.*

Tanya Roberts spent eight seasons playing a mom in Fox-TV's *That '70s Show,* as well as theater productions of *A View from a Bridge, The Hydes of March,* and *Sextette.*

May Day: The Character

Tall, dark, and deadly, May Day was the lover of Max Zorin in *A View to a Kill.* No doubt, she was someone Bond should have kept away from—although they quickly found time to share a night together. With unbelievable strength, she once lifted a KGB agent over her head with little effort.

After killing Aubergine, 007's contact in France, May Day jumped from the top of the Eiffel Tower with a parachute, landed safely, and escaped with Zorin in a speedboat. Later, she killed Bond's associate, Sir Godfrey Tibbett, and tried to kill Bond by sinking the Rolls-Royce in which he was trapped.

But when Zorin flooded his mines and left May Day to perish, she switched her allegiance and helped Bond foil the villain's plan to create an earthquake in California. Pulling a bomb that Zorin planted from a fault in the mine, May Day sacrificed herself and saved Bond. Riding a handcar that contained the bomb, May Day took it out of the mine, where it exploded with no damage to the landscape.

May Day: The Portrayal

Born in Jamaica in 1948, Grace Jones moved with her family to New York when she was in her teens. She studied theater at Syracuse University and Onondaga Community College, then embarked on a career as a successful model.

Along with a few minor film roles in the 1970s, Jones moved to Paris, where her lean and sexy look landed her on the covers of *Essence, Elle,* and *Vogue* magazines, among others. Wanting more, Jones got a recording contract and quickly became the diva of disco music, while still being a major influence on the fashion scene. Her square-cut hair, ruby-red lipstick, and androgynous appearance enhanced her eccentric personality.

Grace Jones as May Day in *A View to a Kill.*

In 1984, Jones teamed up with Arnold Schwarzenegger in the film sequel *Conan the Destroyer.* The role set her up for *A View to a Kill,* with Cubby Broccoli wanting Jones in a Bond film for some time. Seeking someone muscular, he found that person in Grace Jones.

On the set, Jones had heard that costar Roger Moore liked to play jokes during love scenes, usually hiding some sort of device under the bed covers until the director yelled, "Action!," then bringing it out for everyone's amusement. The actress decided to beat him at his own game, working with the prop department to devise a monstrous instrument that she strapped on under her robe. Moore's reaction was priceless.

Jones followed her Bond appearance with the comedy-horror film *Vamp,* playing a vampire-stripper. A few feature and TV movie roles came after, with more music and modeling work to keep Jones busy into the 2000s.

Kara Milovy: The Character

Beautiful, talented, but a bit gullible, Kara Milovy started out *The Living Daylights* movie as the girlfriend of Russian general Georgi Koskov. Before the film's end, she was in the arms of James Bond.

A brilliant concert cellist from Czechoslovakia, Milovy was duped by Koskov to act as his assassin during his defection to the West. Knowing MI6 would thwart any attempt on the life of a defector, Koskov assumed Bond would be sent to protect him and Milovy would be killed during the

Maryam d'Abo as Kara Milovy in *The Living Daylights.*

shooting. But Bond, recognizing the girl with the gun was no professional, only grazed the sniper rifle and injured the cellist.

Bond helped Milovy flee from the KGB and promised to take her to Koskov. But her boyfriend convinced her that Bond was a KGB agent, and Milovy drugged 007. Captured and taken to an Afghanistan airfield controlled by the Russians, Bond and Milovy escaped with the help of Mujahideen leader Kamran Shah. The pair escaped in a huge cargo plane, and Kara stayed at the controls while Bond fought with Necros on the open loading ramp of the plane. With Necros killed and Koskov taken prisoner by the Russians, Milovy was free to return to her concert tour. Although 007 missed her cello playing, there was one performance that he assured her he wouldn't miss.

Kara Milovy: The Portrayal

Blonde, with beautiful big, brown eyes, Maryam d'Abo was born in London in 1960. With her father incapacitated by meningitis, the young girl traveled with her mother, living in France and Switzerland. After studying photography in London, she began to focus on acting in 1980. To support herself, d'Abo modeled and made TV commercials.

Her first film appearance was in the cult horror feature *Xtro* in 1983. She continued in television movies and miniseries, as well as features like *White Nights,* with Mikhail Baryshnikov and Gregory Hines. Auditioning for the role of Pola Ivanova, the KGB agent who joined Bond in the hot tub in *A View to a Kill,* d'Abo was deemed too young. But she remained in touch with the Bond producers, acting in the Tatiana Romanova role during the auditions for actors seeking to be the next 007.

Cast as Kara Milovy, d'Abo learned how to "fake play" the cello, although with soap replacing rosin on the bow, her performance was soundless. Not so soundless were the endless explosions that always accompany a Bond film. With a phobia of explosions, d'Abo didn't enjoy them very much. She also found the three days of shooting the snow ride in the cello case to be no fun, with balance an issue, as well as the constant fear of tumbling into the adjacent ravine.

After Bond, d'Abo starred in the NBC-TV sci-fi movie and series *Something Is Out There* in 1988, as well as a large variety of films and television shows for nearly twenty years. In 2007, she suffered a life-threatening brain hemorrhage, in searing pain for a week before surgery removed the aneurysm. Months of recovery and therapy allowed d'Abo to return to the movies, appearing in the 2009 version of *Dorian Gray*.

Pam Bouvier: The Character

In 1989's *Licence to Kill,* Pam Bouvier was a continuation of what Bond girls were becoming in the 1980s—smart, tough, independent, able to meet 007 on a level playing field.

A pilot for the CIA, Bouvier was originally scheduled to meet Felix Leiter in a bar in Isthmus City. With Leiter in the hospital, Bond kept the appointment, where he immediately found that Bouvier was a heckuva woman—handy with a shotgun and her wits. They agreed to go after the villain named Sanchez together.

Acting as Bond's personal assistant, Bouvier helped Bond infiltrate Sanchez's gang. Later, at Sanchez's drug processing plant, hidden inside the retreat of televangelist Professor Joe Butcher, Bouvier found herself trapped in a bedroom with Joe, who had more than praying on his mind. But she was having none of it, pulled a gun, and got away.

As Sanchez escaped in tanker truck filled with drug-infused gasoline, Bond and Bouvier followed in a small plane. Bond jumped onto one of the trucks, as Bouvier landed the damaged plane. After Bond killed Sanchez, Bouvier came to his aid with an abandoned truck cab.

During a party for the new president, Bond realized he was attracted to Bouvier, and the two of them frolicked in a swimming pool, fully clothed.

Pam Bouvier: The Portrayal

Carey Lowell was born in New York in 1961 and was soon traveling the world with her geologist father. When she was twelve, the family settled in Colorado. When Lowell graduated high school, her stunning looks earned her a modeling agreement with the Ford Agency. She attended the University of Colorado and

Carey Lowell as Pam Bouvier with Timothy Dalton as 007 in *Licence to Kill*.

New York University, while posing for clients like Calvin Klein and Ralph Lauren, along with numerous fashion magazines.

Lowell got her first film roles in 1986, appearing in the action-thriller *Dangerously Close* and *Club Paradise,* which starred Robin Williams. She followed with the quirky comedy *Him and Me,* where a man's private part starts to talk and things are no longer private.

Hearing that producers were looking for a "tough Bond girl" for their new movie, Lowell dressed for the audition in jeans, cowboy boots, and leather jacket. When she arrived for the test, she was sent home and told that no one could audition for a Bond girl dressed like that—come back the next week, properly dressed—meaning, wearing something tight and sexy. The actress bought a cheap fitted dress, returned the next week, and was cast as Pam Bouvier.

On set, the character had to shoot guns—after all, she was a CIA agent. But Lowell hadn't fired many weapons and, naturally, blinked and flinched when pulling the trigger. To be a believable agent, she had to learn to shoot without showing any reaction.

After *Licence to Kill,* Lowell starred in the William Friedkin–directed horror film *The Guardian,* as well as playing Tom Hanks' wife who dies in *Sleepless in Seattle.* She also starred as the Geena Davis role in CBS-TV's short-lived version of *A League of Their Own* in 1993. The actress held a recurring role in the popular NBC-TV police drama *Law and Order,* as well as the ABC-TV and ITV drama *Six Degrees.*

Lupe Lamora: The Character

A dark Latin beauty, Lupe Lamora was the abused girlfriend of villain Franz Sanchez. Fidelity was not her strong suit, as she dallied with another man—until Sanchez burst into the bedroom. Her lack of loyalty was understandable, considering Sanchez regularly beat her with a whip made from the tail of a stingray. Not nice.

Lupe also had her hands full onboard Milton Krest's boat—the *Wavekrest.* Mostly, Lamora's problem was keeping an inebriated Krest from manhandling her in the bedroom where she stayed. No wonder she clung to James Bond when he came upon the scene.

At Sanchez's casino in Isthmus City, the villain was curious about Bond, so he sent Lupe to deal blackjack with 007 and quiz him on his intentions. The secret agent wound up a guest at Sanchez's home, and he took a chance by romancing Lupe—a move that later angered Pam Bouvier when Lamora declared her love for Bond. Later, with Sanchez dead and his reign of terror over, Lupe came on strong to Bond, but he deflected her advances toward the new president of Isthmus City. He didn't seem to mind.

Lupe Lamora: The Portrayal

Casting for Lupe Lamora in *Licence to Kill* involved interviewing actresses from all over the world, searching for a ravishing international beauty. Ironically, Talisa Soto was born in Brooklyn, New York, in 1967. Interviewed early in the search, she got the part several months later.

Soto, whose family was originally from Puerto Rico, moved with them to Massachusetts as a young girl. At age fifteen, she signed a modeling deal with Click Model Management and became one of the world's top cover models. Her gorgeous dark features soon graced the covers of magazines like *Vogue, Elle,* and *Glamour.*

At nineteen years of age, Soto retired from modeling, turning her focus toward a career in acting. She landed her first role in the independent film *Spike of Bensonhurst,* with Ernest Borgnine and Sylvia Miles.

Cast as Lamora, Soto realized her work as a blackjack dealer had to be believable. With a few days off from shooting, she flew to Las Vegas, where she took a two-hour crash course for pro dealers, as well as spent time watching the real dealers in action. The actress spent a portion of every evening deftly fanning a deck of cards, working until it was flawless.

Soto made a few TV movies after Bond, as well as appearing in *The Mambo Kings* and costarring with Sam Neill in *Hostage.* She also appeared in the CBS-TV western series *Harts of the West,* played one of Johnny Depp's girlfriends in *Don Juan DeMarco,* and had a recurring role in the video-game-turned-feature films *Mortal Kombat* and *Mortal Kombat: Annihilation.*

The actress has continued to work in a wide selection of film and TV projects, including ABC-TV's *C-16: FBI* and feature films *Pinero* and *Ballistic: Ecks vs. Sever,* among others.

Natalya Simonova: The Character

In 1995's *GoldenEye,* Natalya Simonova worked at the Russian Space Weapons Control Center, in Severnaya in the Arctic Ocean. As a mid-level computer programmer, Simonova did her job and tried to keep her juvenile and lecherous coworker Boris Grishenko at arm's length.

Traitorous Russian general Ourumov struck the center with an electromagnetic pulse, killing everyone in the facility—except for Simonova, who was getting a fortuitous cup of coffee, and Grishenko, who was having a smoke outside.

Later, Simonova connected with Grishenko via email, happy to see that he survived the blast. But, meeting in a chapel, the devious Boris turned her over to an associate of Ourumov, the villainous Xenia Onatopp.

Bond and Simonova found themselves trapped in a Tiger helicopter, with its missiles set to fire and target itself. The pair ejected just before the rockets struck, but were captured again and tossed in a cell. Once Natalya began to trust Bond, she was able to expose Grishenko and Ourumov as the villains.

A hostage on Ourumov's armored train, Simonova was rescued by 007, with the general killed. Natalya located a second secret GoldenEye system center in Cuba, and she and Bond took off for the island nation. Once there, they made love on a secluded beach, then found the GoldenEye system. Natalya was able to reprogram the GoldenEye satellite to reenter the Earth's atmosphere and burn up.

Alec Trevelyan and Grishenko were eliminated, with Bond and Simonova safe in a quiet field.

Natalya Simonova: The Portrayal

Born in Poland in 1970, Izabella Scorupco moved with her mother to Sweden at the age of eight. She studied music and acting, then was cast at age eighteen in the Swedish romance *Only We Can Love Like This,* shooting her to stardom in the country.

The film introduced Scorupco to the world of modeling, landing on the covers of the world's top magazines. But she quickly became disenchanted with modeling and set her sights on a career in the music industry. Her records scored Swedish gold and expanded her fan base.

The performer returned to acting, appearing on Swedish television in the early 1990s before coming to the attention of Bond producers. Cast in Pierce Brosnan's first shot as James Bond, Scorupco found herself reestablishing a new standard for Bond girls—smart, resourceful, dressed for success, rather than the beach. In fact, her wardrobe consisted of only two outfits.

Izabella Scorupco as Natalya Simonova in *GoldenEye.*

Perhaps unbelievably, Scorupco was never much of a fitness freak, so she prepared for her physical scenes by ripping off ten quick push-ups—a real feat for someone who had never done one before the film began shooting. The actress found the destruction of the GoldenEye control center to be stressful, putting her trust in director Martin Campbell when told she would be perfectly safe with the set crashing down around her.

The actress found the Bond experience to be a bit overwhelming and took a four-year hiatus from filmmaking, returning to star in hits like *Vertical Limit* in 2000; *Reign of Fire,* with Christian Bale, Matthew McConaughey, and Gerard Butler in 2002; and *Exorcist: The Beginning* in 2004, among others.

Xenia Onatopp: The Character

An ex-Soviet fighter pilot in *GoldenEye,* Xenia Onatopp was never one to avoid doing the leg work on her missions. Aligned with Alec Treveylan and his Janus crime syndicate, Onatopp was wild, daring, and deadly.

Bond first noticed the beautiful brunette as she zoomed past him in a racy red Ferrari in the South of France. Later, as she puffed on a cigar at the baccarat table, Bond defeated her and she left in a huff (having left her Ferrari in the parking lot). In a tryst with her Canadian admiral boyfriend, she made like a praying mantis and killed him after making love, choking him with her thighs. She then made a quick escape in a new Tiger helicopter, relying on her skills as a former pilot.

Landing at the Space Weapons Control Center in Severnaya, Onatopp maniacally machine-gunned everyone in the place—except for Simonova and Grishenko. Later, the woman viciously seduced Bond, then tried to kill him. But he survived the attempt, negotiating a meeting with Janus.

Later in Cuba, Onatopp rappelled down a rope from her helicopter, intending once more to kill 007. But he shot the chopper from the sky, ramming the villainess into a tree and to her death.

Xenia Onatopp: The Portrayal

Famke Janssen, born in the Netherlands in 1965, came to New York City at age nineteen, signing a modeling deal with the Elite agency. Having attended the University of Amsterdam, she continued her studies at Columbia University while modeling. She landed on the covers of the world's biggest magazines, including *Elle, Maxim,* and *Glamour,* as well as print ads for Chanel and others.

Janssen studied acting with Harold Guskin, then moved to LA to work with acting coach Roy London. The hard work paid off, as she was cast as Jeff Goldblum's love interest in 1992's *Fathers and Sons.* Television work followed, as she showed up in *Star Trek: The Next Generation, Melrose Place,* and *Model by Day.*

At nearly six feet tall, Janssen's size and athletic abilities were tailor-made for her role as the evil and deadly Xenia Onatopp. Despite her fine performance, everyone could only remember her ability to kill men with her thighs. The skill even showed up on late-night comic Conan O'Brien's show, where the actress personally demonstrated her rib-crushing talents on the host himself while atop his desk.

Fearing being typecast as "the evil woman" in films, Janssen chose smaller films after *GoldenEye,* such as *City of Industry* with Harvey Keitel, director Robert Altman's *The Gingerbread Man, Rounders* with Matt Damon and Edward Norton, and the 1999 remake of *House on Haunted Hill.*

In the 2000s, Janssen's sporty form earned her a spot in the hit super-hero series *X-Men.* As the telepathic and telekinetic Jean Grey, she appeared in the three films made between 2000 and 2006, starring with Hugh Jackman, Patrick Stewart, and others. She also made appearances in the hit TV show *Ally McBeal* and had a recurring role on FX cable network's *Nip/Tuck.*

The actress wrote and directed her first feature in 2011, *Bringing Up Bobby,* with Milla Jovovich as a shady woman who is trying to bring her son up the right way.

Wai Lin: The Character

Clearly Bond's equal—and then some—in *Tomorrow Never Dies,* Wai Lin was an agent of the Chinese People's External Security Force. Highly skilled in weaponry and the martial arts, Lin helped 007 defeat Elliot Carver's plan to start a world war.

Like Bond, she made her way into Carver's gala celebration for the start-up of his new satellite news network, seeking information about the missing Chinese stealth materials. Later, both Bond and Lin broke into Carver's headquarters and made separate escapes from security guards. Later still, Bond dove into Vietnamese waters to find the sunken British ship, the *Devonshire.* Once again, he ran into Lin, and the pair wound up in the hands of Stamper, Carver's thug.

Handcuffed, Bond and Lin escaped down the side of Carver's sky-scraper, stole a motorcycle and sped off, with the villain's men in pursuit. Working well together, Bond and Lin adroitly maneuvered on the bike and escaped the bad guys. Yet Lin picked the handcuffs and left 007 hooked to a water pipe—she only worked alone.

Getting free, Bond wound up in Lin's apartment, where they vanquished a gang of thugs. Lin especially showed incredible skills in hand-to-hand battle. She also smoothly avoided Bond's amorous advances, then agreed to work with Bond to defeat Carver and his secret partner, Chinese general Chang. The agent opened up her arsenal, the pair loaded up, and took off for Carver's stealth ship.

Lin was captured, with Bond believed to be killed by Stamper. The Chinese agent broke free from her captor as Bond turned up, very much alive. Disabling the stealth ship, Bond killed Carver as Stamper chained Lin and threw her into the sea. Bond got the best of Stamper, then pulled the nearly drowned Lin to the surface and saved her with a kiss.

Wai Lin: The Portrayal

Born to Chinese parents in Malaysia in 1962, Michelle Yeoh was always a standout in physical skills. She began ballet at age four and, considered a tomboy, swam, dove and played squash at national levels.

At fifteen years of age, Yeoh moved to England to study at the London Royal Academy of Dance. But a serious spinal injury dashed any hopes of a career in ballet, and she turned her attention to choreography and acting. By age twenty-one, Yeoh had won the title of Miss Malaysia and represented her country in the Miss World pageant.

Yeoh came to Hong Kong to make a commercial with martial arts actor and superstar Jackie Chan. The experience opened up a new world of acting for her, as she began to appear in the highly popular Hong Kong action films. She embraced the martial arts, working ten to twelve hours a day to learn the deadly moves needed for her new career.

By 1992, Yeoh was reteamed with her former TV commercial partner, costarring with Jackie Chan in *Supercop*. She also had her own starring roles in action films like *Butterfly and Sword, The Heroic Trio,* and *Executioners.* Yeoh joined Chan once more in the sequel, *Supercop 2.*

Yeoh was a veteran of action films and perfect for the James Bond series. As such, the role of Wai Lin was written for the actress, and she came in ready to go. Accustomed to doing all of her own stunts, Yeoh had the chance to shine in the attack scene in her apartment. But director Roger Spottiswoode refused to let her descend down the skyscraper or ride the dangerous motorcycle stunt, even though she wanted to. No doubt, it was a good decision as, during her film career, Yeoh had dislocated her joints, cracked a rib, been burned, ruptured an artery in her leg, and torn knee ligaments, not to mention reaggravating her old spinal injury.

Pierce Brosnan as Bond and Michelle Yeoh as Wai Lin in *Tomorrow Never Dies.*

The success of *Tomorrow Never Dies* put Michelle Yeoh squarely on the global silver screen. She starred with action star Chow Yun-Fat in Ang Lee's enormously popular *Crouching Tiger, Hidden Dragon,* nominated for ten Oscars and winning four, including Best Foreign Language Film.

Yeoh continued to make Asian films, along with mainstream action films like the second sequel in Brendan Fraser's *Mummy* series, *The Mummy: Tomb of the Dragon Emperor.* The actress also added her voice to the animated feature *Kung Fu Panda 2.*

Paris Carver: The Character

A trophy wife for media mogul Elliot Carver, Paris Carver had a previous relationship with agent 007, but it couldn't stand up to the stress of James Bond's occupation. In *Tomorrow Never Dies,* Paris represented a conduit for MI6 through Bond, a way to obtain information on Carver's devious activities.

At the billionaire's gala reception for his new business venture—a satellite news network—Bond and Paris renewed their acquaintance, although she lied to her husband about her former relationship with Bond. Carver sent his wife to Bond's hotel to see what he knew, then found out the truth—he wasn't pleased.

Bond couldn't forget Paris, as they romped in his bedroom. Paris clued Bond in to how to sneak into the network headquarters, then was killed in Bond's room by professional assassin, Dr. Kaufman. While 007 discovered the woman dead, Carver prepared to use his dead wife in a messy murder-suicide broadcast—anything for ratings. But Bond killed Kaufman before the story could break.

Paris Carver: The Portrayal

Teri Hatcher was born in Northern California in 1964, taking ballet lessons as a young girl. After high school, she enrolled at De Anza College for a degree in math and engineering. But she also enjoyed acting and studied at the American Conservatory Theater in San Francisco. In 1984, she became a member of the cheerleading squad for the San Francisco 49ers football team.

Moving to Los Angeles the next year, Hatcher joined a friend for moral support at an open casting call. But it was Hatcher who got the role of Amy the Mermaid in ABC-TV's *The Love Boat*. She followed that with recurring roles on TV shows like *Capitol, Karen's Song,* and *MacGyver,* as well as films like director Christopher Guest's *The Big Picture, Tango and Cash,* and *Soapdish.*

Losing out to Helen Hunt in *Mad About You,* Hatcher won the role of Lois Lane for four seasons in the ABC-TV hit *Lois and Clark: The New Adventures of Superman.* She also made several appearances on *Seinfeld.* Around that time, Hatcher took on the role of Paris Carver in *Tomorrow Never Dies.*

With a part that was smaller than she expected, Hatcher didn't find the Bond experience very satisfying. A few years later, the actress regretted taking the role of Paris, saying the character was artificial and gave her no "special satisfaction."

After a line of TV commercials with former footballer Howie Long for Radio Shack, Hatcher landed one of the plum roles in ABC-TV's megahit *Desperate Housewives.* The part earned the actress Golden Globe and Screen Actors Guild awards.

Elektra King: The Character

A powerful and independent woman, Elektra King was both beauty and beast in *The World Is Not Enough.* With her father murdered at MI6 headquarters, she became heiress to his vast financial and business holdings.

Kidnapped by the terrorist known as Renard for a $5 million ransom, she escaped from her captors. M admitted to Bond that the woman was used as a decoy in an attempt to lure Renard out of hiding, but he remained at large. Fearing Elektra was still in Renard's sights, M assigned Bond to protect her and find out who killed her father.

King refused Bond's offer of protection. She calmed the anger of local churchgoers who opposed the King oil pipeline's route that threatened their chapel by choosing an expensive rerouting of the project to save the church. Bond stuck around and saved King from an attack of armed para-wing snowmobiles.

Bond gained Elektra's trust, then watched her lose $1 million to Valentin Zukovsky in his casino. After romancing Elektra, Bond realized she was in cahoots with Renard. But it was too late, as Elektra lured M to her estate and imprisoned her. The head of MI6 would perish—with millions of others along with pipelines competing with King's—when a nuclear weapon was detonated in Istanbul.

Bond visited Zukovsky at his caviar plant, where two of King's tree-trimming helicopters tore up the place, along with Bond's car. Zukovsky's nephew was a sub captain who occasionally delivered machine parts for Elektra—the million she lost in the casino was actually payment. Renard killed the nephew and gave Elektra his captain's hat as a souvenir.

King began to slowly kill Bond in a chair with a choking collar. Zukovsky interrupted, seeking his nephew. The devious King fatally shot the Russian, who freed Bond from his torture as he died. Bond was able to release M and then corner Elektra, who had her doubts that 007 would kill her in cold blood—Bond proved her wrong.

Elektra King: The Portrayal

French beauty Sophie Marceau was born in a suburb of Paris in 1966. Seeking a summer job at age twelve, Marceau registered with a modeling agency, although she was too old for their needs.

Shortly after, the agency forwarded the young girl's name and photo to folks at the Gaumont Film Company. Seeking a fresh face for their new teen film *La Boum* (*The Party*), the filmmakers cast Marceau as the lead. The film was a big hit, and Marceau starred in the sequel, *La Boum 2*, in 1982.

In a bold move for someone so young, Marceau bought her contract back from Gaumont for F1 million (more than $70,000). As an independent actress, she sought more dramatic roles. She got them, with films like *L'Amour Braque* (*Crazy Love*); *Police,* with Gerard Depardieu; and *Mes Nuits Sont Plus Belles Que Vos Jours* (*My Nights Are More Beautiful Than Your Days*).

Marceau hit the international screen as Princess Isabelle in Mel Gibson's *Braveheart* in 1995, *Anna Karenina* with Sean Bean (former Bond villain Alec Trevelyan) in 1997, and the awkward comedy *Lost and Found* with David Spade, among others.

Cast as Bond's first major female villain, Marceau saw the part of Elektra King in *The World Is Not Enough* as "a gift," allowing her to have fun with the character. Seeing the film series as "a fantasy set in a real world," the actress liked being part of an action film.

Entering the 2000s, Marceau returned to French films, as well as select productions like Rob Reiner's comedy *Alex and Emma,* with Kate Hudson and Luke Wilson. She also wrote and directed the French drama *Speak to Me of Love,* adding the role of lead actress as well for *Trivial* in 2007.

Dr. Christmas Jones: The Character

With Elektra King turning out to be the main villain in *The World Is Not Enough,* Bond needed someone to romance at the film's end. Enter Dr. Christmas Jones.

Sophie Marceau as Elektra King in *The World Is Not Enough.*

Although not trusting 007 at first, she came around to his side and helped defeat Renard's plan to disrupt the world's oil supply and kill millions of people.

Posing as Arkov, a nuclear scientist, Bond traveled to Kazakhstan and an underground Russian site for nuclear weapons. There he met Dr. Jones, who was assisting with the dismantling of the warheads as the arms race was being dissolved. But Jones pegged Bond as a fraud (despite the mileage, he didn't look sixty-three years old, Arkov's age), and turned him over to Russian troops.

Chaos reigned as Renard fled the site, while Bond and Jones barely escaped the blast of a bomb the terrorist left behind. At that point, Jones was convinced that she and Bond were on the same side. Later, the pair entered the King pipeline to defuse a nuclear device planted by Renard.

In the film's climax, Renard escaped in a submarine with Dr. Jones. Bond made his way onto the sub as it sunk into deep water. Jones became trapped in a cabin quickly filling with water as the sub was damaged. When 007 defeated Renard, he freed Jones and they escaped through a torpedo tube. In the end, Bond and Jones embraced as MI6 watched them via thermal imaging.

Dr. Christmas Jones: The Portrayal

Pretty Denise Richards was born in the suburbs of Chicago in 1971. Her family moved to California when she was a teen, and she started part-time work as a model. She appeared in print and TV ads for Paul Mitchell hair products and Secret deodorant. Richards set out on her own, moving to Los Angeles at age nineteen to seek a career in acting.

She spent a good portion of the 1990s doing bit parts in movies and television, including *Saved by the Bell*, *Married with Children*, *Doogie Howser, M.D.*, *Beverly Hills, 90210*, and *In Living Color*, among others. She also had a small recurring part on *Melrose Place* in 1996.

Her first major film role was in director Paul Verhoeven's bug-infested flick *Starship Troopers*. She followed that up in a sexy romp with Matt Dillon and Neve Campbell in *Wild Things* in 1998. Richards also starred with Kirsten Dunst and Kirstie Alley in the comedy *Drop Dead Gorgeous*.

Her casting in *The World Is Not Enough* was clearly designed to appeal to the younger segment of the moviegoing public, and much has been made (including in this book) about the believability of Richards as a nuclear scientist. It didn't help to introduce her character as wearing skimpy shorts and a tight tank top (definitely not de rigueur for dismantling nuclear warheads). As well, the choice of her first name seemed to be merely a setup for the double-entendre comment that closed the film.

The prominence of the Bond role opened more doors for the actress, mostly in TV in the 2000s. She had a memorable guest appearance on *Friends* and a recurring role in ABC-TV's hit comedy *Spin City*. Richards also starred in the short-lived UPN network drama *Sex, Love and Secrets*, as well as Spike TV's comedy *Blue Mountain State*.

At the same time, she appeared in a variety of films like *Undercover Brother*, *You Stupid Man*, *Scary Movie 3*, *Edmund*, and *Blonde and Blonder*, teamed with Pamela Anderson, among other films.

Giacinta "Jinx" Johnson: The Character

In 2002's *Die Another Day*, Jinx Johnson was an agent for America's National Security Agency, hot on the trail of North Korean villain Zao. Not coincidentally, so was James Bond.

Immediately attracted to each other when they first met on Isla Los Organos, Johnson and Bond got physical. Jinx then escaped local soldiers by executing a perfect backflip into the ocean and away in a speedboat.

At Gustav Graves' ice castle in Iceland, Jinx pulled up in a new Ford Thunderbird, then was caught breaking into the villain's solarium. Bond saved the woman from being cut in two by a laser, then found out Jinx was with NSA and they were both after Zao and Graves.

Trapped in a flooding room while the ice castle was melting, Jinx was pulled out by Bond, who breathed life back into her with a kiss. The pair then made their way onto Graves' getaway cargo plane, where Jinx squared off against double agent Miranda Frost in a sword fight. Jinx killed Frost with a knife in the chest, then escaped with Bond in a helicopter stored in the cargo bay.

As usual, Bond and Johnson ended the film in each other's embrace.

Giacinta "Jinx" Johnson: The Portrayal

Halle Berry was born in Cleveland, Ohio in 1966, moving to the suburbs with her mother and sister after her father abandoned them. In high school, she was class president, editor of the newspaper, and lead cheerleader.

Berry pursued broadcast journalism at the local community college, but left when she landed in the finals of beauty pageants like Miss Teen Ohio and Miss Teen America. At age twenty, she was first runner-up in the Miss USA contest, then finished sixth in the Miss World pageant. From there, Berry worked in Chicago and New York as a fashion and catalog model.

In 1989, Berry starred in *Living Dolls,* a spin-off of the television show *Who's the Boss?* Several additional TV appearances followed, including a recurring role on *Knots Landing.* At the same time, the actress made her first major film, *Jungle Fever,* written and directed by Spike Lee.

Through the 1990s, Berry appeared in a steady stream of movies, such as *The Last Boy Scout* with Bruce Willis, the live-action version of *The Flintstones,* the searing drama *Losing Isaiah* with Jessica Lange, the action-thriller *Executive Decision, The Rich Man's Wife,* and *Bulworth,* written and directed by Warren Beatty.

Berry's performance as the first black actress to earn a Best Actress Oscar nomination, in HBO's *Introducing Dorothy Dandridge* in 1999, earned her multiple awards, including an Emmy, a Golden Globe, a Screen Actors Guild Award, and an NAACP Image Award.

Joining the superhero franchise of *X-Men,* Berry starred as Storm in all three films between 2000 and 2006. But her appearance as the girlfriend of racist Billy Bob Thornton in 2001's *Monster's Ball* made history, as Berry won

Halle Berry as Giacinta "Jinx" Johnson in *Die Another Day.*

the Oscar for Best Actress—a first for a black woman. With that honor under her belt, she was ready for *Die Another Day.*

Making history again as the first black Bond girl as a heroine, Berry showed her equal as Bond's counterpart in the NSA. The scene of the actress emerging from the sea in an orange bikini and knife belt around her waist was a tribute to Ursula Andress' appearance as the first Bond girl in *Dr. No* forty years before.

Hazards on the set presented themselves, as Berry was briefly hospitalized after a fragment from a smoke grenade became lodged in her left eye. The scene being filmed was Zao's escape in a helicopter as Bond tried to shoot it down. The injury was minor and caused no permanent damage to the actress' vision.

Berry proceeded to make big-budget films after *Die Another Day,* including the horror-thriller *Gothika*, the Batman spinoff *Catwoman, Perfect Stranger* with Bruce Willis, and *New Year's Eve,* among others.

Miranda Frost: The Character

Another case of a spy who wanted her scone buttered on both sides, Miranda Frost was a double agent in *Die Another Day.* It was she who betrayed Bond to the North Koreans, leading to more than a year of captivity and torture for 007.

Schooled at Harvard and a gold medalist in the 2000 Sydney Olympics in fencing (although her boss, Gustav Graves, made sure the fix was in), Frost first appeared in a spirited practice duel with Graves, while coach Verity and James Bond looked on. Later, M briefed an MI6 agent who was scheduled for an Iceland flight—it was Frost, who had volunteered to become Graves' personal assistant to gain access to his operation. While Frost had turned up nothing incriminating, Bond thought otherwise.

In Iceland, Frost flipped her behavior on Bond, going from cold fish to hot tamale as she finally took 007 up on his romantic advances. Later, Bond challenged Graves and discovered whose side Frost was really on.

Graves and Frost escaped in a cargo plane, and the woman engaged Jinx Johnson in a deadly sword fight. Although Frost injured Johnson, Jinx got the final stroke with a dagger, buried in a copy of *The Art of War,* stabbing Frost in the heart.

Miranda Frost: The Portrayal

Born in London in 1979, Rosamund Pike spent most of her childhood traveling through Europe with her musical parents. She played piano and cello as a young girl, then joined the National Youth Theater at age sixteen.

She attended Wadham College at Oxford University, studying English, but broke off halfway through to attend drama school. Unfortunately, she was rejected by everyone she auditioned for and returned to Wadham to finish.

In 1999, Pike was offered a part in the BBC miniseries drama *Wives and Daughters.* Several other TV appearances followed, with the twenty-one-year-old Pike being cast as the two-timing Miranda Frost in *Die Another Day.*

Not that getting the part was easy. After many screen tests, Pike went on holiday to a quaint cottage in the east of England—without a phone. Bond producers and director Lee Tamahori frantically tried to reach her. Once they did, she was thrilled to be a Bond girl.

Having never fenced before, the actress trained for nearly a month with Olympic fencer Bob Anderson and found the sport to be "fast, sexy, and elegant, all at the same time." Pike also found the ice palace set—built on the enormous Cubby Broccoli 007 Stage at Pinewood Studios—to be exciting, comparing it to a theme park.

Pike found herself with actor Johnny Depp in the 2004 period drama *The Libertine,* which earned her the British Independent Film Award for Best Supporting Actress. She then appeared in the 2005 version of the Jane Austen novel *Pride and Prejudice,* followed up in the same year with the videogame-turned-movie *Doom* (talk about variety).

The actress also starred with Anthony Hopkins in *Fracture, An Education,* which resulted in several nominations for Best Supporting Actress awards, the sci-fi thriller *Surrogates* with Bruce Willis, and appeared as Andromeda in 2012's *Wrath of the Titans,* among others.

Vesper Lynd: The Character

Ian Fleming's first novel, *Casino Royale,* presented the world with its first Bond girl: Vesper Lynd. Based on Christine Granville, a British spy who was also one of Fleming's many paramours, Vesper Lynd's name was the author's wordplay on "West Berlin."

In the book, she was an assistant to MI6's head of Soviet activities and assigned to help agent 007 in beating the villain Le Chiffre at baccarat. She had black hair and, of course, was very beautiful.

After Bond defeated Le Chiffre at the gaming table, the villain took his vengeance by kidnapping Lynd and grabbed Bond when he crashed his Bentley in a chase. The pair were taken away, and Bond was tortured by Le Chiffre before an agent from SMERSH shot him dead for gambling with the organization's funds.

As Bond recovered from his ordeal, he and Vesper spent time together, and they fell in love. As he contemplated marriage with Lynd, Bond woke one morning to find she had committed suicide. In a letter she left for Bond, Vesper revealed she had been a double agent, blackmailed by the MWD—the Russian secret police—to foil Bond's assignment. Knowing that SMERSH would make life for her and Bond miserable, she took her own life, leaving 007 crushed and bitter.

The 2006 film held close to the novel in many ways, with some embellishments. Lynd was made an accountant for the Royal Treasury, assigned to keep an eye on the money Bond played with. The game of baccarat was changed to the more popular Texas Hold'em, and Lynd spent a portion of screen time sitting with Rene Mathis as he explained the game to her—and to the audience.

Vesper was used to capture Bond, trussed up and left in the roadway so that 007 had to dump his Aston Martin to avoid striking her. When they were rescued from Le Chiffre, Bond and Lynd fell in love and Bond resigned from MI6. When Lynd went to retrieve Bond's (and Britain's) winnings from a Venetian bank, Bond discovered she had set him up.

With the Quantum organization tied into the scam and grabbing Lynd, the climax took place in a building under renovation. Vesper became locked in an elevator cage, and despite Bond's efforts to save her, she chose to drown. Later, M told Bond of the blackmail scheme and Bond

Eva Green as Vesper Lynd in *Casino Royale* (2006).

retrieved a clue to who was behind everything, left by Lynd on her cell phone before she died.

Vesper Lynd: The Portrayal

Eva Green was born in Paris in 1980, the older of twin girls. Her mother was a French actress and singer, her father a dentist. She attended a private school in Paris, then the American School of Paris. Green had plans to be an Egyptologist.

Seeing a movie with Isabelle Adjani changed the young teen's mind, redirecting her ambitions toward acting. Green attended the Performing Arts Centre, then studied with drama teacher Eva St. Paul for three years.

Starting with stage work for several years, the actress made her screen debut in Bernardo Bertolucci's controversial *The Dreamers* in 2003. Green made the French crime film *Arsène Lupin,* then appeared in director Ridley Scott's historic drama *Kingdom of Heaven,* with Liam Neeson and Orlando Bloom.

The role of Vesper Lynd was supposedly considered for high-profile actresses like Charlize Theron, Scarlett Johansson, and Angelina Jolie before Eva Green took the part at the last minute, just two days before shooting began. The actress was attracted to Lynd's flawed and vulnerable character, seeing she wasn't a "typical Bond girl in a bikini." Her performance led to winning the BAFTA Rising Star Award, along with nominations for other kudos.

Green followed her Bond performance with the fantasy film *The Golden Compass,* then a dual role in the quirky drama *Franklyn.* She also showed up in *Cracks, Womb, Perfect Sense,* as well as the Starz cable channel miniseries *Camelot.* The actress joined an all-star cast in director Tim Burton's big-screen version of *Dark Shadows* in 2012.

Camille Montes: The Character

Continuing to redefine the Bond girl for the twenty-first century, 2008's *Quantum of Solace* introduced Camille Montes, a woman with vengeance on her mind. What's more, she was a rarity—a beautiful lady who didn't sleep with 007.

In Haiti, Bond posed as Mr. Slate, a man hired to kill Camille Montes, the former girlfriend of Dominic Greene. Greene was in cahoots with Bolivian general Medrano, who was responsible for the murder of Montes' family when she was a girl. When Greene tried to make a gift of his former lover to the general, Bond came to her rescue.

Olga Kurylenko as Camille Montes in *Quantum of Solace.*

At a fund-raiser for Greene's ecological efforts, Montes bad-mouthed the philanthropist to potential backers, but Bond intervened to save her once more from Greene. The pair flew to survey a parcel of Greene's property in Bolivia, but the plane was shot down and they parachuted into a sinkhole.

Bond and Montes escaped, catching up with Greene and Medrano in a desert hotel. Camille finally avenged her family by killing the general as he attacked a hotel worker. A car crash set off fires in the resort, and Montes found herself trapped and terrified. Bond pulled her to safety and they grabbed Greene, leaving him in the desert for the Quantum organization as justice. With a simple kiss, Bond and Camille went their separate ways.

Camille Montes: The Portrayal

Born in the Ukraine in 1979, Olga Kurylenko was only thirteen when a modeling coach spied her on a vacation in Moscow. Knowing she was too young at that point, the coach kept in touch with Kurylenko and started working with the teen a few years later. At age seventeen, Kurylenko moved to Paris by herself, showing up on the covers of magazines like *Elle, Glamour, Maxim,* and *Vogue.*

Her first film appearance was in the French erotic thriller *The Ring Finger* in 2005. She followed as a vampire with Elijah Wood in the multisegmented feature *Paris Je T'aime,* in 2006. Kurylenko appeared in the French television miniseries *Secrets* in 2007. She showed up in two video-games-turned-movies: *Hitman* and *Max Payne.*

Cast as a Bolivian (with a Russian mother), Kurylenko surprised herself at being so adept at stunts, which she had never done before. Her scene of skydiving from a plane required a month of training in a wind tunnel—something she grew very fond of. Kurylenko's fight scene with Joaquin Cosio—as General Medrano—was memorable for the actress, as it left her with many cuts and bruises, and was the last scene she shot for the film.

The actress' next films included the Israeli action drama *The Assassin Next Door,* the Roman period drama *Centurion,* and the French drama *Land of Oblivion,* as well as a lead role in the Starz cable channel drama about Miami gangsters called *Magic City.*

Strawberry Fields: The Character

In *Quantum of Solace,* Bond was framed for killing a bodyguard to an associate of the British prime minister and was on the lam to La Paz, Bolivia. Arriving by plane, Bond was met at the airport by a pretty member of the British Consulate, Miss Fields. She had orders to return 007 on the next plane back to London.

Bond had other ideas and found her choice of hotel to be in question. They checked into the opulent Andean Grand Hotel, where, despite her initial instincts, she shared a bed with Bond. The couple attended Dominic Greene's fund-raiser, and when Bond and Camille Montes needed to break away, Fields provided the necessary diversion.

Bond returned to the hotel the next evening, where he received a note left by Fields at the front desk. It simply read "run," and, reaching his room, Bond found Fields' body, dead and drenched in black crude oil, on his bed. In deeper trouble than ever now, Bond insisted on having M note in her report that Fields demonstrated real bravery in the field.

Strawberry Fields: The Portrayal

Gemma Arterton was born in Kent, England, in 1986. Receiving a full scholarship to RADA, Arterton appeared in a wide variety of productions, as well as showing exceptional skill in dance and singing.

Graduating from the academy, she joined the Miskin Theater Company, along with Kent's Masquerade Theater Company. Arterton furthered her experience by appearing in the BBC television drama *Capturing Mary,* with Maggie Smith, in 2007. Her first film role was in the comedy *St. Trinian's,* with Rupert Everett, Toby Jones, and Colin Firth.

She continued with *A Deal Is a Deal*; director Guy Ritchie's *RocknRolla,* with Gerard Butler, Ludacris, and Mark Strong; and ITV's miniseries *Lost in Austen*; as well as starring in the BBC and PBS miniseries *Tess of the D'Urbervilles.*

Out of more than fifteen hundred actresses, Arterton won the role of Agent Fields in *Quantum of Solace.* The twenty-two-year-old actress' first scene was a love scene with Daniel Craig. She enjoyed it so much, reminding herself that she was acting in a film, just playing a character. Her death scene, lying on a bed, covered with black crude oil, was a duplicate of Shirley Eaton's end in *Goldfinger*. Fields never revealed her first name in the film; the name "Strawberry" was shown in the closing credits.

With the success of *Quantum of Solace*, Arterton followed with *Pirate Radio*, with Philip Seymour Hoffman; *The Disappearance of Alice Creed*; and big-budget films like *Clash of the Titans* and *Prince of Persia: The Sands of Time*, both in 2010.

Sévérine: The Character

The beautiful but abused girlfriend of villain Raoul Silva in *Skyfall*, Sévérine first spotted James Bond while he tussled with the hired gun named Patrice. Later, Bond met up with the lady in a Macau casino, where she warned 007 of an upcoming attempt on his life. Sévérine offered to meet up with him at her yacht if he survived.

Bond weathered the attack and connected with Sévérine at the boat. Following a shower for two, the couple found themselves captured by the yacht's crew and they were taken to Silva. Later, 007 spied her trussed up and beaten in a courtyard. Placing a shot glass on her head, Silva challenged Bond to a dangerous game of target shooting—but it was Sévérine who lost the match, and her life.

Sévérine: The Portrayal

Dark, exotic, sexy—Bérénice Marlohe perfectly fits the bill as the latest Bond girl in *Skyfall*. Part of her unique look comes from having a French mother and Asian father. Born in Paris in 1979, Marlohe first set her sights on being an artist, then a concert pianist. She was serious enough to spend ten years studying at the well-regarded Conservatoire de Paris.

She turned her attention to acting, although Marlohe was quickly frustrated with mostly minor roles in French television and the occasional commercial. When she heard about the auditions for *Skyfall*, the actress took matters into her own hands—contacting everyone she could to get the chance to try out. Finding the email address for 007 casting director Debbie McWilliams, Marlohe sent off her demo reel. The aggressive move got her foot in the door and, after her third interview with director Sam Mendes, Marlohe was cast as Sévérine.

Oddly, Marlohe had a dream about working with Javier Bardem—six months before the audition process had even started. Only after the second interview was she told that her co-star would be Bardem—cue the *Twilight Zone* music.

5

The Man with the Golden Guns (and Other Boy Toys)

The Gadgets of James Bond

pen your favorite dictionary and turn to the "G" pages. Find the word "gadget" and you'll find it basically means "a sometimes small mechanical or electronic device with a practical use." In the world of 007, that definition expands to include, "anything, as small as a key chain or as big as a blimp, designed to help or harm the MI6 hero, depending on who wields it."

Ian Fleming's novels and stories kept the gimmicks and gadgets to a minimum, usually an assortment of weapons and other diabolical devices. In many cases, the author relied on his wartime experiences in British Naval Intelligence. In a 1964 interview from *Playboy,* Fleming suggested that his interests in such things were not nearly as exotic as his fictitious friend's. He said, "Quite honestly, the whole question of expertise in these matters [guns and holsters] bores me." Yet he did detail his amusement with a gimmick being used at the time by West German assassins, "a cyanide gas pistol . . . which is more or less a water pistol filled with liquid cyanide." He eventually incorporated the concept when he wrote *The Man with the Golden Gun* in 1965.

The Bond films, on the other hand, have relied on the rapidly advancing technology of the day. (For example, consider the jet pack that saved 007 in the opening sequences of *Thunderball*—an actual experimental flying pack developed by Bell Labs, but more on that later.) At other times, the gizmos, doodads, and thingamabobs seen on screen were strictly the product of the creative minds behind the Bond charter, with no basis in fact or science whatsoever.

In many cases, the gadgets in Bond films have gone from science fiction to science fact. After all, fifty years is a lot of time in terms of technological advancements, and the cinematic world has always been keen to use them, only to see them become real. Fantastic space flights, as suggested in George Pal's *Destination Moon* in 1950 and 1964's *From the Earth to the Moon*, featuring Ray Harryhausen's marvelous special effects, became fact in 1969 as Americans landed on the moon. Fast cars, from the Ford Mustang to the Aston Martin Vanquish, have roared across the big screen and landed in garages and carports around the world. The use of lasers, homing devices, and miniaturized communication devices, among others, have gone from mysterious to mundane.

In a more or less chronological film-by-film process, these are some of the major gadgets that took Bond films from everyday entertainment to sizzling cinema.

Beretta Pistol

Author Ian Fleming considered this pistol to be standard issue to those agents with the 00 prefix, but the Beretta 418 made an interesting choice for those licensed to kill. Originally designed by the Italian weapon-making company right after the First World War, the .25-caliber "pocket pistol" held seven bullets in the magazine and one in the chamber. But it had limited stopping power and got Fleming in big trouble. Upon expert advice, he changed the weapon to a Walther PPK. Fleming described the M-demanded exchange in his 1958 novel *Dr. No.*

In the flicks, the change-out took place in a similar manner, as seen in the first Bond outing, *Dr. No.* But someone on the film team must have noticed the daintiness of the 418, as Bond is forced to hand M a beefier Beretta M1934—with a larger .38-caliber cartridge—in return for the trusty Walther on camera. That Walther prop pistol, by the way, fetched more than $106,000 in a Christie's of London auction in 2006. (M should have held on to it.)

Walther PPK Pistol

Introduced around 1930, the German-made semiautomatic pistol became a favorite of German military and law enforcement. (A certain Nazi warmonger named "Adolf" used his favorite PPK to end his own life as Russians closed in on his Berlin bunker in 1945.) The light but effective gun holds six 7.65mm bullets in the magazine and one in the chamber. (Most American PPKs use a larger .380 ACP caliber round.) Today, the Walther PPK (and its variants) are the choice of many law enforcement and special tactical groups around the world.

The iconic pistol became the favored weapon (and standard issue) for James Bond essentially for the first eighteen films, with one exception. In *Octopussy,* Bond tells Q that he has mislaid his Walther (the PPK), and he's given a P5 to use. In reality, the Walther company had just introduced the P5 and recognized that having it used by the world's greatest screen spy would certainly help sales and acceptance of the new weapon. Perhaps

A Walther PPK pistol, Bond's weapon of choice for more than three decades.

not coincidentally, *Never Say Never Again,* released a mere four months after *Octopussy,* also had Bond wielding a P5. The 9mm pistol is still being produced today.

The PPK was comfortably back in its shoulder holster for Moore's final Bond outing, *A View to a Kill,* and remained there (except when saving the world) through the Dalton films, as well as the first two Brosnan Bonds.

Several Walther PPKs from the Bond films have been sold through Christie's of London auctions over the years. As mentioned, the piece from *Dr. No* went for more than $106,000, while a similar item used by Pierce Brosnan in *GoldenEye* brought about half that amount in the same 2006 auction.

Electronic Bug Detector

In *From Russia with Love,* Bond checks into an Istanbul hotel, where he discovers not-so-secret microphones hidden behind pictures and in the chandelier. He removes a high-tech device from his briefcase, placing it on the bottom of the room's phone. The meter's needle confirms the telephone is also bugged. Bond calls room service and asks for another room.

In actuality, the "high-tech" device used in the film is an Elcometer. Made in the United Kingdom, it was used to measure the thickness of paint on metal items. Propmaster John Chisholm obviously liked the look and size of the playing card pack–sized meter and used it in the scene, with appropriate clicking sound effects added in postproduction.

A similar device helped 007 check out his hotel room at the San Monique in *Live and Let Die*.

Briefcase

From the same film, 007 received this iconic toolkit, loaded with goodies that every secret agent needs on the road, during a meeting with M and Q. What appeared to be an ordinary, black leather briefcase turned out to be the "Swiss Army knife" for all double-oh agents.

Forty rounds of ammunition were concealed in the case, as well as a spring-loaded, flat throwing knife in its top edge. Along with a special rifle (coming right up), the contents included fifty gold sovereigns. These are British coins, minted since the fifteenth century, worth about twenty shillings or a British pound each (about $2.80 at the time the film was made). According to the Royal Mint, the sovereign was a "coin of international status," which would explain why they would be valuable to Bond wherever he roamed.

The case also held a tin of regular talcum powder, although it contained a tear gas cartridge. Magnetized, it fit inside the luggage and was triggered to go off if the briefcase latches were not properly aligned when opened.

The red leather–lined briefcase was first made for *From Russia with Love* by the esteemed London luggage maker Swaine Adeney Brigg. It's still available today, and although they claim it is an exact replica of the Bond item, the modern case has round latch releases, as opposed to the rectangular latches seen in the film. No matter, it can be had for the bargain price of $2,500.

Kerim Bey (Pedro Armendariz) prepares to fire an Armalite AR-7 rifle, using 007 (Sean Connery) for support, in *From Russia with Love*.

AR-7 Rifle

As promised, this little honey was tucked away in the *From Russia with Love* attaché case, along with the ammo, the coins, and the baby powder. The AR-7 is a collapsible sniper rifle, with all components (receiver section with trigger, rifle barrel, and magazines) fitting into the sixteen-and-a-half-inch butt stock for convenient handling. The whole package weighs in at around three pounds and is completely waterproof. An infrared telescopic scope slides onto the top of the receiver.

It comes in handy during the film several times. First, Kerim Bey, head of Station T Turkish espionage, has been the target of Krilencu, SMERSH assassin. He's missed twice, and before he can have a third chance, Bey must vanquish the killer. Using the AR-7, with Bond's shoulder as a gun rest, the Turkish spy shoots Krilencu as he attempts to escape his hideout. Second, Bond and Russian agent Tatiana Romanova have escaped the Orient Express, pursued by a threatening helicopter among the Dinaric Alps. Bond finds safety in the creases of a rock, where he assembles the AR-7. Taking aim, he wounds one of the copter's occupants, who drops a live grenade in the cockpit. It detonates, destroying the chopper and allowing Bond and his lady to escape.

The same AR-7 shows up in *Goldfinger* as Tilly Masterson's weapon of choice as she stalks the flaxen-haired villain.

Unlike the aforementioned bug detector/Elcometer, the AR-7 Explorer was a real survival rifle, made at the time by Armalite. The AR-7 was quickly adopted by the US Air Force as an essential survival weapon for pilots and other military agencies. While Q mentions it's a .25-caliber rifle, it actually uses .22-caliber ammunition. The AR-7 continues to be available today from Henry Repeating Arms.

Dagger Shoe

Obviously considered standard issue footwear for all SPECTRE operatives, the dagger shoe in *From Russia with Love* proves to be an effective means to quickly eliminate unwanted pests. Mounted in the sole of the right shoe, the knife is tinged with an unnamed poison (as if the blade weren't bad enough). Spring-loaded, the dagger is released with a click of the heels— good thing the Nazis weren't wearing these things during their reign of terror.

The deadly device shows up twice in the film, once worn by Morenzy, who gives Kronsteen a swift kick in his shin and dispatches him for not killing Bond. In the film's exciting climax, Bond prepares to leave his hotel room with the lovely Romanova and the prized Lektor decoder. Evil SPECTRE agent Rosa Klebb shows up, disguised as a housekeeper who intends to clean 007 out of the picture and recover the Lektor as her own booty. She pulls a gun on Bond, preparing to shoot, but Romanova knocks the gun from her hand. Out comes the dagger on her right toe, and she begins flailing away, trying to get at 007's shins. He has to do some fancy stepping to avoid being stabbed and uses a chair like a lion tamer to keep

Klebb at leg's length. But before Bond gets the boot, Romanova shoots Klebb with her own dropped gun, and the couple are safe.

Garrote Wire Watch

One of *From Russia with Love*'s brutal baddies was SPECTRE master assassin Donald "Red" Grant. His weapon of choice was a nasty wristwatch with a unique movement—a retractable piano wire that he used as a garrote to strangle his victims.

Grant gets to demonstrate his prowess in the film's opening scenes as he stalks a 007 look-alike through a maze of hedges. He catches the Bond double and swiftly snuffs him out. Later, he tussles with the real McCoy (oh, alright—the real Bond) on the Orient Express. Just as he prepares to choke 007, the tables are turned, and Bond strangles Grant with his own device.

The timepiece was simple—a white-faced watch on a brown leather strap. But a crown ring surrounding the crystal allowed Grant to quickly extend the wire to full length, wrap it around the neck of his prey, then withdraw into the watch body. The process took only seconds—you could count them on a watch.

Aston Martin DB5

In the novels, Fleming had given his hero an appreciation of many fine things, fast cars being one of them. In *Casino Royale*, the first Bond book, it's revealed that an early 1930s Bentley—a two-door, battleship-gray convertible, equipped with a 4.5-liter supercharged engine—is 007's only real hobby. The author once admitted he selected that particular car because he was very close friends with Amherst Villiers, the builder of the Bentley's supercharger.

Of course, the films were another matter. In a 1960s world where Corvettes, Thunderbirds, and Jaguars roamed, the thirty-plus-year-old Bentley might have appeared quaint—if not surely out of place. In *Goldfinger*, it was decided to give James Bond a car that visually matched his smooth and debonair style. What's more, it would be filled with gadgets and weapons that would put the Pentagon to shame.

In the book, Fleming gave Bond a British Aston Martin DB Mark III, equipped with a homing device, which he drove to his golf game with Auric Goldfinger. But the Aston Martin Lagonda Ltd. company had introduced the sleek and sexy DB5 in 1963, and it was tailor-made for the world's best secret agent. It had a V6, 4.0-liter engine, and delivered 282 hp and a top speed of 145 mph.

An Aston Martin DB5, loaded with extras.

On-screen, Bond prepares to leave Q Branch and inquires to Q about his Bentley. "It's had its day, I'm afraid," Q replies, "M's orders, 007." In its place, Q reveals the steel gray DB5—"with modifications." These include bulletproof glass all around and revolving license plates in front and back (valid in all countries, of course). Bond can activate all of his weapons from a control panel located in the center armrest. The car's arsenal includes dispensers for a smoke screen and oil slick, a retractable trunk-mounted bullet shield, and front-mounted .303-caliber Browning machine guns. The top of the gear shifter opens to reveal a red button that should be handled with great care. Why? When it's pressed, it releases a portion of the DB5's roof and fires the passenger ejector seat. Also included, but never seen: a system to eject spikes from the car's tail lights, front-mounted ramming bumpers, a radar scanner in the outside rear-view mirror, a mobile telephone mounted in the driver's door (a phone in a car? What a concept!), and an underseat tray to hold weapons.

The amazing auto held even more surprises, as the film reveals. Bond places a homing device on Goldfinger's 1937 Rolls-Royce Phantom III two-tone luxury car after their golf match. The DB5's dashboard opens to reveal a display screen with a map indicating the location of the homer. Using this, Bond is able to tail Goldfinger through the rolling mountainside of Geneva, Switzerland. When a beautiful blonde lady—Tilly Masterson—in a sporty pale yellow Mustang convertible tries to edge past 007, he quietly extends razor-sharp spinning cutting blades from the DB5's hubcaps. They slash the Mustang's tires to bits and carve a jagged groove through the car's body—no doubt, this baby's going to be in the shop for a couple of days.

Later, Bond is casing Goldfinger's Auric Enterprises smelting plant in the dark of night. Masterson shows up, still intent on shooting Goldfinger. But she trips an alarm, so she and Bond hop in the DB5 in an attempt to escape the villain's Asian henchmen. Pursued by ominous black Mercedes-Benz sedans, Bond quickly dispatches two carloads of bad guys—one with a blinding smoke screen and the other with a slippery oil slick. But a third Mercedes corners the Aston Martin at the edge of a ravine. Bond uses the extended bullet shield as protection while Tilly tries to escape. Unfortunately, there's nothing in Bond's car to guard against the deadly derby hat of Oddjob, and the girl is killed. Bond is taken prisoner and is led, driving the DB5 and flanked by the henchmen's cars, toward the plant. With one of the bad guys occupying the passenger seat in Bond's car, it looks like the secret agent is trapped. But Bond breaks away, quickly chucking his captor by firing the ejector seat. The DB5 deftly speeds through the maze of alleys surrounding Goldfinger's plant, but freedom is short-lived. Bond loses a game of chicken as he races head-on toward an opposing auto. The Aston Martin crashes into a wall of the factory, and Bond, knocked unconscious, is captured.

The Aston Martin Lagonda Ltd. Company actually provided two DB5s to the producers for the filming. One was basically stock and used for the driving scenes, called the Road car. The second was outfitted with gadgets, including the ejector seat, and was called the Effects car. The DB5 proved to be such a star of the film that two more were built to accommodate PR world tours touting *Goldfinger,* making a total of four. Where are they today?

The Road car was purchased from Aston Martin by American car collector Jerry Lee in 1969 for $12,000. He lovingly kept the DB5 in a specially built room in his home, where Lee would proudly show it to visitors. In October 2010, he decided to put the iconic auto up for auction. Handled by RM Auctions of London, the car brought a whopping $4.1 million, sold to Harry Yeaggy, who planned to display it in his private car museum in Ohio.

The original Effects car was sold to several car collectors in the 1980s and wound up being stored in an airplane hangar at the Boca Raton Airport in south Florida. In June 1997, the DB5 disappeared—a victim of grand theft auto. The case remains unsolved to this day, an event worthy of James Bond's crime-solving skills.

The two PR cars reside in Europe. One was sold to a Swiss buyer by RM Auctions in January 2006 for $2.1 million. The other is held by Louman Museum, the Dutch National Motor Museum, in The Hague.

The Ford Motor Company provided the 1964-1/2 Mustang convertible—the first of its kind to be seen on the big screen. Although it appears to be a light yellow color, the shade was called Wimbledon White. With its red leather interior and beefy 289-cubic-inch V8 engine, the Mustang found the perfect avenue to introduce itself to the world. Sadly, its whereabouts are unknown to date.

The Detroit carmaker was originally asked to supply the production with a new Ford Mustang fastback—a gold hardtop with a sleek sloping roof. But it would not be ready in time for shooting, and when it was, it served as a promotional item for Ford after the film's release. It was sold among car collectors across the years, eventually being auctioned by Barrett-Jackson in 2001 for more than $35,000.

The DB5 would show up in the next Bond film, *Thunderball*, sporting another surprise weapon. Advancing henchmen threaten Bond and his beautiful aide Madame LaPointe, and they take cover in the Aston Martin. Bond fires two high-powered water hoses from under the car's rear, dispatching the fiends who—very conveniently—run right into the debilitating wash of water as the opening credits roll.

Bond's Aston Martin DB5 makes brief appearances with Pierce Brosnan in *GoldenEye* and *Tomorrow Never Dies*, although the car really does nothing but carry 007 from one spot to another. It also appears quickly in the 2006 version of *Casino Royale* when Bond wins it in a game of Texas Hold'em, but the DB5 has no apparent "upgrades." In *Skyfall*, the DB5—this time complete with machine guns and ejector seat—returns and whisks M away to 007's boyhood Scotland home, before meeting its end in a hail of bullets and exploding in a ball of fire.

Homing Device

It may be appropriate that a Brit is responsible for the technology behind homing devices. Certainly, the global positioning systems (GPS) of today make the whole idea of tracking someone somewhat quaint, but it was high-tech in the days of the first Bond films.

In *Goldfinger*, Q gives Bond two homing devices for him to use—one about the size of a cigarette pack, the other the size of a piece of "clean your teeth" chewing gum that fits snugly in the heel of one's shoe. The larger one is magnetized and comes in handy when tracking Goldfinger across Europe. The miniature version allows Felix Leiter to keep tabs on Bond (or so he thinks) while they're in Kentucky.

Thanks go to Sir Robert Alexander Watson-Watt, the inventor of radar in 1935, for going further into the world of covert tracking. He basically developed the idea during World War II, and it came to be known as "radio-frequency identification" (RFID). The Royal Air Force fitted each of their planes with a transmitter that reacted to the bounce of a radar beam, which allowed ground stations to recognize friends from foes.

The invention of the transistor in 1948 brought about the concept of miniaturization, although it's highly unlikely the smaller homer from Q would have been possible in 1965. Microchip circuitry had just been introduced in the early 1960s, and even then, the smallest ones were the size of a lipstick tube. Plus, the size and power requirements of the receivers mounted in the DB5 and the CIA car could have been prohibitive as well.

Truth be told, the homing device shouldn't be confused with GPS, which differs in several ways. GPS, as we know it, evolved from the military's need to track munitions movements in the '60s, although nothing would really be operational until the mid-1970s. The technology slowly became available to the general public, until the military-quality information was made accessible to all in the late 1990s. While a homer usually sends out a signal to be directly received by the tracker, a GPS receiver gets its information from a network of satellites that circle the globe. A homer also allows someone to be tracked, while the GPS allows the user to track him- or herself, mostly for navigation purposes.

Like other technologies, the homing device made return appearances in *Thunderball* (in pill form), *The Man with the Golden Gun* (used to track the location of Scaramanga's flying car), *Octopussy* (placed in the Fabergé egg, complete with microphone), Daniel Craig's *Casino Royale* (embedded in his arm), and *Skyfall* (simply kept in Bond's pocket), among other variations.

Laser Table

The art of persuasion can sometimes turn into torture, and in the world of spies and espionage, an operative will do whatever it takes to get the reaction he or she needs. In the *Goldfinger* novel, the villain wants to know why Bond has been following him around Europe. In search of an answer, Oddjob threatens to give Bond a split personality—by means of a circular saw. The 1964 movie, of course, sought to up the ante somewhat and did, replacing the saw with an industrial laser.

The laser (actually an acronym for Light Amplification by Stimulated Emission of Radiation) was another example of cutting-edge technology (pun definitely intended) that was quickly becoming the norm in the 007 flicks. It was not even ten years old, having been developed by Bell Lab scientists in 1958. It's possible that many people in the world had not even heard of or seen a laser when *Goldfinger* was released. No matter, it was new, so it was cool.

Using an industrial laser, Goldfinger (Gert Fröbe) expects Bond (Sean Connery) to talk . . . or die.

In the film, Bond is captured by Goldfinger and finds himself strapped to a metal table, Overhead is a large and menacing device, resembling a metal and glass syringe on steroids. The villain explains that it is an industrial laser, emitting an extraordinary light capable of being bounced off the Moon or cutting through metal. He demonstrates, as the glass tubing glows blue and a thin red beam begins to burn through the golden platform—making a beeline toward 007's crotch. As the sizzling ray nears turning Bond from a stud to a gelding, he quickly convinces Goldfinger that he's more valuable in one piece. The mean millionaire signals for a technician to shut the laser down, and Bond is put out of action with a tranquilizer gun.

As described by one of its developers, the laser was a "solution looking for a problem." As such, the idea of cutting metal with one was only theoretical when *Goldfinger* was released—the feat would be first accomplished several years later. The film effect was created by placing a grip under the table with an acetylene torch, which slowly burned a gaping cut into the metal. The blue glow and red beam of the laser were added via special effects in postproduction.

The laser would make a return appearance when Goldfinger prepares to break into Fort Knox. It was now portable, mounted in the back of a phony

Red Cross ambulance. With its now-familiar colorful glow, the laser made quick work of cutting a loading dock door from its latches.

Lasers became commonplace in the Bond films. A diamond-powered laser mounted on a satellite became a space-placed threat in *Diamonds Are Forever*... There was the solex agitator-powered laser cannon in *Man with the Golden Gun*... A laser gun was used in *Moonraker*... The hubcap lasers in *The Living Daylights* replaced the spinning blades from *Goldfinger*... A laser Polaroid camera took a pretty picture in *Licence to Kill*... A miniaturized version was placed in a Rolex watch, which came in handy for 007 to make his escape in *Never Say Never Again*. The laser was switched into an Omega Seamaster for *GoldenEye* and *Die Another Day*.

Oddjob's Metal-Rimmed Bowler Hat

Goldfinger wasn't accustomed to soiling his own pinkies doing manual labor, so he left the heavy lifting to his mute Korean manservant Oddjob. As if being brutally strong and deftly skilled at karate wasn't enough, Oddjob had a special head garment to add to his arsenal of mayhem.

In the book, Fleming gave Oddjob a black bowler hat, its brim rimmed with a razor-sharp alloy. The Korean demonstrates his deadly skill with it when Bond visits Goldfinger's estate in Reculver, throwing it like a Frisbee with deadly accuracy and burying it into the ceiling's molding. And, although much later into the story than in the film, Oddjob uses the hat to break the neck of Tilly Masterson, killing her.

The 1964 film took the hat and made it capable of severing the head of a marble statue on the golf course grounds, as well as ending Masterson's life in the woods outside Goldfinger's factory. Oddjob doffs his chapeau once more in the depths of Fort Knox as he and 007 wrestle for their lives. The Korean's aim is, for once, a bit off, and it becomes wedged between the protective metal bars of the vault. But the metal brim of the hat proves to be not conducive to living by being too conductive to electricity, as Bond electrocutes Oddjob with a severed power cable when he tries to retrieve it.

While the idea of using a steel-brimmed hat as a weapon came from the inventive mind of Fleming, it could hardly be based on fact . . . Or could it? Discovery Channel's *MythBusters* tackled the concept, seeking to prove or disprove the film's hypothesis that Oddjob's hat could actually sever the head of a marble statue.

Combining equal portions of entertaining theatrics and solid scientific methods, the MythBusters used a hat identical to the cinematic version. Developing a robotic arm to deliver the flying fedora with consistent force over multiple attempts, they acquired concrete and marble varieties of a statue with a head on its shoulders. Their results? Busted. The marble head did tumble, but was discovered to be hollow rather than solid like the film's. The concrete bust, while solid like marble, only chipped and refused to yield. The deadly Oddjob bonnet from Fleming's furtive imagination turned out to be just that: imaginary.

Although the hat was often called a derby, the style was more accurately a square-crowned coke, custom-made by James Lock and Company, hatters in London. Oddjob actor Harold Sakata held on to the hat as a souvenir from the film. It remained in the possession of his family until the estate placed it with Julien's Auctions in June 2006, where it sold for $33,000. The buyer, pop culture collector Anthony Pugliese III, turned around in 2008 and sold it for a whopping $110,000 in the Guernsey's Pop Culture Auction at Palms in Las Vegas.

Jet Pack

A perfect example of an honest-to-goodness, real-life item pulled from the technology of the day and plopped down smack in the middle (or in this case the beginning) of a James Bond flick, the jet pack set the tone of excitement for 1965's *Thunderball*.

In the opening scenes, Bond has just killed SPECTRE agent Jacques Bouvar in his French chateau, and Bouvar's servants are in hot pursuit. Bond pulls on a crash helmet and straps himself into the harness of a jet-propelled backpack. It whines as 007 rises into the air, soaring over the chateau's rooftop. He comes to rest with a great cloud of dust next to his trusted Aston Martin DB5 and stows the pack in its trunk with the help of Madame LaPointe of the French Station.

The jet pack was developed by Wendell Moore at Bell Aerosystems in the late 1950s. The US Army gave Moore a contract in 1960 to develop a one-man flying harness for America's fighting man. It was considered a partial success—it flew but was incredibly noisy, and a full flight lasted about twenty seconds, carrying the pilot a distance of about 850 feet in total. Not bad, as long as the enemy couldn't hear, couldn't wait long, and was closer than a quarter of a mile away.

The design was pretty straightforward—the tanks on the back held a fuel

Sean Connery as Bond (without safety helmet) takes off with the Bell jet pack in *Thunderball*.

of hydrogen peroxide, pressurized with a tank of nitrogen, When the fuel came in contact with a catalyst of specially treated silver mesh plates in the combustion chamber, the silver mesh decomposed. The resulting reaction was a lot of heat and a lot of steam, creating jets of thrust powerful enough to lift a person right off the ground. Handgrips controlled the height, speed, and direction of the pilot.

Of course, producers weren't crazy about having their star, Sean Connery, flying around in a noisy and dangerous jet pack. Bell sent two test pilots—Bill Suitor and Gordon Yaeger (no relation to Chuck)—to fly the jet pack during filming. Suitor would later use a similar jet pack to wow the crowds during the opening ceremonies of the 1984 Summer Olympic Games in Los Angeles.

The Bond jet pack reappeared in *Die Another Day*, hanging around among the Q Branch archives. Bond activates it, asking, "Does this thing still work?" Q has to quickly corral the device as it slowly heads toward the ceiling. This prop now makes tours with 007 vehicles in an exhibit called *Bond in Motion*.

Disco Volante Yacht/Hydrofoil

Ian Fleming's novel of *Thunderball* featured SPECTRE bad guy Emilio Largo traveling the Caribbean in a luxury cruiser yacht called the *Disco Volante*—Italian for Flying Saucer. The ship was said to be large, fast, and of a revolutionary design—a hydrofoil. A large metal blade extended from the hull, raising up the bow of the 100-ton craft and allowing it to reach speeds of fifty knots—more than fifty-six miles per hour.

As had quickly become the norm for the Bond films in the '60s, the 1965 cinematic presentation of *Thunderball* upped the ante when it came to introducing the *Disco Volante*. Like the book, it held several underwater craft to retrieve the hijacked bombs. But it had much more to offer, like a rear "cocoon" section—loaded to the teeth with armaments that could be released from the yacht. This allowed the *Disco Volante* to escape while covering its aft.

The yacht from *Thunderball*, the *Disco Volante*, pictured when it was just the *Flying Fish* hydrofoil.

The actual craft was a PT-20 hydrofoil called the *Flying Fish*, built by Italian-based Rodriquez Cantieri Navali in 1957. The ship was powered by a massive 1,350-hp Mercedes-Benz diesel engine and was very much capable of the fifty-knot speeds of which Fleming had written. In January 1959, the craft began ferry service for up to seventy tourists traveling between Puerto Rico and St. Croix, making the ninety-mile trip in just two and a half hours. By 1961, it was brought to the Pacific Northwest, where it was supposed to journey between Bellingham, Washington, and Victoria, British Columbia, in Canada.

Production designer Ken Adam located the hydrofoil back in Puerto Rico as preproduction began on *Thunderball.* Purchased for $10,000, it wound up needing a complete—and expensive at $300,000—mechanical overhaul, performed in Miami. Adam also designed the backend catamaran, complete with machine guns, an anti-aircraft gun, a smoke generator, and armor plating. The two hulls were joined together by two one-inch slip bolts, which naval experts said would never work (they were wrong).

The *Disco Volante* is one of the stars of *Thunderball,* appearing in a large portion of the film. Much is made of the ship's ability to house and deploy powered underwater sleds, suitable for carrying Largo's men or hijacked nuclear bombs. Everything and everyone go in and out through hinged access located in the bottom of the ship's hull.

Shooting for *Thunderball* was completed in July 1965. The *Disco Volante* (now renamed, once again, the *Flying Fish*) was put up for sale in February 1966. An ad placed in the *Miami Herald* referred to the ship as "a distinctive one-of-a-kind high-speed aluminum hydrofoil cruising yacht." The cocoon was not included in the sale but wound up as a houseboat in Florida for a number of years. As for the *Flying Fish,* it apparently was scrapped in the Miami area sometime in the early 1980s.

Another *Disco Volante* showed up seventeen years later in *Never Say Never Again,* this time translated into English as the *Flying Saucer.* Still belonging to Largo (named Maximillian, not Emilio), the ship was devoid of gadgets and gimmicks—with the exception of the underwater hatch and high-tech control center.

The real ship was a 280-foot luxury yacht called the *Nabila,* costing $100 million to make. Built in Italy in 1980, it had twin diesel engines capable of putting out a total of 6,000 hp. A crew of thirty attended to the needs of up to twenty-two guests. A rich (make that VERY rich) Saudi businessman owned the *Nabila* at the time of shooting, allowing the film crew full access to the opulence it offered: five decks, three elevators, a movie theater, a swimming pool, a disco, a three-bed sick bay, and nearly three hundred telephones. A few years after filming, the *Nabila* was sold to the Sultan of Brunei, who then sold it to real estate magnate Donald Trump for $29 million. Trump then sold it during bankruptcy to a member of the Saudi royal family for $40 million. Refitted in 1993, it's now dubbed the *Kingdom 5KR* and is still considered one of the finest yachts in the world.

Miniature Breathing Device

Q Branch must have figured James Bond was going to be spending a lot of time underwater in *Thunderball*. Why else would they have designed and built a tiny breathing apparatus in case of an emergency?

As usual, Major Boothroyd has an exasperating time running 007 through the latest group of gadgets. He offers a breathing device to help Bond breathe underwater for four minutes or so. It has two finger-sized canisters attached to a mouthpiece in the middle, fitting conveniently into a cigar tube. To clarify, the device is not a rebreather—a source of countless concerns among the amateur prop builders of the world. Q states, "In the event of a rebreather not being available . . ." as he hands the breathing device to Bond.

Being one of those amateur prop builders myself, I used what appears to be the same items that property master John Chisholm used to construct the prop—two empty CO_2 cartridges, along with some brass and plastic fittings. But the film gadget was convincing enough for the British Royal Corps of Engineers to believe it was a real-life device. *Thunderball* chief draftsman Peter Lamont retold a conversation he had with a member of the Corps who wanted to know how long the air in the gadget lasted. Lamont replied, "As long as you can hold your breath . . . It wasn't real."

The device comes in handy for Bond on two occasions. First, 007 finds himself trapped under the closed steel grates of Largo's Palmyra swimming pool. Deadly sharks are released and the breather gives Bond the oxygen

Replica prop of Q Branch's miniature breathing device used in *Thunderball*.

needed to escape them. Later, in the exciting underwater battle climax, Bond dumps his aqualung and uses the tiny breather to sucker some unsuspecting Largo henchmen into a time bomb trap.

The breather showed up thirty-seven years later in *Die Another Day*, as Pierce Brosnan used an identical device to make his way underwater beneath a sheet of ice to reach the lair of Gustav Graves. It must have had plenty of air to last nearly four decades.

Powered Aqualung

Also seen among the Q Branch gadgets in *Thunderball* is the bulky white aqualung, complete with hi-beam headlight, turbocharged in-board motor, liquid dye ejector, and two spearguns, tipped with shotgun shells. It helps 007 save the day as US Marine scuba divers wrestle with Largo's men underwater.

Jumping from a US Coast Guard Sikorsky S-62 helicopter, Bond quickly zooms among the grappling frogmen, yanking face masks and cutting air hoses as he goes. The backpack leaves a trail of green dye as he heads to the rescue. Bond fires one shotgun spear squarely into the midsection of an unfortunate bad guy, then uses the other to accurately blast an iron door down onto a couple of Largo's men, trapping them.

Sea Sleds

Thunderball's Largo knew lugging around heavy nuclear bombs would be a real drag, so he used a custom-designed underwater sea sled to move them from the Vulcan bomber to the *Disco Volante*. The eighteen-foot-long, two-ton orange vehicle carried up to three frogmen and had storage space for two bombs.

Conceived by production designer Ken Adam, the sea sled had three reversible electric motors—two forward and one aft—that delivered a total of 10 hp. Taking the vehicle from drawing board to reality was up to Jordan Klein Sr., an expert in building mini-subs and other underwater transportation. Adam found Klein in Miami, showed him the drawings, and left him to build the sled. The results were amazing, as the sub could travel at nearly five knots underwater for up to four hours on its batteries, and was capable of diving to depths of two hundred feet. Six spearguns were mounted up front. Klein also built the individual sea sleds according to Adam's designs. Nearly ten feet long, these seas scooters were also battery powered and armed with two spearguns.

The idea of an underwater diver propulsion vehicle (DPV) came from the mind of undersea pioneer Jacques Cousteau in the late 1950s. Of course, the military jumped on the idea, with little positive results at the time. By the time *Thunderball* was released, the first recreational DPVs appeared. Today, companies like SeaDoo and Stidd Systems Inc. serve both the pleasure-seeker and military needs for assisted underwater transportation.

BSA Lightning Motorcycle

In the novel of *Thunderball,* the vengeful Count Lippe chases 007, intent on shooting him down. But Lippe becomes the victim of a large grenade explosion, tossed into his rented Volkswagen by SPECTRE's Sub-operator G, who is riding a swift 500-cc Triumph motorcycle.

The flick switches this up, introducing the sexy character of Fiona Volpe, who rides to Bond's rescue on a custom-built 650-cc BSA A65 Lightning. Bond's DB5 is in the lead on a quiet country road. Clad in black leather, a mysterious rider speeds up upon Lippe's 1957 black Ford Skyliner from behind. Riding the golden cycle, the rider fires two missiles into the trunk of the Ford, where they detonate and send the car skidding off the road. It explodes in a ball of fire while Bond watches as a very interested bystander. The cyclist zooms off to the edge of a lake, where the driver dumps the bike in the drink. Only when the driver's helmet is removed does the audience see it is the beautiful, raven-haired Volpe.

With a top speed of nearly 110 mph, the BSA Lightning was known as one of the fastest two-wheeled vehicles around in the mid-1960s. Special-effects designer John Stears customized the bike by adding a sleek, aerodynamic Avon Avonaire fairing to the front. He installed two chrome tubes on either side of the yoke, representing missile launchers.

The scene was shot on the racetrack at Silverstone Circuit, ninety miles north of London. The explosion effect was pulled off by loading five gallons of gasoline and detonating cord into the Ford's trunk, which was then remotely set off on cue by stunt driver Bob Simmons. Some accounts name the motorcycle driver as champion cycle sidecar racer Chris Vincent.

Fear not, as the 650 was not dumped in the water. Rather, an older BSA 10 was painted up to resemble the Lightning and used for the shot. The A65 made the promotional rounds after the release of *Thunderball* and wound up as part of the Cars of the Stars Motor Museum in the UK. In 2011, the museum's entire assets—including one hot BSA Lightning—were sold to super auto collector Michael Dezer. His Dezer Collection Museum in North Miami, Florida, hosts an amazing separate James Bond Museum.

Nikon Underwater Camera

In order to surreptitiously survey the hull of the *Disco Volante* yacht, James Bond makes use of another gift from Q Branch—a nifty underwater camera. With its ability to snap eight images in rapid succession, Q is enamored with it, but 007 is unimpressed. Later, Bond clicks off the pics that reveal the underwater hatch that allows access to the yacht.

The camera that didn't impress Bond was actually pretty impressive. The Nikon Nikonos I began as a custom-built camera body and lens known as the Calypso-Photo for Jacques Cousteau in the late 1950s. Nikon took the design and made it commercially available to serious and recreational underwater photo enthusiasts in 1963. Able to shoot pictures at depths of two hundred feet, the Nikonos accepted all sorts of film, including the infrared kind that Q mentions. However, most photographers agree that using infrared film underwater (especially without a flash) is not effective, as the water greatly reduces the film's special sensitivities. But it sure sounded good on film.

The Nikon underwater camera is not to be confused with the camera/Geiger counter that Bond gives to Domino later in the film (similar to the novel, where Felix Leiter gave the special device to Bond), although close inspection reveals that the camera appears to be a Nikonos model with gray body grips. Nor should the camera/Geiger counter be confused with the Geiger counter watch that Q gives 007 (are you confused yet?). The watch was a Swiss-made Breitling Top Time chronograph with an enlarged case. Truth be told, the watch was too small to be anything but a darned good timepiece.

Little Nellie Autogyro

Here's a perfect example of how the 007 film franchise grew by leaps and bounds in the beginning. In *From Russia with Love,* Q gave Bond a briefcase that held a gun stock and talcum powder. Four years later, in *You Only Live Twice,* Q gave Bond four suitcases that held a helicopter. How's that for progress?

In *You Only Live Twice,* Bond needs to survey a suspicious Japanese island—fast. Fortunately, he called ahead to have Q make the trip to Japan with *Little Nellie.* Tiger Tanaka, head of Japanese Secret Service, watches in amazement as technicians carry four large suitcases into the garage. Under Q's supervision, they quickly unpack and assemble a machine that Tanaka calls "a toy helicopter." But once Q briefs 007 on its capabilities, *Little Nellie* proves her worth. Bond takes off in the tiny chopper, heading toward

Bond (Sean Connery) in the *Little Nellie* autogyro in *You Only Live Twice*.

Matsue Island. (Actually, Matsue Island is located northwest of Kobe and, contrary to what Tanaka says, is nowhere near a direct route between Kobe and Shanghai. Doesn't matter—it's a Bond flick.) Nearing the island, Bond is attacked by four Bell helicopters. Using a full complement of weapons, *Little Nellie* protects her honor and defeats the advancing copters.

Producers must have figured the public had tired of seeing Bond slay people with his tricked-out Aston Martin, so they let him slay people with a tricked-out autogyro. To clarify, an autogyro is very similar to a helicopter, but the top rotor is not powered. It is freewheeling and spins with the forward motion created by the main motor-driven propeller behind the pilot. The spinning top rotor gives the craft lift, allowing it to fly.

To build and pilot the new gadget-laden craft, producers tapped the skills of Ken Wallis. An RAF bomber commander during World War II, Wallis began working with autogyros in the late 1950s. (As a little-known sidenote, Wallis also invented the hobby of slot car racing while in the RAF—tiny cars, the pin that fits into the track—everything!) The pilot quickly embraced the autogyro and began to design and build his own models.

The WA-116 was developed in 1962. It was ultralight, weighing less than 250 pounds. The craft could take off in as little as ninety feet of runway, soar to an altitude of more than 13,000 feet (although without a cockpit or cabin, that could be a little chilly), and zoom around at a top speed of almost 130 mph. If the engine conked out—no worries, mate—the rotor continued to spin, and the craft maintained its aerodynamics to a safe landing. It was the perfect machine to join the Bond legacy.

Effects designer John Stears added two forward-firing machine guns; two canisters holding rocket launchers; two red-tipped, heat-seeking missiles; two rear-firing smoke ejectors and flame throwers; plus parachuted aerial mines. He finished the autogyro with a neat paint job of yellow, silver, and black, and *Little Nellie* was born.

As might be expected, Ken Wallis filled in for Sean Connery for the actual flying sequences, with aerial cameraman Johnny Jordan shooting a total of eighty-five takeoffs and landings. On one such shot in Japan, an updraft carried the rotors of one helicopter into the landing skids of another—as well as the foot of Jordan, severely injuring the cameraman. But quick action got Jordan to a team of surgeons, who saved his leg (although serious pain would lead Jordan to insist it be amputated some months later. Afterward, he resumed his career in aerial photography). Shooting the fighting copters resumed in Spain later, as the Japanese government was not keen on the idea of rockets being fired over their land, and the area in Spain resembled the Japanese region of the first shots.

Little Nellie remained in the Wallis fleet after shooting *You Only Live Twice* was completed. More than forty-five years later, Wallis—aged ninety-six—was still flying autogyros, having set every record in the book since his time on the Bond set.

Toyota 2000 GT

In *You Only Live Twice,* James Bond has left his appointment with the head of Osato Chemicals and is about to be ambushed in the parking lot by a bunch of thugs in a black Toyota Crown 2300. Japanese Secret Service operative Aki roars in to the rescue in a racy white Toyota 2000GT convertible.

The 2000GT zooms through the local streets and countryside, with the Crown in hot pursuit. Aki contacts Tiger Tanaka and orders the "usual reception" (apparently, this kind of thing happens to her a lot). On the open road, an enormous Boeing/Kawasaki KV-107II twin-rotor helicopter swoops in—with a large electromagnet suspended from its belly. The magnet clamps onto the Crown's roof, and as the helicopter pulls up, it takes the car with its startled occupants straight up in the air (the nonplussed driver keeps steering, but finds it to be ineffective from three hundred feet in the sky). The copter pilot cuts the juice to the magnet and—once again—gravity wins as the carload of bad guys ends up at the bottom of Tokyo Bay.

The Toyota 2000GT was a huge hit when it was first viewed by the public at the 1965 Tokyo Motor Show. The Japanese company would eventually make about 350 of the model—all hardtops. The exceptions, of course, were the two customized convertibles made for *You Only Live Twice* (Connery, at well over six feet tall, would hardly fit comfortably in a hardtop). One had the full load of gadgets, while the other would be a backup and had a regular interior. Under the hood was an inline six-cylinder 2.0-liter engine with three Solex carbs, pumping out 150 hp. The 2000GT had independent suspension at the front and rear, as well as disc brakes on all four corners. Equipped with a five-speed manual transmission, it could hit a top speed of 140 mph.

John Stears worked with Sony Electronics to load the car with goodies, many of which never appeared in the film. The two-seat interior had a console behind it that held a color TV monitor, a voice-activated tape recorder, and an FM receiver. In the front glove box were a cordless phone and a video recorder. (Sony had just introduced the first one for the home market, the CV-2000, although it had the dimensions of a full-sized suitcase and was a tight squeeze in the Toyota.) Video cameras behind the front and rear license plates showed where one was going and where one had been.

The backup Toyota 2000GT wound up in the Toyota Automobile Museum in Japan, although their current vehicle inventory does not list it. Many questions surround the fate of the gadget-filled 2000GT—one story says it was scrapped in 1970; another says it ended up in the private collection of a former Toyota exec. The original equipment console supposedly showed up in a replica of the convertible at the Cars of the Stars Motor Museum in the UK, but that can't be verified. It now sits in North Miami, Florida, as part of the Bond Museum.

Electronic Safecracker

Bond happens to find himself in the offices of Osato Chemicals in the first part of *You Only Live Twice*. Seeing a chance to break into the company safe, he pulls a convenient device out of his pocket to assist him in cracking the safe.

The metal case is about the size of a cigarette pack with two coiled wires, each attached to a magnetic sensing bar. The bars are placed in proximity to the lock bolts, and as 007 spins the combination dial, the tumblers inside click. Each click lights one of ten bulbs on the gadget, and with a press of a button, the combination appears on its face. The whole process takes less than forty-five seconds.

In theory, Bond uses the right means to crack the safe—security professionals agree that picking locks using sound sensing (ears, stethoscopes, or in this case, a high-tech device) to detect the tumblers falling into place is the best and cleanest way. However, even the best pros can take an hour or more to do so. (Faster means include pry bars, high-speed drills, thermal lances, and high explosives, but these can get a bit messy, not to mention destroy much, if not all, of the safe's contents.) What's more, the technology of the mid-1960s was ill equipped to build the kind of device Bond uses. Even today, laptop computers can use specialized software to run thousands of combinations to open safes—but they can still take hours.

A similar, but much bulkier, safecracking device showed up in *On Her Majesty's Secret Service*—this time with its own photocopier built in—but was no more feasible than the one in *You Only Live Twice. Moonraker* demonstrates an X-ray version of the safecracker, fitting snugly in a cigarette case—again, a figment of fiction. Sorry, Mr. Bond—you're locked out.

Rocket-Firing Gun and Cigarette

As Bond prepares to train as a ninja warrior with Tiger Tanaka's team in *You Only Live Twice,* he tours the firing range at Tanaka's camp. Tiger demonstrates a unique gun that uses jet propulsion instead of gunpowder. Bond is very impressed with this rocket gun.

Once again, it's a case of art imitating life, as these rocket guns were real. Called the Gyrojet, they performed exactly as Tiger explained: four tiny jets in the base of the bullet gave it thrust and spin (the gun barrels were smooth bored, not rifled). The Rocketeer Automatic Rocket Pistol was the product of MBAssociates in California, who made an assault rifle version as well (also seen on the table in front of Tanaka, Bond, and Aki in *You Only Live Twice*). The US Army showed some interest in the Gyrojet, but two factors spelled its doom: the ammo wasn't very accurate and was very expensive.

Tanaka also shows Bond another weapon: a cigarette that holds a tiny explosive rocket (deadly enough, even without the rocket, but that's another story). Tiger demonstrates, offering that it's accurate up to thirty yards. The "lung dart" comes in handy for 007 later on, when he's held prisoner in Blofeld's control room. Another item from MBAssociates, the rocket inside is a Finjet—molded plastic with a steel tip (not explosive, as seen in *You Only Live Twice*).

Blofeld's Volcano Fortress

The centerpiece of *You Only Live Twice*, a massive Japanese volcano fortress, is used by master villain Blofeld as a launchpad and landing site for his spacecraft-hijacking rocket. It becomes the site for the film's exciting conclusion, complete with dozens of rappelling ninja fighters, thunderous explosions, and bodies flying in every direction.

The idea of a hollowed-out volcano as an outlaw's lair rose from the necessity for a Plan B. Producer Cubby Broccoli, along with director Lewis Gilbert, production designer Ken Adam, and cameraman Freddie Young, flew over coastal mountain ranges of Japan for three weeks. They sought a Japanese castle fortress as described by Ian Fleming in his novel *You Only Live Twice*.

Unfortunately, like Bond himself, Japanese castles on the coast were pieces of fiction (castles don't hold up well in fierce seaside storms and were never built on the coast). Disappointed, the group landed where Ken Adam remembered several large volcanoes they had seen on their trip. He drew up a few quick sketches, suggesting to Broccoli that this would be a great place for Blofeld's base of operations. The producer wondered if the set could be built for $1 million—an enormous amount of money in 1966 (more than then entire budget for *Dr. No*). Adam replied, "Of course I can do it."

Ken Adam's resulting design turned out to be nearly as big as the Bond franchise itself. Built on an outdoor lot at Pinewood Studios near London, the volcano set was 130 feet tall and nearly 450 feet across. It had a 70-foot retractable roof, made up to resemble a crater lake. The opening was big enough to fly a helicopter through (and they really did).

Ken Adam's volcano set from *You Only Live Twice*, complete with *Bird 1*.

Inside were an operating monorail system, a maze of brushed aluminum staircases, a movable heliport pad, a command center and control room protected by adjustable steel shutters, and a mocked-up 110-foot rocket with gantry and elevator. A crane located outside the set lifted the rocket to simulate liftoff. It took seven hundred tons of structural steel and two hundred miles of tubular steel to build—Adam claimed there was more steel in the volcano set than in the

London Hilton Hotel. It also used two hundred tons of plaster and more than a quarter-million square yards of canvas.

The real volcano that impressed Adam, Mount Shinmoedake, was located in southern Japan near the city of Kobayashi. It made news nearly forty-five years after *You Only Live Twice,* as it erupted in 2011, spewing smoke and ash nearly two miles into the sky. It looked just like a scene out of a movie.

Bird I/*Intruder* Rocket

SPECTRE's Blofeld has come up with a nifty plot to create anarchy in the world in *You Only Live Twice.* Communist Russia and the United States are hotly involved in the Space Race. Bald Boy figures he can hijack their spacecraft in orbit, with each of the superpowers pinning the blame on the other. Once war has broken out between the superpowers, China can take over—paying Blofeld and SPECTRE handsomely for services rendered. In order to accomplish this scheme, Blofeld has a rogue rocket that can lift off and return to a launch complex hidden inside a Japanese volcano.

The rocket—referred to as *Bird I* in the film and *Intruder* rocket in the shooting script—was a fictitious design by Ken Adam and John Stears. But the single-stage booster was based on a cut-down version of the American *Atlas* ICBM, used to launch Mercury astronauts into Earth orbit in the mid-1960s.

Once in orbit, the silver-skinned *Bird 1* separates from its booster and takes off after its prey. With two SPECTRE astronauts onboard, the *Bird 1* approaches the target craft from behind. Nearing to within a few feet of the craft, four hinged jaws open on the front of *Bird 1,* engulfing and swallowing the Russian or US capsule. The jaws close, trapping the craft. The *Bird 1* then makes a 180-degree turn, reentering the Earth's atmosphere. Its heat shield turns bright red from the friction, then falls away. Retro-rockets fire, further slowing the rocket's descent, until four spiderlike landing pad legs deploy. The *Bird 1* makes a powered touchdown on the platform inside Blofeld's volcano lair.

The idea of the open jaws came—once more—from the headlines of the day. In June 1966, the astronauts on Gemini 9, part of the US space program to reach the moon, were attempting to join up with an unmanned docking adapter nearly 160 miles in space. When they got close enough to see the target, they noticed the protective cone—used during launch—had failed to come off completely. The gaping jaws of the shroud, said one astronaut, looked like "an angry alligator." Another Bond device was born.

Radioactive Lint

Yes, you read that correctly. *On Her Majesty's Secret Service* was largely deficient in gear and gadgets, except for the previously mentioned safecracking/photocopying device and an upgraded Aston Martin DBS for 007.

The opening scene does feature Q briefing M on the latest in homing technology, as he produces a small plastic container of lint. Once it's placed in the target's pocket, its radioactivity makes tracking the person a cinch (assuming it doesn't get stuck to an atomic-powered sourball and get thrown away). The less said about this, the better.

Whyte's Tectronics Industries Moon Buggy

In *Diamonds Are Forever*, Blofeld has assumed the guise of reclusive billionaire Willard Whyte. Modeled after the real-life mogul Howard Hughes, Whyte holds many financial interests, including Tectronics Industries. The company has developed, among other projects, a moon buggy for NASA at its desert facility outside Las Vegas. The high-tech jalopy provides 007 with a getaway vehicle from the lab's security crew.

The Apollo moon missions were in full swing at the time of *Diamonds Are Forever*'s release. Astronauts on the lunar surface began using a Lunar Roving Vehicle (LRV), traveling many miles from the Lunar Module to collect rock and soil samples. The LRV was battery-powered, looking much like a two-seat roadster with its body removed.

Ken Adam was well aware of the LRV, but when time came to design the film's moon buggy, director Guy Hamilton wanted it to be "more grotesque." The designer responded with something straight out of comic books. The silver buggy had a clear bubble dome for complete 360-degree vision; a tall and angular body; a large, round red oxygen tank behind the cockpit; a rotating radio antenna at the rear; two spindly robotic arms; and four black balloon tires.

Bond finds the buggy sitting among a moon set used by astronauts for simulations. Chased by lab guards, he climbs into the vehicle and crashes through a wall, heading out across the Nevada desert. Military green Ford sedans have a tough time handling the terrain, and Bond abandons the buggy to escape with Tiffany Case.

The moon buggy design was turned over for construction to legendary car customizer Dean Jeffries, who had built the Green Hornet's Black Beauty and the Monkeemobile for TV, among many other cars. Jeffries assembled the buggy according to Adam's design, including conical fiberglass wheels. But once on the sandy set, it became apparent the wheels would not hold up, and heavy-duty rubber tires were substituted. Still, they weren't the best solution, as they kept coming off the buggy during filming. In fact, in one scene in the final cut, a Ford goes tumbling over a sand dune as one of the buggy's lost and lonely tires can be seen rolling in from the opposite side of the screen.

The moon buggy made the regular promotional trips following the release of *Diamonds Are Forever,* then was abandoned and fell into disrepair for years. To the rescue came Graham Rye, the editor of *007 Magazine,* who arranged for its restoration. Once completed, the moon buggy called Caesar's Palace in Las Vegas home, where it was publicly displayed in the Planet Hollywood restaurant for ten years. Despite absurd rumors that Sean Connery had purchased the buggy, it was sold in December 2004 as part of Christie's Film and Entertainment Auction. Appropriately, it was purchased by the new Planet Hollywood Las Vegas Casino for $46,000.

Satellite with Diamond-Powered Laser

In *Diamonds Are Forever,* Blofeld launches a satellite into orbit. But it's not a satellite for communications or weather or global tracking or scientific research. Its one purpose is mayhem—Blofeld plans to disable the major nuclear powers of the world with a deadly laser cannon mounted on the satellite. Once that's done, Blofeld will auction off the rights for nuclear supremacy to the highest bidder.

The satellite's design was attractive, if not practical. Unfolding from the nose of a NASA booster rocket, it had two solar panels and a triad of slender brackets. Once open, they supported an unfurled parabolic dish, encrusted with diamonds and a laser cannon in the center. Designed by Ken Adam, the booster and satellite models were built by Mastermodels Ltd. near London. The booster model was about twelve feet long, with the satellite's parabolic dish about eighteen inches across.

The idea of using a laser as a weapon was not necessarily new (see *Goldfinger*). In this case, the idea was also flawed. First, Willard Whyte may have stacks of cash, but he must have flunked history. He claims the first laser beam was generated through a diamond. Wrong, Mr. GottRox—it was through a ruby in 1960. Second (without turning this into a physics class), while certain gem crystals such as synthetic rubies can be used as a lasing material, they have to be singular tubes, not individual crystals. Third, scientists agree that a diamond is not an ideal medium for lasers (although forty years after *Diamonds Are Forever,* efforts are continuing to use them in lasers). A diamond-powered laser on a satellite made for great fiction but lousy fact.

Study hard—the test will be next Thursday.

Rolex Submariner Wristwatch

In *Live and Let Die,* Miss Moneypenny returns 007's trusty watch, having been restored from unseen rigors and damage to fighting condition by Q Branch. Good thing he's got it back, too. It has a few modifications that come in handy throughout the film.

First, it holds a powerful magnet—perfect for yanking a spoon from the boss' coffee cup, lowering the dress zipper of a comely lady, attempting to pull in a lifesaving boat while surrounded by hungry alligators, or even attracting a compressed-air bullet from a table, to be activated and shoved into the mouth of the evil Dr. Kananga. Second, the saw-toothed black bezel is valuable in cutting through ropes that hold Bond and Solitaire captive over a tank of savage sharks.

Designed and adapted by art director Syd Cain, the watch was a Rolex 5513 Oyster Perpetual Submariner, a favorite of divers and fans of fine timepieces. Originally priced for around $450, the watch was famed for its black dial face and brushed silver body and watchband. Cain removed the inside moving parts, added sharpened teeth to the saw-edged bezel, and allowed the crystal to rotate, turning the white dial markers to red. The inside was signed by Roger Moore 007.

The celebrated watch wound up being sold twice at Christie's Auctions of London. The first sale, in February 2001, fetched more than $37,000, including the buyer's premium. Sold again in November 2011, the price came in at more than $240,000. Not bad for a watch that couldn't even tell the time.

Solex Agitator

In *The Man with the Golden Gun,* Bond chases after the title villain, Scaramanga, who has stolen a device called the Solex Agitator from a British scientist named Gibson after murdering him. The gadget has the ability to harness the sun's power and convert it into enormous amounts of electricity. But the evil Scaramanga plans to auction the powerful Solex Agitator to the highest bidder (have we heard this plot before?).

Sized like a pack of playing cards (a standard size, it seems, in Bond films), the Solex Agitator was made from aluminum with a clear plastic face. Inside were an assortment of resistors, capacitors, and coils mounted to a small circuit board. Etched into the metal was a cryptic engraving: H/220. Perhaps it was a formula, with the etched H representing "henries"—which, in physics, are measurements of stored energy in relation to a magnetic field and . . . Who cares!? The Solex Agitator wasn't real anyway!

The Golden Gun

In Fleming's novel *The Man with the Golden Gun,* Scaramanga is a well-paid assassin who wields a gold-plated .45 Colt revolver to do his dirty work. The cylinder holds six gold-plated bullets—it's no wonder the man got a million dollars per order.

The 1974 film, however, took the historic pistol to new heights of gadgetry. This time around, Scaramanga's weapon broke apart into a few innocent personal items, allowing him to travel with the gun undetected (before the days of the TSA). The gun held only one 4.2mm golden bullet, but with his reputation and skill, Scaramanga only needed one shot. The items were a writing pen, a cigarette case, a cigarette lighter, and a cuff link. The victim's bullet was hidden in his belt buckle.

Scaramanga first pulls his pistol when he dispatches a thug hired to keep his shooting eye sharp by stalking him in a mirror-filled room usually found in a carnival funhouse. Later, he shoots another double-oh agent, the man who created the Solex Agitator, his Chinese employer Hai Fat, and the beautiful Andrea Anders—each with just one shot. But when he comes up against Bond in the funhouse, Scaramanga isn't as quick on the draw as 007 and is shot dead through the heart.

Designed by art director Peter Lamont, the Golden Gun consisted of:

- A Waterman fountain pen for its barrel
- A Colibri Molectric 88 lighter (heavily modified) for the chamber mechanism
- A cigarette case for the handle
- A cuff link that screwed into the opened lid of the cigarette case to act as the trigger

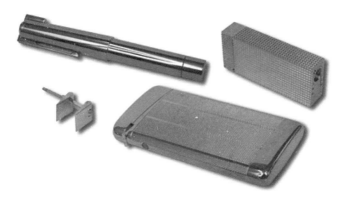

The Golden Gun (some assembly required).

Lamont took a balsawood prototype to the Colibri Company, makers of fine lighters, and asked them to build the prop. They delivered the gun to Albert Luxford, one of the special-effects engineers on the film. Luxford gave the gun to either Roger Moore or Christopher Lee—he couldn't recall which actor—and it came back, broken to pieces. Luxford and an associate were able to fashion another prop—this time in brass—in less than two weeks.

As Colibri's results were not durable or sufficiently high quality, SJ Rose and Son Silversmiths in London were asked to take up the job of creating several additional prop guns. They delivered three gold-plated models for the film: a nonfiring gimmick gun, made to be assembled from the separate parts; a fully assembled, nonfiring gun to be used where it needed to be handled but not fired; and an operational prop, designed to fire a blank.

The Golden Gun became one of the most well-known weapons in film history. But, as seems the case with many of the 007 artifacts, their history after their screen time is somewhat vague. One prop gun was stored at London's Elstree Props, until it was discovered stolen in October 2008. At the time, its value was estimated at more than $125,000, although many fans questioned the authenticity of the item taken. Another Golden Gun is believed to be somewhere within Eon Productions control. Still another was purchased at a 2001 Christie's Auction and is now in the Bond Museum in Florida (yet its Colibri lighter is made of two segments, a version that never appears in the film). Several replica guns have fetched prices of more than $10,000 in Christie's auctions, but they were high-quality copies made by a small prop-making studio and were not connected with the film.

No matter, whoever held them became the man with a Golden Gun.

AMC Matador Flying Car

In *The Man with the Golden Gun,* Bond tracks Scaramanga and Nick Nack to a warehouse in Bangkok. The evil duo enter the building driving a copper-colored 1974 AMC Matador, but when they leave it, they're flying the friendly skies in the car.

AMC—American Motors Corporation—was the fourth US car manufacturer, always seeming to tail the Big Three from Detroit. The company arranged a decent product placement deal for the film, as the Matador was joined by a sporty AMC Hornet, among other AMCs. The Matador, however, was the star of the scene as it rolled down the roadway and took to the air.

In the warehouse, the Matador received a large cowling with wings, a tail section, and a single jet engine. The contraption attached to the roof and rear by means of struts. Special-effects wizard John Stears built the full-sized and model versions, almost sending the actual car-plane into the air during a test run at Pinewood Studios.

Production designer Peter Murton based the flying car on a real-life prototype, as two California builders had married a 300-hp airplane engine, Cessna Skymaster wings, and a Ford Pinto to create the Mizar Flying Car in 1973. They flew it successfully numerous times before a wing folded up and set the craft crashing to the ground in September of that year, killing the duo.

The AMC Matador—sans wings and engine—is found firmly on the ground these days in the Bond Museum in North Miami.

"Wet Nellie" Lotus Esprit

The Spy Who Loved Me introduced a vehicle that dared to rival the iconic Aston Martin DB5. More than a dozen years after *Goldfinger* showed the silver auto to millions of fans around the world, Bond producers figured the time was right to bring out a new star car.

Following the obligatory lecture from Q about taking care of the vehicle (this time, beachside in Sardinia), 007 and KGB agent Anya Amasova take off in a sporty white 1976 Lotus Esprit S1. Tailed by a motorcycle with a deadly bomb-carrying sidecar, Bond eludes it, as well as a carload of gun-firing heavies (including Jaws). But an ominous helicopter, piloted by the ravishing Naomi, threatens to take the Esprit out of commission—permanently. Bond drives the car off a ramp into the sea, and, perhaps not surprisingly, the car becomes a submarine. From beneath the waves, Bond dispatches the helicopter with a well-aimed missile, along with eliminating Stromberg's men on sea sleds. To the amazement of sunbathing beachgoers, Bond and Amasova roll up out of the waters in the Esprit and motor off.

Once again, Production Designer Ken Adam was behind the creation. Being a Lotus owner at the time, he loved the sleek styling and was

In *The Spy Who Loved Me*, the Lotus Esprit emerges from the sea.

acquainted with Colin Chapman, the founder of Lotus Cars Ltd. The company loaned two 1976 Lotus Esprits (originally designed by Italian carmaker Giorgetto Giugiaro) to the Bond people, supplying five more body shells for modifications. Adam sent the bodies to Perry Oceanographics in Riviera Beach, Florida, and asked the company what seemed impossible—to turn the Lotus Esprit into a mini submarine! But since mini-subs were their business, Perry came up with the real thing.

The full-sized model was battery powered by four submersible motors mounted near the rear bumper, with adjustable vanes to change the car's direction. Fore and aft diving planes controlled the depth of the sub. A periscope allowed Bond a 360-degree view above the water's surface. Perry's Lotus could reach a speed of fifteen knots and was capable of diving to more than 300 feet. Extras included surface-to-air missiles from behind the cockpit, front-firing torpedoes and harpoons, rear-firing cement and ink ejectors behind the license plate (PPW 306R), and disc-shaped magnetic mines. The sub version did not have tires, as the wheel wells were permanently sealed. Pressurizing the interior was not possible, so the driver was a diver—oxygen tanks allowed professionals to work submerged.

Additional car shells and a radio-controlled three-foot scale model were used to portray the transformation from car to sub and back again. The shooting script referred to the Lotus as "Wet Nellie"—in honor of *You Only Live Twice*'s *Little Nellie* autogyro. Alas, the scene of the car driving out of the sea was a bit of movie magic: special-effects designer Derek Meddings actually towed the car with a cable and winch along hidden tracks in the sand.

One of the world's master 007 aficionados recovered and restored the sub car in the Bahamas, displaying it in the Bond Museum in North Miami. One of the two land cars sold at Bonham's auction in 2008 for more than $206,000—that's one expensive ride.

Karl Stromberg's Atlantis Underwater Den

In case anyone watching the Bond films hasn't noticed, the super-villain must have one heckuva monstrous lair. Massive in size, scope, and armaments, the baddie's crib has got to be fly (thank God for teenaged kids in my house). Karl Stromberg was no exception in *The Spy Who Loved Me*.

His Atlantis was an underwater paradise—literally a city mounted on four telescoping legs that allowed it to surface and submerge in the Mediterranean Sea off the coast of Sardinia. From there, he planned on initiating a crippling nuclear war between the world's superpowers and starting a new world beneath the sea—with Stromberg as the overseer.

The spiderlike Atlantis was the brainchild of production designer Ken Adam, who drew his influence from the floating city of Aquapolis. The centerpiece of the World's Fair/Expo '75 in Okinawa, Japan, Aquapolis was the ¥13 billion (about $45 million) concept of a human habitat on the sea. The multiple-deck structure occupied nearly 110,000 square feet and weighed 15,000 tons. Built in Hiroshima on the Japanese mainland, it was towed more than six hundred miles to its spot in the ocean. It towered more than one hundred feet above the waves and could fully support a crew of almost 200. Like Stromberg's Atlantis, Aquapolis was self-supporting in terms of energy and even providing fresh water. But once the Expo closed, Aquapolis' days were numbered. Closed in 1993, it was towed to Shanghai, China, and scrapped in 2000.

Stromberg's Atlantis was well equipped, featuring a helicopter pad, boating docks, radar dish, living quarters, dining room, a private aquarium (including a nasty shark tank), and a massive control room. Designer Ken Adam used curved shapes to give the structure an organic quality, although the immense dining room had straight walls and beautiful hanging tapestries.

Unfortunately, it all came crashing down and fell to the sea's bottom when Bond recovered one of the hijacked nuclear subs, then rescued Amasova from Atlantis while the sub sank it with torpedoes. Stromberg wasn't around to see the finish, as Bond had already shot and killed him.

Karl Stromberg's *Liparus* Supertanker

Stromberg's plot to create a new world by destroying the old world was based on hijacking nuclear submarines, then launching their atomic warheads against the nations of the world. To pull this off, he relied on his one million-plus-ton supertanker called *Liparus*.

The huge ship would come upon a sub from behind, its bow would open up, and the vessel would be captured in the hold of the *Liparus*. (Sound familiar? Just imagine a waterlogged version of *You Only Live Twice*'s *Bird 1* and orbiting spacecraft.) Stromberg grabbed Soviet, British, and American submarines, stowing all three of them in the supertanker.

Filmmakers originally planned on using a real supertanker—producer Cubby Broccoli had friends, apparently—but it was deemed too dangerous (open pyrotechnics and flammable oil don't mix well). Special-effects designer Derek Meddings built an eighty-foot-long model (powered by a 45-hp inboard Evinrude motor to provide the proper wake). With additional model work done by Simon Atkinson, the *Liparus* footage was shot in the Bahamas.

Of course, the set for the interior of the *Liparus* would have to be big enough to house three submarines. One problem—no soundstage in the world was big enough to handle such an order. But wait—this is James Bond! Enter the Pinewood Studios, where the world's biggest shooting stage would be erected. Production designer Ken Adam learned his lesson from *You Only Live Twice,* where he built the enormous volcano set, only to see its use limited just to that film. Knowing what he wanted and needed, Adam designed the set and the stage simultaneously, with the understanding the stage would be completely functional for future films of all kinds.

Finished in December 1976, the structure was more than 300 feet long and 130 feet wide—nearly large enough in which to play soccer. It was more than 40 feet tall and held a water tank nearly 200,000 cubic feet in size, with a capacity of almost 1.5 million gallons of water. At the time, it cost $1.8 million to build.

Each submarine mockup inside the *Liparus* set was built to 60 percent of full size, fabricated from plywood, and covered with fiberglass. As the subs were still 300 feet in length, cameraman Claude Renoir (yes, the grandson of the famous French artist) was very concerned about properly lighting the set. Ken Adam had the answer.

He called a friend with whom he'd worked on several films before and asked him to come over to take a look at how he would light such a large set. The friend—a man well known in the industry—feared being seen tampering or being mixed up with a Bond film, so Adam agreed to sneak him in on a Sunday. They spent four hours arranging the lighting, and it worked wonderfully. Of course, the friend insisted on no credits, so don't look for the name of multiple Oscar and BAFTA Award–nominated writer and director Stanley Kubrick at the end of *The Spy Who Loved Me.*

The 007 stage has suffered through a tough life following *The Spy Who Loved Me.* In 1984, with the shooting of Ridley Scott's *Legend* complete, the stage caught fire and burned to the ground. Rebuilt, it was renamed the Albert R. Broccoli 007 Stage. Then in July 2006, as *Casino Royale* finished, the stage burned once more. The ruins were demolished and rebuilt in 2007.

Seiko Teletype Watch

Don't you hate it when the phone rings at the most inopportune times? Watching your favorite Bond film, or eating dinner, or lying in bed trying to sleep (or not?). In *The Spy Who Loved Me,* it wasn't the phone but the wristwatch that caught 007 at a bad time.

Bond's Seiko LCD 0674 quartz watch was customized with a ticker-tape-type printout, delivering messages wherever he might be. In this case, Bond was in a log cabin in Austria, keeping time with a lovely lass in front of a roaring fire when his watch spit out the following: 007 TO REPORT HQ. IMMEDIATE M.

The gadget was simple, with a pre-printed Dymo embossed tape chugging out the top of the watch. Sometimes, low-tech can look high-tech.

Drax Industries' Moonraker Space Shuttles

Moonraker introduced filmgoers to Hugo Drax, a man of ambition (aren't they all?). His company, Drax Industries, manufactures the Earth-orbiting space shuttle for NASA. Underneath it all, though, he has plans similar to those made by a certain Nazi despot from the 1930s and '40s—develop a "master race" of humans and eliminate the rest of the world's inferior population. (It didn't work the first time—why would he think it would work now?)

Drax's shuttle fleet—six, by visual count—was no cheap operation. At $1.7 billion per vehicle (according to NASA), he had more than $10 billion flying around in space . . . a lot of dough-ray-me! At least one shuttle was equipped with a laser weapon, and they all had snazzy orange racing stripes, adding to the sticker price as well.

The space shuttle program was NASA's next step following America's successful landing on the Moon in 1969. Designed to be a reusable vehicle, it launched into space on the back of two solid rocket boosters (also reusable), as well as its own onboard liquid-fueled engines. Completing its mission, the Shuttle reentered the Earth's atmosphere and landed on an airplane-style runway, gliding on its own momentum. NASA had a fleet of six Shuttles, each about the size of a DC-9 airplane—*Enterprise* (never flown in space, but used for testing), *Columbia, Challenger, Discovery, Atlantis,* and *Endeavour.* Sadly, *Challenger* and *Columbia* were lost in tragic in-flight accidents in 1986 and 2003, respectively.

The *Moonraker* shuttles, however, preceded the actual shuttle flights by two years. In fact, the first shuttle—*Columbia*—was delivered to NASA only three months before the theatrical release of *Moonraker* in 1979. *Moonraker* production designer Ken Adam spent extensive time with NASA, ensuring the film shuttles were as accurate as possible.

Hugo Drax's Space Station

In *Moonraker*, Drax plans to keep his select group of "master race" men and women in space while the Earth's population is wiped out by a deadly toxin. Once cleared, the globe would be repopulated by Drax's folks, ferried by Shuttles from his space station.

The space station featured a spherical center, with floors for living quarters, operations, communications, as well as a laser defense system and radar-jamming antenna to assure stealth activities in space. An asymmetrical array of tubular corridors connected the center with docking platforms for up to five shuttles. The entire assembly rotated, creating simulated gravity.

Ken Adam was very intent on getting away from the "giant rotating wheel" concept seen in Stanley Kubrick's *2001: A Space Odyssey*, hence the odd shape of the Drax space station. Adam wanted to give the station the artistic appearance of a mobile, making its destruction in the film's climax all the more tragic—the filmmakers used shotguns to blow the model to pieces.

Venetian Gondola Hovercraft

A scene in *Moonraker* finds 007 taking a relaxing gondola ride through the Grand Canal of Venice. The calm is broken as a small funeral barge passes, with the coffin's obviously not-dead occupant emerging and throwing knives at Bond. Missing its target, the blade is retrieved and our favorite agent shows much better aim. But the danger is not yet over, as a motorboat pulls out and takes chase. Bond flips open a control panel, and the gondola shows some muscle of its own, becoming a high-speed motorboat. As the villains get close, Bond throws another switch, and the gondola grows an enormous inflatable air bag, becoming a hovercraft. It emerges from the water and drives through St. Mark's Square, an amazing sight for tourists, diners, waiters, artists—even a dog and a double-taking pigeon.

Glastron/Carlson Boat

Another *Moonraker* scene has Bond traveling up the Amazon to locate a rare plant from which a highly toxic poison is made. The trip is made possible by means of a special boat, which Q has given Bond with his usual nervous reluctance. He is soon pursued by a speedboat of gun-toting, mortar-firing thugs. Once more, a handy control panel gives Bond access to all sorts of goodies, including a series of mines that quickly destroy the speedboat.

Unfortunately, two more take its place, one with the gigantic Jaws at its helm. A heat-seeking torpedo blows one boat from the waters, but the other boat has 007 cornered as he approaches the edge of a treacherous waterfall. But he has one more button to push, releasing the roof of the boat and revealing a hang-glider. Bond grabs on and soars to safety as the Q Branch boat tumbles over the falls—closely followed by Jaws in his vessel.

Producers secured the services of boat manufacturer Glastron/Carlson to customize a twenty-three-foot CV23HT for the film. The limited edition craft (only three hundred total were made) had a 5.7-liter in-board motor that produced 300 hp. The company produced three custom boats for *Moonraker.* The hardtop was extended to accommodate the folded hang-glider, and the hull was finished in a special silver flake over gray paint.

A completely restored model identical to the movie boat was sold at auction in 2011 for $30,000, while only one of the three film boats survived, residing in the Bond Museum in North Miami.

One- and Two-Person Mini-Submarines

In *For Your Eyes Only,* Bond is sent to the Adriatic Sea to recover the ATAC—Automatic Targeting Attack Communicator—a British device capable of controlling the country's entire fleet of nuclear submarines. The ATAC was sunk along with the *St. George,* a surveillance vessel disguised as a fishing trawler. Bond enlists Melina Havelock, a marine archaeologist, to aid in the recovery.

The pair take to the deep waters in a compact two-person research sub called the *Neptune.* Finding the *St. George,* they don diving gear and venture into its damaged hold, where they locate the ATAC. Disconnecting it from an explosive charge, they try to leave but are confronted by a menacing diver in a rigid pressurized suit—complete with powerful mechanical pincers for hands. Melina is injured, but 007 eliminates the diver with the explosive charge. The two retreat to the safety of their sub, only to be attacked by a one-person Mantis sub that begins to dismantle the *Neptune* by tearing out cables and pipes with vice-gripped mechanical arms. Bond uses the more powerful *Neptune* to force the Mantis into the jagged opening of the *St. George.* Bond and Melina escape to the surface.

Production designer Peter Lamont came up with the two-person research submarine *Neptune,* based on real-life examples of similar craft. He built two full-sized versions for *For Your Eyes Only*—one to be used in the Bahamas and one for the water tank at Pinewood Studios. As the Bahamas prop was not designed to be fully functional, it was not watertight, which required divers in scuba gear to operate it. The vessel was twenty-three feet long and eight feet wide.

The one-person pressurized diving gear was known as a JIM Suit, one of a series of atmospheric diving suits—ADS—originally developed around World War II. The JIM Suit was named after its first user, Jim Garrett. The suit was capable of diving to depths of four thousand feet and intended for research and rescue applications (and might fill in for a certain marshmallow man in a pinch). An external tank could provide up to three days of oxygen, although no one dared to stay down for that period of time. Its menacing and futuristic look was tailor-made for a Bond film.

Models and props of the marine vehicles were built and detailed by the talented Terry Reed of Otter FX, who also performed duties as model supervisor on *Moonraker* and *The Living Daylights*, as well as other films and TV shows.

The menacing Mantis one-man sub was also designed in the real world for scientific research and underwater industrial work. It was piloted in *For Your Eyes Only* by Graham Hawkes, the vessel's actual oceanic designer and engineer. Who knew an engineer could look so scary?

Bede BD-5J Microjet

The opening scene of *Octopussy* places James Bond on a mission to destroy a secret fleet of jets in a Latin American "banana republic." The plot fails and Bond is captured, but he escapes with the aid of the beautiful Bianca. Climbing into a horse trailer, 007 reveals the horse's behind is actually a shroud for a mini-jet. He unfolds its wings and soars into the skies. The army fires a tracking missile that closes in on the jet. Bond's skillful piloting eludes the missile, and as he flies the tiny aircraft through the hangar housing the jet fleet, the missile explodes. Bond accomplishes his mission after all. The jet runs low on fuel and lands on a highway. Bond taxis into a local gas station, where he requests a fill-up.

The jet was real, developed as a revolutionary kit by Jim Bede in the early 1970s. Originally designed as a prop-driven one-person plane for the handy builder at home, the BD-5 was truly an amazing craft. The jet version was only thirteen feet long, 350 pounds (empty), and capable of speeds more than 300 mph. The turbojet engine carried the plane as high as 26,000 feet. The prop-driven kit sold for only $3,000 in 1973.

Producers brought in a veteran stunt pilot from *Moonraker*, J. W. "Corkey" Fornof, to fly the BD-5J for the scene in *Octopussy* (the mini-jet sequence had originally been planned for *Moonraker* but was moved to *Octopussy*). But much of the thrilling aerial stunts were done with movie magic and miniatures, rather than precision piloting.

The scene of the BD-5J entering and leaving the hangar was accomplished by "forced perspective." A model of the jet—about four feet long—was flown behind a model door, lined up in front of the real hangar, but perhaps 150 feet closer to the camera. With proper alignment, the plane appeared to fly directly into the hangar, although it was nowhere near it. The same effect was used when the plane flew out the other side.

The BD-5J's quick trip through the hangar used a real-sized jet but with a special setup—it was on top of a pole mounted to a topless Jaguar XJ-6. Driven by special-effects designer John Richardson, the car was traveling at 75 mph. An off-camera assistant tilted the plane so its wings covered the pole during the drive-through. Strategically placed set pieces in the foreground conveniently blocked the car.

The Octopussy BD-5J resides in the Pima Air and Space Museum in Tucson, Arizona, although the Bond Museum in Florida also displays a similar jet.

Bajaj Tuk-Tuk Taxi

Much of *Octopussy* is set in India, where streets are crowded and narrow. As such, big yellow taxis are not available to ferry folks from one spot to another. Like many cities in Europe and Asia, personal public transportation is provided via small, three-wheeled vehicles known as auto-rickshaws or tuk-tuks, named for the sound they make. (Just imagine brightly colored golf carts with drivers who get paid to cuss.)

Bond arrives in India, where he meets Vijay, MI6's operative there. After beating the evil Kamal Khan in a spirited game of backgammon, Vijay and Bond take off in a three-wheeler. But they have company, as Khan's henchman, Gobinda, follows in another tuk-tuk—armed with a double-barreled blunderbuss. When Bond mentions they're being tailed, Vijay confidently states, "No problem—this is a company car." He steps on the gas and pops a wheelie, roaring away—obviously, Q has been fooling around under the hood.

The tuk-tuk chase was designed by Remy Julienne, veteran car stuntman and coordinator of six Bond films, who also modified the vehicles. The tuk-tuk in which Gobinda rode was sold at Coys Auction in July 2009 for almost $2,900.

Montblanc Acid Pen

In *Octopussy*, Bond stops by Q Branch to see the latest creations by Major Boothroyd and receives a special Montblanc Model 149 fountain pen. Twisting the top releases a combination of highly concentrated nitric and hydrochloric acids (a very corrosive mixture known as aqua regia, Latin for "royal water"—it even dissolves precious metals like gold and platinum). The pen's cap also holds a highly sensitive listening earpiece, tuned to the transmitting microphone Q places in the coveted Fabergé egg.

The pen comes in handy a bit later when 007 finds himself captive in the compound of Kamal Khan. The acid makes quick work of two iron bars, allowing Bond to escape. The earpiece then lets him eavesdrop on a conversation between Khan and Russian general Orlov.

Yo-Yo Saw

In *Octopussy*, Kamal Khan hires some swarthy locals to get rid of Bond, who has made his way to Octopussy's floating palace. One of the villains has a unique weapon—a large yo-yo handle with two razor-sharp circular saw blades. He kills Vijay, who is keeping watch on the mainland, then moves on to the island. Bond nearly winds up torn in two at the hands of the assassin, but disarms him and fights him until an alligator butts in and has the killer for lunch.

The 007 films spawned many toys over the years, but *Octopussy* produced perhaps the oddest of all. English toymaker Wembley Playcraft Ltd offered

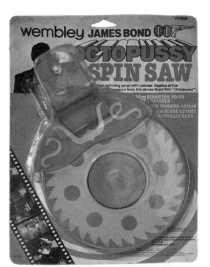

a plastic replica of the yo-yo weapon in 1983 called "Octopussy Spin Saw," complete with six-inch blades. Not to worry, the package assured parents the toy was "totally safe."

Yeah . . . sure.

Octopussy Spin Saw toy by Wembley.

Zorin Industries Airship

The master villain in *A View to a Kill* was Max Zorin, a high-tech industrialist. His selected mode of transportation was the blimp, proudly proclaiming his name in green letters, accented with red stripes.

There were actually two airships in the film. Zorin first conducts a meeting with potential investors for his plan to destroy

Silicon Valley in California and corner the market in microchips (think Goldfinger with skinny little gold bars). One man opts out of the scheme—and winds up opting out of the airship, as May Day dumps him overboard into San Francisco Bay.

Later, Zorin attempts to escape in another blimp (which inflates and bursts out of a collapsible storage building), with Stacey Sutton onboard and Bond hanging from a mooring line. Zorin tries to ram Bond into the Golden Gate Bridge, but 007 turns the tables by wrapping the mooring line around one of the towers, tying the airship to the bridge. The enraged villain comes after Bond with an ax, but 007 wins the match, sending Zorin to a watery grave. A vengeful Dr. Mortner, Zorin's longtime mentor, attempts to blow Bond and Sutton off the bridge with a bundle of dynamite, but Bond quickly cuts the mooring line, causing Mortner to drop the explosives, and they go off, destroying the blimp and proving—once again—what goes up, must come down.

The blimps were part of a fleet built by an English company known as Airship Industries. The first was a fictitious ship called the Skyship 6000, represented by models, but the second was the very real Skyship 500. Registered as G-B1HN, the airship was 170 feet long and 47 feet in diameter. The gondola held eight passengers and two pilots.

As a Fuji Film Skyship 500 airship happened to be in the SF area during the filmmakers' initial visits, long shots were captured and later used in the final film, as the colors of the Zorin ship were designed to resemble those of the Fuji ship. Effects crews built blimp models in four-foot, twenty-foot, and forty-foot versions, as well as mocking up full-sized sections of the gondola and bridge tower and rigging.

Walther WA2000 Sniper Rifle

The Living Daylights finds Bond selected as personal protection for defecting Russian general Koskov. A beautiful lady sniper prepares to shoot the general, but Bond is at the ready across the street in a hotel room. As a "sniper for a sniper," he shoulders an enormous rifle but sees his target is a lovely blonde. He carefully aims and shoots the rifle from her hands, sparing her life.

The fancy-looking rifle chosen for 007 was not a creation of the prop department, but a real Walther WA2000 sniper rifle (yes, the same gun maker of the trusty 007 PPK pistol). Made from the late 1970s to the late 1980s, the

Bond (Timothy Dalton) with a Walther WA2000 sniper rifle in *The Living Daylights*.

WA2000 was considered a dream rifle—if sniping is your thing. Weighing in at a hefty sixteen pounds, the gun was extremely accurate up to more than three thousand feet and sold for $9,000 in its day (collectors will pay nearly ten times as much for one today!). The WA2000 was a very limited edition, as only 175 or so were built.

Bond used steel-tipped .300 cartridges, as he notes that KGB snipers usually wear body armor. His weapon was also equipped with a high-power infrared scope, laser sight, and muzzle flash suppressor. Good thing he was properly armed, or he might have accidentally hit his target.

Philips Keyfinder Key Chain

Bond has his obligatory meeting with Q in *The Living Daylights*, where Major Boothroyd gives him a keyring finder—a little device that beeps when it hears a whistle. Of course, Q has modified it a bit. Once armed, it responds to the first bars of "Rule, Britannia" by emitting stun gas, effective for a range of five feet. The gadget also holds a small amount of plastic explosive, customized to go off when 007 gives out a wolf whistle. An attached skeleton key opens 90 percent of the world's locks—according to Q.

Bond uses the stun gas feature to disable a captor while he and Kara are imprisoned in an Afghanistan jail. Later, the wolf whistle topples a head bust of mercenary Brad Whitaker—ironically—on Brad Whitaker, killing him.

Amsterdam-based Philips Electronics—inventors of the audio cassette tape and compact disc—had their keyfinder selected for the film, and their logo showed prominently on it. Special James Bond 007 promotional keychains were available from Philips during the release of *The Living Daylights* in 1987. These, of course, were minus the stun gas, the plastic explosive, and the skeleton key, making for a rather boring keyring finder.

Aston Martin V8 Vantage Volante

The Living Daylights decided to update Bond's transportation, staying with an Aston Martin but going with a model nearly twenty-five years newer than his classic DB5. Still, Q remembered to jam-pack the new car with plenty of special goodies.

Introduced in 1974 and upgraded in 1978, the Aston Martin V8 Vantage was truly an elegant but powerful British auto. The V8 engine delivered nearly 400 hp, and the car could reach speeds of almost 170 mph. The Volante was a convertible model brought out in 1985, and Aston Martin produced about 170 of them in the three years they were made.

Bond is first seen pulling into the grounds of the safe house where Koskov is hiding. The dark gray convertible in the scene was actually a pre-production edition belonging to Aston Martin chairman Victor Gauntlett. The Vantage next appears in the workshop of Q Branch, where it is winterized with a hard top, along with other goodies (this model was actually a Vantage V8 saloon).

Later, Bond and Kara Milovy run into a Czechoslovakian police car that pulls alongside in an effort to stop the Vantage. Bond smiles and flips a switch, firing a laser beam from the front wheel hubcap (so much for the old-fashioned tire cutters from the Goldfinger days). The laser cuts the car's body cleanly from its chassis, and when the cops hit the brakes, they slide right off the auto's frame. Bond next encounters a semi truck set up as a roadblock. Using a tracking system that appears on the windshield, he fires two missiles from behind the fog lights—truck destroyed, travels continue.

A personnel carrier loaded with soldiers follows the Vantage onto a frozen lake, with another police car in pursuit. When a mortar shell blows one of 007's tires off its wheel, he pulls a tight circle around the cop car, and the rim cuts the ice into a perfect disk—sinking the police. Another pair of switches extends a pair of outrigger skis from the Aston Martin's rocker panels and traction spikes from the tires, allowing the couple to elude another squadrol. But they are quickly surrounded, and Bond flicks one more switch, firing a rocket motor from behind the rear license plate, vaulting over a guard post and into a thatch of trees. Not wanting the car to be captured, Bond sets a self-destruct timer before leaving with Kara. The Aston Martin explodes just as a group of armed skiers arrive (Q is not going to be happy).

A replica of the *Living Daylights* V8 Vantage sold at a Bonham's Auction in May 2011 for $251,000. One of the effects car shells enjoys retired life at the Bond Museum in North Miami.

Dentonite Toothpaste with Cigarette Pack Detonator

In *Licence to Kill*, Bond gets on the good side of drug kingpin Franz Sanchez. But he plans on killing the villain in his headquarters in Isthmus City, once he can get past the two-inch protective glass in his office windows.

Rappelling off the roof, 007 lays out a glop of plastic explosives from a seemingly harmless tube of toothpaste along the base of the window frame. From a hard box of Lark cigarettes, he pulls a detonator and plants it in the goo.

Many fans think Dentonite is a type of explosive, but it's just a play on a fake brand name of toothpaste. The plastic explosive is most likely PE4, a type of C4 compound used by the British military. The stuff is one and a half times as powerful as TNT, so Q Branch made a good choice. Just don't brush your teeth with it.

Signature Camera Gun

In the same scenes from *Licence to Kill*, Bond makes his way across the street to a condemned building, carrying a special gun from Q Branch in a nicely gift-wrapped box (how thoughtful). The gun is disguised as a camera with a handle programmed to recognize only Bond's handprint. Assembling the gun, he blows out Sanchez's windows with a remote control, but his shot is skewed by stealthy ninjas. One tries to shoot Bond with the camera gun, but the signature handle does not recognize the shooter's palm print, so he uses the gun butt to knock out 007.

The gun started with a Hasselblad 500 C/M body, equipped with a prism viewfinder, a sniperscope that fit into the camera's hot shoe, a pistol grip/palm reader programmed with an external keypad, a film magazine that holds .220 high-powered bullets, and a barrel extension.

The prop was seen as part of the *Bond, James Bond* Exhibition at the London Science Museum in 2003.

Polaroid Laser Camera

Another goodie from Q's bag of tricks in *Licence to Kill,* this instant camera took pictures that lasted a lifetime—assuming one lived long enough to see them develop.

The Polaroid Spectra System camera was modified to fire a deadly laser beam, as well as take X-ray pictures of whatever was captured by the 125mm lens. Bond's lovely CIA partner, Pam Bouvier, nearly burned 007 and Q to a crisp, thinking the camera was a normal picture-taking device.

Grenade Pen

In *GoldenEye,* Q gives Bond a ballpoint pen guaranteed to write a death sentence to anyone who uses it. Fortunately, it comes in handy for 007 later in the film.

Appearing to be a normal stainless-steel Parker Jotter pen, it actually is a Class 4 grenade (more on that in a moment) that is primed when clicked three times. At that point, a four-second fuse should give Bond enough time to get out of the way. Clicking three more times will disarm the weapon.

Bond and Russian programmer Natalya Simonova infiltrate Alec Trevelyan's Cuban compound, where he controls the GoldenEye satellite. Another programmer, Boris Grishenko, has set the satellite to explode a nuclear weapon, which will create an electromagnetic pulse that will cripple England's computer systems. But Grishenko has a nervous habit of toying and clicking a pen while he programs (how convenient). Unknowingly, he begins the tic with Bond's confiscated pen. Bond knocks the grenade pen into a pool of spilled fuel as it explodes, and the control center bursts into flames, allowing Natalya and him to escape.

Q's reference to a Class 4 grenade most likely indicated the explosives used were Class 4, recognized as a flammable solid hazardous material, which is actually a Class 1 dangerous compound, made safe for transportation by wetting (welcome to Chemistry 101). In other words, the film's writers thought it sounded cool.

Q's demonstration of the exploding pen blew the top half of a mannequin clean off. Discovery Channel's *MythBusters* took on the task in a 2008 episode of proving or disproving whether a pen loaded with explosives could actually cause such damage. What did they find? Using three cubic centimeters of explosives—an amount determined that could fit into the pen—the MythBusters were able to blast a hole in a dummy that probably would be fatal to the user, but came nowhere near destroying the entire top half as *GoldenEye* showed. A second attempt, this time with six times the amount of explosives, was better—but still required more to replicate the film's carnage. A third try, with a novelty pen the size of an adult's forearm, did the trick, and the MythBusters came through again.

BMW Z3

Demonstrated by Q in *GoldenEye*, the beautiful metallic blue (called Atlanta Blue) 1995 BMW Z3 convertible wound up being a case of "all dressed up and nowhere to go." Teased with all sorts of gadgetry, the car barely shows up later in the film.

Boothroyd shows 007 a rear-mounted parachute and touts a self-destruct system, all-points radar (whatever that is), and Stinger missiles behind the headlamps. Later, Bond takes a leisurely jaunt with Natalya in the BMW, until CIA agent Jack Wade shows up in a small prop plane and trades it for the car. After being seen earlier driving a POS Soviet ZAZ-965A (with a big 27-hp engine), Wade is only too happy to drive off in the BMW, although it might be better if he didn't know the Z3 had only a four-cylinder engine and delivered a paltry 138 hp.

What happened to Bond's reliable Aston Martin? BMW wooed the producers away with a cross-promotional marketing deal worth millions of bucks. BMW let *GoldenEye* feature their new two-seater, and Pierce Brosnan appeared in two BMW TV commercials. The give and take resulted in plenty of exposure for both factions—BMW sold out their first year's production of Z3s before the first one even hit the BMW showrooms.

Omega Seamaster Watch

The humble wristwatch has become many things in the Bond films—a reservoir for a garrote wire, a powerful magnet, a circular saw, a teletype machine, among others—so it was only a matter of time before gadgets were repeated. The non-Eon-produced *Never Say Never Again* featured 007 with a black watch of undetermined make that had a laser in the watch band.

Similarly, *GoldenEye* had Bond wearing a blue-dialed Omega Seamaster Diver 300M, also equipped with a frickin' laser beam. It comes in handy when Bond and Natalya have only seconds to escape the crashed Russian train. Bond cuts a hole in the floor, and they barely make it out before it blows to smithereens. Later, the remote-control feature of the Omega is pressed and accidentally disarms explosives planted by 007 in Treveylan's control center.

Walther P99 Pistol

James Bond uses his trusted Walther PPK sidearm throughout most of *Tomorrow Never Dies*. But when he's loading up at Wai Lin's hidden armory, he notes the "new" Walther P99, already having asked Q to get him one.

The new Bond gun was a major change for the secret agent, considering he carried the PPK for more than thirty-five years. The P99 was heavier by a third (thirty ounces versus twenty ounces). It had a higher muzzle velocity, meaning it packed a bigger wallop than the PPK. The new gun also held twice as many bullets

A Walther P99 pistol, used by Bond in four films.

as the old model (sixteen versus eight). Although both weapons could use a variety of cartridge calibers, both were capable of firing 9mm bullets.

The new P99 would be Bond's weapon of choice for the next three films, although he returned to his old favorite, the PPK, in *Quantum of Solace.*

Carver's Stealth Ship with Sea-Vac Drill

Tomorrow Never Dies' villain was a bit different from all the others that 007 came up against. Elliot Carver was a media mogul who felt, when it came to war, the pen was mightier than the sword. The journalist sought to orchestrate a war between China and the UK by sinking a British warship and framing the Chinese military. Of course, Bond came to the rescue.

Carver made this all happen from his stealth ship. Oddly shaped and coated with reflective paint, the ship was invisible to radar and heat-signatures, allowing the warmonger to travel the seas unnoticed. Riding on two large pontoons, the ship sat high in the waters, fortified with surface-to-air missiles and a satellite navigation and tracking system. It also carried a vicious device called the Sea-Vac Drill.

Deployed from the underside of the ship, the jet engine–sized Sea-Vac Drill was turbine-powered, with three razor-toothed cutting wheels in its front. It chewed its way into the hull of the HMS *Devonshire,* sinking it and leaving everyone to believe it was torpedoed by Chinese MIG jets. Toward the film's end, Carver finds out—all too closely—the drill can chew through humans as easy as (or easier than) steel hulls of ships.

The stealth ship was based on an actual vessel designed by the United States in the mid-1980s and revealed to the world in 1993. Called the *Sea Shadow*—numbered IX-529—the real thing cost nearly $200 million to build and operate. The navy, however, never used the ship for any missions, but designed and built it to test the feasibility of using stealth technology on a sea vessel.

In 2006, the *Sea Shadow* was designated for donation to a museum for public display, but to date, there have been no takers. It sits in San Diego, waiting to be scrapped. Or perhaps sunk by a Sea-Vac Drill.

BMW 750iL and Ericsson Cell Phone

Disguised as a rental car aide in a Hamburg airport, Q presented Bond with a new car in *Tomorrow Never Dies.* The Silver BMW 750iL came with "all the usual refinements—machine guns, rockets, and GPS tracking system." Fortunately, 007 took the insurance waiver, too.

Q also gave Bond a prototype Ericsson cell phone—model JB988—customized with a fingerprint scanner and 20kv security system. More, it opened up to reveal a complete control unit—complete with video screen—to allow remote driving of the BMW. (The prop sold in a 2006 Christie's Auction for nearly $9,500.)

Although Bond had quickly tooled around London in his Aston Martin early in the film, the BMW finally gave 007 his first four-door auto after a lifetime of coupes. The big V12 engine (yes, twelve cylinders) delivered a muscular 326 hp and a top speed of more than 150 mph.

Bond left the 750iL parked in a public garage, where Carver's thugs tried to break into it. First, they were shocked whenever they touched the car and found that crowbars, sledgehammers, and machine gun bullets were totally ineffective, bouncing off the auto. Bond remotely started it, hopped in an open back window, and drove from the comfort (and safety) of the rear seat. Like playing a full-sized video game, 007 fired a rocket from a sunroof-mounted array and blasted a car apart. From a tray beneath the rear bumper, he released sharp metal spikes that blew the tires off a vehicle in pursuit. Bond was forced to make a U-turn, driving right over the spikes and blowing his own tires. Fortunately, they were reinflatable, so no worries there. Confronted by a stranded steel cable blocking his escape, 007 extended a cable-cutter from the car's hood badge, snapping it in two. Jumping from the vehicle, Bond sends it crashing off the top of the garage, over the street, and right into the front window of the rental car agency. At least he returned the BMW from where he got it.

BMW R1200C Motorcycle

BMW continued its cozy relationship with Eon Productions by giving a new model of motorcycle in *Tomorrow Never Dies* for a scene of grand stunts featuring Bond and Wai Lin.

The two are running from Carver's headquarters and a band of his thugs. To complicate things they're also handcuffed. Arm in arm and riding tandem, Bond and Wai Lin share steering and shifting duties on a stolen BMW R1200C motorcycle.

Eluding a couple of Range Rovers along the streets of Saigon, the couple make their way to the rooftops of the neighborhood. A helicopter takes up the chase, as Bond and Wai Lin make a daring forty-foot jump from one rooftop to another, soaring over the rotating blades of the chopper beneath them. They get back to the streets but are cornered by the helicopter. Bond and Wai Lin head directly toward it and wrap a cable around the tail rotor. They dump the bike as the chopper crashes into the side of a building.

The ivory-colored motorcycle was a real beauty—a 1200-cc, two-cylinder machine capable of hitting more than 100 mph. Eight bikes were used for shooting—four survived and one of those is part of the collection held by the Ian Fleming Foundation.

Q Boat

The opening of *The World Is Not Enough* finds an explosion rocking MI6 Headquarters in London on the Thames River. A lady sniper in a speedboat is the likely culprit, and Bond hops into a dark, compact boat, taking chase. Zooming headlong into machine gun fire from the speedboat, 007 hurdles over the vessel, spinning 360 degrees. He comes upon a lowered bridge and amazingly throws the boat into a submarine-type dive, actually passing under the barrier.

Tracking the speedboat on a GPS screen, Bond takes a shortcut—firing twin rocket motors—scooting across land, crashing through a restaurant, and coming face-to-face with the villain. He fires two heat-seeking torpedoes, and, trying to elude them, the lady beaches her craft at the base of the Millennium Dome. As the torpedoes find their mark, Bond vaults his boat over the burning speedboat, grabbing a rope from the escaping woman's hot-air balloon. But she blows up a fuel tank, killing herself, while Bond tumbles to a rough but safe landing on the roof of the dome.

It turns out the boat was intended as a retirement indulgence for Q, who planned on fishing in it before Bond turned it into scrap (fishing for what—nuclear submarines?). The Q Boat was tiny, but packed a big wallop.

The fourteen-foot aluminum-hulled, fiberglass-decked Bentz jet boat was powered by a Chevy 350-hp V8 engine. (While the twin rocket engines looked cool, they were merely for show and didn't add to the boat's motive power.) Even so, the Q Boat was capable of reaching speeds of more than 80 mph. Built for the Bond producers by Riddle Marine in Idaho, a total of fifteen Q Boats were delivered (only nine came out in one piece). Instead of a propeller, the powerful engine sucked in water and blew it out the rear of the craft, making travel in shallow water possible.

Special-effects supervisor Chris Corbould loaded up on the gadgets, some of which never made it into the final cut. The Q Boat was equipped with .30-caliber machine guns, rocket launchers, the aforementioned twin torpedoes (just where did Q plan on fishing?), as well as a computer-controlled navigation system. Unfortunately, it had no live well for fish.

Bond (Pierce Brosnan) in the Q Boat in *The World Is Not Enough.*

Parahawk Snowmobile

In *The World Is Not Enough,* M has asked Bond to protect Elektra King. They wind up skiing in the Caucasus Mountains in Azerbaijan, where a fleet of flying snowmobiles attack.

Gliding in on black parasails and propelled by rear-mounted fans, the vehicles hit the snow with their drivers throwing grenades and firing machine guns. The parasails detach, and the snowmobiles continue under fan power. Bond leads them into a thatch of evergreens, where they recklessly crash into themselves.

Known as powered parachutes, these vehicles usually have wheels and a tubular frame. But the movie producers contacted Blue Heron Industries in upstate New York, who provided fifteen XC-70s for shooting. Of course, the machines would have never gotten off the ground if they had snowmobiles built into them, so three additional shells were fitted over Polaris snowmobiles for the Parahawk land machines. Although they had built-in machine guns, drivers never used them, relying on handheld weapons.

Ski-Suit Escape Pod

Bond gets an eyeful of goodies during his briefing with Q in *The World Is Not Enough* (where he meets Q's eventual replacement, whom Bond refers to as R). An ordinary ski jacket can, with a pull of the ski tag, transform into a large inflatable protective sphere (because you just never know when . . . well, you just never know).

The device actually does become useful later, when Bond and Elektra are escaping the Parahawks on the snow-covered mountainside. The last two vehicles collide and the resulting explosion starts a deadly avalanche. Bond quickly inflates the pod, which surrounds the pair with a protective pocket of air. Alas, Elektra is claustrophobic and begins to freak out. Bond calms her, as they cut their way out of the pod and climb out of the snow to safety.

Lock-Pick Credit Card

In *The World Is Not Enough,* Bond must make his way into an office to find out who might want to kill Elektra King. Lacking a set of keys, 007 pulls out a Visa card that separates, revealing a lock pick to open the door and easily gain access to the information.

Q's credit card—Don't leave home without it.

BMW Z8

The partnership between BMW and 007 continued in *The World Is Not Enough*, as this time Bond drove a silver 1999 BMW Z3 convertible. Introduced at MI6 headquarters, the Z3 had titanium armor and, sparing no expense, six beverage holders.

Later, Bond visits an old acquaintance, Valentin Zukovsky, at his pierside caviar factory near the Caspian Sea. Two menacing and heavily armed helicopters break the darkness (more on the toothsome armaments shortly). Bond needs his Z8, but it's on the other side of the pier. Pulling out the ignition key, he uses its remote controls to start and drive the car to him. Getting into the BMW, he opens a control panel on the steering wheel and sights one of the copters on the screen. Bond quickly fires a missile from the side air vent, hitting its target and blowing up the helicopter. But the victory is short-lived as Bond has to split—and so does his car (be patient).

The BMW Z8 finally had the muscle missing from his Z3 in *GoldenEye*. Its 5.0-liter V8 engine put out 400 hp and had a top speed of more than 150 mph. But there was one small problem—the filmmakers needed the Z8 nearly a year before it would be ready for public release (timed to mark the release of *The World Is Not Enough*). BMW was able to give three to the

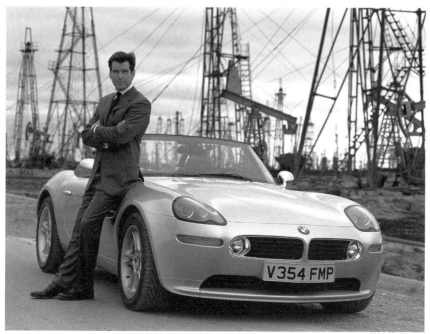

Pierce Brosnan with a BMW Z8 in *The World Is Not Enough*.

production, while special-effects supervisor Chris Corbould pieced together additional cars at Pinewood Studios.

Helicopter Tree-Trimming Saws

In the aforementioned scene at the caviar factory, Bond's BMW Z8 meets a dire end that definitely left a mark.

The helicopters arrived on the scene with an impressive array of circular saws designed to aid tree-trimming in remote areas. The five sets of double blades were powered by an onboard gasoline engine. While Bond was able to down one of the choppers with a missile, the other brought its spinning blades straight through the Z8, cutting it cleanly in two pieces and barely missing 007.

Chris Corbould planted soft material between two halves of a Z8 shell and placed a full-sized helicopter cockpit (complete with whirling saw blades) on Europe's largest crane at Pinewood Studios, giving him complete control on the impressive scene. The saw blades were relatively safe, cutting through the flimsy car material, as well as soft wood planks on the pier.

Resembling the yo-yo saw weapon from *Octopussy,* and a scene originally planned for *GoldenEye,* the *World Is Not Enough* helicopter saws were based on real contraptions used by tree-trimming services around the world, clearing parts of tall trees from areas with communication and power lines.

Elektra King's Torture Chair

As the climax approaches for *The World Is Not Enough,* Bond has become the captive of Elektra King in the Maiden's Tower near Istanbul. As she reveals her plot to corner the oil market—at the cost of millions of people in a nuclear explosion—she slowly chokes Bond in an ornate chair designed for just such a torture.

Just like King, the chair is beautiful and deadly, built from mahogany and inlaid with ivory. When turned, a wheel mounted to the upright crosspost slowly moves a brass fitting into the back of the victim's neck. Shackled at the wrist and throat, the movement forces the victim to gradually asphyxiate.

The prop chair was built by craftsman and carpenter Terry Reed at Otter FX, based on drawings by production designer Peter Lamont. The chair had a plywood core, laminated with assorted woods and inlaid with ornate designs. As the chair was actually functional, certain scenes required the garrote device be partially dismantled, lest Pierce Brosnan be really asphyxiated!

Zukovsky's Walking Cane Gun

Before King's chair leaves Bond all choked up, Valentin Zukovsky bursts in and realizes Elektra is responsible for the death of his favored nephew. She fatally wounds Zukovsky but, before he expires, cocks the hammer on his beautiful silver-handled walking stick, revealing it is a gun. He takes aim at King, then changes direction and fires at Bond as he slumps. Elektra notes Zukovsky's poor aim, but his shot was actually on its intended mark—breaking one of Bond's wrist shackles. He breaks free and goes after King.

The idea of a cane gun actually came from Ian Fleming's first novel, *Casino Royale*. It was carried by one of Le Chiffre's bodyguards, who threatens Bond with it during the baccarat game—although Bond cleverly disarms him and turns the weapon over to Felix Leiter.

Aston Martin V12 Vanquish

In *Die Another Day*, James Bond had tired of driving German sports cars, so he decided to go back to what brought him to the dance in the first place—the Aston Martin. Of course, it had been updated along the way.

MI6 has a new Q (Bond called him R in the previous flick), and he has no more tolerance for 007 than his predecessor. Bond receives his latest company car—a silver 2002 Aston Martin Vanquish (or the Vanish, as Q notes). It features the latest in adaptive camouflage—a series of onboard cameras and a polymer coating that reflects the car's surroundings and renders it essentially unseen. Of course, the car has the usual refinements, such as ejector seat, torpedoes, and target-seeking shotguns.

Later, the Vanquish's adaptive camouflage system fails, and Bond engages Zao in a car chase on a frozen lake outside the Ice Palace. Bond fires rockets from behind the front grill but is upended by one from Zao's auto (sit tight, we'll talk about it shortly). Bond skids on the car's roof, but cleverly fires the ejector seat, forcing the Aston Martin back onto its wheels. Machine guns fire from behind the grill and the target-seeking shotguns under the hood intercept rockets launched by Zao.

Graves fires the laser from the Icarus satellite, striking the Ice Palace and causing it to melt rapidly. Bond beats Zao to the palace, crashing through the front doors. The adaptive camouflage system restores, just in time for 007 to fake Zao into trying to ram his car. But he quickly pops spikes out from the tire treads and secretly zooms out of the way, causing Zao to crash into a rapidly filling well of water. Using an onboard thermal imaging system, Bond locates Jinx and saves her from drowning.

The Vanquish sported a beefy twelve-cylinder, 460-hp engine that gave it a top speed of more than 200 mph. Aston Martin was good enough to give Eon Productions three standard Vanquishes for close-up work, while four more effects cars were built by the special-effects team.

Jaguar XKR

In *Die Another Day,* Zao must have figured why should Bond be the only one to have a tricked-out car? So he found his own Q and wound up with one crazy 1998 Jaguar XKR.

Not so fast. The Jag was a Jag in body only (well, half of them). Jaguar provided eight XKR convertibles to the film, half equipped with standard two-wheel drive. The other four were drastically modified for the film. Underneath each was a throaty Ford Mustang 302 V8 engine, a Ford Explorer front suspension and a four-wheel-drive chassis. All eight were finished with a gorgeous green exterior.

As for extras, Zao added a GE Mini gun that popped out of the trunk, Sidewinder missiles in the door panels, a missile array behind the front grill, mortar launchers in the trunk, steel ramming bars that extended from the grill, and a high-tech thermal imaging system.

The XKR gives Bond's Vanquish a run for its money during the chase on the frozen lake and in the Ice Palace. But Zao crashes through an ice wall, trashing the Jag and dying from a dangling chandelier that Bond shot from its anchor.

One of the green Jaguar XKRs from the movie (actually, SFX1 or Special Effects Car One) was sold complete by RM Auctions of London in October 2010 for a hefty price of almost $88,000.

Aston Martin DBS

As Daniel Craig assumed the role of 007, producers decided it was time to reboot the franchise (ah, what would our lexicon be without computers?). In doing so, it was time to downplay the gadgets, as well as the winking at the camera and outrageous plotlines, and get back to the basis of the series: story and performance. As such, *Casino Royale* in 2006 offered only one real item for geekdom review, but what an item it was.

The 2006 Aston Martin DBS is first seen in the lot of the Casino Royale in Montenegro. Charcoal gray and a real beauty, Bond reveals two sliding trays in the glove compartment. One holds armaments, including a Walther P99 with silencer. The other's contents come in handy later on.

During a game of Texas Hold'em that includes Le Chiffre, Bond consumes a martini containing a major mickey, courtesy of Le Chiffre's girlfriend. He leaves the table and makes his way to the DBS in the lot, where he begins to go into cardiac arrest. Connecting with MI6 headquarters for instructions, 007 opens the second tray and uses the AED—automated external defibrillator—it holds. But a lead has come loose, and Bond, bathed in sweat, passes out—flatlining as MI6 techs and M stand by helplessly. But Vesper Lynd rushes to the car, attaches the lead, and fires the defibrillator. Bond jumps back to life, adjusts his clothes, and returns to the poker game, where he beats Le Chiffre.

Later, Lynd is kidnapped by the vengeful villain's thugs, and Bond roars off in the DBS. He closes in, only to find Vesper tossed from the car, bound and lying in the roadway. Swerving to avoid her, the DBS rolls endlessly, finally coming to rest on the roadside, totally trashed (a scene taken almost verbatim from the Ian Fleming novel, except Bond had his Bentley instead of the Aston Martin).

The DBS was a fitting car for Bond in the twenty-first century. Again, Aston Martin took advantage of their 007 connection, introducing the brand-new model in the film. The massive 6.0-liter, twelve-cylinder engine put out an awesome 510 hp and hit speeds of over 190 mph.

A darker 2008 DBS showed up in the opening minutes of *Quantum of Solace*, but following a harrowing chase scene in Siena, Italy, it wound up bent, battered, and bruised (obviously lowering its resale value).

Aston Martin supplied seven cars for *Quantum of Solace*. Four were demolished during the shooting (including three in accidents that put several stunt drivers in the hospital), one sold at a charity auction, one wound up with Eon Productions, and the last went back to Aston Martin.

An Aston Martin DBS, Bond's ride in *Casino Royale* (2006) and *Quantum of Solace*.

6

Thunderpals

Bond's Best Buds

While it may be true that dog is man's best friend, it's doubtful that 007 could have taken on Max Zorin with a trusty cocker spaniel at his side. Could James Bond have faced Dr. No's fiery Dragon Tank while a Saint Bernard slobbered at it? Highly unlikely (unless the tank rusted like the Tin Man in *The Wizard of Oz*). How far would JB have traveled in the tuk-tuk in *Octopussy* with an Alaskan malamute behind the wheel? Not far (especially if it stopped at every fire hydrant it spied).

Needless to say, Bond relied on support (and we're not talking tuxedo cummerbunds here). No, he knew he could count on the backing of the folks at MI6 headquarters, the field operatives, allies with similar causes to fight, and vengeful vixens across the world. While they all couldn't be BFFs, James Bond had people he could trust when the chips were down.

M: The Character

At the top was M, the administrative head of MI6. Like many bosses, M was often frustrated with his subordinate, perhaps a bit envious, but he (or she) always knew they could call upon Bond to handle the toughest of cases.

Seldom acknowledged, M (the male) was named Admiral Sir Miles Messervy, revealed in Ian Fleming's final Bond novel, *The Man with the Golden Gun*. Fleming never disclosed

Bernard Lee as M in *From Russia with Love*.

the true identity of his source for M, but many suggest it was largely based on the man he assisted during the war—Admiral John Godfrey, Director of Naval Intelligence for the Royal Navy. Although he became a great personal friend of Fleming, Godfrey was quoted in a London *Times* article, "He turned me into that unsavoury character, M."

Judi Dench as M in *Casino Royale* (2006).

Other sources believe Fleming used M since that was the appellation he used for his mum. John Pearson's biography *The Life of Ian Fleming* said, "Fleming often called his mother M . . . While Fleming was young, [her ways were] an echo in the way M handles . . . 007." Most likely, Fleming made an amalgam of the aforementioned folks, plus other members of the British naval intelligence and secret service communities with whom he was acquainted.

Turning M into a woman in the films was a reflection of the real world. In 1992, Stella Rimington, a woman with more than twenty years of experience in the British intelligence world, was named the director general of MI5. While MI6 concerned itself with British security outside the country's borders, MI5 focused on its internal security. Coincidentally, *GoldenEye* introduced M as a female in 1995, naming her Barbara Mawdsley.

With Pierce Brosnan's Bond, this M made no bones about it; she viewed him as a dinosaur, whose rough methods were frowned upon. Defensive of her "bean-counter" reputation, M still showed 007 the respect he had earned. When Daniel Craig took the reins, M now viewed Bond as a young but capable member of an elite group of professional spies.

In 2012's *Skyfall*, M moved into the field with 007, winding up at Bond's childhood home in Scotland. A climactic faceoff against villain Raoul Silva and his men resulted in a fatal wound for M. When the pieces were put back together, Gareth Mallory—chairperson for the Intelligence and Security Committee—was seated behind M's desk.

M: The Portrayals

Born in 1908, John Bernard Lee played M in the first eleven Bond films, giving orders to Sean Connery, George Lazenby, and Roger Moore. His father was an actor, leading Lee to join the Royal Academy of Dramatic Arts in the mid-1920s. Touring the theaters of Britain, he began making films, including *The Third Man* and *Beat the Devil*.

Stern and intolerant of Bond's cheeky nature, Lee's portrayal of M spanned the groovy 1960s and the disco days of the 1970s. Lee became ill during *Live and Let Die* in 1973, leading producers to consider a replacement. But he recovered to continue the role through *Moonraker* in 1979. His death prior to 1981's *For Your Eyes Only* prompted filmmakers, out of respect to the actor, to place M "away on leave," rather than recast the part. Like Connery, Lee had created a prototype franchise character for others to follow.

Robert James Brown was born in 1921 and studied acting in New York City. Appearing in small roles in British film and television, Brown played Gurth in ITV's *Ivanhoe* in 1958, companion of the handsome Roger Moore. In 1977, he was featured in *The Spy Who Loved Me* as Admiral Hargreaves of the Royal Navy. When he picked up the role of M in 1983's *Octopussy*, it was never established whether the character was a promoted Hargreaves or a continuation of Messervy. No matter, Brown was M in Moore's last two Bond films, as well as Timothy Dalton's two turns in the role. He retired at age seventy in 1991 and passed away in 2003.

The gap of nearly six years between *Licence to Kill* and *GoldenEye* left plenty of time to allow Dame Judi Dench to completely reestablish the role of M in 1995. Born Judith Olivia Dench in 1934, she had thoughts of being a theater designer but wound up studying acting at the Central School of Speech and Drama in London. Dench had a prominent career on the English stage, performing with the Royal Shakespeare Company and the National Theater. In the 1960s, she began appearing in British TV shows, moving on to film in the 1970s.

Following up her first two films as M in *GoldenEye* and *Tomorrow Never Dies*, Dench won an Academy Award for Best Supporting Actress as Queen Elizabeth I in 1998's *Shakespeare in Love*. She continued as M for Brosnan's last two Bond films, then the first two featuring Daniel Craig. Despite battling macular degeneration, compromising her eyesight, Dench undertook the seminal role for a seventh time in *Skyfall*, released in 2012.

With Dench's version of M killed off at the end of *Skyfall*, actor Ralph Fiennes took over the role. Born in England in 1962, he studied painting before deciding on a career in acting. Fiennes attended the RADA and then worked in English theater before making his screen debut in the 1992 version of *Wuthering Heights*.

The actor began to land plum parts in major movies like director Steven Spielberg's *Schindler's List* in 1993 (earning an Oscar nomination for Best Supporting Actor), 1994's *Quiz Show*, and *The English Patient* in 1996 (with another Oscar nomination, this time for Best Actor). He was the suave John

Steed in 1998's *The Avengers*, the film version of the 1960s British detective show, with Uma Thurman as Emma Peel.

Fiennes' next decade included playing a nasty villain in the third of the Hannibal Lecter films, *Red Dragon*, in 2002; assuming the lead role in the 2005 mystery *The Constant Gardener*; taking the part of Lord Voldemort in four of the hugely popular Harry Potter films; and appearing in the Oscar-winning *The Hurt Locker* in 2008.

Edward Fox, born in 1937, took the role of M in *Never Say Never Again*, playing the part with a great dose of upper-class snobbery. A grad of RADA, he made his mark in films with roles such as the assassin in 1973's *The Day of the Jackal*, among others.

Q: The Character

If M found James Bond to be intolerable, then Q found him to be impossibly insufferable. The Q Branch of MI6 was responsible for keeping 007 up to his shoulder holster in gadgets and vehicles, lest he find himself at the edge of death without a wristwatch equipped with a rock climber's piton spike and cable.

Ian Fleming, during his war years with British Naval Intelligence, was no doubt familiar with Charles Fraser-Smith, the master gadget-maker with MI6. Fraser-Smith fashioned items for British agents, such as shoelaces that doubled as garrotes, a fountain pen that contained a map and a compass, and radios small enough to fit into cigarette tins. He called these items "Q gadgets," after the "Q ships" during the war—British gunships disguised as freighters. Many consider this the source of Q and Q Branch in Fleming's novels.

The author occasionally brought Q into his books, actually naming him Major Boothroyd in *Dr. No*. Like many of his characters, Fleming drew the name from a real-life acquaintance—Geoffrey Boothroyd—a Scotch weapons expert who had written a letter to Fleming, claiming Bond's Beretta 418 was "a lady's gun."

The comment was appropriately adapted for use in the first Bond film, *Dr. No*, as the world met Major Boothroyd for the first time. Bond had his questionable Beretta replaced with M's choice—the Walther PPK—delivered in a wooden case by the master MI6 armourer.

Desmond Llewelyn as Q in *The Living Daylights*.

The character of Q disappeared with the 007 reboot in 2006's *Casino Royale*. He finally resurfaced in 2012's *Skyfall*, trading a mastery of mechanics and electronics for full digital computer geekdom.

Q: The Portrayals

Born in 1921, Peter Burton was a journeyman English actor who occupied about one minute of screen time in *Dr. No*. He played Major Boothroyd as a relatively nondescript worker of MI6, knowledgeable of weapons and not much else. His misfortune of not being available for the next Bond flick, *From Russia with Love*, became great fortune for the next Q.

Desmond Wilkinson Llewelyn was born in South Wales in 1914. Following a brief thought of becoming a minister, he turned toward acting. He attended the Royal Academy of Dramatic Arts, but World War II interrupted his plans. Llewelyn became a POW in a Nazi prison camp in France for five years before liberation in 1945.

He resumed his acting career, appearing in small roles on British TV and in films. When Peter Burton was unavailable for the role of Q in *From Russia with Love* in 1963, director Terence Young remembered working with Llewelyn in a war film during the early '50s. The part would be his for seventeen Bond flicks across the next thirty-six years. (Although, contrary to what one might think, the part didn't make him particularly rich. He was paid at a day rate and received no royalties.)

His work with the first five Bonds left a mark on them all. The actor understood that, while the world loved Bond, Q hated him—he showed no respect for his brilliant devices. By his own admission, Llewelyn was "hopeless" with technology and gadgets, and needed cue cards for much of the technospeak he had to deliver. Roger Moore admitted that, more than once, he would rewrite the cards, adding mild curses like "bollocks" to them.

At age eighty-four, Llewelyn had completed *The World Is Not Enough* in 1999. While he planned on continuing the role, a deadly car accident foiled those plans in December of that year.

As a hedge against retirement, *The World Is Not Enough* had introduced Q's assistant, played by former Monty Python funnyman John Cleese. Born John Marwood Cleese in 1939, he scored well in school and had intentions of becoming a lawyer. But his penchant for writing and performing comedy prevailed, first as a member of Monty Python's Flying Circus, a zany troupe that performed on TV, stage, and in feature films. In the mid-1970s, he created and starred in TV's *Fawlty Towers*, playing a rude, intolerant hotel owner (good training for his future role of Q).

Cleese took the impatience of Llewelyn and added the quick, acerbic wit of Basil Fawlty. The result was enough for two Bond films, and probably more, if the reboot of *Casino Royale* in 2006 had felt humor would have helped. He did voice the role of Q in the 2003 video game *James Bond 007: Everything or Nothing.*

Never Say Never Again featured a dreary and forgotten Q Branch, run by someone named Algernon, who envied Bond's exciting adventures. The minor part was played by Alec McCowen, who had appeared in many British and American films, including Alfred Hitchcock's *Frenzy* in 1972 and Martin Scorsese's *Age of Innocence* in 1993.

The new Q in *Skyfall* was Ben Whishaw, who, at age thirty-one, became the first MI6 armorer to be younger than Bond. Born in England in 1980 and a graduate of RADA, Whishaw found himself cast as Hamlet in the hit 2004 production staged at the Old Vic in London's West End.

Whishaw appeared with future 007 Daniel Craig in 2004's *Layer Cake*, played Rolling Stones guitarist Keith Richards in the 2005 Brian Jones bio-flick *Stoned*, and starred in the award-winning BBC limited series *Criminal Justice* in 2008.

As Q, Whishaw intentionally avoided seeing the performances by Llewelyn and Cleese as Major Boothroyd. He did admit that, like Llewelyn, he was a total Luddite, having difficulty with the simplest of gadgets. The actor prepared for his part by reading up on MI6 and current technology.

Following *Skyfall*, Whishaw was set to appear in director Terry Gilliam's *Zero Theorem*, with Oscar winners Matt Damon, Christoph Waltz, and Tilda Swinton.

Felix Leiter: The Character

The character of Felix Leiter holds different spots in the world of 007. In the novels, he is clearly a friend, as well as associate, of Bond. He's an outgoing Texan with a broad sense of humor. Leiter arrives in *Casino Royale* as a member of the CIA who helps Bond defeat Le Chiffre at the gaming table. The next novel, *Live and Let Die,* has Leiter fed to the sharks, costing him an arm and a leg (literally). Skipping a book, Leiter shows up with a hook for a hand and a false leg in *Diamonds Are Forever,* now a private detective with Pinkerton's Agency. Bond's ally appears in four more Fleming novels.

In the films, Felix Leiter does little more than put out the "welcome mat" for Bond when he comes to America. Seriously, his role, if nothing else, demonstrates American support for Britain's security efforts in the world. The character has been played by no less than eight actors.

Jeffrey Wright as Felix Leiter in *Casino Royale* (2006).

Ian Fleming named his CIA agent by taking the middle name of longtime friend Ivar Bryce—Felix—and joining it with the last name of another, Marion "Oatsie" Leiter, his friend in Washington, D.C., and frequent dinner guest of the First Family, the Kennedys.

Felix Leiter: The Portrayals

Born in 1920, Jack Lord was a film and TV actor who first took the role of Felix Leiter in *Dr. No.* When asked to return for *Goldfinger*, Lord asked for a lot: cobilling with Sean Connery, a meatier role, and more bucks. Producers gave thanks to Lord and moved on.

Cec Linder was born in Poland in 1921 and raised in Canada. He was originally cast as Simmons, the suckered card player in *Goldfinger*, but switched roles with Austin Willis, and became Felix Leiter.

Rik Van Nutter was born in 1929 and was married to movie starlet Anita Ekberg when cast as Leiter in *Thunderball*. At least he resembled Fleming's description. Van Nutter was offered an extended contract to return as Felix, but the character did not appear in the next two Bond films.

When he did return in *Diamonds Are Forever*, the part went to Norman Burton (who, like Cec Linder, played Leiter like a worn-down flatfoot hotel detective). Born in 1923, Burton had roles in TV and film, including *Planet of the Apes* and *Towering Inferno*.

Live and Let Die in 1973 featured David Hedison as Leiter, making him the most prominent actor cast as the character to that point. Born in 1927, he had appeared as the doomed doctor-turned-bug-eyed-pest in 1958's *The Fly* and Captain Lee Crane in TV's *Voyage to the Bottom of the Sea*.

Hedison was favored with the chance to return as Leiter—in a much expanded part—with Timothy Dalton in *Licence to Kill* sixteen years after *Live and Let Die*. Interestingly, Fleming's scene from the *Live and Let Die* novel where Leiter is fed to the sharks, losing his arm and leg, appeared in this film. The scene of Bond finding a barely alive Leiter with a handwritten note stating, "He disagreed with something that ate him," is directly from the novel.

Born in 1944, John Terry showed up briefly as Felix Leiter in 1987's *The Living Daylights,* sandwiched by Hedison's portrayals. Terry's career has mostly focused on television appearances, including extended roles on *ER* and *Lost.*

The new direction that brought Daniel Craig also brought a new Felix Leiter—Jeffrey Wright. Although former Pro Bowl football player and actor Bernie Casey became the first black Leiter in *Never Say Never Again,* Wright brought a major presence and performance to *Casino Royale* and *Quantum of Solace.* Unfortunately, Wright—and Leiter—did not show up in *Skyfall.*

Quarrel: The Character

Fleming's second novel, *Live and Let Die,* led Bond to Jamaica, where he hooked up with Quarrel. Originally from the Cayman Islands, his affable and confident demeanor created a good ally for 007 and a strong character in the reader's eye. He would appear again in *Dr. No,* the author's sixth book, where he dies on the villain's island, burned by the "dragon."

The film of *Dr. No,* being the first in the cinema series, delivered Quarrel as a much more one-dimensional character. At first suspicious of Bond, Quarrel then becomes his aide, although he meets the same fiery end on Dr. No's island.

When *Live and Let Die* was made eleven years later, filmmakers were forced to create Quarrel Junior to accommodate the few story fragments taken from the novel. In *Licence to Kill,* a black fishing guide named Sharkey essentially carried on the role of Quarrel Junior.

Quarrel: The Portrayals

John Kitzmiller, born in Battle Creek, Michigan, in 1913, held a degree in engineering and was a veteran of World War II. Enamored with Italy, he made it his home after the war and began a busy career making films there. After winning Best Actor at the 1957 Cannes Film Festival, Kitzmiller gained the role of Quarrel for *Dr. No.*

Jamaican-born in 1925, Roy Stewart became one of Britain's top black stuntmen and actors. He opened a popular gym and a Caribbean-styled restaurant before playing Quarrel Junior in *Live and Let Die.*

Former NFL football player Frank McRae, born in Memphis, Tennessee, in 1942, played Sharkey in *Licence to Kill* in 1989.

Darko Kerim/Kerim Bey: The Character

Fleming's *From Russia with Love,* published in 1957, featured the head of Station T, the Secret Service branch in Turkey. A wild and colorful character named Darko Kerim, he was very likable, and Bond easily took to him and his outlook on life. Bond saved the former circus strongman's life during a Russian attack on gypsies, and the Turk joined Bond and Tatiana on the Orient Express. Assassin Red Grant got to Kerim and secretly killed him.

In September 1955, Ian Fleming attended the Interpol Conference in Istanbul, Turkey. While there, he met an Oxford-educated Turkish ship owner named Nazim Kalkavan. The man became a good friend with Fleming, as they both shared a love of life, an enthusiasm for food and women. Kalkavan admitted he smoked and drank and loved too much, and Fleming knew he had found his next best friend for Bond. Nazim Kalkavan became Darko Kerim in *From Russia with Love.*

Darko Kerim/Kerim Bey: The Portrayal

Pedro Armendariz, born in 1912, was one of Mexico's greatest cinema stars. After earning an engineering degree at California PolyTech, he began an international film career, working with Mexico's finest directors, as well as Europe's Luis Buñuel and America's John Ford.

His portrayal of Kerim Bey, the name given to the character of Darko Kerim, is spot-on. Armendariz gives the Turk a lusty outlook and broad swagger—an amazing performance, considering he was dying of cancer during the shooting of *From Russia with Love.* Very ill, he insisted on completing the picture (his cancerous hips caused a bad limp, visible in many of his scenes), as he desperately wanted his family to get his salary. He confided his condition to director Terence Young, and production schedules were rearranged to accommodate Armendariz's close-ups. Afterward, long shots and over-the-shoulder shots with Sean Connery would be done using Terence Young himself as Armendariz's stand-in.

In June 1963, while shooting on *From Russia with Love* continued, Armendariz lay in a UCLA Med Center. Knowing the pain would be unbearable for his family and himself, he shot and killed himself with a smuggled pistol. The great actor was only fifty-one years of age.

Dikko Henderson: The Character

Ian Fleming's eleventh novel, *You Only Live Twice,* brought Bond to the Far East land of Japan. Brokering an introduction to Japanese Secret Service,

Australian intelligence agent Richard Lovelace "Dikko" Henderson also
tutored 007 in the ways of Japan. He was big in body and voice, and like
Bond, enjoyed his liquor. They made a quick friendship.

As foreign manager of the London *Times,* Fleming traveled quite a bit
in penning a series of travel essays called *Thrilling Cities.* In Asia, he met a
Times correspondent named Richard Hughes, a huge ex-boxer who knew
Tokyo like the back of his hand (Richard, nicknamed "Dick" or "Dikko,"
hence the character name). Richard Hughes made a great prototype for
Dikko Henderson.

Dikko Henderson: The Portrayal

Donald Marshall Gray was born in 1928 and attended primary school
with future funnyman Benny Hill. Gifted with a strong voice and physical
presence, Gray changed his name to Charles and appeared in Shakespeare
productions with the Old Vic and Stratford-on-Avon companies in England,
as well as on Broadway in New York.

Like the book, the film character of Henderson in *You Only Live Twice*
serves to introduce Bond to Japan and Tiger Tanaka. Gray uses his wonderful voice to give Henderson a strong air of aristocracy, while his broad face
and size fit into Fleming's original description. Just as Henderson is about
to spill his theories on who is behind the hijacked spacecraft, he's fatally
stabbed in the back by a Japanese thug.

Imagine the surprise of Bond fans all over the world when, four years
after *You Only Live Twice,* good guy Henderson had been resurrected
and gone over to the other side. Charles Gray became bad guy Blofeld in
Diamonds Are Forever.

Continuing to show up in films like *The Rocky Horror Picture Show* and *The
Seven-Per-Cent Solution,* Gray died from cancer in 2000.

Tiger Tanaka: The Character

Like Darko Kerim in *From Russia with Love,* Tiger Tanaka in *You Only Live
Twice* provides contrast to Bond's solemn pursuit of life in Fleming's novels.
Yes, they all drink and fool around, but Tanaka enjoys it, while 007 seems
to embrace those pleasures out of habit or force.

Tanaka is head of Japanese Secret Service (SIS—Secret Intelligence
Service although, in reality, Japan did not have an agency comparable to
MI6 or the CIA until 2008). An Oxford graduate and former pilot for the
Imperial Navy, he takes Bond under his wing in Japan, schooling him in the
deadly art of the ninja warrior. He is big and has an easy smile. In the film,

Tetsuro Tamba as Tiger Tanaka in *You Only Live Twice.*

Tiger Tanaka performs similar activities with Bond. He has an underground headquarters and a private train for traveling in Tokyo.

Fleming's influence was again from his Far East travels for the *Thrilling Cities* project. Like Dikko Hughes, Torao "Tiger" Saito was a journalist and accompanied Fleming during his journey through Japan.

Tiger Tanaka: The Portrayal

Born in 1922, Tetsuro Tamba appeared in more than three hundred Japanese films, as well as TV shows. Like many international stars in early Bond films, his voice was dubbed (this time around by Robert Rietty), although Tamba's real voice is heard when ordering a bath in the geisha house.

The son of the emperor's personal doctor, Tamba made movies in practically every genre. Later in life, he embraced spiritualism and theories on life after death. He died in 2006, moving on to his own afterlife.

Marc-Ange Draco: The Character

Another warm body in the cold life of James Bond, Marc-Ange Draco appears in Fleming's tenth 007 novel, *On Her Majesty's Secret Service.* Draco, a Corsican native, is the head of the French Mafia, known as the Union Corse. He is also Bond's future father-in-law.

Not surprisingly, Draco's characterization is not far from those of Kerim, Tanaka, and others—gregarious, where Bond is introverted. Of course, Draco is the "good" bad guy, being the don of a European crime syndicate. He only wants his daughter to be happy, enough to bribe Bond into marrying her (007 does it without the monetary incentive). Fleming liked the sound of the name Draco, basing it on El Draco—the nickname of historic seaman Sir Francis Drake.

Marc-Ange Draco: The Portrayal

Gabriele Ferzetti, born in 1925, began his long film career while still a teen. He eventually worked with some of Italy's top directors, including Michelangelo Antonioni. He prefaced his part in *On Her Majesty's Secret Service* by appearing in Sergio Leone's *Once Upon a Time in the West.*

Ferzetti moved proudly and gracefully through his role as Marc-Ange Draco, although his speaking performance was dubbed by David de Keyser.

Sheriff J. W. Pepper: The Character

Found nowhere in the Fleming novels was the cartoonish character of Sheriff J. W. Pepper. First appearing in 1973's *Live and Let Die,* the St. Tammany Parish, Louisiana, sheriff functioned to provide comic relief (who asked for any?). Although considered a Bond ally, Pepper did nothing in the film to help him.

Pepper was painted as a stereotypical Deep South redneck—biased toward anyone not a local, calling everyone "Boy," chewing and spitting tobacco. Following a destructive car and boat chase, authorities shared with Pepper the fact that 007 was a secret agent. The sheriff incredulously wondered for whose side.

The comedic character returned, with more to do this time, in *The Man with the Golden Gun.* Like all Louisiana sheriffs, Pepper and his wife were vacationing in Thailand (!), where Bond was following Scaramanga. Even better, the sheriff was contemplating the purchase of a new car (despite the fact there were dozens of dealerships back home). Bond jumped in a model that Pepper was considering, and before you know it, the cracker sheriff teamed up with 007 in the chase. After a harrowing 360-degree roll across a river, the pair cornered Scaramanga in a warehouse, but he escaped in his car/plane. When last seen, Pepper was in handcuffs with the Thai police.

Sheriff J. W. Pepper: The Portrayal

Surprising to many fans, the thick-drawled Pepper was played by New York City–born Clifton James. Born in 1921, James studied at the

Clifton James as Sheriff J. W. Pepper in *Live and Let Die.*

Actors Studio and had a long career onstage, on TV, and in films, including playing the floor-walking jailer Carr in 1967's *Cool Hand Luke*, the DA in 1987's *The Untouchables*, and White Sox owner Charles Comiskey in 1988's *Eight Men Out*.

James, a decorated veteran of World War II, understood his role of Pepper was for laughs. He wore an umpire's chest protector under his police uniform, knowing Southern sheriffs seemed to be proud of their prominent stomachs. The expert performer also noted his character had some of the best dialogue he'd ever seen.

With a diverse acting career of more than fifty years, James retired to New York in 2006.

Milos/Enrico Columbo: The Character

Ian Fleming's short story of "Risico," in the collection *For Your Eyes Only*, introduced a character named Enrico Columbo. Fleming, ever the car enthusiast, took the name of Columbo from Gioacchino Columbo, the great designer of the Ferrari car engine.

Columbo is identified to 007 as a drug smuggler by a CIA operative named Kristatos. While he is a smuggler, drugs are one thing Columbo wants no part of. When Bond finds this out, he enlists Columbo to help track down Kristatos, who turns out to be the real drug smuggler.

The 1981 film of *For Your Eyes Only* combined many elements from the short story of the same name with much of "Risico." The Columbo character had his first name of Enrico changed to Milos and identity changed from Italian to Greek. But his function in the story remained the same—being an ally to Bond.

Milos Columbo: The Portrayal

Once again, this 007 ally was cute and cuddly, like a big teddy bear. At first, Bond was leery of this Greek bearing the gift of friendship, but he quickly warmed to Columbo. The pair led a small team of fighters to defeat Kristatos on his mountaintop monastery retreat of St. Cyril's.

The pivotal role of Columbo was larger than many of 007's film allies. As such, a big-time star was cast—Topol. Born in Israel (then Palestine) in 1935, Chaim Topol first performed in amateur plays to entertain Israeli troops. He started his own acting troupe and by the early 1960s was performing in films.

The charismatic performer established the role of milkman Tevye in the musical *Fiddler on the Roof*. He first took the stage with it in 1965, did the film version in 1971 (for which he was nominated for an Academy Award), and seemingly owned the part for nearly forty-five years. As Columbo, Topol brought class, as well as an affinity for pistachios, to a character usually on the other side of the law.

General Anatol Gogol: The Character

Purely a cinematic concoction, General Anatol Gogol (although referred to as Alexis by M in *The Spy Who Loved Me*) became the icon for all things Russian in the Bond films. The recurring character—showing up in all six films between 1977 and 1987—toed the party line (the Communist Party) while maintaining a moderate philosophy and open-minded desire for peace among the world's superpowers. First, Gogol was head of the KGB, while he eventually wound up his career with a diplomatic promotion to the Foreign Service. He also had an attractive assistant named Rubelvitch (the monetary-sounding name was a takeoff on Moneypenny).

With the loss of British and Soviet subs in *The Spy Who Loved Me*, Gogol is brought together with his counterpart, M. The occurrences can only strengthen Anglo-Russo relationships, and Gogol gets an eyeful of British ingenuity on a visit to Q Branch's field operations in Egypt. In *For Your Eyes Only*, the Russian chase for the British ATAC ends with Bond destroying it so that no one gets it. Gogol, instead of being angered, is amused at 007's logic and leaves, laughing. In *Octopussy*, he shows no sympathy for the mortally wounded, traitorous General Orlov, whose actions may have seriously damaged the British-Russian relationship. In *A View to a Kill*, General Gogol shows his extreme displeasure with former KGB agent Max Zorin, who has (supposedly) killed 007 without approval. In *The Living Daylights*, he heaps praise on the musical talents of Czech cellist Kara Milovy, hoping she can visit Moscow.

General Anatol Gogol: The Portrayal

Born in Germany in 1924, Walter Gotell's experience with the James Bond films spanned nearly twenty-five years. Like several other performers, he played two different characters in that time.

Gotell appeared in 1963's *From Russia with Love* as the head of SPECTRE Island, Morzeny. It was Morzeny who killed Kronsteen with the poisoned shoe dagger for not eliminating Bond. The secret agent outsmarts a group of SPECTRE motorboats, led by Morzeny, who jumps from a burning boat with his clothes afire.

The actor had a diverse career starting in the early 1940s. Smart, with the ability to speak five languages, Gotell mixed acting with the world of business. He eventually became business manager for a group of engineering firms, but never strayed far from the stage or screen. He appeared in films like John Huston's *The African Queen,* Alfred Hitchcock's *The Man Who Knew Too Much,* and Franklin Schaffner's *The Boys from Brazil,* among many others.

He was given the role of General Gogol partly because of his uncanny resemblance to the former head of the Soviet secret police, Lavrentiy Beria. Where many actors would have played a Russian KGB head with a loud, blustery swagger, Gotell maintained a quiet and thoughtful demeanor.

Working in film and TV into his late sixties, Gotell retired to his farm in Ireland. He died in 1997.

Vijay: The Character

In *Octopussy,* Bond needed a connection in India. Enter, playing the role of a snake charmer, Vijay. As a field operative with MI6, he was ready and able to give Bond a hand. As a tennis pro at Kamal Khan's club, he was privy to all sorts of info.

After 007 defeated Khan in backgammon (using Khan's own loaded dice), Bond made a quick getaway as Vijay deftly handled a tuk-tuk taxi though the crowded streets. He was also quite amused at Bond's reaction to Q's briefing. Unfortunately, while keeping an eye on Bond's visit to Octopussy's Floating Palace, Vijay was murdered by Khan's hired goons.

Vijay: The Portrayal

When in need of a young actor pretending to be a tennis pro, hire a young tennis pro pretending to be an actor. Vijay Amritraj, born in India in 1953, turned tennis pro in 1970 and became one of the world's top players.

Sickly as a child, he started tennis as a way to get outside, and it paid off. Amritraj eventually won sixteen singles and thirteen doubles tennis titles while getting a chance to perform in his favorite hobby—the movies. Producer Cubby Broccoli was a great fan of tennis and thought Amritraj would be perfect for the part of the Indian agent.

The experience wasn't completely fun and games, as the first-time actor was highly fearful of snakes and had to be convincing as a snake charmer when Bond arrives in India. Actor Roger Moore was no help, often spooking the young man between takes by trying to upend the basket in which a live cobra sat while Amritraj held it.

Although Amritraj appeared in a few TV series and other films, he used his international notoriety to establish the Vijay Amritraj Foundation. Following five years as a United Nations Messenger of Peace, he started the charity to focus on helping those in need in India.

Sir Godfrey Tibbett: The Character

In *A View to a Kill,* Zorin's horse won the Ascot Race easily, and horse trainer (and MI6 operative) Sir Godfrey Tibbett believed the fix was in. As Zorin was having a sale of thoroughbreds at his farm, Tibbett took the guise of Bond's chauffeur and the pair investigated, becoming part of the crowd.

Some sleuthing around the stables by Tibbett and Bond revealed that Zorin was using microchip-controlled steroid injections to make a super-horse. When Bond sent Tibbett into town to contact M, Sir Godfrey was killed by Zorin's girlfriend, May Day.

Sir Godfrey Tibbett: The Portrayal

Tibbett was played by Patrick Macnee, who had established his own secret agent reputation for much of the 1960s on TV. The suave and sophisticated John Steed, replete in bowler hat and umbrella, was the male half of *The Avengers,* a syndicated British show that was very popular on both sides of the Atlantic.

Born in 1922, Macnee came from an upper-class family—including a father who was a successful horse trainer (shades of Sir Godfrey Tibbett!). With a scholarship to Webber Douglas Academy of Dramatic Art, Macnee quickly took to acting. Unfortunately, World War II took to him, and he became an officer in the Royal Navy.

Following the war, he worked on the stage, TV, and in films in England, Canada, and America. During his years on *The Avengers,* he shared the screen with Bond ladies Honor Blackman and Diana Rigg. He also shot much of the series next to where *The Saint* was being made—starring Roger Moore.

Much of the excitement about having Macnee in a Bond film focused on the pairing of "John Steed" with "James Bond." As always, Patrick Macnee kept his end up.

Kamran Shah: The Character

The Living Daylights found Bond and Kara Milovy locked up in an Afghan jail during the Soviet occupation. But at least they weren't alone—the cell next to theirs was taken by a shabby-looking local. Once Bond overpowered the jailers, he tossed the cell keys to the prisoner as Bond and Kara escape to the grounds.

Later, they find their cellmate was Kamran Shah, Deputy Commander of the Eastern District of the Mujahideen—the Afghan resistance to the Russians. The tall, dark, and handsome Shah was educated in Oxford and committed to leading his rebels against the Soviet invasion of Afghanistan.

Rogue Russian general Koskov had arranged an opium-for-diamonds-for-arms three-way deal with Shah and illegal weapons dealer Brad Whitaker. Bond convinces Kamran Shah to help him derail the arms deal between Koskov and Whitaker. When Bond gets stuck on a truck full of opium bound for a Soviet air transport, Kara persuades the reluctant Shah to help save him. Trading his horse for a frontloader, Shah leads his gang against the Russian troops as Bond takes to the skies with the opium.

Later, with the Russians defeated and the opium destroyed, Shah arrives at an Austrian concert hall, only to miss Kara's brilliant cello recital. Apparently, he and his rebels ran into some "trouble at the airport."

Kamran Shah: The Portrayal

Born in Pakistan in 1952, Art Malik moved with his family to England when he was four. With a scholarship to Guildhall School of Music and Drama, he soon was performing in Shakespeare with the Old Vic and Royal Shakespeare Company.

In 1984, Malik made a big impression in the British television miniseries *The Jewel in the Crown,* and on the big screen in David Lean's *A Passage to India* the same year. Following his well-turned portrayal of Kamran Shah in *The Living Daylights,* he hit a short period of inactivity. But director James Cameron cast Malik without an audition as the Islamic fundamentalist terrorist against Arnold Schwarzenegger in the 1994 megahit *True Lies.*

His work since has been split among film, television, and the stage, although he admits—as a dark-skinned Brit—to having interesting experiences in airports since the terrorist attacks of 9/11.

General Leonid Pushkin: The Character

Truth be told, General Pushkin was lucky to be around during *The Living Daylights.* Only by a twist of fate did he ever come to exist.

The story point of General Koskov attempting to frame General Pushkin originally targeted General Gogol, head of Russian KGB. But actor Walter Gotell, as Gogol, was ill and couldn't commit to such a strenuous role. Gogol was cleverly promoted to the Foreign Service (and a cameo appearance for Gotell at the film's end), and that led to the creation of General Leonid Pushkin as the new head of the KGB.

Pushkin is all business, as one might expect out of the Russian military. Visiting the Tangiers headquarters of mercenary arms dealer Brad Whitaker, the general cancels the gun deal brokered by Koskov. When Bond discovers Koskov's plot to frame Pushkin, he arranges to fake Pushkin's assassination (with the general's full cooperation), leading Koskov to think his plan has worked.

Later, after Bond has eliminated Whitaker, Pushkin storms the stronghold with Russian troops. Koskov feigns relief at being rescued, embracing the general. Pushkin orders him sent home to Moscow—in a diplomatic bag. Placing a friendly arm around Bond's shoulder, the pair discuss what to do about Kara's defection.

General Leonid Pushkin: The Portrayal

This was another relatively high-profile performer in a secondary role for a Bond film, as John Rhys-Davies was well known as the Egyptian digger Sallah, sidekick of Indiana Jones, in Steven Spielberg's *Raiders of the Lost Ark*.

Rhys-Davies, born in Wales in 1944, studied English and history at the University of East Anglia at Norwich. Accepting a scholarship to RADA, he taught secondary school for a short period before taking various roles onstage and in British TV.

An imposing figure with a rich, deep voice, Rhys-Davies was featured in the BBC miniseries *I, Claudius,* as well as the NBC-TV movie *James Clavell's Shogun.* After a return to the role of Sallah in *Indiana Jones and the Last Crusade,* he enjoyed doing plenty of voice work and episodic TV. Into the twenty-first century, he took the role of Gimli in Peter Jackson's *Lord of the Rings* trilogy, as well as video games in the series.

Jack Wade: The Character

Another function of cinematic creativity, Jack Wade appeared in the first two Pierce Brosnan films: *GoldenEye* and *Tomorrow Never Dies.* As CIA agent Felix Leiter found himself pretty well chewed up in *Licence to Kill,* Wade became Bond's new CIA connection.

Meeting Bond at the Pulkovo Airport in St. Petersburg (freezing Russia, not sunny Florida), Wade quickly establishes his disdain for "stiff-assed Brits," secret codes, and passwords in *GoldenEye.* He also, somewhat reluctantly, reveals a tattoo on his hip of a rose and the name "Muffy." The big guy soon takes to 007, calling him "Jimbo." His timing, however, could use some work, as he arrived with the marines while Bond was having a romantic interlude with Natalya in a Cuban field at the film's end.

In *Tomorrow Never Dies*, Commander Bond arrives at a US airbase in the South China Sea, where Jack Wade gets a GPS decoder back—the same one used to send the HMS *Devonshire* off course and sunk by Carver. Bond asks a favor of Wade and gets it—a HALO suit (high-altitude, low opening—basically, skydiving from five miles up in a scuba outfit into the ocean) and a jump from the back of a C-160 transport plane.

Jack Wade: The Portrayal

Joe Don Baker squared off against Bond as bad guy Brad Whitaker in *The Living Daylights*. But let's face it—anyone who can appear in great films like Barry Levinson's *The Natural* and Martin Scorsese's *Cape Fear,* while also showing up in *Leonard Part 6* (often regarded as one of the worst films ever made), has got to be some kind of actor.

Born in Texas in 1936, Baker received a bachelor's in business administration from North Texas State College. Following a stint in the US Army, he began studying at the Actors Studio in New York City.

His first film role was as the Fixer in *Cool Hand Luke,* but Baker made his first impact as brother to Steve McQueen in Sam Peckinpah's *Junior Bonner.* His imposing size made him a natural as the crime-busting Buford Pusser in *Walking Tall.*

Baker's work continued in TV and film, but his two different characters in the Bond series gave him a distinction shared only with actors Charles Gray and Walter Gotell—their first role as a Bond baddie, returning as a Bond ally.

Valentin Zukovsky: The Character

In *GoldenEye*, Bond needs an introduction to a Russian mafioso called Janus, seeking information on a stolen helicopter. He visits a seedy St. Petersburg nightclub, run by ex-KGB agent Valentin Zukovsky. Bond has a history with the man, having wounded him in the leg some years before.

In *The World Is Not Enough,* Bond seeks information (always looking for information!) and visits the L'or Noir—Black Gold—casino in Baku, Russia. The owner is Zukovsky, who has moved up in the world since last seen. Not only does he own the casino, but he also produces Zukovsky's Finest Caviar.

The man is big and broad, with a streak of sarcasm when he speaks. He carries a silver-handled cane and has a gold-toothed bodyguard named

Bullion. Later, at Zukovsky's caviar plant, Bond demands to know what the deal is between the Russian and Elektra King, but before Valentin can answer, his office—and Bond's BMW Z8—is cut apart by helicopters with tree-trimming circular saws. Escaping one of the spinning blades, Zukovsky ends up in a vat of caviar, where Bond pulls him to safety.

Robbie Coltrane as Valentin Zukovsky in *The World Is Not Enough.*

Later, Elektra King has Bond captured and slowly chokes him in a torture chair. Zukovsky bursts in, demanding to know where his favorite nephew is, a sub commander who was doing a job for King. He finds Bullion, who was spying for King, and kills him. When Zukovsky finds that King has killed his nephew, she shoots him in cold blood as well. Dying, Zukovsky reveals his cane is also a single-shot rifle and aims it at Bond, seemingly in anger. But the Russian actually saves 007, shooting away one of the shackles that binds him. As he succumbs to his wounds, he offers a slight and knowing smile to Bond.

Valentin Zukovsky: The Portrayal

Born in Scotland in 1950, Robbie Coltrane (originally Anthony Robert McMillan) attended Glasgow Art School, receiving credentials in drawing, painting, and film. He appeared onstage with the Traverse Theater in Scotland, as well as pursued an interest in stand-up comedy.

By 1980, he began to land small film roles, as well as episodic comedy TV. In 1990, he costarred with former Monty Python member Eric Idle in the comedy feature *Nuns on the Run*. Coltrane's introduction as Zukovsky in *GoldenEye* led to a second appearance in *The World Is Not Enough* four years later, this time in a meatier part.

Coltrane made an entire new generation of fans by playing the bearded giant Rubeus Hagrid in all eight *Harry Potter* films between 2001 and 2011.

Damian Falco: The Character

In *Die Another Day*, Damian Falco is introduced as the chief of the American NSA—National Security Agency. He's present when Bond is traded by the North Koreans for Zao, but Falco has little admiration for the secret agent.

Later, Falco butts heads with M, angered that Bond easily slipped away from the medical facility where he was recovering from his months in captivity. Falco expects MI6 to get Bond in line, or the NSA will do it for them.

Later, Bond and NSA agent Jinx Johnson are brought up to speed by Falco and M in a bunker near the DMZ of South Korea. When Bond decides to sneak into North Korea to find Gustav Graves, Falco insists that Jinx go along to protect America's interests.

Damian Falco: The Portrayal

Like many performers, Michael Madsen just wanted to be in a Bond film. Of course, it helped that he had worked with *Die Another Day* director Lee Tamahori on an earlier film *and* his neighbor down the street was Pierce Brosnan. He didn't care that his role would be small, he just knew he'd get the chance to work at Pinewood Studios.

Born in Chicago in 1957, Madsen first worked with John Malkovich at Steppenwolf Theater in his hometown. Moving to LA, he was pumping gas when he received a lead on an agent. Soon, he was appearing in small film roles, like the prima-donna outfielder Bump Bailey in 1984's *The Natural.*

In the 1990s, he snared the role of Susan Sarandon's boyfriend in *Thelma and Louise,* but made a lasting impression playing the psychopathic Mr. Blonde in Quentin Tarantino's *Reservoir Dogs* in 1992. Avoiding typecasting, he took the role of the father in the first two *Free Willy* family films. Yet he continued with tough-guy roles in *Mulholland Falls, Donnie Brasco,* and the *Kill Bill* films.

When cast in *Die Another Day,* Madsen believed he would become a recurring character, a la Felix Leiter. Alas, the reboot of the series with Daniel Craig sealed the fate of Damian Falco, although Michael Madsen carried on.

Rene Mathis: The Character

With the return to Bond's roots in *Casino Royale,* the film also returned to characters found in the Ian Fleming novel. Rene Mathis was one such character.

Mathis was a member of the French intelligence agency once known as the Deuxième Bureau (Second Bureau). He returned in *From Russia with Love,* now the head of the bureau. Mathis is also referenced in Fleming's sixth novel, *Doctor No,* as having once saved 007's life.

The 2006 film greatly alters the character and function of Rene Mathis. A field operative of MI6, based in the southeastern Europe country of

Montenegro, Mathis first meets Bond and Vesper Lynd at an outdoor cafe. Mathis has been keeping tabs on Le Chiffre.

After Bond has a particularly nasty tussle with two thugs (whom he kills with his wits and bare hands), Mathis arranges for the bodies to be found in the trunk of one of Le Chiffre's men. Later, at the gaming table, Bond plays with Le Chiffre and Felix Leiter, among others. Mathis watches with Lynd, explaining the game of Texas Hold'em to her (and, conveniently, to the filmgoing audience who do not know the game). After Bond beats Le Chiffre, it appears that Mathis is on the villain's side—his text to Lynd has set up her kidnapping and Bond's capture.

Bond and Lynd are saved, and as 007 convalesces, Mathis visits him. But MI6 agents taze Mathis, bro—and he's taken away.

Mathis reappears in *Quantum of Solace,* retired and bitter, having been found innocent of setting up Lynd and Bond. He joins Bond on a trip to Bolivia, since he spent seven years in South America and has useful contacts there. He works his phone and arranges an invitation for Bond to attend a party thrown by bad guy Dominic Greene.

When Bond leaves the fete, Bolivian police stop him and demand he open the car's trunk. In it is the badly beaten body of Mathis. When Bond lifts his friend out, the cops shoot Mathis in the back, killing him. Bond quickly shoots the officers, killing them. As he passes away, Bond holds him, then coldly carries the body to a dumpster, noting that Mathis wouldn't care. Later, Bond confronts the chief of Bolivian Police, shooting him dead as they had "a mutual friend."

Rene Mathis: The Portrayal

Born in 1942, Giancarlo Giannini received a degree in electronic engineering, then turned toward acting, studying at the Rome Academy of Drama. By the mid-1960s, he had begun a long and diverse working relationship with director Lina Wertmüller.

In 1973, he won the Cannes Best Actor award for *Love and Anarchy,* starred in 1974's *Swept Away,* and was nominated for a Best Actor Oscar in 1975's *Seven Beauties.* Giannini's versatile style made him a favorite to dub American films for the Italian market, including performances by Al Pacino, Jack Nicholson, and others. He also played the Italian inspector in 2001 in Ridley Scott's *Hannibal.*

Giannini, silver-haired and bearded, plays Mathis in both Bond films as the experienced continental. He's a resourceful man with plenty of answers and contacts.

7

Toonmaker

The Music of James Bond

Here's a challenge for you—imagine watching a feature film without any music. (No, I'm not talking about silent movies). Yes, there are some—Hitchcock's *The Birds,* James Bridges' *The China Syndrome* (not including the cool opening credits song), Fritz Lang's classic German film *M* (in 1933; yes, it was a sound picture), among others. But by and large, a stirring film score can usually turn a good film into a great film. Think about Bill Conti's score in *Rocky,* almost anything from Bernard Herrmann (*Citizen Kane* to *Taxi Driver*—and his myriad of avian sound effects in the aforementioned *Birds* was considered a score by many). Add in Max Steiner, Henry Mancini, John Williams, Randy Newman, and (insert your favorite here) among many, many others, and you've got a wonderful film.

The Composers

Consider then the eight composers who have graced the twenty-two Bond films (nine, counting Thomas Newman's work on 2012's *Skyfall*). Their musical works have created drama, suspense, relief, humor, and other emotional accompaniments to the other elements that make Bond pictures truly unique in the world of cinema.

Monty Norman

Born in 1928 in London, Monty Norman's original name was Noserovitch. As a young man, he apprenticed as a barber for a bit more than five pounds a week. But Norman soon realized he wanted a career in music.

He developed a fine voice, singing with big bands led by notables such as Cyril Stapleton and Stanley Black around England, and at the London Palladium Sunday Concerts. Norman continued as a solo act, sharing the bill with comics such as Benny Hill, Peter Sellers, and Spike Milligan.

In the late 1950s, he began writing songs for other singers, including Cliff Richard and Tommy Steele. Norman also started to write film scores, including features like sci-fi's *The Day the Earth Caught Fire,* Hammer Films' *The Two Faces of Dr. Jekyll,* and Bob Hope's *Call Me Bwana.*

In 1961, producers Cubby Broccoli and Harry Saltzman asked Norman to consider scoring a film based on one of Ian Fleming's spy novels. He agreed, as he was told there might be as many as two films and a TV series (talk about understatement!). Norman took a trip to Jamaica, along with the rest of the production crew and cast, to pick up the vibes of the local scene.

Norman responded with "The Kingston Calypso" (based on the kids' rhyme "Three Blind Mice"), "Underneath the Mango Tree" (for Bond to serenade Honey Ryder with), and "Jump Up Jamaica," among others. For some songs, Norman used a local Jamaican band, Byron Lee and the Dragonaires.

Across the years, while composing for many more stage shows, Monty Norman has had to fend off claims that John Barry actually composed the main theme. The courts have found in Norman's favor three times, keeping the credit where it belongs.

John Barry

Sean Connery and Bernard Lee, to name two examples, seem to be forever linked to the James Bond series. While others took their places over the years with varying degrees of success, they were the ones to define the roles. Similarly, John Barry will be forever linked to the Bond films as "the" composer. Others did fine and admirable jobs, but Barry set the bar toward which they could reach.

He was born in York, England, in 1933, as John Barry Prendergast. With his mother a classical pianist and his dad owning a few movie theaters, Barry had the right roots from which to draw. Joining the National Service (drafted in the military), he became a young man with a horn—trumpet, to be exact, in the army band. Barry also studied composition and arranging through a correspondence course.

At age twenty-four, he started the John Barry Seven, a rock 'n' roll combo with horns. The band enjoyed success with recordings and television in Britain, as well as backing up performers like Paul Anka and Adam Faith.

After arranging the main theme song for *Dr. No,* Barry was brought on to compose the entire score for *From Russia with Love,* except for the theme song. Barry would go on to compose for eleven more Bond films, often working on theme songs with lyricists like Don Black, Leslie Bricusse, or Hal David. Barry made the series music unmistakably his—blaring horns, percussive, dynamic—practically "Barry-esque."

John Barry —"the" James Bond composer, who scored eleven Bond films.

Barry's prolific career stretched far beyond just scoring for James Bond films, writing for films like *Born Free, Midnight Cowboy, Out of Africa,* and *Dances with Wolves.* His film work garnered five Oscars (out of seven nominations), five Grammy awards, three BAFTA nominations (and one award), two Emmy nominations, and two Golden Globe nominations. Barry was inducted into the Songwriters Hall of Fame in 1998.

John Barry missed out on a number of Bond films other than the eleven he did score. For *Live and Let Die,* he was unavailable and had a falling-out with producer Harry Saltzman. For *The Spy Who Loved Me* and *For Your Eyes Only,* owing large amounts of tax money to England, he lived in self exile and was unable to work. Eventually working those problems out, Barry was asked to score *Licence to Kill,* but was still recovering from a ruptured esophagus. He was also approached for *GoldenEye,* but had other works underway and wished to spend time with his young son. For *Tomorrow Never Dies,* he asked for complete creative control (which, after working on the series for thirty-five years, was probably not unreasonable), but did not receive it.

Suffering a sudden heart attack in 2011, John Barry passed away at age seventy-seven.

George Martin

Most of the world has heard George Martin's work, even if they haven't seen *Live and Let Die,* his only foray into scoring a Bond film. Renowned as one of the world's greatest music producers, he spent most of the 1960s working with a little group known as the Beatles.

Born in London in 1926, Martin was naturally drawn to music, playing piano and forming his own band when still in his teens. After the war, he attended the Guildhall School of Music and Drama, studying composition and orchestration, becoming an oboe player.

A chance interview at Abbey Road Studios in 1950 led to his hiring as the assistant to Oscar Preuss, the head of the EMI/Parlophone label. Five years later, when Preuss retired, George Martin was named the new head of the label at only twenty-nine. Through the 1950s and early 1960s, Martin produced classical, jazz, even comedy records for EMI/Parlophone.

In the 1960s, Martin's time was heavily spent with the Beatles, although he did produce the recording of Shirley Bassey's performance of "Goldfinger," as well as sign singer Matt Monro—vocalist on "From Russia with Love"—to an EMI contract.

Following the Beatles' breakup in 1970, Martin had the opportunity to produce other rock performers, including Jeff Beck, America, and the Mahavishnu Orchestra, among others.

Cubby Broccoli asked Paul McCartney to contribute the title track for *Live and Let Die* in 1973. Impressed with the demo, which featured George Martin's orchestral arrangement, Broccoli asked Martin to score the entire film. Instead of trying to copy the style of John Barry, Martin supplied his own take on 007. Many of the cues relied on the chromatic V–♭VI–VI against the minor root, a staple in many Bond pieces (yes, I've been a musician for more than forty years).

George Martin received six Grammys, spanning 1967 to 2007, and was inducted into the Rock and Roll Hall of Fame in 1999. He retired from studio recording in that same year, citing a progressive loss of hearing. Moving into the twenty-first century, he continued to receive accolades and did take the opportunity to work with his son Giles on a remix of Beatles music for a Las Vegas–based show called *Beatles—LOVE*.

Marvin Hamlisch

With John Barry not available, Bond producers turned to Marvin Hamlisch to score *The Spy Who Loved Me*. Not a bad choice, considering he had pulled down three Oscars for his music on *The Way We Were* and his ragging good-time score for *The Sting*, both in 1974.

Considered a child prodigy on piano, Hamlisch was born in NYC in 1944. Just seven years old, he was entered into the Juilliard School of Music. At age twenty-one, he cowrote the hit single "Sunshine, Lollipops, and Rainbows" for singer Lesley Gore. His early experiences continued to be diverse, as he scored several films for Woody Allen and played piano for Groucho Marx's live stage tour. Hamlisch also hit it big on Broadway, writing the musical score for *A Chorus Line*.

Hamlisch's approach to the Bond score was, in some cases, updating classic 007 melodies and themes to the current music genres of the day. In 1977, of course, disco was the rage, so "Bond 77" has the pumping four-beat drive of the dance floor, complete with Bee Gees–style guitar accents. But a tune like "Ride to Atlantis" might have been better suited for an interlude scene from a naughty film. Other motifs are properly represented, including Latin, Russian, orchestral, and Middle Eastern.

Hamlisch's musical career has continued full bore since then, with varied work for stage, screen, and TV. He was selected as musical director and arranger for Barbra Streisand's stirring 1994 concert tour and has been guest conductor for many symphony orchestras across America.

Marvin Hamlisch's musical successes over the years have led to the incredibly rare distinction of earning him an Emmy, a Grammy, an Oscar, a Tony, and a Pulitzer Prize. It's an honor shared with composer Richard Rodgers—and no one else. The composer passed away in Los Angeles in 2012.

Bill Conti

With a simple horn fanfare that built to a heart-pumping climax, Bill Conti composed a theme for every underdog on the globe. His "Gonna Fly Now" theme from the *Rocky* film series stirred people of all ages to assume a boxer's stance and prepare to take on the world. His score in *For Your Eyes Only* was just as effective.

Conti was born in Rhode Island in 1942, with early lessons on piano from his father, himself an accomplished musician. He received a bassoon scholarship to Louisiana State University, then moved on to the Juilliard School of Music, where he earned bachelor's and master's degrees.

Conti spent the late 1960s and early 1970s in Italy, scoring films and conducting musicals. Upon his return to America in 1974, he scored two Paul Mazursky films, *Blume in Love* and *Harry and Tonto*. The big payday was next—*Rocky* in 1976.

More film and TV work followed, and when John Barry was unable to do *For Your Eyes Only*, he recommended Conti to the producers. They took the suggestion, and the composer did not disappoint.

Bill Conti's score on *For Your Eyes Only* is an effective array of styles, again avoiding the trap of trying to copy Barry's work. Yes, there are stabbing horns at times, but Conti uses percussion and traditional instruments well, with synthesizers added for the right mix at the right times. He sets the moods well throughout the film.

Soon after *For Your Eyes Only*, Conti scored the American spaceflight story of *The Right Stuff*, winning an Academy Award for Best Musical Score.

Conti has maintained a busy career since then—composing for four of the five additional *Rocky* films and the four original *Karate Kid* films, and writing many signature themes for TV shows and news programs. He also has been musical director for many Academy Award telecasts, earning him three Emmys.

Michael Kamen

With a résumé of scoring action films like *Lethal Weapon, Die Hard,* and *Road House,* Michael Kamen was well qualified to take on the task of writing music for *Licence to Kill* in 1989.

Born in New York City in 1948, Kamen studied oboe at Juilliard. Always a rocker, he formed the New York Rock Ensemble in the late 1960s, releasing four albums between 1968 and 1971. Yet Kamen also wrote ballet scores during the period. He also directed musical tours for David Bowie and arranged the orchestral portion of Pink Floyd's *The Wall* in 1979.

Kamen's score for the Bond film is rousing where it needs to be and appropriately thematic when called for, with tropical steel drums used for the Felix/Della wedding scene, for example. He was also sure to include the signature James Bond theme whenever called for.

After *Licence to Kill,* Kamen scored many more films, including *Robin Hood: Prince of Thieves, Don Juan DeMarco, Mr. Holland's Opus,* and *X-Men,* among others. His work earned a Grammy among many nominations, as well as Oscar nods for several films.

Only fifty-five years old, Kamen had a heart attack and died in 2003.

Eric Serra

For *GoldenEye,* producers wiped the slate clean and decided to use a relative newcomer to score the film. Eric Serra, a French guitarist, got the call.

Born in Paris in 1959, Serra came from musical roots, as his father Claude was a popular songwriter during the 1950s and 1960s. Eric began playing at age five and, by the mid-1970s, was a session player for many French performers. He also had his own rock and jazz-rock bands during that time.

Serra became the bass player for Jacques Higelin, one of France's biggest rock stars, in 1980. Around the same time, he connected with French film director Luc Besson and began to score the filmmaker's productions. By the mid-1980s, Serra was scoring for other European directors as well. Into the 1990s, he scored two of Besson's best-known films: *La Femme Nikita* and *The Professional.*

The chance to score *GoldenEye* put Eric Serra on the global film scene, with mixed reaction. Many hardcore Bond fans didn't care for Serra's use of electronic, industrial, and synthesized music, while other fans welcomed the new direction and his embracing of current music trends.

Following the Bond film, Serra continued to score films, including *The Fifth Element,* the 2002 version of *Rollerball,* and *Bulletproof Monk,* among others. In 2008, he collaborated with illusionist Criss Angel and performing artists Cirque Du Soleil on a Las Vegas show called *Believe.*

David Arnold

Just like the composers before him, David Arnold knew he could never replace John Barry's stirring scores for the Bond films. The only thing he could hope for is to deliver the best David Arnold score for a Bond film and let the world decide. Something went right, because Arnold scored five Bond films, a number only matched and exceeded by Barry himself.

David Arnold was born in England in 1962—the same year as *Dr. No*—and, like many of the newer composers, is largely a self-taught musician (clarinet, guitar, and keyboards) and writer. As a young boy, he befriended Danny Cannon, and the pair made short films. When Cannon attended the prestigious National Film and Television School, Arnold continued to score his student films. At age twenty-five, Cannon got the chance to direct Harvey Keitel and Viggo Mortensen in the British thriller *The Young Americans.* Arnold scored the picture and drew the attention of the film team of Roland Emmerich and Dean Devlin.

Impressed with David Arnold's work, the duo asked him to score *Stargate,* followed by *Independence Day,* for which Arnold won a Grammy. At the same time, Arnold had produced an album of James Bond film cover tunes called *Shaken and Stirred.* Bond producers heard the music and, with the assent of John Barry, invited Arnold to score *Tomorrow Never Dies.* Rave reviews followed.

David Arnold, composer for five Bond films, from *Tomorrow Never Dies* through *Quantum of Solace.*

Returning to Emmerich and Devlin for *Godzilla,* Arnold was invited back to Bond for *The World Is Not Enough* and *Die Another Day.* Even with the series reboot, producers stayed with David Arnold for *Casino Royale* and *Quantum of Solace.* Each one was a stellar effort.

Though Arnold was ready and able to return for 2012's *Skyfall,* Oscar-winning director Sam Mendes had a long-established relationship with composer Thomas Newman. Mendes and Newman had collaborated on five of the director's major films. Arnold completely understood the selection and stands ready for the next Bond film if his services are once again called for.

Thomas Newman

Born in Los Angeles in 1955, Newman hails from the famed musical Newman family. His father, Alfred (no middle initial "E"), won Academy Awards for original and adapted scores, including ones for musicals like *The King and I* and *Camelot.* His uncle Lionel worked in television and film, winning an Oscar in 1969 for *Hello, Dolly!* and acting as musical supervisor for *Star Wars, The Empire Strikes Back,* and *Return of the Jedi,* among other movies. Cousin Randy is a singer-songwriter who has penned pop favorites like "Short People" and "I Love L.A." and scored diverse films like *The Natural, Three Amigos, Toy Story, Monsters, Inc.,* and *Cars.*

Schooled at USC and Yale before entering the world of music, Thomas Newman began his career writing songs for films like *Reckless* and *Revenge of the Nerds,* both in 1984. He went on to compose the scores for films like 1985's *Desperately Seeking Susan* with Madonna, *The Man with One Red Shoe* with Tom Hanks in the same year, and director Ron Howard's *Gung Ho* in 1986. Newman's scoring credits would eventually encompass a vast range of movies, such as the vampire film *The Lost Boys* in 1987, the cult mystery *The Rapture* in 1991, the drama *Scent of a Woman* with Al Pacino in 1992, director Frank Darabont's *The Green Mile* in 1999, the animated children's classic *Finding Nemo* in 2003, and the racial drama *The Help* in 2011, among dozens of others. Incredibly prolific, he's scored nearly ninety films and earned ten Oscar nominations---without a single win.

For *Skyfall,* Newman felt compelled to honor the classic James Bond themes while adding his own take on the twenty-first-century 007. His score is often percussive, combining Eastern and Western motifs with orchestral instruments and plucked guitars. He establishes his theme for Séverine with a reverbed flute amid lush strings. As might be expected, his score for *Skyfall* does not disappoint.

The Title Songs

Dr. No: The James Bond Theme

Knowing a strong and memorable theme would be needed for the very first Bond film, composer Monty Norman tapped into a piece of music he had written for an unperformed stage show called *A House for Mr. Biswas*. Originally composed to be played by East Indian instruments—with the seventeen-stringed sitar carrying the melody—he took the song, called "Bad Sign, Good Sign."

Although Burt Rhodes was considered to be the orchestrator for *Dr. No*, everyone agreed a more contemporary arranger was needed for the main theme. John Barry was suggested and brought in to handle the job.

Knowing the popularity of the electric guitar, Barry called on Vic Flick, his guitar player from the John Barry Seven, to handle the low staccato notes that establish the basis for the tune. Flick would play on eight more soundtracks for Bond films.

The theme starts with a statement of suspense—the previously mentioned three-note progression of V–♭VI–VI against the E minor chord never seems to resolve, leaving the viewer to wonder what's going to happen. The low guitar melody offers more anticipation, with soft horns underneath, then finally, with a crashing gong, a resounding brass chorus breaks loose. Accompanied by the skeleton-like tones of a mallet-driven vibraphone, now the audience is getting some action.

Soon, the drummer is slamming the snare, the bass is walking, and the horns are trading in question-and-answer fashion—the end is near. Wait—it starts over again . . . the suspense is building once more (just as James Bond's assignments never cease). The guitar restates its melody, horns build a four-note phrase, from root, minor third, fifth, to octave. Then everything finishes with a suspended second chord from the guitar—Heavens! What could be next?

A James Bond film, what else?

"From Russia with Love"—Matt Monro

While John Barry had secured writing the soundtrack for *From Russia with Love*, Cubby Broccoli felt a more proven hit maker would be better for the theme song. That's where Lionel Bart came in.

Being unable to formally read or write music didn't seem to bother Bart, as he penned hit songs for English rockers Tommy Steele and Cliff Richard in the 1950s. But his big claim to fame was writing the enormously successful musical *Oliver!* in 1960. Popular songs from the show like "Consider Yourself" and "I'd Do Anything" kept theatergoers singing for years.

Bart's melody to *From Russia with Love* is very nice, although the lyrics do not relate at all to the film (save for the title itself). The song's voice tells of someone who regrets leaving his lover and, with tail firmly between legs, decides to return to her. Nowhere is there a mention of Bond, guns, saving the world, or even Rosa Klebb's dagger shoe.

Chosen to croon the tune was Matt Monro, known in the UK as "the singing bus driver," a nod to one of his former occupations. Recognized in 1961 by *Billboard* magazine as the Top International Act, Monro worked closely with Beatles' producer George Martin to record songs that charted in England and America in the 1960s.

Monro's version of *From Russia with Love* did not open the film like other themes. Conveniently, it was heard, in part, on a radio during the film and was played in its entirety over the end credits. The song opens with a traditional lush flourish of strings (John Barry's orchestrations, of course), and Monro delivers the tune with Sinatra-like clarity and phrasing, using a strong vibrato throughout. The song's finale features the singer holding the finishing D note for twelve strong seconds. (If that doesn't sound like much, grab your watch and try it.)

"Goldfinger"—Shirley Bassey

Creating a song to become the pure personification of a film's character is pretty tricky business, but then, John Barry really knew his business. With George Martin producing and Shirley Bassey singing, the theme for *Goldfinger* clearly achieved that goal.

Barry was known to agonize over writing a piece of music, usually doing many versions until he had something he liked. When working on the *Goldfinger* theme, he had a houseguest who later complained of not being able to sleep, since the composer pounded away at his piano through the night. The droopy-eyed houseguest? Actor Michael Caine.

Lyrics were penned by the team of Leslie Bricusse and Anthony Newley, who had scored big with stage musicals like *Stop the World—I Want to Get Off* and *The Roar of the Greasepaint, the Smell of the Crowd.* In 1971, they did words and music for the film musical *Willy Wonka and the Chocolate Factory.* When the pair heard the first three notes of *Goldfinger,* they immediately thought of the song "Moon River," which had the same three opening notes. Barry was not amused.

Chosen to sing was popular singer Shirley Bassey. Gifted with a strong voice at an early age, the singer had multiple hit records in the UK during the 1950s. Bassey was touring England at the time *Goldfinger* was starting production, and her musical director—who just happened to be John Barry—asked her to record the song at EMI studios.

The opening chords—E to C or I– ♭VI (for those taking notes) are bold, yet discomforting, just like Goldfinger. The responding sassy brass instantly brings shiny metal to mind—perhaps, gold? The orchestra softens and Bassey clearly enunciates the name as the first line. The story proceeds as a warning to avoid this callous fellow at all costs, for he only cares for one thing—gold. The singer purrs, growls, and nearly pops a vein by the end in trying to get the message across. Bassey admitted to nearly passing out after hitting and holding the final note.

Not everyone viewed the iconic song as a masterpiece. Producer Harry Saltzman said he hated the tune, as John Barry recalled on a National Public Radio interview. He said Saltzman called it "the worst song he'd ever heard in his life."

He obviously never heard anything by the Shaggs (go ahead—do an Internet search).

"Thunderball"—Tom Jones

In the days of Top Forty radio, there was a slogan—"The Hits Just Keep on Coming!" Such was the case for John Barry and James Bond theme songs. The lead track from *Thunderball*, sung by Tom Jones, was another success for the franchise.

Composer John Barry teamed with a young lyricist named Don Black, who would write the words for four more Bond film themes over the years. He also penned the lyrics for "Born Free," "To Sir with Love," and "Ben"—a number one hit for Michael Jackson in 1972.

The final theme used for the opening credits was not the first one chosen. Originally, Barry had teamed once again with lyricist Leslie Bricusse to write "Mr. Kiss Kiss Bang Bang." It was a title describing the two things 007 did best, taken from either Japanese filmgoers or an Italian journalist, depending on which rumor is to be believed. The song was recorded by Shirley Bassey (again) and then by Dionne Warwick. However, the title and lyrics neglected to use the name of the film, causing United Artists distributors to fret over the lack of connection between theme song and picture. An instrumental version of the tune showed up in the film.

Country legend Johnny Cash submitted his version of a theme song for the film. Aptly titled "Thunderball," it told the story of a downed plane, the potential fury of the bombs, and the possibility of someone who could save the world. Complete with muted guitar and answering chorus, the song sounded like a countrified commercial for a big pickup truck. As great as Cash was, it's perhaps better that the theme wasn't used.

At the last minute, Barry worked with Black to write a nebulous song—the lyrics actually describe Largo, much like "Goldfinger" did—and called upon pop sensation Tom Jones to sing it. The young singer (like Bassey, a native of Wales) asked Barry what the song was about. The composer replied, "Tom—Don't ask, take a leaf out of Shirley's book. Just get in the studio and sing the hell out of it!"

And he did. Jones later related that, upon finishing the final note, he opened his eyes and the room was spinning. As for the song, it's pure Barry—whining horns, booming percussion, and the unveiled progression from, once again, the original James Bond theme.

"Thunderball" was another hit, reaching twenty-five on the *Billboard* Top 100 chart and going all the way to number five on their Adult Contemporary chart, both in January 1966.

"You Only Live Twice"—Nancy Sinatra

Hey, John Barry—the next Bond film is set in Japan . . . Could you do an Asian-tinged theme? Of course he could.

"You Only Live Twice," like other themes for Bond films, took a circuitous route on its way to opening the 1967 film. Yes, the team of Barry and Bricusse put together the music and words, respectively, but it was tough to get everyone on the same page in terms of a singer.

A version of a song with the same title—not at all sounding like the film theme—was written and recorded, using UK pop singer Julie Rogers. The lyrics talked about dice (rhymes with "twice") and gambling, while Rogers had a fine voice, full of power. But producers weren't impressed and wanted something else.

The writers went back to the piano and came up with the final version, but who would sing it? Harry Saltzman had a musical consultant brought in, who recommended a young unknown talent named Aretha Franklin, but Barry felt she wasn't right for the song. Cubby Broccoli decided to quit pussyfooting around, recommending his good friend—Frank Sinatra. Frankie declined, but suggested his daughter Nancy, who had just scored hits with "These Boots Are Made for Walkin'," "Sugar Town," and a duet with Daddy, "Somethin' Stupid."

Nancy Sinatra, by her own admission, was "scared to death" to sing the theme for the world's biggest film series at the time. Who wouldn't have been—she was only twenty-six years old. Plus, the song's enormous melody range was intimidating to her. Regardless, Sinatra did her best.

The theme is quite different from the pounding tunes that opened the previous two pictures. Lush strings and French horns set up a lilting ballad, with a soft guitar and faux Oriental instruments leading into the vocal. Again, the lyrics have no relevance to the film, but at least they kept "dice" out this time around.

Barry recorded twelve takes with the singer and, after she'd gone, had the engineers get out the razor blades and tape to assemble one usable mix from the various tracks. Nancy's performance was good enough to take the song to number three on the *Billboard* Adult Contemporary charts in 1967.

Why not? Her name was Sinatra, after all.

On Her Majesty's Secret Service: "We Have All the Time in the World"— Louis Armstrong

When George Lazenby took the reins of Bond in *On Her Majesty's Secret Service,* composer John Barry knew his work was cut out for him. With a new lead actor, Barry "poured everything in," writing a score that practically yelled "Bond" from every musical piece.

Yet the title song was instrumental, with the signature vocal theme reserved for later in the film. Barry switched up roles between combo and orchestral instruments—where the traditional James Bond theme used a horn background under an electric guitar melody, *On Her Majesty's Secret Service* opens the vamp with electric bass and muted electric guitar, and full horns state the melody.

Barry was leery of using the film's title as a lyric—usually the case in Bond films up to that point. The composer called upon the usual wordsmith partner of Burt Bacharach, Hal David, to write the lyrics. It was decided to take the last line Bond says—in both film and novel—to use as the title. Presented over a montage of Bond courting and wooing Teresa di Vicenzo, "We Have All the Time in the World" became an ominous foreshadowing of what would come at the film's climax.

Jazz legend Louis "Satchmo" Armstrong was asked by Barry to sing the tune. Long known for his trumpet playing and one-of-a-kind raspy voice, Armstrong had been in failing health and the recording was the last he would make. He died of a heart attack two years later.

Completing the session in one take, Satchmo delivered the hope and wonder of what new love is all about, yet with a sense of irony at the limits and frailty of a person's life (OK, OK . . . I'll lighten up). Just think of it as a music video years before MTV made them mundane.

"Diamonds Are Forever"—Shirley Bassey

The old gang was back in the saddle for *Diamonds Are Forever*—Connery was behind the Walther, and Bassey was behind the microphone. Barry was at the piano, and Black had pencil and paper in hand.

The singer is bitter in the lyrics, firmly convinced that compressed carbon is the only way to go. Having obviously been a casualty of a broken heart, she is now only interested in the reliability of diamonds being a girl's best you-know-what. She has no faith in a man's onions, but can trust in a diamond's carats (sorry).

A harp flourish and repeating arpeggio set up Bassey's opening lines, but with John Barry—can the horns be far behind? Of course not, and they arrive as the second verse begins. The full orchestra makes it to the party at the chorus, and soon, Bassey's voice flexes its muscles as wah-wah guitar adds to the arrangement. Again, Shirley has a big note at the end, but maintains consciousness this time.

"Live and Let Die"—Paul McCartney and Wings

The opportunity to tap a former Beatle for a Bond film was tempting. Since the band's breakup in 1970, everyone had gone their own ways, and Paul McCartney made the best commercial choice to write a title song.

McCartney had been considered to score *Diamonds Are Forever* (it wouldn't have been his first, as he had written the film music for 1967's *The Family Way*), but it never happened. With another new Bond (Roger Moore), it was as good a time as any to shake things up (John Barry was busy on another project anyway). McCartney was quickly approached to write the title tune for *Live and Let Die*.

Harry Saltzman, in his infinite wisdom (remember, he thought "Goldfinger" was no good), asked who they should get to sing the theme, believing a black vocalist would better attract a wider audience. George Martin, who was onboard to score the film, reminded him that the song had been written by one of the greatest pop singers around.

The arrangement and orchestration fits the mood more than the lyrics. A lone piano and voice open the song, reminiscing about youth and letting bygones be bygones. Today's world seems to have changed that philosophy by 180 degrees. At that point, everything blows up (if you've ever seen Macca perform this song live in concert, that's exactly what happens). A long and winding orchestration ensues, with suspense-like overtones—then a short break for reggae (written by Paul's wife, Linda). Why? Who knows . . . Fortunately, the orchestra breaks that up and the lone piano and voice return to restate the opening, completing the circle.

The theme song reached number two on the US *Billboard* Hot 100 charts and number nine in the UK and became the first Bond theme to receive an Oscar nomination for Best Original Song. (It lost out to "The Way We Were.")

"The Man with the Golden Gun"—Lulu

With John Barry back to score *The Man with the Golden Gun,* it was time for another title song. Scottish pop singer Lulu, famous for her hit recording of "To Sir with Love," was picked to sing it. The tune came from Barry and lyricist Don Black, but it was nearly knocked out by Mr. Nice Guy.

Shock-rocker Alice Cooper and his band of the same name wrote and recorded a title song called "The Man with the Golden Gun" with the intention of submitting it for inclusion in the film. Relying on Barry's former scores for inspiration, Cooper called on folks like the Pointer Sisters, Ronnie Spector, and Liza Minnelli as background singers. With a pulsing rhythm track, appropriate guitar riffs, and horn stabs, the song is an interesting attempt at molding Cooper's signature sound into a movie theme song.

Unfortunately, the rocker was one day late in submitting the song to the producers, who had signed Lulu to sing the Barry/Black theme by then. While Cooper included his track on the album *Muscle of Love* and performed it live in concert, it never made it to the Bond film.

The resulting song was received with indifference or dislike—even from its creators. With its provocative lyrics that referred to a man with "a powerful weapon" and asks, "Who will he bang?," Black brushed the song off as "cartoon hokum." John Barry claimed it was the song he hated the most from what he had written, although his trademark horns are present and the melody itself isn't bad. Even Lulu suggested her performance was a poor impression of Shirley Bassey.

And Alice Cooper says everyone he talked to was amazed that they picked the Lulu tune over his version.

The Spy Who Loved Me: "Nobody Does It Better"—Carly Simon

Coming to a Bond film with a boatload of impressive credentials didn't make the job any easier for Marvin Hamlisch. So, tapping into a Mozart-inspired piano phrase to open the song, Hamlisch scored a winner.

The composer went against type, choosing to pen a ballad instead of a frantic, power-packed opening song. Since Bond was always cool and in control, Hamlisch figured there was no reason to come in with guitars drawn and trumpets blaring. With lyrics by then-girlfriend Carole Bayer

Sager, the first line said it all: Nobody does it better. It would be hard to argue with an understatement like that. The lyrics continued forward to soft-sell the idea that the song's subject (Bond himself—a first) was more adept at . . . making love, saving the world, you fill in the blanks.

But producers didn't care for the fact that for the first time also, the song's title was not the film's title (some traditions die hard). Sager tweaked the lines with "like heaven above me, the spy who loved me" and all was well.

A hit maker in her own right, Carly Simon was chosen to sing the song, having scored in the 1970s with songs like "That's the Way I've Always Heard It Should Be," "Anticipation," "You're So Vain," "Mockingbird," and many more. Having seen *Dr. No* as a teen, she dreamed of hearing her singing voice pumping out of the theater's speakers one day.

The song did well on the music charts, going to the number two spot for three weeks on *Billboard*'s Hot 100 and number seven on the UK Singles Chart.

"Moonraker"—Shirley Bassey

Third time was a charm for Shirley Bassey, having sung the title songs for *Goldfinger* and *Diamonds Are Forever* before tackling *Moonraker*. But, popular as she had been, she wasn't the first choice to sing the Barry/David collaboration.

Pop singer Johnny Mathis was tapped to croon the smooth and somewhat sad ballad. But, with the track completed, the vocal just didn't seem to work. Barry didn't fault Mathis—sometimes things just don't click. By chance, Barry ran into Bassey, and on short notice she agreed to sing the tune. Although she didn't feel particularly comfortable with the tune, Bassey wanted to help Barry out with time running out to deliver a finished theme song.

The lyrics are from someone who dreams of finding love, referring to a "moonraker" as a person who searches for treasure. While the Moonraker was a rocket designed and built by Hugo Drax (in the book and the movie), English slang defined a moonraker in several ways: a simpleton or dunce, like someone so stupid he would try to rake the moon's reflection out of a pond, or a top sail on a schooner ship. Whatever the meaning, Hal David found a way to work it into the lyrics for a Bond film.

"For Your Eyes Only"—Sheena Easton

With Bill Conti taking the job of scoring *For Your Eyes Only*, producers figured the man who hit the charts with "The Theme from *Rocky*" would strike gold once more. The composer originally wanted supertalent Barbra Streisand to write the lyrics for the *For Your Eyes Only* theme, then have disco diva Donna Summer sing it.

When those plans fell through, Conti turned to hit maker Deborah Harry and Blondie. Even though the band submitted their idea of a Bond theme (unlike Alice Cooper, they were on time), producers only wanted Harry and not the band, and passed on their song. The singer didn't want to do it without her band, so Conti had to look elsewhere. Sheena Easton, a young Brit gifted with a powerful voice, had scored a hit single with "Morning Train," so she seemed to be a good selection to sing the theme.

Maurice Binder, longtime designer of the unique James Bond opening credits, had a problem with the song. He always liked to have the title being sung in sync with its appearance on the screen. But lyricist Mick Leeson had left it for the end, so Conti and Leeson went back to the drawing board.

When they came back, Binder had an inspired thought—Easton would sing on-camera, the first time that had been done. While the lyrics spoke of committed love and insight, Easton looked right into the camera lens, as Binder's usual female silhouettes undulated around her.

The song was a hit, reaching number four on *Billboard*'s Hot 100 Chart and number eight on the UK Singles Chart. It also received an Oscar nomination for Best Song.

Octopussy: "All Time High"—Rita Coolidge

Barry was back for *Octopussy*, teaming with lyricist Tim Rice for the theme. Rice was world renowned, having written the lyrics for musicals such as *Joseph and the Amazing Technicolor Dreamcoat, Jesus Christ Superstar,* and *Evita.* (He would continue to break the bank with hits like *Beauty and the Beast* and *The Lion King,* among others.)

Of course, the challenge for Rice was to work the film's controversial and suggestive title into the song's lyrics. He chose to follow the old saying: When there's an elephant in the room, don't mention it. He didn't, basing the lyrics on the phrase "all-time high."

The resulting storyline spoke of serendipitous love (missing were mentions of Bond, fake Fabergé eggs, circuses, or atomic bombs). After considering vocalists like retro-pop star Mari Wilson and Laura Branigan (1982's "Gloria"), singer Rita Coolidge was chosen by Cubby Broccoli, albeit with a little family influence.

Daughter Barbara Broccoli was an assistant director on *Octopussy*. She liked Rita Coolidge, a two-time Grammy award winner who hadn't had a major hit in the last five years. But Barbara kept playing Coolidge's records around the house until her dad stopped one night and said, "That's the voice I want for the new film!"

Getting the track on tape was a bit of a challenge, as Rice had yet to finish the lyrics by the time the recording session started. The situation put the song's producer, Phil Ramone (another Grammy winner), on edge until the words were delivered and another Bond theme was in the can.

The song reached number thirty-six on the *Billboard* Top 100 Chart (making it a hit in the days of "Top 40" radio). Even better, "All Time High" reached number one and stayed for four straight weeks on *Billboard*'s Adult Contemporary charts, making Barbara Broccoli's efforts a worthy campaign.

"A View to a Kill"—Duran Duran

Part of the success of the Bond franchise over the years has been the ability to embrace change, rather than deny it. In John Barry's case, *A View to a Kill* allowed him, for the first time, to collaborate with a popular rock band on the theme song. The result was a first-time occurrence as well.

English-based Duran Duran scored several megahits in the early 1980s, and with the help of cable's MTV, the quintet pioneered the music video as a device of promotion and entertainment. Some of their international hits included "Hungry Like the Wolf," "Is There Something I Should Know?," "Union of the Snake," and "The Reflex."

Bassist John Taylor—a huge Bond fan—told of having an inebriated conversation with Cubby Broccoli, where he asked the producer when he was "going to get someone decent" to record a Bond theme. An intrigued Broccoli took Taylor up on his query.

The writing process was, unfortunately, not very streamlined. Duran Duran was experiencing internal struggles—on the verge of falling apart—and John Barry now had five partners with whom to communicate, rather than the customary one. But everyone got through it and crafted a song loaded with gated drums, orchestra hits, and synth pads under a solid Simon LeBon vocal. Barry's influence is evident with his brass stabs throughout. The lyrics are somewhat abstract and aloof, but they still carry the theme of danger, espionage, and romance.

The efforts of all involved with the theme song paid big dividends. For the first and only time, a James Bond theme song hit the number one position on the *Billboard* Hot 100 Chart in July 1985, and went to number two on the UK Singles Chart.

"The Living Daylights"—a-ha

In 1987, Bond had been around for twenty-five years on the screen. And for most of those years, John Barry had been behind the piano and the podium, writing and conducting the scores. *The Living Daylights* would be Barry's last Bond film.

The composer had enjoyed his work with Duran Duran on the previous film, but the same couldn't be said this time around. Producers noted that the incorporation of a pop band into the mix had resulted in the first number one hit for a Bond theme song, so they went to the well once more. This time, they picked Norwegian trio a-ha, who had an international hit with "Take on Me." The song also produced an award-winning video that combined creative use of pencil-drawn animation with live action.

The title song was cowritten by Barry and a-ha's guitarist, although he claimed Barry wasn't working at the same level as the band's input. Barry seemed to brush off the issues as a lack of personality connection between himself and a-ha. Musically, the piece is very eighties driven—slamming drums, prominent synthesizers, and David Bowie–like vocals, but nicely mixed with strings and flutes by Barry. The lyrics basically describe the white-knuckle world of spying.

The song landed on the Top Ten of several European charts—obviously going to number one in Norway, but the tune failed to chart in the US.

Barry also decided to add a completely different song for the closing credits, tapping American band the Pretenders, with singer Chrissie Hynde, to write "If There Were a Man." The band laid a basic rhythm track to which Barry orchestrated strings. Once again, the lush ballad speaks of a search for love, seeming never to be found. The Pretenders also had a tune, "Where Has Everybody Gone?," featured in the film—playing on the Walkman of the dastardly Necros.

"Licence to Kill"—Gladys Knight

With John Barry recovering from his ruptured esophagus, producers turned to composer Michael Kamen to write the score for *Licence to Kill*. Wanting to get back to the basics of Bond music, Kamen envisioned something with low guitar notes and knew just who to call.

Famed Bond guitarist Vic Flick tells of getting that phone call in 1989. In response, he walked into a recording studio one day in 1989, only to find superstar guitarist Eric Clapton working on a riff. Trading licks with "Slowhand" was something many players could only dream of. The session went smoother than silk, and the very next day, everyone assembled on a London wharf to shoot a high-profile music video that would herald the coming of a new Bond film.

Two weeks later, Flick was told that producers didn't care for the resulting music and were going in another direction. Flick was disappointed but knew those things happened all the time in the music business. Even more disappointing, the music and video recordings from those days have been lost to the ages—never seen and considered to be the holiest of Grails for Bond fans around the world.

The other direction taken was soul singer Gladys Knight, who had R&B hits (with and without the Pips) with "I Heard It Through the Grapevine," "Neither One of Us," "Midnight Train to Georgia," among many others. The main theme song was written by Grammy-winning writers N. Michael Walden, Jeff Cohen, and Walter Afanasieff.

With a nod to the *Goldfinger* theme (very intentional, according to Walden), "Licence to Kill" opens with the same I–♭VI interval (albeit G to D♯ this time). Highly dynamic, with a slamming snare and clicking claves, the song speaks of loyalty in love—perhaps to the point of smothering—as Knight's voice soars in her soulful way (although she was somewhat uncomfortable with the whole violent "licence to kill" idea). With a slight hesitation in tempo, the song comes full circle, returning to the beginning theme as the film opens.

While the tune didn't make much of an impact on American music charts, it did reach the Top Ten in the UK. Faring better in the US was the end credits theme, "If You Asked Me To." Sung by Grammy-winning singer Patti LaBelle, the song hit number ten on the *Billboard* R&B Chart and number eleven on the Adult Contemporary Chart.

"GoldenEye"—Tina Turner

A trend had started to emerge in Bond films, as one composer worked on the film score and another writer or writers were charged with penning the theme song. Buoyed by the added exposure and promotional value of the music videos produced for the songs, it made sense to tap top pop, rock, and soul writers and performers. In the case of "GoldenEye," singer Bono and guitarist the Edge from the Irish rock band U2 wrote the main tune, to be sung by R&B superstar Tina Turner.

Under thumping bass and pizzicato strings, Turner sings with her usual sass. Horns reminiscent of Barry, plus bits from the Monty Norman theme, are tapped as the lyrics focus on domination and revenge for being left behind. (In love? At the circus? In a crowded elevator? It's not really revealed.) Turner's range is amazing, and the main theme does a fine job of setting the opening for the film.

Turner considered herself to be in "good company" as she joined the ranks of Bond singers, although she had originally dreamed of being a Bond girl herself in the film series. In a 1995 interview on television's *Entertainment Tonight,* she said, "My reputation is so strong as a singer that, unfortunately, it may be hindering my movie career . . . but I'm still here, I'll wait."

Originally half of the husband-wife team in the Ike and Tina Turner Revue, the Tennessee-born singer had a monster hit in 1971 with "Proud Mary." Later, as a solo performer, the eight-time Grammy winner struck gold with songs like "What's Love Got to Do with It," "Better Be Good to Me," "Private Dancer," and "We Don't Need Another Hero."

Her *GoldenEye* theme song reached into the Top Ten across Europe and hit number twenty-two on the *Billboard* Dance Music Chart in America.

"Tomorrow Never Dies"—Sheryl Crow

Since it was now fair game, everyone wanted a piece of the Bond theme song pie. For *Tomorrow Never Dies,* song submissions were received from Brit pop group Saint Etienne, Brit alternative rockers Pulp, and singer/songwriter Marc Almond (who scored a worldwide Top Ten hit, "Tainted Love," with the band Soft Cell), among others. Even David Arnold, scoring his first Bond film and figuring to have the inside track, made a submission—but all lost out on the title song.

The winner was folk-rocker Sheryl Crow, who had Top Ten hits in the US and UK with "All I Wanna Do," "If It Makes You Happy," and "Everyday Is a Winding Road." Written with composer/producer Mitchell Froom, "Tomorrow Never Dies" didn't match the success of Crow's earlier singles, which was why producers chose her in the first place.

Arnold's title offering, sung by Canadian pop star k. d. lang, was retitled "Surrender" and became the end credit song, although many fans thought it should have been placed upfront of the film. Since Arnold was under the impression that his song would open, variations on it appear throughout the film as part of the soundtrack.

Crow's theme song does not carry the magnificence that normally comes with a Bond title song. The descending verse progression sounds a bit like the verse in "A Taste of Honey," made popular in the sixties as a vocal number by the Beatles and an instrumental by Herb Alpert and the Tijuana Brass. Going into the chorus, a faint staccato piano reminds one of "The *Perry Mason* Theme." Crow's voice is somewhat harsh and doesn't have the power of Bassey or other Bond theme singers.

Many reviewers and fans of the day agreed.

"The World Is Not Enough"—Garbage

Perhaps it was time to take some of the control back in the Bond theme songs, allowing the composer—David Arnold—to create a title song that would be in sync with his accompanying score that would follow. To write the lyrics, old hand Don Black was brought in for the fifth time. And chosen to perform the title—"Garbage."

No, that's not a critical assessment of the resulting song, it's the name of the American-based alternative rock/techno-pop band who did it. Fronted by Scot-born singer Shirley Manson, the band had scored successful singles, such as "Stupid Girl," "Push It," and "Special." Their first two albums reached multiple platinum sales status in the US and UK.

Arnold's orchestration was lush, and Manson's vocal was sultry, both appropriate to the Bond formula. Black's lyrics were sung from the villain's perspective, addressing an insatiable and selfish greed for power and love. While the singer was "terrified" that she wouldn't be able to pull the vocal off, her performance proved her wrong, and like many before Manson, she fulfilled her dream of being a "Bond girl."

An effective music video for the song featured a very Bondian yarn, with Manson playing a robotic version of herself, constructed with a powerful bomb inside her. Dispatching her real self with a single kiss in a concert venue dressing room, she and her bandmates complete the song's performance, just as the bomb's timer reaches zero. Fade to black, cue explosion.

The title song reached into the Top Twenty on many music charts across Europe, although it failed to make a dent in the American market. Shortly after the song's release, a lawsuit was filed for copyright infringement, claiming it took a four-note sequence from a song, "This Game We Play," submitted for another MGM film. The resulting ruling found that David Arnold knew nothing about the other song and had actually written his song before "This Game We Play" was even submitted.

"Die Another Day"—Madonna

With *Die Another Day*, Bond had stormed into the twenty-first century. So, then, did the theme song. Once again, David Arnold was doing the soundtrack, but one of the biggest performers in the last twenty years of music was chosen to write and perform the theme song—Madonna.

The resulting piece was received with differing opinions, largely based on what side of the century your tastes sat. Those fans and reviewers who grew up with Connery and Barry felt the tune was in no way worthy of the Bond opening credits. And those who lapped up music videos and dance mixes loved the "new direction."

Heavily reliant on string stabs, electronic drums, and an Auto-Tuned Madonna voice that's barely recognizable as her, the song's lyrics lean strongly on dance potential and much less on storytelling. Suffice it to say, the movie title shows up quite a bit.

In a 2002 interview with CNN's Larry King, Madonna indicated she was reluctant to do the job, claiming everyone wanted the chance to record a James Bond theme, and she didn't want to be like everyone else. She changed her mind when it occurred to her that the franchise needed to "get techno."

No matter the critics' opinions, the public ate the song up. Madonna's take on James Bond spent eleven weeks in the number one position on America's singles charts. Around the world, "Die Another Day" hit the top of the music charts.

Once again, a sharp and inventive music video boosted visibility and sales, featuring the singer enduring water torture (much like Brosnan's Bond in the film's opening), fencing with herself (in a nod to her small role in the film as a fencing teacher), writhing around (standard in all Madonna videos), multiple icons from past Bond films (Oddjob and his hat, the Golden Gun, a speargun from *Thunderball,* et al.), and, fittingly, a gun barrel scene, complete with animated blood drip.

All in all, another action-packed four-plus minutes from Madonna.

Casino Royale: "You Know My Name"—Chris Cornell

New Bond, new direction—not the first time this had been heard. Composer David Arnold, now behind the pen and staff paper for the fourth time on a Bond film, collaborated with singer/songwriter Chris Cornell to produce a theme song worthy of the Bond name.

Although not a megastar in the Madonna/Tina Turner mold, Cornell was something the others weren't—a male. Arnold and producers felt a rougher approach—think Tom Jones—was needed to herald the new Bond. They chose Cornell, singer/guitarist with alternative bands Soundgarden and Audioslave, as his wide vocal range would suit whatever he and Arnold came up with.

The result was a powerful tune, opening with the crunching power chords of B–G–E. As the dynamics of the verse come down, they stop cold to set up the chorus. The lyrics—written first by Cornell and some of the best in a long time—describe a nascent Bond, new to the double-oh ranking, and what being an agent is all about. Although the potentially awkward film title of *Casino Royale* does not show up in the lyrics, the grandeur of the piece easily identifies it as a Bond theme song. The original Bond theme barely sneaks under the end of the song, as the opening power chords repeat.

That traditional James Bond theme, newly orchestrated and performed, covers the closing credits, with composer (and guitarist) Arnold stepping into Vic Flick's shoes for the signature guitar licks.

"You Know My Name" was nominated for a Grammy Award and hit the Top Ten on many European music charts, though it only reached number seventy-nine on the *Billboard* Hot 100 chart.

Quantum of Solace: "Another Way to Die"—Jack White and Alicia Keys

After twenty-one Bond films and twenty-one Bond theme songs, what remained that had yet to be done? How about a duet? Yeah—that'd never been done before.

After efforts to corral Brit soul and blues singer Amy Winehouse for the lead track never made it, producers tabbed Jack White, singer/songwriter/drummer/guitarist with the alternative rock duo the White Stripes, to write and record the theme song for *Quantum of Solace.* In turn, he called in a vocalist with whom he'd wanted to work for several years—R&B Grammy winner Alicia Keys.

The result was percussive, staccato, with White's drums mixed up-in-your-face. A power-packed guitar intro—broken by a single piano B octave—led to sassy vocals by White and Keys. The effective lyrics described the various characters in the film and death—from mistrust or no trust at all.

White relied heavily on analog instruments and technology in a digital world. The tracks were recorded—on tape, not hard drive—in Memphis, with the legendary Memphis Horns backing up the performance.

Fan reaction was widely mixed, as the song appeared at various positions among the top one hundred on European music charts. In America, the tune reached number eighty-one on the *Billboard* Top 100 chart. Worse, Jack White himself was irate to hear his song attached to a diet soda commercial. He was under the impression he'd written a theme song for a James Bond film.

"Skyfall"—Adele

British pop singer Adele was only eighteen years old when her first music was posted to the social media website MySpace in 2006. A record contract quickly followed, and she won her first Grammy awards three years later, earning Best New Artist and Best Female Pop Vocal Performance for her debut album, *19*. With the release of her follow-up album, *21*, in 2011, the singer dominated the Grammys once more—six nominations, six wins, including Album of the Year and Song of the Year.

Gifted with a powerful voice and an amazing range, the singer was the perfect choice to write and perform the theme song for *Skyfall*. Producers Wilson and Broccoli had once sought another Brit singer, Amy Winehouse, for the Bond theme, but her untimely death in 2011 closed that door. Adele first hinted at her own involvement with *Skyfall* in September of the same year, saying she was working on a special project. Her musical producer, Paul Epworth, assisted with the composition once they read the top-secret screenplay.

Perhaps not coincidentally, the theme opens with the same chordal intervals as "You Know My Name" from *Casino Royale,* although a half step up from the Chris Cornell song. And where he came crashing in with crunchy guitars, Adele comes in with single block chords on a piano. The lyrics are then set up with a typical suspended fourth chord that resolves to its root. (Think "Pinball Wizard"—that has suspended fourth chords resolving to their roots. Class dismissed.)

Adele's smooth and soft voice sings about coming face-to-face with the final moment (of life, we assume) and about the chances of surviving the turmoil. With strings joining in at the second verse, everyone is ready by the time the chorus comes around (entering with the requisite snare snap and drum fill). By now, Adele sings of making it through the mayhem, at least not alone, but together. (Perhaps "together" with 007? The lyrics don't say.) The chorus ends with the favored 007 chromatic V–♭VI–VI against the minor root.

The lyrics continue the story of conflict, with a mixed choir echoing Adele's vocal in the choruses this time, along with John Barry--esque horns for good measure. While her acrobatic expression never reaches the majesty of her earlier hits like "Rolling in the Deep" and "Set Fire to the Rain," Adele still ends the theme on a strong and soulful note.

Released three weeks before the world premiere of the film, the single for *Skyfall* commemorated the fiftieth anniversary of the release of *Dr. No*. The song quickly moved up the musical ladder, including iTunes download sales, the *Billboard* Hot 100, and charts all around the world. Most listeners, fans and critics alike, agreed that Adele's song had returned to the greatness of themes like "Goldfinger" and "Nobody Does It Better."

8

The Living Highlights

The Films of James Bond

Dr. No

(1962—British/UNITED ARTISTS—110 MIN/COLOR) Based on the Ian Fleming novel.
DIRECTOR: Terence Young
ORIGINAL MUSIC: Monty Norman
FILM EDITING: Peter Hunt
PRODUCTION DESIGN: Ken Adam
CAST: Sean Connery (007/James Bond)
Ursula Andress (Honey Ryder)
Joseph Wiseman (Dr. Julius No)
Jack Lord (Felix Leiter)
Bernard Lee (M)
Anthony Dawson (Professor R. J. Dent)
John Kitzmiller (Quarrel)
Zena Marshall (Miss Taro)
Eunice Gayson (Sylvia Trench)
Lois Maxwell (Miss Moneypenny)
Peter Burton (Major Boothroyd)

In Kingston, Jamaica, three blind men turn out to be not so blind, as they ambush and kill MI6 field operative Strangways, then quickly toss his body into a black hearse. At his office, a similar fate meets his secretary, and secret files on Crab Key and Doctor No are stolen.

In London, a suave and handsome tuxedo-clad man plays baccarat in a posh club called Le Cercle. His name is Bond, James Bond. He defeats the beautiful Sylvia Trench and then must leave the table on an urgent matter.

The offices of Universal Exports are merely a cover for the headquarters of MI6, the British Secret Service. Bond arrives, a member of the branch. He is labeled 007—licensed to kill. Miss Moneypenny ushers Bond into the

HARRY SALTZMAN and
ALBERT R. BROCCOLI PRESENT

IAN FLEMING'S

THE FIRST JAMES BOND FILM!

DR.
NO

TECHNICOLOR

SEAN CONNERY AS 007 ... URSULA ANDRESS · JOSEPH WISEMAN · JACK LORD ... ANTHONY DAWSON · MARSHALL KITZMILLER · GAYSON ... BERNARD LEE

Screenplay by RICHARD MAIBAUM, JOHANNA HARWOOD and BERKELY MATHER   Directed by TERENCE YOUNG   Produced by HARRY SALTZMAN and ALBERT R. BROCCOLI ... EON PRODUCTIONS LTD

Dr. No—British quad poster.

inner office of their boss, known only as M. Strangways was investigating interference with Cape Canaveral rocket launches that seemed to be coming from Jamaica when he disappeared. After changing his Beretta pistol for a Walther PPK—thanks to Major Boothroyd—Bond is off to Jamaica to find out what happened to Strangways.

In Jamaica, a chauffeur from the Government House picks up Bond, and they find themselves tailed leaving the airport. Losing the tail, it seems the chauffeur isn't really from the government and he commits suicide rather than reveal his identity to Bond. Later, Bond checks Strangways' place, where he finds two leads—a fisherman named Quarrel and a geologist named Dent.

Bond looks up Quarrel, who's leery of the British stranger. After Bond roughly convinces Quarrel and the barkeeper Puss-Feller that he's one of the good guys, he connects with Felix Leiter from the CIA. Everyone agrees that Crab Key, a private island owned by a mysterious Chinese man named Doctor No, deserves a closer look.

First, Bond visits Professor Dent about some rock samples Strangways had from Crab Key, but finds out nothing. Dent rushes to Crab Key, reporting to Doctor No. Bond is to be eliminated immediately, and Dent is given a poisonous tarantula to accomplish the task. That night, while 007 sleeps, the arachnid slowly crawls up his body. At the last minute, Bond throws the spider to the floor, smashing it with his shoe.

Bond finds that Strangways' rock samples were radioactive and has to check out Crab Key. Quarrel balks, telling of a dragon that breathes fire, but eventually relents. Before they go, Bond takes off for a quick afternoon tryst with Miss Taro, but it's a trap, as the familiar black hearse takes chase. The car loses control and tumbles down a mountainside in flames.

Taro seems surprised to see him, but she keeps their appointment. That evening, Bond sends for a car to pick him up at her place, but the driver is a policeman, and the vixen is whisked away instead. Waiting in the dark of Taro's home, Bond surprises Dent, who entered with intentions of shooting the supposedly sleeping agent. With Dent's gun emptied, Bond coldly kills him.

Bond and Quarrel arrive at Crab Key late at night. The next morning, Bond is awakened to the singing of a beautiful, bikini-clad blonde walking out of the water. She is Honey Ryder, collecting shells, and does not trust this stranger. He reassures her, and with Quarrel, they evade a patrol boat. When dogs come after the trio, they fashion breathing tubes from reeds and hide underwater. Later, Bond sees for himself—the fire-breathing dragon is a tank with flamethrowers. But Quarrel is killed in the fire, and Bond and Honey are captured.

Taken to Doctor No's hideout, the pair are discovered to be highly radioactive and have to be washed and scrubbed down. The Chinese staff are unusually kind to them, until they drug the two with spiked coffee.

After a long nap, they join Doctor No for dinner and finally get a look at the villain. Soft-spoken and proper, he has metal hands, as his were lost in a nuclear accident. The doctor is a member of SPECTRE—Special Executive for Counter-intelligence, Terrorism, Revenge, and Extortion—a rogue organization of the world's greatest criminals. Tiring of the conversation, Doctor No leaves while Honey is taken away and Bond is beaten.

Placed in a solitary cell, 007 makes his way into an air duct, where searing heat and a flood of water make his escape a true challenge. He comes out into the decontamination area, where Bond subdues a worker and gets into his radiation suit.

His identity hidden by the suit, Bond finds himself in Doctor No's immense control center, powered by a nuclear reactor. No is preparing to disrupt another American rocket launch, and Bond has to stop him. Spinning a control wheel, Bond runs the reactor into a dangerous meltdown condition. As workers flee the room, Doctor No tackles Bond, and they fight on the slowly sinking frame of the water-cooled reactor. Bond climbs to safety, while Doctor No's claws have no grip on the metal structure, and he sinks beneath the water in the reactor pool.

Meanwhile, the rocket launch goes off without a problem. Bond rescues Honey, shackled to the floor, from a slow drowning, and they escape in a small motorboat as Doctor No's complex explodes behind them.

At sea without fuel, Bond and Honey are found by Leiter and the Coast Guard. Felix throws them a rope, but Bond thinks better of it and lets it go, sinking into an embrace with Honey.

From Russia with Love

(1963—British/UNITED ARTISTS—115 MIN/COLOR) Based on the Ian Fleming novel.
DIRECTOR: Terence Young
ORIGINAL MUSIC: John Barry
FILM EDITING: Peter Hunt
ART DIRECTION: Syd Cain
CAST: Sean Connery (007/James Bond)
Daniela Bianchi (Tatiana Romanova)
Pedro Armendariz (Kerim Bey)
Lotte Lenya (Rosa Klebb)
Robert Shaw (Donald "Red" Grant)
Bernard Lee (M)
Eunice Gayson (Sylvia Trench)
Walter Gotell (Morzeny)
Lois Maxwell (Miss Moneypenny)
Vladek Sheybal (Kronsteen)
Desmond Llewelyn (Boothroyd)
Fred Haggarty (Krilencu)

A garden maze on a dark night—James Bond, gun drawn, is being tracked by a tall, blonde—assassin. But the agent is attacked from behind, strangled with a garrote wire hidden in a wristwatch—Bond is dead. Or is he? It's merely a training exercise, with a latex mask removed from the dead man's face—it's not 007.

In Venice, cunning Czech champion Kronsteen squares off against the Canadian Macadams in the final match of the Grandmasters Championship of Chess. With a brilliant move, Kronsteen defeats his opponent and quickly leaves the arena. He has been summoned to a yacht.

Kronsteen is director of planning for the underworld organization known as SPECTRE—Special Executive for Counter-intelligence, Terrorism,

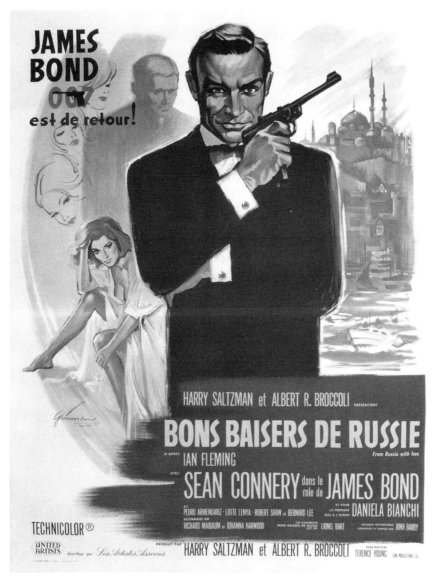

From Russia with Love—French 31 × 24 poster.

Revenge and Extortion. Meeting with its cat-loving leader, Blofeld, and the mannish-looking Number Three Rosa Klebb (a former Russian Intelligence agent), Kronsteen outlines his latest scheme.

SPECTRE will arrange for the capture of a secret Russian decoding machine called a Lektor. To achieve this, a Russian clerk and the British Secret Service will unknowingly be manipulated into action. The clerk will think she's acting on behalf of her superiors, and the British, long desiring a Lektor, will very likely send James Bond out to retrieve it. Kronsteen's calculating mind has anticipated every possible countermove—his plan is foolproof.

Klebb meets with Morzeny, the leader of SPECTRE Island. She has chosen Donald "Red" Grant to carry out the mission. He's the tall, blond assassin, and he's tough, showing no reaction when Klebb slams him in the belly with brass knuckles.

In Istanbul, beautiful Russian Consulate clerk Tatiana Romanova receives her orders from "Colonel" Klebb. Romanova is to push false information to the British—or else. Shown a picture of Bond, she is to do whatever he says.

Along an English stream, James Bond enjoys a moment with old friend Sylvia Trench—until the office calls. Using a mobile phone in his Bentley, Bond agrees to meet M in an hour—or maybe an hour and a half.

M reveals Romanova's desire to defect, with a Lektor in hand—only if Bond is the agent in Istanbul to receive her. Skeptical, he agrees. He meets Major Boothroyd, the equipment officer from Q Branch, who gives Bond a special briefcase, loaded with weapons, money, and a booby trap.

Bond meets Kerim Bey, the gregarious head of Station T, the Secret Service branch in Istanbul. He's been the contact with Romanova and will help arrange the deal. Bond discovers bugs in his hotel room—the electronic kind—and changes the arrangements to the bridal suite.

Bey's office is bombed and he suspects the Russians. Using the secret waterways under the streets and a conveniently placed periscope, Bey and Bond spy on the Russian Consulate. Later, Kerim Bey takes Bond to a gypsy camp for a wild time, including watching a violent cat-fight between two love-torn vixens.

The camp is attacked by Bulgar men led by Bey's old Bulgarian nemesis, Krilencu. Bey is wounded, and Bond lends his combative expertise. Krilencu retreats with his group, and 007 receives the two girls as his reward.

Bey must kill Krilencu before another attempt is made on his life. Outside Krilencu's apartment hideout, Bond lends the wounded Bey his AR-7 survival rifle, and his shoulder as a guide, to shoot Krilencu as he escapes from an upper-floor window.

Bond returns to his room, only to find someone sleeping in his bed—Romanova. While they make love, Klebb captures the whole episode on film, hidden behind a two-way mirror. The next morning, Romanova slips Bond a map of the Russian Consulate during a trip to Hagia Sofia. She describes the Lektor in great detail to Bond, verifying the machine as genuine. If a bomb can be planted at the consulate, it may create an appropriate diversion for 007 to grab the Lektor and escape with it and the girl.

Bey sets off the bomb, and the plan goes perfectly—almost. With the Lektor and Romanova in hand, and Bey alongside, Bond boards the Orient Express en route to London, but a Russian KGB agent, Benz, recognizes the girl and quickly gets on. Unknown to all, Grant is already on the train.

Bey spots Benz and detains him while Bond waits with Tatiana. But Grant kills them both, making it look like they killed each other. Bond finds Bey dead and accuses Tatiana of setting it up, slapping her. When the train stops in Belgrade, Yugoslavia, Bond finds one of Bey's sons and tells him of his father's death. He also asks for M to have someone from MI6 rendezvous with Bond in Zagreb.

At the Zagreb station, MI6 agent Captain Nash waits to meet Bond. But Grant kills him, takes his identity, and meets Bond instead. Dining on the train, Grant slips a sleeping pill to Tatiana in her wine, while he and Bond make plans to jump off the train with the Lektor near Trieste, Italy. With the girl passed out in her compartment, Grant subdues Bond in the adjoining room. Bond discovers it was SPECTRE behind it all, and Grant has been tailing him since Istanbul. Now that SPECTRE has the Lektor, Bond and Tatiana are goners. Plus, with the secret film taken of the lovers in Turkey released to the press, SPECTRE will be able to smear the Russians and Brits at the same time.

Bond bargains with Grant, offering him money from his briefcase. When Grant opens it, the booby trap tear gas canister goes off. Bond and Grant fight in the tight quarters of the room. As Grant prepares to finish 007 off with his garrote wire, Bond gets the advantage and kills Grant with his own weapon.

Bond grabs the drowsy and drugged Tatiana, and they leap from the train, taking Grant's waiting escape truck and driver. A SPECTRE helicopter threatens to blow up the truck with hand grenades, but Bond draws them away into the hills. Taking cover under a boulder, Bond assembles his AR-7 rifle and shoots the assailant in the copter, causing him to drop a live grenade in the cockpit. It explodes and crashes to the ground.

Bond drives the truck to a motorboat waiting on the coast of the Istrian peninsula. He dumps the driver and races off to Venice with Tatiana. Meanwhile, Blofeld is not happy with the outcome of Kronsteen's plan and has him killed by Morzeny's poison-tipped boot. He orders Klebb to kill Bond.

With a group of speedboats, Morzeny catches up with Bond in the Mediterranean Sea. They fire on Bond, puncturing his extra fuel tanks. Bond dumps them in the water, then sets everything ablaze with a flare gun. Boats and Morzeny burn while Bond and Tatiana escape.

In Venice, the pair get ready to leave for London. A maid comes to clean up, but it's really Klebb, trying to grab the Lektor and Tatiana while killing Bond. Preparing to shoot 007, Klebb has her gun knocked to the ground by Romanova. Klebb then tries to give Bond a fatal kick with her dagger shoe, but Romanova kills her with the dropped gun.

Bond and Tatiana take a romantic trip down the Venice canals. In an embrace, Bond tosses the incriminating reel of film into the water and out of their lives.

Goldfinger

(1964—British/UNITED ARTISTS—110 MIN/COLOR) Based on the Ian Fleming
  novel.
DIRECTOR: Guy Hamilton
ORIGINAL MUSIC: John Barry
FILM EDITING: Peter Hunt
PRODUCTION DESIGN: Ken Adam
CAST: Sean Connery (007/James Bond)
Honor Blackman (Pussy Galore)
Gert Fröbe (Auric Goldfinger)
Shirley Eaton (Jill Masterson)
Tania Mallet (Tilly Masterson)
Harold Sakata/Tosh Togo (Oddjob)
Bernard Lee (M)
Martin Benson (Solo)
Cec Linder (Felix Leiter)
Austin Willis (Simmons)
Lois Maxwell (Miss Moneypenny)
Burt Kwouk (Mr. Ling)
Desmond Llewelyn (Q, aka Major Boothroyd)
Margaret Nolan (Dink)

A black bird floats innocently on a moonlit pond. But it's merely a decoy, the headdress of secret agent 007—James Bond. Clad in a black wet suit, he emerges from the water, subdues a guard, and plants plastic explosives in a secret heroin factory. Outside, he removes his wet suit to reveal a white dinner jacket, complete with red carnation. The bomb destroys another illegal operation, and he returns to the hotel room of his mistress. He embraces her, and the reflection in her eye reveals an approaching assailant. Bond tussles with the thug, tossing him into a bathtub. But the mugger reaches for 007's gun, and the resourceful agent knocks an electric fan into the bath water, electrocuting the villain. "Shocking," observes Bond dryly, "positively shocking."

Miami Beach and CIA's Felix Leiter finds Bond in the capable hands of the lovely Dink. Leiter has orders from Bond's boss to watch Auric Goldfinger, who enjoys a game of gin by the pool. Goldfinger cheats, using a radio transmitter and a comely accomplice named Jill Masterson. Bond's suave ways convince Jill to defect, and they force Goldfinger to lose $15,000 to his former card pigeon. Later, Goldfinger has his revenge by subduing Bond in his hotel suite and murdering Masterson by covering her, head to toe, in gold paint.

Back at London headquarters, M, the head of British Secret Service, orders Bond to meet him for dinner. His lovely secretary, Miss Moneypenny, counters the offer by suggesting she bake an angel cake for James. M, of course, wins out and briefs 007 on Goldfinger's suspected operation of smuggling gold bullion. Bond must find out how he's getting the gold out of the country.

Goldfinger—US three-sheet poster.

In the equipment department, Bond meets up with Q, who runs Q Branch. The no-nonsense Q replaces Bond's stately Bentley motorcar with a sleek gray Aston Martin DB5 that's loaded with special features.

Using a gold bar as bait, Bond engages the rotund Goldfinger in a game of golf. In a neat double play of ball switching, Bond wins the match and nearly $12,000 from the angered loser. Goldfinger's massive and mute manservant, Oddjob, is not one to be taken lightly. He wears a razor-edged bowler hat that can sever the stone head from a statue with one throw. Bond taunts Oddjob with the real golf ball after the match, and the huge tuxedoed Korean crushes the pellet in one hand.

Bond tracks Goldfinger's Rolls-Royce Phantom III to Geneva, Switzerland. Stopped on a winding mountain road, 007 is nearly killed by a mysterious gunshot. A blonde in a sharp Ford Mustang convertible plays bumper tag with Bond, and he shreds her tires with razor-tipped hubcap covers on the Aston Martin. He innocently offers to help her, and she introduces herself as Tilly Soames. He drops her at a garage and resumes the hunt for Goldfinger.

Arriving at Auric Enterprises, Bond spies on the operation and discovers the smuggling secret—Goldfinger has his Rolls-Royce cast out of gold bullion. Bond meets Soames again and discovers she's really Tilly Masterson, sister of the murdered Jill. The errant shot that missed 007 was hers, meant for Goldfinger. They flee from Goldfinger's Asian thugs in the DB5. Spraying slick oil and clouds of thick smoke from the rear, two carloads of villains are thwarted. Protected by the bulletproof shield on the trunk, Bond and Masterson take off on foot. But Oddjob kills Tilly with his deadly derby. Captured, Bond is taken to the factory, but not before blasting a guard through his car roof with the ejection seat. He nearly escapes, but crashes into a building and is knocked out cold.

He wakes to find himself strapped to a golden table, as the evil Goldfinger intends to eliminate the secret agent with a powerful industrial laser. "Do you expect me to talk?" asks 007. "No, Mr. Bond," Goldfinger replies bluntly, "I expect you to die!" But the clever Bond mentions the mysterious Operation Grand Slam and convinces the villain that he's worth more alive than dead.

Hustled aboard a private plane, Bond meets Goldfinger's beautiful but icy-cold pilot Pussy Galore. Airborne, they're bound for the bluegrass of Kentucky, where Goldfinger has a stud farm for thoroughbred horses. Once there, Bond is locked in a dungeon cell, but he cleverly escapes the lone guard. Hiding under a model of Fort Knox, he watches as Goldfinger reveals Operation Grand Slam to a roomful of top underworld figures. He plans to break into Fort Knox and explode an atom bomb. It will render the US gold supply of $50 billion radioactive, making the villain's gold reserves infinitely richer in value. Bond is found by Pussy and tossed back in his cell, now guarded by a phalanx of Goldfinger's men.

Fearing the watchful CIA will become suspicious when Bond isn't seen, Goldfinger and Pussy decide that it's better to release him and let him have the run of the farm. Pussy rebukes Bond's amorous advances, and they trade judo flips in a barn. But Bond wins this "roll in the hay," as Pussy Galore surrenders to his charms.

The next morning, Pussy Galore's Flying Circus puts Goldfinger's plan into action as they soar over Fort Knox, spraying the deadly Delta-9 nerve gas and killing everyone in the area, including Felix Leiter. Goldfinger dynamites the fence surrounding the gold reserve and uses the laser to cut his way into the vaults.

Bond is handcuffed to the atomic bomb, donated by the Red Chinese. Armed, it's set to explode in four minutes. But it's all a grand trap, as the supposedly "dead" military forces of Fort Knox return to life and descend on Goldfinger and his men. Dressed as an army general, Goldfinger escapes. But Oddjob is trapped in the locked vault with Bond, as the seconds tick away on the A-bomb.

Bond frees himself but has to contend with the powerful Oddjob. The huge butler attacks Bond with his bowler but misses, cutting a large electrical cable. Bond retaliates, hurling the hat at Oddjob. He too misses, wedging the derby in some metal bars. As Oddjob retrieves the hat, Bond shoves the sparking electrical cable up against the bars, and Oddjob is finished.

The army blasts their way into the vault, and a scientist shuts the bomb off with just "007" seconds to spare. Leiter tells Bond it was Pussy Galore who double-crossed Goldfinger, helping the army to switch the Delta-9 with a harmless substitute. Bond was the cause of her change of heart, as he "must have appealed to her maternal instincts."

The British hero is spirited off in a private plane to a congratulatory lunch meeting with the president, but things quickly go awry. Goldfinger shows up with Pussy at the controls. Bond tackles Goldfinger, and his gold-plated revolver goes off. It shatters a window, and the plane violently depressurizes. While Bond holds on for his life, the evil Goldfinger is sucked out into the wild blue yonder. Bond tells Pussy, "He's playing his golden harp."

The plane spirals to a fiery crash in the ocean, but Bond and Pussy bail out at 4,000 feet. While a copter searches for them, Bond hides himself and Pussy under a parachute, saying as they embrace, "This is no time to be rescued."

Thunderball

(1965—British/UNITED ARTISTS—130 MIN/COLOR) Based on the Ian Fleming novel.
DIRECTOR: Terence Young
ORIGINAL MUSIC: John Barry
FILM EDITING: Ernest Hosler
PRODUCTION DESIGN: Ken Adam
CAST: Sean Connery (007/James Bond)
Claudine Auger (Domino Duval)
Adolfo Celi (Emilio Largo)

Luciana Paluzzi (Fiona)
Rik Van Nutter (Felix Leiter)
Guy Doleman (Count Lippe)
Molly Peters (Patricia)
Martine Beswick (Paula)
Bernard Lee (M)
Desmond Llewelyn (Q)
Lois Maxwell (Miss Moneypenny)
Philip Locke (Vargas)

A funeral in France—SPECTRE agent Colonel Jacques Bouvar is dead. James Bond receives the grief-stricken wife at her chateau to offer condolences. But she is a he—Bouvar is not dead after all, posing in disguise as his own widow. A brutal fight ensues, with Bond making sure Bouvar is really dead this time. As servants chase 007, he straps on a Bell Jet-pack and soars away. Landing next to his Aston Martin, he stows the rocket pack in the trunk and makes his escape.

Emilio Largo attends an executive meeting of SPECTRE, led by Blofeld. An embezzling member of the group is outed and executed, completing old business. New business outlines a plot to hold a threat over NATO countries for a ransom of $280 million. Field agent Count Lippe is making arrangements at Shrublands, a health sanitarium in England, where Bond happens to be recuperating.

While there searching Lippe's room, Bond sees a bandage-wrapped patient lurking about. Therapist Pat Fearing puts Bond in a traction machine to straighten him out. Lippe slips in and sets the machine to violently pull 007 to pieces, but Fearing fortunately saves him in time. He generously shows his appreciation to the lovely woman. Later, Bond returns the favor to Lippe by trapping him in a steam cabinet and setting it to "permanent press."

NATO pilot Francois Derval lounges with voluptuous Fiona Volpe in his room, but when he answers a knock at the door, he comes face-to-face with himself and Count Lippe. Derval is killed and the plot is revealed. The dupe Derval is Angelo, the bandaged patient Bond saw earlier. He will take the real pilot's place during a NATO training mission flying a Vulcan jet carrying two atomic bombs. But at the last minute, Angelo demands more money. Volpe is a SPECTRE agent, and she quickly agrees to his demand.

The training flight begins, and Angelo kills the flight crew by poisoning the air supply, then crash lands the jet into the Atlantic Ocean near the Bahamas. Largo, aboard his luxury yacht, the *Disco Volante,* watches, then deploys a sea sled to recover the bombs from the downed plane. He also kills Angelo in cold blood during the process—no wonder Volpe was so agreeable.

Bond leaves Shrublands and Lippe gives chase, shooting at 007. But before he can respond, a motorcycle roars up from behind, fires missiles into Lippe's car, and destroys it in a ball of flames. The bike zooms off, and the rider dumps it in a lake. It's none other than Volpe, who was ordered by Blofcld to eliminate the incompetent Lippe.

At MI6 headquarters, a tape released by SPECTRE outlines their demands—£100 million ransom or a major city in England or the US will be hit with one of the nuclear bombs now held by the villains. Bond is briefed on Operation Thunderball, the mission to recover the bombs before payment has to be made in four days—before a bomb is detonated. Bond is off to Nassau, where Derval's sister, Domino, is staying.

Bond makes the acquaintance of the beautiful Domino, who happens to be the niece of Largo, although mistress is more accurate. Bond defeats Largo at the baccarat table and wins an invitation for lunch at Largo's estate, Palmyra. Later, Bond discovers one of Largo's henchmen lurking around his hotel room and, with the help of CIA agent Felix Leiter, sends him on his way.

Largo finds his man was discovered by Bond and throws him into a swimming pool full of man-eating sharks. Meanwhile, Bond meets up with Q, who equips him with a special underwater camera, a Geiger counter watch, and other goodies.

Leiter takes Bond to check out the *Disco Volante* underwater, but Largo torments him by dropping hand grenades around him. Bond escapes and just happens to catch a ride with Fiona Volpe. Bond's pictures taken of the yacht reveal an underwater hatch, allowing the bombs to be hidden onboard.

Bond keeps his lunch date with Largo, where 007 is invited to be Largo's guest at the Junkanoo—the local festival that evening. Later, Bond slips onto Palmyra, where he gets trapped in the pool with the sharks. Using a small breathing device, Bond escapes back to his hotel. He's taken hostage by Volpe and Largo's men, but escapes into the crowds at Junkanoo. Volpe catches up with Bond at the Kiss Kiss Club and, while dancing, is shot dead with a bullet meant for 007.

Time is running out, and NATO prepares to deliver the ransom to SPECTRE. Bond searches the waters of the Bahamas and finally locates the Vulcan, but the bombs are gone. Later, Bond shows Domino her brother's watch and dog tags—he's dead, at the hands of Largo. Bond asks Domino to help locate the bombs onboard the *Disco Volante*.

Largo leads a team of scuba divers—with Bond hidden among them—to move the bombs from an underwater grotto to the yacht. Bond is discovered and escapes, as Largo catches Domino looking for the bombs. He binds her and tortures her, demanding to find out what Bond knows. Leiter finds 007, and he joins dozens of para-diving marines, taking the fight to Largo and his men.

A tremendous underwater battle develops, with 007 arriving with a motorized scuba tank, zooming among the combatants. He rips face masks and air hoses from the bad guys as the hand-to-hand fighting continues. The marines capture Largo's men, but he escapes to his yacht. Extending hydrofoils, the boat jettisons its aft section and takes off at tremendous speed as the Coast Guard approaches. Bond has made his way aboard, while one of Largo's technicians releases Domino.

Bond fights with Largo and his men, while the yacht races away out of control. Largo has Bond cornered with a gun, but Domino shoots him dead with a speargun. Bond and Domino jump overboard as the *Disco Volante* crashes into a reef and explodes.

A Skyhook rescue plane drops a raft, where 007 inflates a large balloon and straps into a safety harness, as Domino watches with curiosity. The plane returns, catching the balloon and cable in its yoke. It pulls Bond and Domino into the air and away.

You Only Live Twice

(1967—British/UNITED ARTISTS—117 MIN/COLOR) Loosely based on the Ian Fleming novel.
DIRECTOR: Lewis Gilbert
ORIGINAL MUSIC: John Barry
FILM EDITING: Peter Hunt
PRODUCTION DESIGN: Ken Adam
CAST: Sean Connery (007/James Bond)
Akiko Wakabayashi (Aki)
Mie Hama (Kissy)
Tetsuro Tamba (Tiger Tanaka)
Teru Shimada (Mr. Osato)
Karin Dor (Helga Brandt)
Donald Pleasence (Blofeld)
Bernard Lee (M)
Desmond Llewelyn (Q)
Lois Maxwell (Miss Moneypenny)
Charles Gray (Henderson)
Tsai Chin (Ling)
Ronald Rich (Hans)

Two-man US spacecraft *Jupiter 16* orbits the Earth, as an astronaut exits the ship for a spacewalk. Suddenly, a rogue spacecraft approaches from behind. Amazingly, its nose opens, like the jaws of an alligator. It surrounds *Jupiter 16* and closes, cutting the lifeline of the astronaut. The Soviets deny any

You Only Live Twice—US one-sheet poster.

involvement, to the doubts of the Americans. England arbitrates the heated discussion, suggesting the rocket may have come from the Sea of Japan. They will have one of Her Majesty's agents check it out.

In Hong Kong, James Bond has his romantic interlude with Ling interrupted by machine-gunners, who shoot Bond dead. He's given a proper naval burial at sea, but scuba divers recover the body and take it to a submarine. Cutting open the shroud, it seems 007 is just fine.

The sub is one of M's field offices. Bond's mission is to find out just who is behind the spacecraft hijackings—before the next launch. He's loaded into a torpedo tube and launched toward the shores of Japan.

In Tokyo, Bond meets a beautiful girl, Aki, at a sumo arena. She introduces him to field operative Dikko Henderson. But before Henderson can offer his thoughts on who's stealing the spacecraft, he's murdered and Bond goes after the assailant. Catching and killing him, 007 takes his place in a waiting getaway car, feigning an injury.

Bond ends up at Osato Chemical Engineering, carried in by a massive Japanese thug. They struggle and Bond finally brains him with a stone statue. He breaks into a wall safe with a combination detector, grabs some papers, and runs. Bond escapes with Aki, who takes him to Tiger Tanaka, head of the Japanese Secret Intelligence Service.

Bond and Tanaka inspect the papers, which reveal a photo of a freighter ship and supply orders for what could be rocket fuel. Bond suspects Osato could be fronting the hijack operation for SPECTRE. Later, Tanaka hosts a Japanese bath for Bond, then leaves him with Aki for the night.

Bond meets Mr. Osato the next day, pretending to seek doing business with the company. After the meeting, Osato tells his beautiful helicopter pilot, Helga Brandt, to have Bond killed. Leaving the offices, Bond and Aki are chased by a carload of goons. Aki calls Tiger for assistance, and a large helicopter flies in, grabs the villains' auto with a huge magnet, then dumps the gunmen and their car in Tokyo Bay.

It turns out the freighter ship in the photo belongs to Osato Chemicals and is moored at the Kobe Docks. Bond and Aki arrive there, but run into a group of unsavory dockworkers. Aki escapes, but Bond is captured by the men, who take him to Helga. She threatens 007, but he convinces her to leave Osato and come away with him. Flying away in Brandt's plane, she traps Bond and escapes by parachute. Bond breaks free at the last moment and safely crash-lands the plane.

Japanese SIS have identified the island in the photo and Bond needs to take a closer look. Q arrives with something Bond requested—*Little Nellie,* a weapons-loaded autogyro. Packed in four suitcases, the copter is assembled by technicians, and Bond flies off. Inspecting the islands, Bond finds nothing but volcano craters. When four enemy helicopters attack, Bond swiftly zooms among them, defeating them with *Little Nellie*'s bag of deadly tricks.

The Russians launch a manned spacecraft, and it's quickly hijacked by the marauding missile. It comes down as a false lake opens in a volcano crater, revealing the hideout, rocket pad, and headquarters of Blofeld and SPECTRE. Meanwhile, tensions between Russia and the US continue to escalate over the affair.

In his apartment, Blofeld discusses his plan with Red Chinese officials, who will benefit from the turmoil between the superpowers. He also wants $100 million from them as payment. He then admonishes Osato and Brandt for not knowing they were with James Bond and should have eliminated him. Blofeld feeds Brandt to his piranhas and orders Osato to kill Bond.

Tanaka will have Bond train as a ninja warrior, then infiltrate the island with them. Bond is made up to look Japanese, then learns the way of the ninja. As they prepare to leave for the island, a stealthy assassin kills Aki with poison intended for Bond.

On the island, Bond weds Kissy, a local girl, to help create his cover. To confound the Russians, the Americans have moved up the launch schedule of their next Jupiter mission, so 007 and Tanaka's men have to move fast. Bond and Aki inspect a cave where a local girl was found mysteriously dead. Loaded with poisonous gas to keep people away, the cave leads to the top of a volcano—Bond and Aki have to head there next.

The Americans launch their rocket, as Bond discovers the crater lake is fake. Aki goes to get Tanaka and his ninjas, while 007 heads into Blofeld's lair. Thinking quickly, Bond plans to pose as a rogue astronaut, intending to get on Blofeld's rocket and sabotage it before it can grab the American spacecraft. But Blofeld sees through the ruse, and 007 is brought to the control room as the countdown continues.

The rocket lifts off as Tanaka's ninjas surround the crater. Blofeld leaves the key to explode his rocket once the hijack in completed with his gargantuan assistant, Hans. Bond creates a diversion to open the crater and allow the ninjas to get in. They drop their rappel lines and attack. Explosions flare and bodies fly as Blofeld's men fight back.

Blofeld shoots Osato for his continued failures and escapes on his bubble-shaped monorail. Bond fights Hans in Blofeld's apartment for the key. He grabs it and flips the henchman into the pond of piranhas—Look, Ma—no Hans.

Bond gets to the exploder button and blows the hijack rocket to bits as it nears the US craft. The threat is over, but Blofeld still lives. He throws a lever and starts a series of explosions designed to destroy the volcano and everyone in it. Bond and Aki swim through the cave and out into the open sea.

Safe on a raft, they watch as the volcano explodes. Thinking they're alone, the pair are interrupted as M's submarine surfaces directly under their raft. M orders Moneypenny to get 007 below—at once.

On Her Majesty's Secret Service

(1969—British/UNITED ARTISTS—142 MIN/COLOR) Loosely based on the Ian
  Fleming novel.
DIRECTOR: Peter R. Hunt
ORIGINAL MUSIC: John Barry
FILM EDITING: John Glen
PRODUCTION DESIGN: Syd Cain
CAST: George Lazenby (007/James Bond)
Diana Rigg (Tracy di Vicenzo)
Telly Savalas (Ernst Stavro Blofeld)
Gabriele Ferzetti (Marc-Ange Draco)
Ilse Steppat (Irma Bunt)
Angela Scoular (Ruby Bartlett)
George Baker (Sir Hilary Bray)
Bernard Lee (M)
Desmond Llewelyn (Q)
Lois Maxwell (Miss Moneypenny)
Catherina Von Schell (Nancy)
Bernard Horsfall (Campbell)

At MI6 headquarters, Q briefs M on the latest technical developments, but the boss only wants to know one thing: Where is 007?

He's in Portugal, saving a beautiful young woman from drowning herself in the ocean. When Bond is interrupted by two thugs, he turns his attention to defeating them. Doing so, he finds the woman has driven off, and he wryly notes that things like that never happened to "the other fellow."

Bond catches up with the lady at a posh hotel and casino. She's Countess Teresa di Vicenzo—Tracy—and she's wild, daring, and reckless. Inviting Bond up to her room, he finds a goon waiting instead. Taking care of him, 007 returns to his room, and, of course, Tracy is waiting for him there. In the morning, she's gone.

Bond is taken hostage to an industrial complex where he meets Marc-Ange Draco, who apologizes for the rough treatment. Draco is the head of Unione Corse, the biggest crime syndicate in Europe. He's also Tracy's father.

On Her Majesty's Secret Service—US Style B one-sheet poster.

Knowing how Bond has looked after Tracy, Draco offers him £100 million to court and marry her. Bond refuses the offer, but wants to find Blofeld and knows Draco can help.

With M in London, Bond is taken off the Blofeld case (Operation Bedlam), and in a fit of anger, Bond resigns from MI6. M gives him two weeks leave instead, and Bond is back to Portugal, with Tracy and her father. Draco knows Blofeld is connected to a lawyer named Gumbold in Bern, Switzerland. Meanwhile, James and Tracy spend a lot of time together, and love develops.

Bond sneaks into Gumbold's office where, using a huge safecracking device, he finds correspondence from Blofeld. The villain wishes to assume a royal title as the Swiss Count Bleuchamp and will meet with a British expert in heraldry from the London College of Arms—Sir Hilary Bray—to pursue the matter. Bond consults with Bray and arranges to pose in his place in order to connect with Blofeld.

Arriving in Switzerland, Bond/Bray is collected by Irma Bunt, a stout and stern woman who is personal secretary to Bleuchamp. The Count operates the Bleuchamp Institute, a private lab for allergy research on a remote mountaintop retreat, Piz Gloria.

Dressed in Scot kilts and frilly shirt, Bray dines with Bunt and twelve beautiful women, all patients of the count. He then meets with Bleuchamp, who has developed a cure for allergies based on vaccines and psychological therapy. He is eager to assume his royal position, but hesitates when Bray asks for his time to further investigate his lineage.

Bray slips into the room of a pretty and frisky patient named Ruby, where he discovers Bleuchamp is using hypnosis as part of his treatment. Returning to his own room, he finds Nancy, another patient, waiting for him. The next morning, a mountain climber is roughly turned away from Piz Gloria as the girls play a game of curling and continue to make evening engagements with Sir Hilary.

When Bray comes to Ruby's room, he is surprised to find Irma Bunt waiting instead, and he's knocked cold. Bond and Blofeld now know who each other truly are, and the villain reveals his plot. He has developed strains of viruses that can render flora and fauna infertile—destroying entire species of plants and animals, including man. Blofeld's patients will unknowingly carry the deadly toxins all over the world, disguised as cosmetics, to be released on Blofeld's remote command.

It turns out the mountain climber was Campbell, a British agent sent to help Bond—Blofeld had him killed. He has the same fate planned for 007. Locked in a motor room for the tram car, Bond climbs out through an opening for the cable and slips into skis. He takes off down the mountainside, followed by Blofeld and his armed men. Bond breaks a ski and, amazingly, continues downhill on one ski.

At the bottom, Bond blends into the crowd and finds Tracy. They drive away into town, where Bunt nearly catches them. But Tracy shows some real driving skills, pulling into the midst of a stock car race and slipping away. Bunt's car crashes and explodes, as she and her men escape injury. Tracy and Bond weather a snowstorm in a horse stable, where he proposes marriage—and she accepts.

The next morning, the pair ski away as Blofeld and his men continue their chase. Almost in the clear, Bond and Tracy are trapped in an avalanche started by Blofeld. The villain takes Tracy away as Bond makes his way back to London.

Bond implores M to attack Piz Gloria, save Tracy, and destroy Blofeld and his headquarters, but he refuses. The United Nations has decided to accept Blofeld's demands of amnesty for all past crimes and acknowledgment of his royal title. Undeterred, Bond contacts Draco and seeks his help to attack Piz Gloria.

As Bond, Draco, and his men, posing as a medical mission, approach in three helicopters, Blofeld offers himself to Tracy. Draco attacks, easily defeating Blofeld's men. Bond rescues Tracy, and the complex is blown to pieces. Bond chases Blofeld, as the two race down an icy course in bobsleds. The secret agent reaches Blofeld, and they wrestle on the same sled. Bond gets Blofeld upright, just in time to catch the villain in an overhanging tree branch. A trusty St. Bernard dog comes to Bond's aid as the bobsled flies away and crashes.

Bond and Tracy are wed in a grand celebration. Draco and M reminisce over the Goldfinger caper while Q offers fatherly advice to Bond. The happy newlyweds drive away to their honeymoon as the crowd applauds.

Along a country road, Blofeld—in a neck brace—drives past Bond's Aston Martin, and Irma Bunt fires an automatic weapon out a backdoor window. Bond is unharmed, but Tracy is killed instantly. As a police officer arrives, Bond cradles his dead wife and assures the officer there's no hurry—they have "all the time in the world."

Diamonds Are Forever

(1971—British/UNITED ARTISTS—120 MIN/COLOR) Loosely based on the Ian Fleming novel.
DIRECTOR: Guy Hamilton
ORIGINAL MUSIC: John Barry
FILM EDITING: Bert Bates and John W. Holmes
PRODUCTION DESIGN: Ken Adam
CAST: Sean Connery (007/James Bond)
Jill St. John (Tiffany Case)
Charles Gray (Ernst Stavro Blofeld)
Lana Wood (Plenty O'Toole)
Jimmy Dean (Willard Whyte)
Bruce Cabot (Bert Saxby)
Bruce Glover (Mr. Wint)

Putter Smith (Mr. Kidd)
Bernard Lee (M)
Desmond Llewelyn (Q)
Lois Maxwell (Miss Moneypenny)
Norman Burton (Felix Leiter)
Joseph Furst (Dr. Metz)
Leonard Barr (Shady Tree)
Joe Robinson (Peter Franks)
Margaret Lacey (Mrs. Whistler)
Lola Larson (Bambi)
Trina Parks (Thumper)
David Bauer (Morton Slumber)
David De Keyser (Doctor)

James Bond, a grieving widower, scours the globe in search of Ernst Stavro Blofeld. Bond finally finds the supervillain at a facility where he is creating clones of himself with plastic surgery. Eluding several armed guards, Bond tosses Blofeld into a bubbling pit of mud.

In the diamond mines of South Africa, workers make extra money by slipping diamonds to the company dentist, who pays cash under the table. He then delivers the load to the slimy Mr. Wint and weasely Mr. Kidd, who thank him by dropping a deadly scorpion down his shirt. They keep the diamonds for themselves. MI6 must find out who's really behind the diamond smuggling.

Kindly Mrs. Whistler takes the diamonds from Wint and Kidd, intending to take them to Amsterdam. Unfortunately, the duo dump the lady in the Amstel River, drowning her. Meanwhile, smuggler Peter Franks is detained by M's staff, and Bond takes his identity en route to Holland.

The beautiful Tiffany Case is Franks' smuggling contact there, so Bond makes the connection. His job is to get fifty thousand carats of diamonds into the US. But the real Franks escapes and makes his way to Case's apartment. Bond catches him in the elevator, and they fight in the close quarters of the car. Bond blinds him with a fire extinguisher and throws him over a railing, six floors to his death. He quickly switches IDs, and Case thinks the dead man is James Bond. The diamonds, cleverly arranged as a crystal chandelier by Mrs. Whistler, make their way into America hidden in the body of Peter Franks. His "brother," actually Bond, makes the trip with the corpse, as does Case. Quietly, so do Wint and Kidd.

Arriving at LAX, Bond connects with CIA's Felix Leiter. Three thugs from Slumber Incorporated pick up the body and Bond in a black hearse, traveling to a funeral home outside Las Vegas. The undertaker, Morton

Slumber, relieves Franks of the diamonds, which Bond deposits in a mausoleum crypt in exchange for an envelope of money—$50,000. But Wint and Kidd knock Bond out and take him away, while Las Vegas comedian Shady Tree retrieves the urn full of diamonds. Wint and Kidd throw 007 into a coffin, with the intent of cremating him alive, but Tree and Slumber stop the process. Bond has switched the diamonds for fakes and will get them—when he receives payment with real money.

In Vegas, the reclusive billionaire Willard Whyte runs the luxurious Whyte House Hotel and Casino. By coincidence, Shady Tree happens to be the featured comic in the Lincoln Lounge there. Bond goes to his dressing room, but Wint and Kidd have been there first—Tree has been chopped down. Casino manager Bert Saxby stops the duo, but the deed is already done.

At the craps table, buxom Plenty O'Toole joins Bond for a roll of the bones. Saxby spots him and phones up to Whyte's penthouse, but the mogul can't be bothered. All he wants is the diamonds. When O'Toole retires with Bond to his room, the Slumber thugs are waiting and toss her out a window into a pool—courtesy of Miss Case, who has made herself comfortable in Bond's bed. She'd like to know what happened to the diamonds, but Bond is keeping his mouth shut. Case convinces Bond to get the diamonds, and the two will run away to Hong Kong.

At the Circus Circus Casino, Bond and Leiter watch as Case retrieves the diamonds, hidden in a stuffed dog. Case slips away from Leiter's men, but Bond finds her at her place. O'Toole, mistaken for Case, has been drowned in the pool. Tiffany knows Bond isn't Franks, and Bond wants to know what she did with the diamonds.

At McCarran Airport, Saxby picks up the stuffed animal, while Bond and Case follow in a sleek red Mustang Fastback. When Saxby stops for gas, he switches vehicles with Dr. Metz, an expert in laser technology, who takes the van while Bond slips into the back. Metz drives to Tectronics, a Willard Whyte research facility in the desert.

Bond sneaks into Metz's lab, where a large satellite is being assembled using the diamonds. When 007 is discovered, he escapes through a NASA moon simulation and out the building in a NASA moon buggy. He leads security cars and all-terrain vehicles through the desert and speeds away with Case, who's waiting outside the fence. On Fremont Street, local sheriffs chase the Mustang, but some fancy driving on two wheels gets Bond and Case out in the clear.

Comfortable in the Whyte House bridal suite, Bond would like to meet with the hotel's owner, but Leiter says no. With his men guarding Case and Bond, 007 decides to make his own introduction to Whyte. Riding outside an elevator to the top of the building, Bond rappels his way into the penthouse—where he finds Blofeld has taken the place of the secluded tycoon. What's worse, there are two Blofelds—one of the clones survived Bond's earlier wrath.

The rogue is using an electronic box to duplicate Whyte's voice, while the real thing is being kept hostage somewhere. Bond takes a chance and kills one of the Blofelds—but he chooses the wrong one. He gasses Bond into unconsciousness, and Wint and Kidd take him into the desert. They dump him into a sewer pipe and drive off. Bond escapes a dangerous automatic welding machine in the pipe and makes his way to the surface.

With Q's help, Bond duplicates Saxby's voice and tricks Blofeld into revealing that Whyte is being held in his own summer home in the desert. Bond and Leiter head out to the house. Alone, Bond runs into Bambi and Thumper, Whyte's comely and athletic bodyguards. At first, it seems Bond will be beaten to a pulp by these women, but he eventually forces them to reveal where they're hiding Whyte. He's freed, but Saxby tries to shoot him. Agents quickly get Saxby with their own weapons, and he tumbles down the hillside, dead.

Dressed as a woman, Blofeld sneaks out of the hotel, grabbing Case as he leaves. Bond, Leiter, and Whyte discover Blofeld has built a command center on an oil rig off the coast of Baja California. NASA has launched the diamond-laden satellite—powering a deadly laser ray—and now he is controlling it as it orbits the globe.

First, he destroys a missile installation in North Dakota. Then, he takes aim on a Soviet submarine, blowing it up underwater. Lastly, he sets his sights on a rocket location somewhere in Red China, where the weapons explode. Blofeld is holding the world's superpowers for ransom, with the highest bidder winning the right to nuclear supremacy.

At the oil installation, Bond arrives by inflatable balloon and is taken prisoner immediately. His plan was to replace the cassette tape that controls the satellite in space. In the control room, Bond switches the tapes. But Case, who has been pretending to be on Blofeld's side, switches them again—actually putting the real tape back in the controller.

Blofeld sets the laser's sights on Washington, D.C., and while time counts down, Bond is locked into a storage room. He escapes while Leiter and military helicopters attack Blofeld's lair. Metz wants to surrender, but Blofeld refuses. Blofeld prepares to make a cowardly escape from the melee in a bathosub, but Bond takes control of its crane and slams it repeatedly into the command center. As everything explodes, Bond and Case dive into the ocean and to safety.

The couple relax on a luxury cruise, courtesy of Willard Whyte, but their amorous evening is interrupted by a waiter and wine steward. Unfortunately, they are Wint and Kidd, and they plan on serving Bond his last meal. Kidd attacks 007 with flaming skewers, but Bond douses him with liquor, and he dives over the railing in flames. Wint then seizes Bond, but 007 shoves a bomb disguised as a cake between Wint's legs and tosses him overboard, where the bomb explodes.

A relieved Case has just one question for Bond—how will they get the diamonds back from space?

Live and Let Die

(1973—British/UNITED ARTISTS—121 MIN/COLOR) Loosely based on the Ian Fleming novel.
DIRECTOR: Guy Hamilton
ORIGINAL MUSIC: George Martin
FILM EDITING: Bert Bates, Raymond Poulton, and John Shirley
ART DIRECTION: Ken Adam
CAST: Roger Moore (007/James Bond)
Yaphet Kotto (Kananga/Mr. Big)
Jane Seymour (Solitaire)
Clifton James (Sheriff J. W. Pepper)
Julius Harris (Tee Hee Johnson)
Geoffrey Holder (Baron Samedi)
David Hedison (Felix Leiter)
Gloria Hendry (Rosie Carver)
Bernard Lee (M)
Lois Maxwell (Miss Moneypenny)
Earl Jolly Brown (Whisper)
Roy Stewart (Quarrel Jr.)

At the UN General Assembly, the UK representative is killed by an electronic signal shot through his headset. In New Orleans, an MI6 agent watches a Dixieland band lead a funeral procession, until it becomes his own—killed by a quiet bystander. In the Caribbean island country of San Monique, a voodoo ceremony ends with the killing of another agent from the bite of a poisonous snake.

Bond receives M and Moneypenny at his apartment for an early-morning wake-up call. While 007 tries to quietly slip his female houseguest out, M assigns him to find out who's behind the killings and why. Bond is off to New York City.

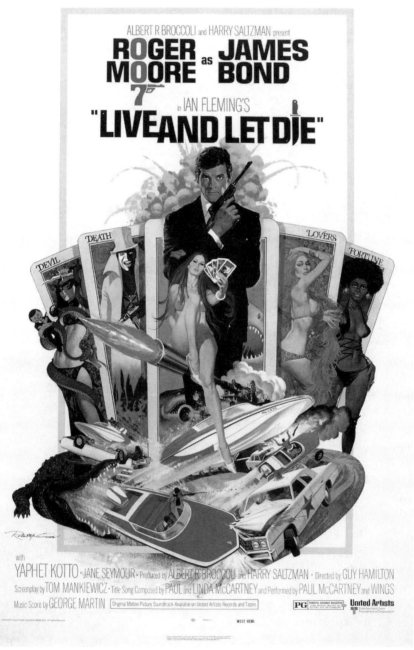

Live and Let Die—US one-sheet poster.

In the Big Apple, 007 is picked up by a CIA agent to meet up with Felix Leiter. But a fancy pimped-out Cadillac pulls alongside their car and kills the driver with a dart to the temple. The car careens through the streets of New York until it crashes into a van.

Meanwhile, the elegant and soft-spoken Dr. Kananga, head of San Monique, arrives at his New York office, accompanied by his beautiful tarot card reader, Solitaire, and the hook-handed Tee Hee. Bond, safe from the accident, stops in a nearby voodoo shop. He sneaks through a back door, where he spots the guilty Cadillac in a parking garage. Solitaire and an entourage of Kananga's men take off in another Cadillac, and Bond grabs a cab to take chase into uptown Harlem.

Arriving at the Fillet of Soul Bar, Bond appears somewhat out of place. Brought into the secret office of Mr. Big, a loud and brash black gangster, Bond finds that Solitaire knows all about him and Mr. Big orders his men to kill 007. A CIA agent comes to his rescue—somehow Kananga and Mr. Big are connected. Bond is off to San Monique.

While the tall, dark, and mysterious Baron Samedi offers voodoo-themed entertainment in the lounge of a San Monique hotel, Bond arrives to discover his "wife" has already checked in. Finding his room empty but full of hidden microphones, Bond hops in the tub for a shave. When someone slips a deadly asp into his bathwater, Bond thinks fast—igniting his spray aftershave with his cigar and searing the snake. "Mrs. Bond" turns out to be Rosie Carver, a new CIA agent sent to help 007. When a voodoo warning scares her, Bond offers his bed as comfort.

The next morning, Bond and Rosie take a fishing charter, run by old friend Quarrel Junior, to see where the MI6 agent was killed. The uncanny Solitaire sees Bond's arrival in her cards and keeps Kananga informed at his estate on the island. And something is shady about Rosie—she's working for Kananga. But before she can talk, she's killed by him. The ruler had a plot to kill Bond underway, but Solitaire's cards didn't tell everything, so it failed. Kananga is angry and wants to know why. He fears his assistant is losing her powers.

Bond parasails behind Quarrel's boat, breaking free and quietly slipping into Kananga's compound. In Solitaire's room, Bond says the tarot cards predict they will be lovers. Solitaire, her abilities apparently based on her long-standing virtue, refuses to believe. Bond seduces her anyway, and she now fears her powers are gone. He convinces her to help him defeat Kananga.

Bond and Solitaire try to escape the island, while Kananga's men watch every move. Bond discovers the leader's poppy fields, hidden under camouflaged nets. Kananga is involved with heroin smuggling. Bond and Solitaire steal a double-decker bus, and local police take off after them. When the bus meets a low bridge, the upper deck comes off and stops the police, while the lower deck drives on to the dock, where Quarrel is waiting. Bond and Solitaire are off to New Orleans.

As luck would have it, Bond and the woman get the same cab driver/ henchman of Mr. Big in the Big Easy as 007 had in New York. Bond hijacks a student plane from the Bleeker Flying School and leads Mr. Big's men on a wild chase through the local airport. Bond escapes them, nearly wrecking the plane in the process.

While Leiter cleans up the aftermath, another agent is killed during a Dixieland funeral. Bond and Leiter find the local Fillet of Soul Bar, and when Felix is called away to the phone, Bond drops through a hole in the floor. He is now face-to-face with Mr. Big. With Solitaire as prisoner, Mr. Big fears Bond has slept with her. Bond will only tell Kananga himself. Pulling off latex prosthetics and a wig, Mr. Big reveals himself to be Kananga.

Using voodoo as a fearful cover, Kananga has grown poppy fields to produce heroin, and as Mr. Big, he will distribute two tons of the drug through the chain of Fillet of Soul Bars—for free. The action will put Mafia suppliers out of business, and then Kananga will have a corner on the heroin market in America.

Kananga tests Solitaire on her ability to read the cards—if she errs, Tee Hee will cut Bond's little finger off. Other extremities will fall if she errs again. Although she fails his test, Kananga has Tee Hee and the enormous Whisper take Bond to a crocodile and alligator farm. Kananga will deal with Solitaire later.

The farm is a cover for heroin processing, and Bond is left as lunch for the toothy reptiles in their pond. As they advance, they happen to form a natural bridge for Bond, and he scampers across their backs to safety. Then he leads them into the processing plant and sets it afire. He hops into a speedboat and takes off into the bayou.

Chased over the water by Kananga's gunslingers, Bond deftly evades them—at one point launching his boat over a roadway, while hick sheriff J. W. Pepper detains one of Kananga's men for speeding. Bond's boat runs out of gas—he grounds it and grabs another. When the chase is over, Bond is in one piece, although various boats and state police cars are not. Sheriff Pepper wonders just whose side Bond is on.

Kananga has escaped back to his island with Solitaire and Baron Samedi. At a voodoo ritual, Solitaire will be the guest of honor, and that's not a good thing. Bond and Quarrel make their way to the island, where Quarrel plants bombs to destroy the poppy fields. Bond watches as Solitaire is tied to a sacrificial altar and a coffin full of poisonous snakes is brought forward. A lifelike mannequin of Baron Samedi rises from a grave, while the native crowd cowers in fear. Bond fires his gun and blows the figure to pieces.

He cuts Solitaire free as the poppy fields explode. Another figure of Baron Samedi rises, but this time it's really him. He attacks Bond with a machete, but is quickly knocked into the coffin of snakes. Bond and Solitaire use the grave's hydraulic platform to reach Kananga's underground base of operations.

Captured by Kananga, Bond and Solitaire are suspended over a shark pond. Using a watch equipped with a powerful magnet, Bond attracts a compressed gas pellet from a desk and the duo are slowly lowered to the water's surface. The watch also has a rotary saw, which cuts through Bond's binding ropes, and he swings free.

Kananga comes at Bond with a knife, and the two fall into the shark pond. As the ferocious fish approach, Bond pulls the pin from the gas pellet and forces it into Kananga's mouth. He swallows it and the gas expands, blowing Kananga to pieces. Bond lowers Solitaire to safety.

Bond and Solitaire hop a train for New York. The vengeful Tee Hee has stowed away, and with Solitaire locked away in a folding berth, he attacks Bond. They struggle and Bond grabs a pair of cuticle clippers. He snips the cables controlling Tee Hee's mechanical arm and tosses the villain off the train through a window.

The lovers bed down as Baron Samedi rides the train's cowcatcher and laughs demonically.

The Man with the Golden Gun

(1974—British/UNITED ARTISTS—125 MIN/COLOR) Loosely based on the Ian
   Fleming novel.
DIRECTOR: Guy Hamilton
ORIGINAL MUSIC: John Barry
FILM EDITING: Raymond Poulton and John Shirley
PRODUCTION DESIGN: Peter Murton
CAST: Roger Moore (007/James Bond)
Christopher Lee (Francisco Scaramanga)
Britt Ekland (Mary Goodnight)
Maud Adams (Andrea Anders)
Herve Villechaize (Nick Nack)
Clifton James (Sheriff J. W. Pepper)
Richard Loo (Hai Fat)
Bernard Lee (M)

Lois Maxwell (Miss Moneypenny)
Desmond Llewelyn (Q)
Soon-Tek Oh (Lt. Hip)
Marne Maitland (Lazar)

Famed assassin Francisco Scaramanga, tall and handsome, relaxes on his private beach with beautiful Andrea Anders, while manservant Nick Nack welcomes an armed thug into the estate to kill Scaramanga. Or is it all sport? The game of cat-and-mouse proceeds into a funhouse-like room, full of mirrors, wax figures—one of James Bond—and sound effects. Amid flashing lights, Scaramanga shoots and kills his stalker.

At MI6 headquarters, M quizzes Bond on his knowledge of Scaramanga, who gets a fee of $1 million per killing. He uses a golden gun and golden bullets—one of which has been delivered to M's office, with Bond's double-oh number engraved in its side. For safety's sake, M pulls Bond from his current mission of locating the Solex Agitator—a device capable of converting solar energy to electricity—and its creator, Gibson. Tracing the death of 002 at the hands of Scaramanga to Beirut, Bond heads there.

He connects with a belly dancer who was with the agent when he was shot. She has kept the spent bullet as a lucky charm, wearing it like a jewel in her navel. Bond accidentally swallows it when attacked by some local toughs. Beating them, he eventually retrieves the bullet, and Q identifies it as a bullet custom-made by an armorer in Macau named Lazar.

Bond finds Lazar and discovers the bullet was made for Scaramanga. A new load is picked up by Anders, and Bond tails her on a hydrofoil transport to Hong Kong harbor. But he loses her when Mary Goodnight, a field operative, shows up.

At the posh Peninsula Hotel, Bond finds Anders and roughly demands to know where he can find Scaramanga. The killer has an appointment at the Bottoms Up Club that evening. Bond will be there. But outside the club, Scaramanga shoots Gibson, and Bond is arrested by Lt. Hip as the killer.

Hip takes Bond to the wreck of the *Queen Elizabeth* ocean liner in Hong Kong harbor. It's actually a field office for MI6, where Bond finds Gibson's device has been stolen from his body after being shot. The shooting may have been orchestrated by a Chinese gangster named Hai Fat, whose heavily guarded complex is in Bangkok.

Bond poses as Scaramanga and meets with Hai Fat. Unfortunately, the real Scaramanga is already there, and Bond may be walking into a trap. That night, Hip drops Bond at Hai Fat's for dinner. Subdued by two sumo wrestlers and Nick Nack, Bond is taken to Hai Fat's dojo, where 007 squares off against several top martial arts students. He crashes through a window to escape and is met by Hip and his two innocent-looking teenaged nieces.

The Man with the Golden Gun—British quad poster

The girls' innocence is a front, as they expertly beat the tar out of more than a dozen kung fu students, with Bond and Hip joining in the melee. Hip and the girls take off by car, as Bond hops into a small speedboat and races down a canal. On the way, he splashes a tour boat, occupied by Sheriff J. W. Pepper and the missus, who just happen to be on vacation.

Scaramanga assembles his golden gun, disguised as simple items like a fountain pen, a cigarette lighter, a cigarette case, and a cuff link. Once done, he kills Hai Fat and now holds the Solex Agitator—and control over Hai Fat's empire.

Bond dines with Goodnight, then prepares for a romantic evening with her. The tryst is interrupted by Miss Anders, who warns Bond of Scaramanga's intent to kill him. It was she who sent the 007 bullet to MI6. Anders needs Bond's help to escape from the assassin, and 007 needs Anders to retrieve the solar device. Bond resumes his romancing, this time with Anders, while Goodnight hides in the closet.

Bond meets Anders at a mixed martial arts match, but she's been shot dead through the heart. Bond rifles through her purse, looking for the device, when Scaramanga boldly sits down next to Bond, revealing he couldn't find the Solex Agitator either. Nick Nack holds a gun to Bond's back when he spies the solar device on the ground. He sneaks it into his hand and passes it to Lt. Hip, disguised as a peanut vendor, who then passes it to Goodnight.

Scaramanga and Nick Nack leave, and Goodnight, placing a homer in the trunk, is tossed in by the killer. Bond steals a car from an auto showroom—a car conveniently occupied by a potential buyer known as Sheriff J. W. Pepper. The two race off to follow Scaramanga, who's made his way to the other side of the canal. Bond runs his car onto a twisted dock—sending the vehicle into a full 360-degree roll—and landing on the other side. The villains duck into a deserted warehouse. As local police arrive to arrest Bond and Pepper, Scaramanga attaches wings and a jet engine to his car and flies off, with Goodnight still in the trunk.

Scaramanga's hideout is located on a small island off the coast of China. Bond flies in, low under Chinese radar, and lands his sea plane near the island. Scaramanga and Nick Nack welcome him with champagne and offer pleasantries. With Goodnight held hostage, Scaramanga gives Bond a firsthand view of his Solex-powered energy plant, run with superconductors cooled by liquid helium. The villain has intentions of selling the technology to the highest bidder. Scaramanga also demonstrates the power of a solar ray gun by blowing up the plane Bond came in on.

The killer has dreamed of going one-on-one with Bond in a gun duel. Back to back, the shootists line up on the beach. Nick Nack begins the count, but when Bond turns and fires, Scaramanga has disappeared. The hunt for the killer leads to the funhouse once more. Bond loses his Walther and must take Scaramanga on unarmed. When the assassin passes the wax figure of Bond, it turns out to be the real thing, and, using the wax figure's gun, he shoots Scaramanga dead.

When Goodnight knocks a plant technician into a vat of liquid helium, it upsets the delicate temperature balance of the generators and threatens to destroy the whole island. Bond struggles to retrieve the Solex Agitator and, with Goodnight's help, grabs it from its fittings. As the island explodes, Bond and Goodnight hop a Chinese junk and escape. But Nick Nack has stowed away and attacks 007 with a knife. Bond traps him in a suitcase, tethers him to a mainsail mast, and takes Goodnight to bed.

The Spy Who Loved Me

(1977—British/UNITED ARTISTS—125 MIN/COLOR) Loosely based on the Ian Fleming novel.
DIRECTOR: Lewis Gilbert
ORIGINAL MUSIC: Marvin Hamlisch
FILM EDITING: John Glen
PRODUCTION DESIGN: Ken Adam
CAST: Roger Moore (007/James Bond)

Barbara Bach (Major Anya Amasova/Agent XXX)
Curt Jurgens (Karl Stromberg)
Richard Kiel (Jaws)
Caroline Munro (Naomi)
Walter Gotell (General Anatol Gogol)
Milton Reid (Sandor)
Geoffrey Keen (Sir Frederick Gray)
Bernard Lee (M)
Lois Maxwell (Miss Moneypenny)
Desmond Llewelyn (Q)
Edward De Souza (Sheikh Hosein)
Vernon Dobtcheff (Max Kalba)

A British nuclear sub has disappeared. In Moscow, General Gogol hears similar news about one of their Russian subs. Agent XXX, Major Anya Amasova, is assigned to investigate. In London, M assigns their best agent—James Bond—to look into their sub's disappearance as well.

In Austria, Bond skis down a mountainside, chased by Russian agents. Evading their gunfire, Bond fires a ski pole–rifle and kills one of his pursuers—who just happens to be the lover of Agent XXX. Reaching a sheer cliff, Bond skis off it and pulls a ripcord, releasing a billowing parachute—emblazoned with the Union Jack.

Gogol sends Amasova to Cairo, but before she leaves, he also has the unenviable task of informing her of her lover's death. Vengefully, she wants to meet the British agent who is responsible.

At a British naval briefing, Q notes that the wake of a submarine can now be traced, much like the heat-signature of a missile in flight. It's feared the Russians may have this technology and are suspected of hijacking the Brit sub. Bond is off to Cairo to trace the source of the technology.

In his undersea headquarters, Karl Stromberg pays $10 million each to two scientists responsible for designing and building the submarine tracking system. But Stromberg's mistress has tried to sell microfilm of the plans, so he feeds her to the sharks.

With a press of a button, Stromberg can raise his Atlantis headquarters to the ocean's surface. He orders his two henchmen—the broad and brawny Sandor and enormous, metal-toothed Jaws—to kill anyone associated with the microfilm. Stromberg also coldheartedly kills the scientists.

In Egypt, Bond finds an old college friend, Sheikh Hosein, who gives him the name of Aziz Fekkesh, a man who has contact with Max Kalba. Kalba has been trying to sell the microfilm. Looking for Fekkesh, 007 is ambushed by Sandor. Chased to a Cairo rooftop, Bond gets Fekkesh's location—the Pyramids—before letting Sandor fall to his death.

Fekkesh is with Agent XXX at the Pyramids. When the Egyptian spots Jaws in the shadows, he bolts. But Jaws catches up with the man and kills him with his chrome-plated teeth. Bond finds Fekkesh's body and gets the address for Kalba from a notebook—the Kasava Club. Anya accuses Bond of killing Fekkesh, but is interrupted by two Russian assailants. Bond quickly dispatches them and bids goodnight to Amasova.

Later, Bond and Amasova meet up at the Kasava Club, where it's obvious they've been studying each other's dossiers. Both meet Kalba and compete to buy the microfilm. Before the deal can be made, Jaws kills Kalba and gets the microfilm. Bond and Amasova hop into Jaws' getaway van. Driving through the night, the van arrives at ancient ruins in the desert. Stalking Jaws, the pair become the hunted as the giant attacks them. Pulling her gun, Amasova gets the microfilm, and the duo escape from Jaws.

In an MI6 field office, located inside the Abu Simbel Temple, Bond finds Gogol, and the Russians have joined forces with M and the Brits to locate their missing subs. The microfilm reveals a connection to industrialist Karl Stromberg. Bond and Agent XXX are headed to his facility in Sardinia.

On the train there, a hiding Jaws assaults Amasova, but Bond subdues him and kicks him off the train. Bond and Anya spend the night and arrive in Sardinia, where Q gives them a sporty Lotus Esprit. Met at the beach by the beautiful Naomi—Stromberg's assistant—Bond and Amasova pose as husband and wife, with 007 as a marine biologist, in order to meet Stromberg.

James and Anya marvel at the grandeur of Atlantis as they arrive. Naomi gives Anya the tour as Bond meets Stromberg. He believes that living underwater is the only hope for the future of the world. As Bond and Amasova leave, they note a model of Stromberg's latest development—the *Liparus,* an enormous supertanker ship. Stromberg orders Jaws to kill them both once they are ashore.

Cruising in the Lotus, the duo are tailed by a motorcycle with sidecar. The sidecar is released with a roar from its onboard rocket motor—it misses the Lotus and blows up a semi rig. The cyclist flies through a guardrail and crashes below, but a dark sedan—with Jaws inside—picks up the chase. Bond lowers his rear license plate and shoots a load of concrete onto the windshield of the pursuer. It careens out of control and crashes, nose down, into a village hut. Jaws, a bit dusty but otherwise fine, emerges from the house as its owner curses in Italian.

A helicopter, piloted by Naomi and its machine guns blazing, takes the trail of the Lotus. Bond drives the car off the pier into the sea, but not to worry—the Lotus converts into a mini-sub. He fires a surface-to-air missile and blows the helicopter out of the sky. Cruising the water's depths, the Lotus is challenged by Stromberg's scuba divers with armed sea sleds. Bond and Amasova eliminate the intruders, and—to the amazement of sunbathers—they drive up on the sands of the local beach and off to their hotel.

Anya discovers it was Bond who killed her lover. Once their mission is complete, she vows to kill Bond.

Bond and Amasova are airlifted to a US submarine. As they prepare to board Stromberg's *Liparus,* the sub is hijacked by the supertanker, its bow opening up to swallow the sub into the hold. Alongside it are the Brit and Soviet subs. As the crew disembarks, Bond and Amasova are brought to Stromberg.

His plan is now clear—Stromberg will launch the Polaris nuclear missiles onboard two of the subs to attack New York and Moscow, creating international panic. The world above the seas will destroy itself, with his new undersea world surviving. The Russian and British subs are sent on their deadly missions.

Stromberg takes off to Atlantis with Anya in a speedboat, while Bond escapes his captors and rallies the captured Allied sailors to revolt against the *Liparus'* crew. Explosions rattle the supertanker, and bodies fly as the crew is quickly subdued, even though the command center remains sealed. Bond removes the detonator from a Polaris missile and uses it to blow a hole in the command center gates, and the sailors pour in. But the subs are on target to launch their missiles in three minutes. Bond reprograms the subs' targets, and they launch on each other, destroying themselves.

The *Liparus* begins to break up with explosions, and the remaining sailors climb into the US sub, torpedoing their way out of the bow of the ship. As the sub clears the *Liparus,* the supertanker continues to explode as it sinks.

The Pentagon has ordered Atlantis destroyed, but Bond must rescue Anya first. With a jet-ski sent from Q, 007 makes his way to Atlantis. Confronting Stromberg in his dining room, Bond shoots him dead. Jaws threatens 007, but a huge industrial magnet traps Jaws by the teeth, and Bond feeds him to the sharks—although the giant wins the fight and swims away.

Bond frees Anya as torpedoes strike Atlantis. Water engulfs the two as they make their way into an escape bathysphere. Whiling away their time under the sheets, Bond and Anya—who's given second thoughts to killing Bond—are caught by M and Gogol as the vessel is loaded onto the deck of a British destroyer.

Moonraker

(1979—British/UNITED ARTISTS—126 MIN/COLOR) Loosely based on the Ian
   Fleming novel.
DIRECTOR: Lewis Gilbert
ORIGINAL MUSIC: John Barry
FILM EDITING: John Glen
PRODUCTION DESIGN: Ken Adam
CAST: Roger Moore (007/James Bond)
Lois Chiles (Dr. Holly Goodhead)
Michael Lonsdale (Hugo Drax)
Richard Kiel (Jaws)
Corinne Cléry (Corinne Dufour)
Bernard Lee (M)
Geoffrey Keen (Sir Frederick Gray)
Lois Maxwell (Miss Moneypenny)
Desmond Llewelyn (Q)
Blanche Ravalec (Dolly, Jaws' Girlfriend)
Walter Gotell (General Gogol)

Two stowaways hop into the cockpit of a Moonraker space shuttle, mounted
piggyback on a 747 jet. Firing its booster engines, the shuttle flies off,
destroying the jet in its wake. MI6 needs Bond to investigate, but he's busy
being thrown out of an airplane by Jaws—last seen swimming away from
Stromberg's Atlantis.

Without a parachute, 007's only hope is to reach the pilot, who has
already jumped. Bond wrestles the chute away from the pilot, but Jaws is
now soaring toward him. Bond breaks away—as does Jaws' ripcord handle.
Flapping his arms in an attempt to fly, Jaws finally lands on a circus big top,
breaking his fall.

Arriving at MI6 headquarters, Bond is briefed by M and Q on the
Moonraker hijacking, determining that the California plant where the
shuttles are built is a good place to start. Once there, Bond is ferried by helicopter to Drax Industries, thanks to the beautiful pilot, Corinne Dufour.
Bond gets a bird's-eye view of the immense and magnificent Drax estate—
everything owned by industrialist Hugo Drax.

Drax receives Bond, expecting an apology for the loss of his shuttle.
Bond corrects him, pointing out he builds them for the US government.
Dufour takes the agent into the plant, as Drax quietly urges his servant
Chang to ensure that Bond gets in harm's way.

Bond meets Dr. Holly Goodhead, a NASA scientist heading up Drax's operations. Bond gets the chance to try out a zero-gravity simulator, but the machine is pushed into the red by Chang. Bond nears a fatal twelve G's, but is able to shut the machine down at the last minute. Shaken but not stirred, Bond staggers out of the room.

Romancing Dufour in her bedroom, Bond makes his way to Drax's safe and cracks it. He photographs the contents with a spy camera and leaves Dufour—with Chang watching all the time.

At a pheasant hunt on the grounds, a sniper climbs a tree to assassinate Bond. With gun in hand, 007 appears to miss his pheasant, but scores a direct hit on the sniper. As Bond leaves for the airport, Drax sets his hounds on Dufour as punishment for aiding 007, killing her.

Bond arrives in Venice, visiting a glass-blowing firm and museum. Spotting Goodhead on a tour, Bond finds she is addressing an international space conference there. Taking a relaxing gondola ride on the Venice canals, Bond is attacked and turns the quaint gondola into a high-powered speedboat. Approaching shore, 007 deploys an airbag under the boat, and it becomes a hovercraft, speeding through St. Mark's Square and away from his pursuers.

Bond makes his way into a secret lab, where strange vials of liquid are loaded into glass forms he saw at the glass plant. When one of the vials breaks, Bond watches as two technicians die—while lab rats remain alive.

In the glass museum, Chang attacks 007, and the resulting carnage will take a while to clean up. Bond finally beats Chang, throwing him through a stained-glass window and into the middle of an evening opera performance. Intermission is quickly taken.

Sneaking into Goodhead's bedroom, Bond finds she is actually a CIA operative planted to keep an eye on Drax. The pair agree to collaborate—personally and professionally. Bond notes the woman has a plane ticket to Rio.

Curiously, when Bond summons M to personally see the secret lab, it turns out to be gone, replaced by a grand ballroom—with Drax inside. The British government is forced to quickly offer its apologies. But Bond offers a sample of the secret vial's contents to M, proving the lab really was there once. Bond is next off to Rio de Janeiro, while Drax hires Jaws to replace Chang.

Bond gets local help in Rio from Manuela, a field agent. While a carnival fills the streets, Bond and Manuela find a local import/export company where Drax shipments have been moving through. A large costumed partier turns out to be Jaws, and he attacks Manuela, but before he can put the bite on her, he's swept away in a mass of jolly revelers.

Taking a cable car from the top of Rio's Sugarloaf Mountain, Bond and Goodhead are stopped by Jaws, who bites through the cable with his steel teeth. Jaws rides another car toward the first, then jumps onto theirs to attack Bond and Goodhead. The two team up to trap the giant inside the car while they slide down the cable on a chain. As the car races toward them, they jump to safety, and the cable car crashes into the base station. Jaws pulls himself from the wreckage, as a pretty and buxom young lady in braids—Dolly—comes to his aid. They walk off, hand in hand.

Bond and Goodhead are taken hostage in an ambulance, but Bond is able to escape. Dressed as a gaucho, he finds Moneypenny, Q, and M in a field office. Q Branch has identified a sample of the liquid Bond recovered from the lab in Venice. It's a highly toxic nerve agent—to humans only—made from a rare orchid found in the Amazon rain forest.

Using a heavily armed speedboat from Q, Bond makes his way down the river, quickly assaulted by enemy speedboats, with Jaws at the helm of one. With mines and heat-seeking torpedoes, 007 evades the attackers until a sheer waterfall threatens to crush Bond. He unveils a parasail and soars to safety. Jaws is not quite as fortunate and tumbles over the falls.

Deep in the jungle, Bond spies a bevy of beautiful women in a lush setting, but is quickly thrown into a pond and grabbed by a deadly python snake. Killing it, he climbs out—right into the hands of Jaws and Drax. Bond is led into Drax's control center, where he watches the launch of several Moonraker shuttles. Bond and Goodhead are placed directly beneath the nozzles of a shuttle booster, where Drax expects them to die when the rocket lifts off. They escape through a ventilation shaft just in time.

Dressed as astronaut-pilots, Bond and Goodhead board a Moonraker shuttle and blast into space. Six shuttles have carried virile young men and women to Drax's space station, where the villain will create a new master race of superhumans. He will use the nerve gas to eliminate everyone in the world, leaving his population perfect.

Bond and Goodhead remove a radar-jamming device, and the space station is now visible to Earth and the military. Russian KGB head Gogol is notified that the US is sending a shuttle immediately to investigate. On the space station, Jaws finds the agents, and they are taken prisoners.

But as Drax prepares to throw the duo into the vast vacuum of space, Bond cleverly notes that Drax desires a perfect world—obviously, a world with no room for a giant like Jaws and a small woman like Dolly. The consequences give Jaws pause to ponder their future together, and he mutinies, becoming a prisoner like Bond and Goodhead. As a laser prepares to blow the US shuttle out of space, Bond flips a switch to stop the space station's rotation, throwing all aboard into weightless panic.

Drax's armed crew ventures out into space, engaging the US forces in a laser battle. As the soldiers enter the station, Bond, Goodhead, and Jaws stage their own attack. As Drax prepares to kill 007, Bond disables him, and he's thrown out into space to die.

The space station begins to break apart, and the US shuttle leaves. Bond and Goodhead try to take off in one of the other shuttles, aiming to stop three nerve gas pods before they reach Earth, but their release bolts are jammed. Jaws and Dolly toast each other with champagne on the doomed space station, and in a last noble effort, the big man sets the stuck shuttle free.

With an onboard laser, Bond destroys the pods. In the weightlessness of space, Bond and Goodhead romance as onboard cameras beam the scene to M, Q, the White House, and Buckingham Palace.

For Your Eyes Only

(1981—British/UNITED ARTISTS—127 MIN/COLOR) Loosely based on the Ian
  Fleming short stories "For Your Eyes Only" and "Risico."
DIRECTOR: John Glen
ORIGINAL MUSIC: Bill Conti
FILM EDITING: John Grover
PRODUCTION DESIGN: Peter Lamont
CAST: Roger Moore (007/James Bond)
Carole Bouquet (Melina Havelock)
Topol (Milos Columbo)
Lynn-Holly Johnson (Bibi Dahl)
Julian Glover (Kristatos)
Michael Gothard (Locque)
Cassandra Harris (Lisl)
John Wyman (Eric Kriegler)
Geoffrey Keen (Minister of Defence)
Lois Maxwell (Miss Moneypenny)
Desmond Llewelyn (Q)
Walter Gotell (General Gogol)
James Villiers (Tanner)
John Moreno (Ferrara)

A somber James Bond visits the grave of his beloved Teresa. A helicopter, sent by MI6, picks Bond up at the cemetery. But a bald man stroking a white cat sits in a wheelchair, with a console at his fingertips. He remotely kills the pilot and takes control of the chopper. Toying with Bond, he recklessly

For Your Eyes Only—US one-sheet poster.

swoops the copter over rooftops. But Bond is able to reach the cockpit and disables the remote. Taking the controls, he snatches the disabled villain with one of the copter's runners and dumps him down a smokestack.

The *St. Georges* fishing trawler is actually a British surveillance vessel off the coast of Albania, equipped with ATAC—Automatic Targeting Attack Communicator—a defense system used to control the Royal Navy's nuclear subs. The ship is torpedoed and sinks, with all hands aboard lost. In Moscow, KGB general Gogol seeks to recover the ATAC for Russia's use.

Beautiful Melina Havelock arrives by seaplane to join her parents on a yacht they use for their marine archaeological studies. But the plane's pilot, a Cuban assassin named Gonzalez, fires his machine guns and kills Melina's parents.

With M on leave, Bond meets with the minister of defense and Bill Tanner, chief of staff. If the ATAC were to fall into the wrong hands, the Brit subs could be forced to target each other. The Havelocks had been asked to quietly locate the device, but were killed before anything could be learned. Under the name of Operation Undertow, Bond is assigned to find out who hired Gonzalez to kill the Havelocks.

In Madrid, Bond is caught spying on Gonzalez's estate, where an unknown figure delivers a suitcase of money as payment for the Havelocks' killing. When Gonzalez dives into his pool, he's struck and killed with an arrow. In the confusion, Bond escapes and runs into Melina Havelock, who happens to be holding a crossbow. They take off in Melina's less-than-trustworthy yellow Citroen, and despite its shortcomings, the pair evade their pursuers.

MI6 is not happy with Bond, since Gonzalez was killed. But, using a device known as an Identigraph, Bond and Q are able to describe and identify the man who gave the killer the money. His name is Emile Locque, a known criminal and killer. Bond is off to Cortina, in northern Italy, to find him.

At the top of Mount Tofana, Bond meets up with local contact Ferrara. They travel to the Olympic Ice Rink, where they find Aris Kristatos, a wealthy Greek informant for MI6. He is the benefactor for a promising but precocious young ice skater named Bibi Dahl. Locque is employed by a Greek gangster named Milos Columbo, part of a crime syndicate known as the Dove.

Bond spies Melina purchasing a crossbow, and two motorcyclists try to run her down. Bond saves her and finds she's been summoned to Cortina by a fake telegram. She wants the man who hired Gonzalez, but Bond needs to know more. The agent tells Melina to return to Corfu.

Back at his hotel room, Bond refuses the seduction efforts of Bibi Dahl, and they attend the biathlon, where brawny Eric Kriegler is the East German champ. Bond skis off into the woods, where gunmen, including Kriegler, attack. Locque is also on the prowl for 007, but Bond escapes the threat.

Bond stops at the ice rink to ask Bibi about Kriegler, but when she leaves, hockey thugs attack 007. He beats them, scoring a hat trick with their bodies. At Bond's car, he finds Ferrara dead, with a pin of the Dove in his hand.

In Corfu, Kristatos warns Bond that he may have to kill Columbo, who happens to be seated in the same restaurant. Columbo overhears the conversation and has an argument with his escort, Countess Lisl. She leaves in a huff, and Bond escorts her home.

On the beach the next morning, a dune buggy driven by Locque strikes and kills Lisl. He drives off as Bond is taken aboard a sailing ship owned by Columbo. The gangster reveals that Kristatos has been lying; Locque works for him, not Columbo. He is the drug smuggler, not Columbo. Bond believes him and drinks to their association.

Columbo and his men, accompanied by Bond, attack one of Kristatos' ports of operation. In the melee, Bond spots Locque and gives chase. He wounds Locque, and the villain's car skids to a precarious point on the edge of a cliff. Bond vengefully kicks the car off the cliff, and it smashes to pieces.

Bond and Havelock review her father's notes concerning the ATAC. Using a special two-person *Neptune* research submarine, the pair search the ocean floor and find the sunken *St. Georges*. They don deep-sea diving gear and venture out into the water. They recover the ATAC, but an intruder in a JIM deep-sea suit enters, takes the ATAC, and threatens to kill Bond and Melina. Bond grabs the ATAC and fixes a time bomb to the JIM suit. The pair make it safely back to the *Neptune* as the bomb explodes on the diver.

A small one-person sub then approaches and begins to pull the *Neptune* apart with its vice-grip arms. Bond forces it into the gaping hole in the *St. Georges*, trapping it, and the duo escape to the surface. On the Havelock boat, Kristatos has boarded and takes the ATAC, with Kriegler as the bagman for the KGB.

Meanwhile, Bond and Melina are bound together and dragged behind a fishing boat. Bond is cut by the coral, and his blood attracts sharks. But he's able to wrap the tether line around some rocks and break free. Using a scuba tank Melina left below earlier, Bond and the woman are able to convince Kristatos they're dead, and he leaves.

In a Greek Orthodox church, Bond meets Q in a confessional, where they discuss Kristatos' possible escape to somewhere called St. Cyril. Q notes there are hundreds of them, but Bond is sure Columbo will know where the villain has gone.

Bond, Melina, Columbo, and a few of his men arrive at the base of St. Cyril, a monastery isolated by sheer cliffs and accessible only by a basket elevator. Bond scales one of the cliff walls with pitons and climbing ropes. As he reaches the top, a guard kicks him off, and only his climbing rope saves him. The guard climbs down to remove the pitons, but Bond kills him with a throwing knife. The secret agent reaches the basket house and lowers it to his party.

Kristatos and Kriegler wait for Gogol to arrive by helicopter. Meanwhile, Bibi Dahl and her coach have tired of Kristatos' shabby treatment and seek to leave. Bond agrees to help them get out if they will help him to get in. Most of Kristatos' men are captured in a surprise raid on their quarters as the helicopter arrives.

Bond fights with Kriegler, who topples out a window to his death. Columbo and Kristatos wrestle, and as Kristatos prepares to ambush Bond, Columbo kills him with a knife. Gogol wants the ATAC, but Bond wisely throws it over the cliffs, smashing it to pieces—no one will have it. Gogol laughs approvingly and leaves. Bibi and her coach tend to the injured Columbo.

Bond and Melina enjoy a midnight swim from a boat, while a mimicking parrot—believed to be Bond—receives well wishes and congratulations from the prime minister.

Octopussy

(1983—British/UNITED ARTISTS—131 MIN/COLOR) Loosely based on the Ian
  Fleming short story.
DIRECTOR: John Glen
ORIGINAL MUSIC: John Barry
FILM EDITING: John Grover, Peter Davies, and Henry Richardson
PRODUCTION DESIGN: Peter Lamont
CAST: Roger Moore (007/James Bond)
Maud Adams (Octopussy)
Louis Jourdan (Kamal Khan)
Kristina Wayborn (Magda)
Kabir Bedi (Gobinda)
Steven Berkoff (General Orlov)
David Meyer (Mishka)
Anthony Meyer (Grishka)
Desmond Llewelyn (Q)

Robert Brown (M)
Lois Maxwell (Miss Moneypenny)
Geoffrey Keen (Minister of Defence)
Walter Gotell (General Gogol)
Vijay Amritraj (Vijay)

In a military-run Latin American country, James Bond assumes the guise of Army colonel Toro, aided by a dark and beautiful woman. Bond is caught in a hangar—trying to plant a bomb in the nose of a radar-equipped jet—by the real Toro. Taken away in a military truck, Bond is followed by his accomplice, who is towing a horse trailer. While she distracts the guards, Bond hops into their getaway car and opens the trailer in back. The horse is really a protective cover for a miniature jet. Bond soars into the sky, deftly evading a surface-to-air missile. He flies through the hangar as soldiers try to quickly close the doors. He slips out the front, but the missile does not make it, exploding and destroying Bond's original target. When his plane runs low on fuel, Bond lands, pulls into a gas station, and, in a blasé manner, says, "Fill it up, please."

In East Germany, a clown runs for his life, finding nothing funny about being chased by knife-throwing twins Mishka and Grishka. Reaching the border of East and West Germany, he is mortally wounded, but makes his way to the British Embassy. As he dies, the clown—MI6 agent 009—reveals an elegant Fabergé egg in his hand.

Octopussy—British quad poster.

At MI6 headquarters, Bond finds the egg, made for Russian royalty, was actually a fake—the real egg is going up for auction at Sotheby's. The Russians may be behind the sale, and Bond takes on Operation Trove to investigate the mystery.

A meeting of Russian military and government leaders reveals a split in opinions. General Gogol recommends continued talks with NATO for peaceful weapons disarmament, but the hawkish General Orlov—commander of the East German territory—proposes an all-out attack on Europe.

At Sotheby's, the egg is purchased by handsome Kamal Khan for £500,000, after Bond runs the price up on him—and switches the real egg with the fake. Khan leaves with his beautiful assistant, Magda, and his huge bearded bodyguard, Gobinda.

Bond, with the real egg, tails Khan to India. Once there, 007 connects with Vijay, a field operative whose cover is that of a tennis instructor at Khan's club. Bond engages Khan in a game of backgammon, seeing he's a cheat. Bond outfoxes him and, putting the egg up as security, wins big.

Bond and Vijay head off in a tuk-tuk through the crowded streets, while Gobinda follows with shotgun in hand. Bond hot-foots it over glowing coals, then escapes the henchman by throwing his winnings from Khan into the streets. Q Branch has a field office nearby, and Bond has a homing device placed into the egg.

Bond dines with the beautiful Magda, who relays an offer from Khan—the egg for 007's life. He beds the lady, then watches as she escapes out the window with the egg—just what Bond intended. Gobinda then subdues 007, while Khan arrives at an island in a boat helmed by beautiful women. He shows the recovered egg to Octopussy, the original owner.

At Khan's palace, Bond joins his host and Magda for dinner. Khan wants answers and will get them from Bond, one way or another. With an acid-filled pen, Bond breaks out of his room and carefully climbs along the parapet. He sees General Orlov arrive by helicopter and ducks through Magda's room unnoticed.

Orlov and Khan meet, where the Russian receives counterfeit Soviet relics made by Khan in exchange for the real items supplied by Orlov. Destroying the fake egg, the general orders 007 killed. Bond heads into the jungle as Khan and Gobinda hunt him safari-style from elephant-back. Avoiding the hunters, as well as natural killers in the wild, Bond escapes.

Using a submarine disguised as an alligator from Q, Bond gets to Octopussy's floating palace, a place for women only—Octopussy is a woman of great wealth. He finds her, and she relates that one of Bond's previous missions involved her father and how Bond had treated him with respect.

With the lady an apparent ally of 007, Khan finds himself as the odd man out. Bond will be Octopussy's guest for a while.

Khan hires local thugs—one with a large yo-yo made of saw blades—to kill Bond. On her island, Octopussy reveals her wealth is based on diamond smuggling as well as legitimate businesses like carnivals and circuses. She also heads up the Octopus Cult—a haven for women who need spiritual direction in their lives.

Vijay is killed with the yo-yo-saw as he stands guard on the mainland. Bond romances Octopussy and they barely escape the saw. Bond and Octopussy team up to stop the intruders, and 007 takes the alligator back to the mainland.

Bond heads to Karl-Marx-Stadt, east of Berlin, where Octopussy's circus is scheduled to appear for Soviet troops. At the circus, Octopussy is joined by Khan, Gobinda—and General Orlov. When the show tears down for its next stop—a US Air Force base in West Germany—Bond slips onto the circus train. But Gogol is now on to the fake jewelry scam and is looking for Orlov. The general's plan is to detonate an atomic bomb at the circus, escalating the tensions he desires between East and West while weakening Europe's defenses. Bond has four hours to stop it.

On the train, Bond barely escapes Mishka, one of the knife-throwers, and kills him. But he confronts Orlov and chases him off the train. Needing to get back on, Bond drives alongside and hops onto a boxcar. He hides in a gorilla costume as soldiers search the train at the border. Gogol catches Orlov as he runs after the departing train and is killed by machine-gun fire.

Gobinda chases Bond to the rooftops of the train's cars, where Grishka joins the fight and he and Bond are thrown from the train. Seeking vengeance for killing Mishka, Grishka corners Bond, but 007 turns the tables, killing Grishka—as vengeance for killing 009.

The circus arrives to cheering crowds, while Bond hoofs it to the base—until a large couple picks him up in a small VW. But Bond then steals a car and ends up evading the police as he barrels onto the base. Meanwhile, Khan and Gobinda make their excuses to Octopussy and the US general at the circus and quickly leave.

Bond changes into a clown outfit and makeup to escape the police, with only five minutes left before the bomb goes off. Bond winds up in the center ring, then implores the US general to evacuate the tents before the bomb goes off. Octopussy identifies Bond, and he's allowed to disarm the bomb. Everyone at the circus is safe.

Khan and Gobinda plan to leave India, but Octopussy's circus troupe invades the palace, using guile, acrobatics, and sheer force. She confronts Khan, but Gobinda grabs her and they get away. Bond and Q arrive on the scene via hot-air balloon. Bond takes off after Khan, while Q entertains the women at the palace.

Khan, Gobinda, and hostage Octopussy take off in a prop plane, but not before Bond jumps onto the tail. Reluctantly, Gobinda agrees to go out and tangle with Bond as they soar thousands of feet in the air. Bond sends Gobinda off the plane to meet his maker and gets into the cockpit as the plane makes a rough landing. He grabs Octopussy and they jump out, as the plane careens out of control and crashes into a hillside.

Officially, General Gogol denies any of the events, but East and West agree to continue friendly relations. Meanwhile, Bond and Octopussy find a way to occupy themselves on her boat.

A View to a Kill

(1985—British/UNITED ARTISTS—131 MIN/COLOR) Loosely based on the Ian
 Fleming short story "From a View to a Kill."
DIRECTOR: John Glen
ORIGINAL MUSIC: John Barry
FILM EDITING: Peter Davies
PRODUCTION DESIGN: Peter Lamont
CAST: Roger Moore (007/James Bond)
Christopher Walken (Max Zorin)
Tanya Roberts (Stacey Sutton)
Grace Jones (May Day)
Patrick Macnee (Sir Godfrey Tibbett)
Patrick Bauchau (Scarpine)
Alison Doody (Jenny Flex)
David Yip (Chuck Lee)
Willoughby Gray (Dr. Carl Mortner)
Desmond Llewelyn (Q)
Robert Brown (M)
Lois Maxwell (Miss Moneypenny)
Geoffrey Keen (Minister of Defence)
Walter Gotell (General Gogol)
Jean Rougerie (Achille Aubergine)
Daniel Benzali (Howe)

In the frozen snows of Siberia, James Bond recovers a microchip from murdered Agent 003. Soviet soldiers chase 007, and, taking a broken ski from a destroyed snowmobile, he snowboards his way to safety aboard a submarine disguised as an iceberg.

At MI6 headquarters, Q reveals a new microchip that would be unaffected by the electromagnetic field created by a nuclear blast—which renders all chips useless. The chip Bond recovered in Siberia is identical, so the KGB must have a connection to the chip's developer—now owned by Zorin Industries. Its owner, Max Zorin, is a well-respected industrialist.

At Ascot Race Track, Pegasus, a horse owned by Zorin, wins the big race but under suspicious means, according to Sir Godfrey Tibbett, a former horse trainer now working with MI6. When the winning horse bolts, May Day—Zorin's exotic associate—calms the beast. Tibbett has a French detective friend, Achille Aubergine, who is investigating Zorin's horses.

In Paris, Bond meets the detective at the Eiffel Tower. Drugs are suspected, but before he can say more, Aubergine is killed by May Day. Bond chases her to the top of the tower, but she parachutes to freedom. Bond steals a taxi and follows the chute. Day lands in the Seine River, zooming away in a speedboat steered by Zorin.

Bond and Tibbett attend a horse sale held by Zorin at his impressive stables. Posing as James St. John Smythe and his chauffeur, the duo arrive in a silver Rolls-Royce and are met by Scarpine, head of Zorin's security. Bond finds his guest room—conveniently bugged—with the help of the beautiful Jenny Flex, one of Zorin's aides. Tibbett notes that Pegasus has disappeared from his stall.

At an evening reception, Bond sneaks into Zorin's office and discovers he's written a $5 million check to Stacey Sutton. He then meets Dr. Mortner, a horse-breeding consultant for Zorin. Bond tries to make the acquaintance of Sutton, but she coldly snubs him—with the interference of May Day.

Bond and Tibbett find Zorin's hidden laboratory, where Pegasus is being kept. Bond discovers Zorin's secret—he implants a chip into the horse, controlling a steroid injection with a switch in a jockey's whip. They also find Zorin's enormous warehouse of microchips.

Bond and May Day share a bed, and Zorin discovers Bond is not who he claims to be and challenges him to a steeplechase. Tibbett leaves to contact MI6, but May Day kills him in a local car wash. The steeplechase race between Bond and Zorin is spirited—and crooked—and with a press of a button on Zorin's crop, Bond's horse bolts into the woods, and he is captured by the villain and his men. Day pushes the Rolls into a lake to drown Bond, but he swims to the surface and escapes.

KGB general Gogol visits Zorin at his empty race track. As a former KGB agent, Zorin's bold and commercial activities are not appreciated by the general and the current heads of the agency. Another KGB agent refers to Zorin as a "biological experiment," as Gogol reminds Zorin that "no one ever leaves the KGB."

Aboard a Zorin Industries airship over San Francisco, the villain meets with his investors and reveals Operation Main Strike. It's a plan to completely destroy Silicon Valley, giving Zorin a corner on the microchip market. He expects $100 million from each of his investors, as well as 50 percent of their net income. When one of the investors opts to back out, he's thrown from the blimp into the bay.

Bond arrives in Frisco, meeting with Chuck Lee of the CIA. It seems Dr. Mortner is actually a former Nazi researcher who tried making geniuses with steroids during the war. Most died, although a few survived—but became psychotic. Zorin may be one of the survivors.

With a cover as a financial reporter, Bond finds that a productive crab patch near one of Zorin's oil plants has completely disappeared. Bond dives to investigate and is nearly killed in a seawater intake pipe. He unstraps his air tanks and jams the vent, allowing him to escape. But a KGB agent sent to blow up the plant is not so lucky.

Bond connects with Stacey, who is a state geologist working with WG Howe, an oil company that Zorin has just acquired. The check that Zorin had written was to buy out Stacey's holdings in a family oil interest, but she has decided against it.

Zorin has been pumping seawater into a nearby fault, and when Stacey tells Howe, she is fired. Lee is killed, as Bond and Sutton steal files on Zorin's plans from city hall. But Zorin and Day catch the pair, shooting Howe in an effort to frame Bond for the killing. The building is set afire, with Bond and Stacey trapped in an elevator. They climb out the top, just as the cable breaks and the elevator falls.

Police try to arrest Bond for killing Howe, but he and Stacey drive off in a fire engine. After a harrowing trip through traffic, they drive out to one of Zorin's mines. He has packed it with tons of explosives and a triggering bomb—once detonated, the San Andreas Fault will separate and earthquakes will ravage the region—including Silicon Valley.

Zorin discovers Bond and Sutton in the mine and sends May Day after them. With no regard for Day or hundreds of miners, Zorin sets off an initial explosion to flood the mine shafts. Laughing maniacally, he kills many of those trapped with a machine gun. Zorin, Scarpine, and Mortner take to the air in a Zorin blimp.

Bond and Day fall into the rushing waters and wade into the mine center. Knowing that Zorin left her to die, Day saves Bond and sacrifices herself to move the triggering bomb away from the explosives, where it harmlessly goes off.

Zorin takes Sutton hostage in the airship, and Bond grabs a mooring line as the craft rises. It heads toward the Golden Gate Bridge, where 007 is able to wrap the line around one of the towers. Sutton jumps Zorin, and the gondola breaks open. She's able to escape to the tower, as Zorin grabs a fire ax and chases after her. Bond and Zorin grapple high on the bridge when the villain loses his grip and falls to his death in the water below.

A revengeful Mortner prepares to toss a bundle of dynamite at Bond. But the secret agent cuts the mooring line, suddenly setting the blimp free and sending the doctor tumbling into the cab. The explosives go off, destroying the airship while killing Mortner and Scarpine.

For his efforts, General Gogol awards Bond the Order of Lenin—a first for a non-Soviet. But Bond is absent, recuperating with the gentle help of Stacey.

The Living Daylights

(1987—British/UNITED ARTISTS—130 MIN/COLOR) Loosely based on the Ian
  Fleming short story.
DIRECTOR: John Glen
ORIGINAL MUSIC: John Barry
FILM EDITING: Peter Davies, John Grover
PRODUCTION DESIGN: Peter Lamont
CAST: Timothy Dalton (007/James Bond)
Maryam d'Abo (Kara Milovy)
Jeroen Krabbé (General Georgi Koskov)
Joe Don Baker (Brad Whitaker)
John Rhys-Davies (General Leonid Pushkin)
Art Malik (Kamran Shah)
Andreas Wisniewski (Necros)
Thomas Wheatley (Saunders)
Desmond Llewelyn (Q)
Robert Brown (M)
Geoffrey Keen (Minister of Defence)
Walter Gotell (General Gogol)
Caroline Bliss (Miss Moneypenny)
John Terry (Felix Leiter)

MI6 conducts training exercises on Gibraltar, with double-oh agents taking part. But someone's not playing the game—they're using real bullets. James Bond takes off after the killer, who is escaping in a jeep loaded with explosives. Bond wrestles with the driver as the car careens down a mountain road. When it heads over a cliff, 007 pulls his chute and is pulled to safety, while the jeep explodes. Bond lands on a yacht, where a lovely lady invites him for a drink.

In Yugoslavia, Bond meets with Saunders, a field operative. At a concert featuring the brilliant and beautiful cellist Kara Milovy, the agents prepare to assassinate a KGB sniper who is out to kill defecting KGB general Georgi Koskov. Seeing the potential sniper is Milovy, Bond shoots to only disable her weapon, rather than kill her.

Koskov successfully makes his escape to Austria, where he embraces Bond as his savior. Koskov is whisked across the border through an oil pipeline in a "pig," a capsule used to clean the lines. Q welcomes the general to the West, and he is taken to England in a Harrier jet. But Saunders is livid at Bond for not killing the sniper as ordered.

Debriefed at the countryside Bladen safe house, Koskov accuses KGB general Pushkin of reinstating an old Soviet initiative called Smiert Spionom—Death to Spies—which will target English and American agents for assassination. Koskov proposes eliminating Pushkin.

The Living Daylights—US one-sheet poster.

But a tall blond man named Necros poses as a milkman to infiltrate the safe house. He kills many of the guards, uses bombs disguised as milk bottles to set the place on fire, and escapes in a helicopter with an unconscious Koskov.

MI6 has a hard time believing that Pushkin has gone psychotic, but an order for his assassination in Tangiers is made, with Bond as the gun man. Q Branch arms 007 with field equipment and gadgets, as well as a new Aston Martin.

Bond returns to Bratislava, where he sees Pushkin and KGB agents take Milovy into custody. But her cello case is left behind and Bond retrieves it; inside he sees her sniper rifle was loaded with blanks—and her address.

At her apartment, Bond finds Milovy released by the KGB, but still under their watchful eye. He also discovers that Koskov is Milovy's boyfriend.

Bond and Kara slip off to Austria in the Aston Martin, after first using its wheel-mounted laser to cut a pursuing police car from its frame. Bond blows a semi trailer in half with a front-mounted missile when it is set up as a roadblock. Chased onto an ice-covered lake, the Aston Martin sprouts tire spikes and skis to evade Soviet troops, then crosses into a forest with the help of a rocket engine. Bond and Milovy use the musician's cello case to slip down a snow-covered mountain, crossing safely into Austria.

In Tangiers, Pushkin meets with Brad Whitaker, an army outcast who maintains his own paramilitary troops. He's also a devious weapons dealer, but Pushkin cancels a pending deal for arms with Whitaker and wants a $50 million deposit returned. The general knows Whitaker and Koskov are in cahoots in some way, and he does not approve.

Bond and Kara enjoy the Vienna sights, and despite the woman's relationship with Koskov, 007 is slowly courting Milovy. Meanwhile, Koskov and Necros lounge with beautiful women by Whitaker's pool. The despot needs Pushkin eliminated, but Koskov insists that Bond will take care of him.

After attending the opera, Bond and Milovy take a romantic moonlit ride in a Ferris wheel, while Saunders arranges a passport for Kara. Bond connects with Saunders, who has discovered that Brad Whitaker paid for Kara's expensive cello—proving Koskov and Whitaker are working together. Necros murders Saunders, attempting to convince Bond that Pushkin is still pushing Smiert Spionom.

In Tangiers, Bond confronts Pushkin, who denies any connection to Smiert Spionom. Later, addressing a Soviet conference, Pushkin is shot and killed by Bond. Chased by local police, Bond escapes across the rooftops of Tangiers. But actually, Pushkin is very much alive. It is a deception created between the general and Bond, allowing everyone to believe Whitaker's plan succeeded. Bond is picked up by the CIA's Felix Leiter while Whitaker, Koskov, and Necros celebrate the apparent killing of Pushkin.

Kara finally speaks with Koskov, who continues to lie and tells her Bond is a KGB agent out to kill everyone. On her boyfriend's orders, she spikes 007's martini and knocks him out. When Koskov and Necros arrive, the plot becomes clear to Milovy—she has been duped.

Escaping in an ambulance, Koskov and Necros pose as doctors, with a human heart for transplant on ice. But the ice is actually a load of diamonds, and they board a military transport plane for Afghanistan. Koskov will be a Russian hero for turning in Bond—the man who killed Pushkin. The conniving Koskov also turns in Milovy as a defector.

Bond and Kara are locked away in a cell at an Afghan military air base. Another cell holds a disheveled Middle Eastern prisoner. Bond subdues a sadistic jailor and his men and escapes with Kara, dressing as soldiers, and they toss the cell keys to the other prisoner as they leave.

Bond, Kara, and the other prisoner bolt the camp, and they join a group of stealthy desert dwellers. The released prisoner turns out to be Kamran Shah, leader of the area's Mujahideen—Afghan resistance fighters against the Russians. Bond needs Shah's help to stop Koskov, but the fighters have their own mission to complete.

The Mujahideen are trading opium to Whitaker and Koskov for the load of diamonds. Bond stows away in the opium-laden truck caravan, and Kara implores Shah to help. When he refuses, she heads after Bond on horseback—and Shah reconsiders, taking off with her.

Bond plants a time bomb in one of the packs of opium, while Shah and his men quietly begin to eliminate the Russian soldiers. Discovered by Koskov and Necros, Bond hijacks the plane as Shah and his men continue to ravage the Soviet troops. Just before taking off, Kara drives a jeep onto the plane's loading ramp. At the last minute, Necros jumps aboard as well.

In the cargo section, Bond frantically looks for the time bomb and is attacked by Necros. The loading ramp opens, and the two continue their fight outside, on a bundle of cargo tethered to the plane. When Necros grabs Bond's boot, 007 quickly cuts its laces, and Necros tumbles to his death.

Bond finds the bomb, resets the timer, and blows up a bridge, saving Shah and his men from advancing Soviet soldiers. But the plane is losing fuel and altitude, and Bond has to think quickly. He and Kara jump into the jeep, and as the plane nears the ground, they safely eject from the plane and drive off near Pakistan.

With Leiter providing backup, Bond infiltrates Whitaker's villa. The would-be soldier gets the jump on 007 with a high-tech weapon. But Bond is able to topple a marble bust of Wellington onto Whitaker with a small explosive in his key ring, killing him.

Pushkin enters and Koskov feigns appreciation, claiming Whitaker was holding him hostage. Pushkin will have none of it and orders Koskov returned to Moscow—in "the diplomatic bag."

Milovy performs at an Austrian concert hall, where she receives the praise of M, as well as General Gogol, now with the Foreign Service. Shah and his men arrive a bit late, but Kara is quietly crushed that Bond missed her performance. But Bond is waiting in her dressing room, with flowers and martinis.

Licence to Kill

(1989—British/UNITED ARTISTS—133 MIN/COLOR) Based on an original
  screenplay by Michael G. Wilson and Richard Maibaum.
DIRECTOR: John Glen
ORIGINAL MUSIC: Michael Kamen
FILM EDITING: John Grover
PRODUCTION DESIGN: Peter Lamont
CAST: Timothy Dalton (007/James Bond)
Carey Lowell (Pam Bouvier)
Robert Davi (Franz Sanchez)
Talisa Soto (Lupe Lamora)
Anthony Zerbe (Milton Krest)
Frank McRae (Sharkey)
David Hedison (Felix Leiter)
Wayne Newton (Professor Joe Butcher)
Benicio Del Toro (Dario)
Anthony Starke (Truman-Lodge)
Everett McGill (Ed Killifer)
Don Stroud (Colonel Heller)
Desmond Llewelyn (Q)
Robert Brown (M)
Priscilla Barnes (Della Churchill Leiter)
Caroline Bliss (Miss Moneypenny)
Cary-Hiroyuki Tagawa (Kwang)
Pedro Armendariz Jr. (President Hector Lopez)

In the Florida Keys, CIA agent Felix Leiter prepares to marry his fiancée, Della. James Bond will be his best man, and local fishing guide Sharkey will be a groomsman. But Franz Sanchez, a drug smuggler long on the CIA's list, turns up in the Keys to retrieve Lupe, his mistress. Since this is the chance they've been waiting for, the tuxedo-clad Leiter and Bond set out with the DEA after Sanchez, leaving Sharkey to make excuses to Della. As Sanchez attempts to flee in a private plane, Bond drops from a Coast Guard helicopter on a cable and winch. Wrapping the line around the plane's tail, they reel in Sanchez like a champion marlin. Felix and James skydive to the wedding, top hats in hand.

Sanchez is transferred under heavy guard, with US marshal Ed Killifer leading the team. But Sanchez's standing offer of $2 million to anyone who helps him escape tempts Killifer to dump the truck carrying the drug lord off a bridge and into the waiting arms of scuba divers, who take him away.

After the wedding reception, Felix and Della are attacked by Sanchez's crew, while the criminal hides out at the offices of marine specialist Milton Krest. Leiter is brought to the warehouse there and is savagely fed to sharks. Hearing of Sanchez's escape, Bond rushes to Leiter's house, where he finds Della murdered and Leiter's office in shambles. A badly maimed Felix has been left, barely alive.

On a hunch, a vengeful Bond slips into Krest's warehouse, where he finds millions of dollars' worth of drugs. Caught by Killifer, Bond gets the upper hand and feeds him to the sharks, along with Killifer's $2 million. But the authorities intercept Bond and bring him to a seething M, who admonishes his agent for shirking his duties. M suspends Bond, and he takes off in haste.

Krest has his research boat, the *Wavekrest*, out in deep waters, with Lupe aboard for safekeeping. Sharkey brings Bond out to investigate what Krest is up to and makes his way onboard the *Wavekrest*. Bond quizzes Lupe, and they watch as Krest's men pull alongside with the dead body of Sharkey. Bond grabs an aqualung and dives overboard, where he sees Krest exchange bundles of cash into a seaplane for bundles of Colombian drugs. He cuts the bags open and dumps them into the water, then escapes on the plane.

Bond returns to Leiter's house, where he finds that a CIA pilot named Bouvier is scheduled to meet Felix in the Central American town of Isthmus City. Once there, he sees the pilot is a beautiful woman named Pam Bouvier. In a local bar, the two fight with Dario and other members of Sanchez's crew, then escape in a powerboat. Bond needs Bouvier's help to bring in Sanchez, and they become cozy under a setting sun.

Moneypenny is concerned about Bond's whereabouts and contacts Q Branch to find him. In Isthmus City, Bond and Bouvier make themselves known, flashing millions of dollars of the money Bond flew away with. Even better, Bond deposits the money into the same bank as Sanchez's.

Sanchez and his financial expert Truman-Lodge escort Asian drug investors through the mogul's operations. He sets drug pricing and receives orders through coded messages, delivered by TV evangelist Professor Joe Butcher. Meanwhile, Bond intentionally loses hundreds of thousands—then wins it all back—at blackjack, drawing the attention of Sanchez and his head of security, Colonel Heller. Sanchez sends Lupe to deal the cards and find out more about Bond.

But Bond forces his way into Sanchez's office, where he introduces himself as a former British agent and offers his services as a bodyguard to the criminal. Sanchez is impressed with Bond's credentials—and chutzpah. Bond returns to his hotel with Pam, finding Q has come out to check on 007 and deliver some handy weapons.

Sanchez meets with his Asian drug partners. One of them, Kwang, insists on seeing the processing plant, and Sanchez agrees to take everyone the next day. Posing as a waiter, Bond sneaks up to the roof of Sanchez's casino, where he rappels down to the office windows. He quietly lays out plastic explosives along the window ledge, as well as a remote detonator. From an abandoned building across the street, Bond assembles a sniper rifle and takes aim on Sanchez. Surprisingly, he spies Bouvier in an adjoining office, talking with Heller. Bond blows out the windows, but before he can fire, 007 is attacked by two ninjas. They trap Bond and knock him out.

Bond wakes to find the ninjas are part of an elite government agency based out of Hong Kong. Kwang is actually the leader of the group and fears Bond's reckless assassination attempt hasn't botched their plan to nab Sanchez and the others. But Heller leads a paramilitary raid against the Asian agents and finds an unconscious Bond in the wreckage.

Waking in Sanchez's lavish estate, Bond is warmly welcomed by the drug lord. Bond plants the idea with Sanchez that there is a snitch inside his organization—Sanchez suspects Krest. Lupe helps Bond leave the island back to his hotel, where he accuses Pam of being in cahoots with Heller. She sets him straight, revealing that Sanchez has acquired Stinger missiles and intends on downing an American plane if the DEA doesn't back off. Bouvier was offering Heller a deal of immunity if he could recover the missiles, but Bond's attempted shooting scared Heller off. Pam reminds Bond there's more going on than just his personal vendetta against Sanchez.

Bond pulls his millions from the bank. With Pam posing as a harbor pilot, she and Bond board the *Wavekrest*, sneaking the money in and planting it in a decompression chamber. Sanchez confronts Krest and accuses him of stealing the drug money. When they search the boat, Krest is surprised to find the money in the chamber where Bond left it. Sanchez throws Krest in with the money, then seals the door. He builds up the pressure in the chamber, then cuts the hose, causing rapid decompression and turning Krest into a living balloon—until he pops.

Bond sends Q and Pam off, returning to Sanchez's estate. The villain thanks Bond for the tip about an inside informer, but he further puts doubts into Sanchez's head, suggesting there might be another insider. Lupe slips in and reveals she's in love with 007.

The next day, Sanchez takes Bond along to tour the drug processing plant with the Asians. It's based on the campus of Professor Joe Butcher's meditation institute. With everyone wearing breathing protection, Bond is safe from being recognized by Dario.

Pam makes her way onto the campus, where Professor Joe turns out to be a womanizer. But Pam will have no part of it, and she breaks out from his private bedroom chamber.

Sanchez's process involves suspending the drug in gasoline, which is then transported in tanker-trucks—four of which are ready to head out the door. Later, the gas can be separated from the cocaine. But Dario has recognized Bond, and he sets off an explosion and fire, sending the investors running. The trucks take off, and Sanchez prepares to dump the British agent into a pulverizer. But the wily Bond puts one more idea into Sanchez's head—Heller will take the Stinger missiles and run. Dario tries to finish Bond off, but Pam distracts him, and Dario falls to his death instead.

Sanchez leaves with Truman-Lodge and the missiles, which Heller was trying to escape with as Bond suggested. Heller is killed, while Pam and Bond take off in a private plane. Bond jumps down onto one of the tankers and dumps the driver, taking control of the semi rig. He runs another tanker into the roadside, as Sanchez's men prepare to fire a missile at Bond. He quickly brings the truck up onto its side wheels, allowing the missile to fly under and past it—exploding as it slams into the other truck.

Bond is under heavy fire from machine guns wielded by Sanchez's men. Pam flies in to help out, dumping a large load of pesticide dust on the gunmen. Bond releases the tanker from its cab, sending it down a hillside and crashing into one of the two remaining trucks, where they explode in enormous balls of fire. Truman-Lodge carps over the drug lord's continued financial losses, and Sanchez cuts him down with gunfire.

Sanchez takes off in the remaining tanker, and Bond, in the cab of his tractor, pops a wheelie to drive safely through a wall of blazing gasoline. Bond puts his rig into cruise control and makes his way onto the back of Sanchez's tanker. Sanchez fires a Stinger at Pam's plane and barely misses, allowing her to land safely. Jumping out with machete in hand, the villain swings at Bond, missing him and cutting the brake line to the truck.

Sanchez and Bond wrestle on the truck as it crashes out of control and spills its load of gas everywhere. Sanchez prepares to kill Bond, but 007 quickly flicks his lighter—a gift from Felix and Della—setting Sanchez afire and killing him as the final truck explodes. Pam has corralled an abandoned truck cab, and she drives away with James.

At a lavish reception for newly elected President Lopez, Lupe tries to seduce Bond, but he's more attracted to Pam. Diving into a pool fully clothed, Bond pulls Pam in with him and they kiss.

GoldenEye

(1995—British/UNITED ARTISTS—130 MIN/COLOR) Inspired by the Ian Fleming
   home in Jamaica.
DIRECTOR: Martin Campbell
ORIGINAL MUSIC: Eric Serra
FILM EDITING: Terry Rawlings
PRODUCTION DESIGN: Peter Lamont
CAST: Pierce Brosnan (007/James Bond)
Sean Bean (006/Alec Trevelyan)
Izabella Scorupco (Natalya Simonova)
Famke Janssen (Xenia Onatopp)
Joe Don Baker (Jack Wade)
Judi Dench (M)
Robbie Coltrane (Valentin Zukovsky)
Tcheky Karyo (Dimitri Mishkin)
Gottfried John (General Ourumov)
Alan Cumming (Boris Grishenko)
Desmond Llewelyn (Q)
Samantha Bond (Miss Moneypenny)
Michael Kitchen (Bill Tanner)
Serena Gordon (Caroline)

Bungee-jumping more than seven hundred feet from the top of a dam, James Bond sneaks into a Soviet chemical weapons factory. Accompanied by Alec Trevelyan, Agent 006, Bond sets timers to destroy the stockpile of weapons. Soldiers capture 006, held at gunpoint by Soviet colonel Ourumov. Trevelyan is shot in the head, and Bond escapes on a conveyor belt. He speeds off in a motorcycle, chasing a small plane taking off from a high, remote airstrip. As it plunges off the mountain's edge, Bond follows on the bike—skydiving to the cockpit of the plane and flying away safely as the factory explodes.

Nine years later, Bond is behind the wheel of his trusted Aston Martin DB5 in the South of France, accompanied by Caroline, a pretty MI6 psychologist sent to evaluate him. A sharp red Ferrari, driven by the sharp-looking Xenia Onatopp, engages Bond in a dangerous race on a mountainous road. Avoiding a disaster with an oncoming bicycle race, Bond cedes the win to

Onatopp, then engages Caroline in some physical therapy.

Bond meets up with the cigar-smoking Onatopp at the baccarat table, where she shows what a sore loser she can be. Onatopp also demonstrates what strong thighs she has, crushing and killing a Canadian admiral with them during their lovemaking. Bond finds the dead admiral, then rushes to the demonstration of a brand-new Tiger helicopter, capable of withstanding the electromagnetic pulse from a nuclear weapon. Onatopp, a former Soviet chopper pilot, steals the helicopter and leaves 007 to take the rap.

At the Space Weapons Control Center in Severnaya, Russia, in the Arctic Ocean, pretty satellite programmer Natalya Simonova tries to tolerate the obnoxious taunts and boasts of her coworker, computer

GoldenEye—US one-sheet poster.

whiz (and hacker) Boris Grishenko. Onatopp, with now-General Ourumov in tow, lands the copter at the center, which controls the GoldenEye satellite weapons system. The general takes the command disk and keys for the system, then Onatopp kills everyone in the building—except Simonova, who was out getting coffee, and Grishenko, out having a smoke. Ourumov starts the GoldenEye, sets the center itself as the target, then leaves with Onatopp in the copter. Scrambled MIGs are destroyed as the electromagnetic weapon fires a pulse that strikes Severnaya. Pure luck and perseverance save Simonova amid the carnage.

At MI6 headquarters, Bond confers with the new M (now female) and Chief of Staff Tanner while they review satellite images of the Severnaya area. Bond suspects a Soviet insider—possibly Ourumov—is responsible for the catastrophe. Somehow, the Russian-based Janus crime syndicate is involved, as well. M doesn't particularly care for Bond's womanizing reputation, but knows he is a very good agent. She assigns 007 to find the GoldenEye and whoever stole it. Before leaving for St. Petersburg, Bond receives a new BMW, a belt that contains climbing gear, and a pen grenade from Q.

In Russia, Ourumov reports to Defense Minister Mishkin, where the general discovers there were two survivors in the Severnaya disaster. When Bond arrives, he meets up with CIA operative Jack Wade. He briefs 007 on Janus, which isn't much—he travels by armored train and has competition from an ex-KGB agent named Zukovsky, whom Bond has met before.

Simonova contacts Boris, who also escaped Severnaya, but when they meet, the devious Grishenko turns her over to Onatopp. Bond asks Zukovsky to set up a meeting with Janus. Meanwhile, Bond is roughly seduced by Onatopp, who then tries to kill him. Bond comes out on top, insisting on meeting Janus.

In a junkyard of rusting Soviet icons, Bond is startled to find his friend 006 still alive—scarred and bitter at Bond—and that he is Janus, the leader of the crime syndicate. Shot with a tranquilizer, Bond is knocked out. He wakes to find himself, and Simonova, bound inside the Tiger copter. Its missiles have been set to launch and target themselves right back at the chopper. Bond is able to eject Simonova and himself before the rockets strike. Before they can flee, the two are captured and locked in a cell, where Bond gains Simonova's trust and she reveals Grishenko to be the traitor. Mishkin accuses Bond of stealing the GoldenEye, but Simonova exposes Grishenko and Ourumov as the terrorists behind the Severnaya disaster. Ourumov bursts in, killing Mishkin and a guard with Bond's PPK, setting up 007 as their killer.

Bond overpowers the general and escapes in a Russian tank, as Simonova is taken prisoner by Ourumov and his troops. The tank crashes through buildings and over cars in pursuit of the general's car. Ourumov takes Simonova onto Trevelyan's armored train, with Onatopp along for the ride. Bond drives the tank onto the tracks to intercept the train. Trevelyan orders the engineer to ram the vehicle, but Bond fires the tank's cannon first. It hits the locomotive, and the train smashes into the tank, derailing as 007 jumps to safety.

Bond faces Janus and Onatopp in a standoff, with Ourumov holding a gun to Simonova's head. Falsely claiming the girl means nothing to him, Bond kills Ourumov, as the other two villains escape by helicopter. The train car is shut tight and set to explode, trapping Bond and Simonova. The girl is able to locate Grishenko's computer in Cuba, identifying Trevelyan's destination—he has secretly maintained a second GoldenEye system there. Bond cuts his way out of the train with his laser watch, and the pair run free as the car explodes.

In Cuba, Wade trades 007 a private plane for the BMW. Bond and Simonova know that the GoldenEye uses an enormous satellite dish, but Wade insists there's nothing like that in the country. Simonova knows Bond is troubled by chasing his old friend, now the villain. On a secluded beach, they make love.

Bond flies the plane in search of the GoldenEye dish. Over a small lake, a missile emerges from below the water, damaging the plane and forcing Bond to down it in a jungle. Onatopp drops from a helicopter, attempting to kill Bond. But he is able to shoot the copter down with a machine gun, and Onatopp dies.

Grishenko drains the lake, revealing the GoldenEye antenna. Bond and Simonova climb onto the structure as Trevelyan targets London—the electromagnetic pulse from the GoldenEye satellite will stun and destroy the entire British economy, while allowing the villain to rob the Bank of England undetected. Avoiding Trevelyan's troops, Bond and Simonova slide down the parabola, reaching an access hatch to the control center.

Planting a bomb with a timer, Bond surrenders, as Simonova reaches a computer terminal and sends the satellite into reentry, where it will burn up in the atmosphere. Grishenko innocently holds Bond's pen grenade, and his playful ticking with it secretly arms the device. Bond throws it into spilled fuel, leaking from gun shots. The center explodes in walls of fire, and Bond and Simonova move to the antenna, as Boris may still be able to reprogram the satellite antenna.

Trevelyan chases Bond onto the support structure of the antenna. Bond stops the dish, but gets into a vicious fight with 006. They grapple on a ladder high above the dish, but Trevelyan slips and falls to his death. Bond jumps to a helicopter commandeered by Natalya, as Boris' claim of invincibility is short-lived. The bomb planted by Bond detonates, showering Grishenko in waves of liquid nitrogen, freezing him solid.

Bond and Simonova drop from the copter and commiserate in a quiet grove, as Wade and US Marine troops interrupt the moment.

Tomorrow Never Dies

(1997—British/METRO-GOLDWYN-MAYER/UNITED ARTISTS—119 MIN/ COLOR) Based on an original screenplay by Bruce Feirstein.
DIRECTOR: Roger Spottiswoode
ORIGINAL MUSIC: David Arnold
FILM EDITING: Dominique Fortin and Michel Arcand
PRODUCTION DESIGN: Allan Cameron

CAST: Pierce Brosnan (007/James Bond)
Jonathan Pryce (Elliot Carver)
Michelle Yeoh (Wai Lin)
Teri Hatcher (Paris Carver)
Joe Don Baker (Jack Wade)
Judi Dench (M)
Ricky Jay (Henry Gupta)
Götz Otto (Stamper)
Vincent Schiavelli (Dr. Kaufman)
Desmond Llewelyn (Q)
Samantha Bond (Miss Moneypenny)

Along the Russian border, wanted terrorists from around the world gather to purchase weapons of all kinds. Secret surveillance cameras beam the scene back to MI6, where M and her associates watch with interest. Terrorist Henry Gupta holds a new GPS encoder developed by the American military. Against M's disagreement, Royal Admiral Roebuck orders a guided missile launch, despite the MI6 agent still being on-site of the attack. When Russian nuclear weapons are spotted as part of the cache, Roebuck orders the launch aborted, to no effect. The agent in harm's way is 007, who takes off in the jet carrying the nukes. Its copilot chokes Bond, while another jet takes off in pursuit. Pulling up under the pursuing jet, 007 fires the copilot's ejection seat, launching him into the other jet and destroying it. Bond flies to safety with the nuclear weapons.

In the South China Sea, the HMS *Devonshire* is buzzed by Chinese jet fighters, warning the frigate that it has illegally entered territorial waters. In reality, Henry Gupta has fed false location coordinates to the ship, using the GPS encoder. It's part of a plot by Elliot Carver, head of Carver Media Group Network (CMGN), to provoke hostilities between China and the British.

In a nearby stealth ship, Carver accomplice Stamper deploys a robotic sea drill called a "sea-vac" to breach the hull of the *Devonshire*. The result will look like the impact of a Chinese torpedo fired from one of the jets. The British ship sinks, with all aboard lost. The stealth ship also destroys one of the Chinese jets, as if the *Devonshire* had retaliated before going under. At CMGN, a smug Carver prepares the next day's sensationalist headlines—"British Sailors Murdered." The tragedy will provide a perfect introduction for Carver's new satellite news network.

Admiral Roebuck advocates a full naval retaliation against the Chinese, but M convinces him to wait forty-eight hours before moving out. She suspects Carver may be behind the incident and wants Bond to investigate.

As it is, Bond happens to have known Carver's wife, Paris, before she was married to the media mogul.

Arriving in Hamburg, Bond gets a new BMW 750, equipped with a remote control built into a cell phone. At a gala reception at CMGN headquarters, Bond catches up with Paris, while Carver meets beautiful journalist Wai Lin. Carver orders Bond taken to a soundproof studio and beaten, which doesn't go well for his men—the beaters become the beatees. Bond kills the power on the mogul's live satellite broadcast, then makes an escape to his hotel, leaving Carver in an embarrassing position. He has Paris visit Bond to find out what he knows.

Bond beds his former female friend, while Gupta hacks around to discover Bond is a government agent—and a past lover of Carver's wife. The media magnate is not amused. Paris tips Bond on how to sneak into CMGN headquarters. Entering through a roof hatch, 007 makes his way to Gupta's office, where he finds—and retrieves—the GPS encoder. He also finds Wai Lin breaking in as well, and the two make separate escapes from security guards.

Bond finds a murdered Paris in his hotel bed, and Carver plans to broadcast a murder-suicide story—once 007 is assassinated by the malevolent Dr. Kaufman, Paris' killer. But Bond gets the upper hand and shoots Kaufman dead.

In the parking garage, Bond remotely starts the BMW, then hops into the back as Carver's men follow the speeding car. He dispatches them with sunroof-mounted rockets, tire spikes, then cuts a thick stranded cable with a metal-cutting hood emblem, all from the safety of the backseat. Bond hops out, just as the BMW careens off the six-story roof, landing back at the rental office—albeit crashing through the front window.

Bond delivers the GPS encoder to a US airbase in the South China Sea, met by CIA agent Jack Wade and other experts. They determine the real location of the sunken *Devonshire*—actually Vietnamese waters—and Bond dives to the site in a HALO suit—High Altitude, Low Opening—a combination of parachute and scuba gear.

Inside the damaged ship, Bond finds Wai Lin—and two guided missiles have been hijacked. As the ship sinks into deeper waters, the pair make a last-minute escape. They find refuge on a Vietnamese fishing boat, although Stamper has commandeered the vessel and takes them to Carver's regional headquarters in Saigon. The villain is composing Bond's obituary for tomorrow's news. To Carver, words are the newest weapons and satellites are the newest artillery—he relishes the impending war that he's creating between China and Britain.

Carver leaves Bond and Lin—handcuffed—in Stamper's hands for torture, but before he can get started, the couple escape out the window of the skyscraper. They rip down along a CMGN banner and crash through a lower-story window. The pair speed off on a motorcycle—still cuffed together—as Stamper and his men follow in cars. Bond and Lin team up to evade the bad guys, zooming down the streets, speeding along rooftops, and soaring over a low-flying helicopter. The copter crashes into a building and explodes, ending the chase.

Lin picks the handcuffs open but traps Bond to a water pipe, insisting she's on her own. But 007 gets free and follows Wai Lin to her apartment, where they both beat a group of invading thugs. Lin is no journalist but a Chinese agent of Bond's equal. Carver has a secret partner—Chinese general Chang—who has provided the media man with stealth materials from which he built his boat. Bond and Lin load up on weapons from a hidden cache and agree to work together to find Carver's boat.

The pair get to the boat in the Vietnamese harbor of Ha Long Bay, just as Carver launches one of the stolen missiles at a British naval target, with Chinese MIGs approaching. Bond and Lin are discovered, and, believing Bond to be shot and killed, Stamper brings Wai Lin aboard. Carver readies the second missile against Beijing. General Chang's part in the plot is to assume power after the attack, arrange a truce, and become a revered world leader. Carver will get exclusive—and lucrative—broadcast rights for a century.

British and Chinese governments get word of the plot, while Bond sneaks into the control room and takes Gupta as a hostage and shield. Carver kills Gupta, since the missile is set to launch in five minutes. Lin breaks free as Bond detonates a grenade, damaging the hull and making the stealth ship visible.

As a British ship fires on Carver's escaping boat, Bond works at defusing the missile while Wai Lin disables the boat's control system, slowing the boat. The pair bust up the place with gunfire as the British ship starts to find its mark. Carver corners Bond, but 007 activates the sea drill, and it tears Carver to pieces.

Stamper gets the drop on Lin and threatens to drop her, chained, to her death in the water below if Bond doesn't get away from the missile. Bond doesn't and Stamper does, and the two fight on the missile gantry. Stamper's leg becomes trapped by the missile, and he holds Bond in a grip guaranteed to keep him in the path of the rocket's exhaust flames. Bond cuts himself free and drops into the water, where he revives the nearly drowned Wai Lin with a kiss of life. The rocket and ship explodes, killing Stamper.

M fabricates a story about Carver's demise, implying suicide, while Bond and Wai Lin dally atop the wreckage of the stealth ship.

The World Is Not Enough

(1999—British/METRO-GOLDWYN-MAYER/UNITED ARTISTS—128 MIN/ COLOR) Based on the family motto of James Bond.
DIRECTOR: Michael Apted
ORIGINAL MUSIC: David Arnold
FILM EDITING: Jim Clark
PRODUCTION DESIGN: Peter Lamont
CAST: Pierce Brosnan (007/James Bond)
Sophie Marceau (Elektra King)
Robert Carlyle (Renard)
Denise Richards (Dr. Christmas Jones)
Robbie Coltrane (Valentin Zukovsky)
Judi Dench (M)
Goldie (Bullion)
David Calder (Sir Robert King)
Desmond Llewelyn (Q)
John Cleese (R)
Maria Grazia Cucinotta (Banker's Assistant/Cigar Girl)
Samantha Bond (Miss Moneypenny)
Ulrich Thomsen (Davidov)
John Seru (Gabor)
Jeff Nutall (Arkov)

In Bilbao, Spain, James Bond recovers a large sum of money from a Swiss banker on behalf of Sir Robert King, an oil industrialist and old personal friend of M. The money was recovered from a murdered MI6 agent, and Bond wants the name of the killer. The banker is murdered by his personal assistant before he can tell, and 007 returns to MI6 headquarters with the money.

Bond meets Sir Robert, who commiserates with M before retrieving his money. But 007 notes something is amiss and tries to stop King from leaving. Too late, as King's lapel pin triggers an explosion in the stacks of currency, killing him and blowing a large hole in the side of the building.

Bond spies the Swiss banker's assistant, armed with a mounted machine gun on a speedboat in the Thames. He takes off after the beautiful but deadly woman in a small experimental power boat from Q Branch. Jet-powered, it quickly overtakes the speedboat, but the driver is able to slip past Bond and through a lowering bridge. Bond's boat submerges to pass under the bridge, then hops a canal, skids down a street, through a restaurant, reenters the river, and fires two torpedoes at the speedboat, now grounded just outside the Millennium Dome. But the woman escapes injury, hopping into a hot-air balloon. Bond grabs one of its ropes as it ascends, and he pleads with the woman to reveal who is behind all the carnage. But she detonates a fuel tank, killing herself and sending 007 tumbling to the roof of the dome. With a rough landing, Bond is in one piece.

Favoring a dislocated collarbone, Bond sees King's beautiful daughter Elektra at her father's funeral. At the Scot branch of MI6, experts reveal King's lapel pin was a fake, with a hidden radio transmitter that set off the explosion. As the pin was given by someone close to him, there must be an inside connection in his company. M resolves to bring the terrorists responsible to justice, but Bond is off the case for medical reasons. He uses his charm to convince the lovely MI6 doctor to clear him for duty.

In Q Branch, it turns out the boat Bond took (and trashed) was a fishing boat for Q's impending retirement. His assistant, whom Bond refers to as "R," has as much or more contempt for the agent as Q does. Bond picks up a gadget-loaded BMW and other essentials.

Researching the background on Elektra, Bond finds she was kidnapped for a $5 million ransom. Although she escaped, the ransom demand was strangely the exact amount of the money Bond recovered for Sir Robert. M tells Bond that, against her judgment, Elektra was used as a decoy and the ransom was not paid. Bond believes the recovered money is a message that the terrorist has returned.

He is Renard, the anarchist. An independent mercenary, he was shot in the head by MI6 agent 009 but, amazingly, survived. The result is Renard can feel no pain, and while the injury will eventually kill him, his stamina and endurance will be superhuman. His next target will be Elektra, and Bond is sent to protect her and find out who switched Sir Robert's pin.

Elektra has taken over her father's pipeline project in Azerbaijan near the Caspian Sea. Locals are angered, as a church is scheduled for demolition, but King makes an expensive decision to reroute the pipeline and save the church. Elektra has no trust in or need for MI6 and Bond, but he persists in staying at her side.

Bond and Elektra ski the Caucasus range to survey the pipeline, but armed para-wing glider/snowmobiles attack them. Bond leads them into the forest, where they crash and collide with trees. One explosion creates an avalanche, and Bond quickly activates his jacket, turning into a protective inflatable sphere around the couple. But Elektra is claustrophobic, and Bond soothes her, gaining her trust as well.

At her lavish home in Baku, Bond waits with King's head of security Davidov and bodyguard Gabor. Elektra seems afraid, wanting to know who's after her and asking Bond to stay with her. But 007 calms her fears and heads to the L'or Noir Casino, run by his old nemesis, Valentin Zukovsky. The Russian fingers Renard as being behind the paraglider attack and says he used to be part of the KGB. Showing she's not intimidated, Elektra comes to the casino and promptly loses $1 million. Bond chides her, but she suggests, "There's no point in living, if you can't feel alive."

The World Is Not Enough—US one-sheet poster.

In a remote cave, Renard meets with Davidov, who is secretly in cahoots with the terrorist. A nuclear scientist, Arkov, was trusted to kill Bond but failed. Renard kills him and puts Davidov in his place.

Bond romances Elektra, then searches Davidov's office and car, where he finds the deceased Arkov. Bond kills Davidov and, posing as Arkov, boards a KGB plane for Kazakhstan in central Asia. He meets a lovely nuclear scientist, Dr. Christmas Jones, who is breaking down an underground nuclear weapon site for the Russians.

Bond finds Renard there working on an atomic weapon and threatens to kill him. Renard is unaffected, saying, "There's no point in living, if you can't feel alive." Bond is caught by Jones and Russian troops, who know he is not Arkov. Renard grabs his shoulder, knowing about his previous injury. Bond realizes King is aligned with Renard, who fires on the troops and takes the bomb. Bond and Jones escape being killed by a bomb planted by the fleeing Renard. When they figure he can be tracked by the locator card stored in the weapon, Bond shows Jones the card is in his hand, not the bomb.

Elektra lures M into coming to Baku, while Bond confronts the heiress about being on Renard's side, a result of "Stockholm Syndrome," where the kidnapped victim sympathizes with and falls for his or her captor. King denies the accusation, but Bond is not convinced.

Renard has attached his stolen nuclear weapon to an inspection rig in the pipeline, and it is headed for the oil terminal, where Bond, King, M, Jones, and everyone else are threatened. Bond and Jones fly out to enter the pipeline, intercept the bomb, and defuse it. As it speeds toward the terminal, Jones finds only half the plutonium in the bomb, and Bond lets the detonator explode as they hop out of the rig. King thinks 007 and Jones were killed in the mishap and reveals to M her part in Renard's plot and imprisons her.

In Istanbul at the Maiden's Tower, Renard embraces King, showing her the other half of the plutonium, which will be used to destroy the city, and the Russian pipelines that were King's competitors. The villain intends to let M die in the explosion.

In the Caspian Sea, Bond visits Zukovsky at his caviar-processing plant, and the Russian's golden-toothed aide Bullion turns out to be an ally of King. Bond wants to know what kind of deal Zukovsky has with King, but he's cut short when two King helicopters, carrying deadly circular saws used to trim forests, start slicing through the building. Bond remotely summons his BMW, climbs in, and blows one of the choppers out of the sky with a missile. But the other saws the BMW in two, nearly getting 007 in the process. Bond blows up that chopper, and Zukovsky falls into a vat of his own caviar. Bond pulls him to safety after he reveals that his nephew, a Russian sub captain, occasionally smuggled machine parts for King and the million dollars she lost in his casino was payment for the service. The last delivery was due in to Istanbul.

Renard's plan becomes clearer—using the Russian sub, he will replace the fuel-grade uranium in its reactor with the weapons-grade plutonium. The resulting explosion will look like an accident and contaminate the Bosphorus between Europe and Asia for decades, shutting down any chance of shipping oil in the region. King's pipeline is sure to prosper.

M uses the locating card Bond gave her to send out a tracking signal, while Bullion attempts to kill everyone in MI6 with a bomb hidden in a briefcase. The traitor captures Bond and Jones, while Renard kills Zukovsky's nephew and the rest of the sub crew. Renard gives the nephew's captain's hat to King as a souvenir.

Bond is locked into an ornate chair, with a device that Elektra uses to slowly strangle him. She resents her father's refusal to pay her kidnapping ransom and seems to hate the entire world for it. Zukovsky bursts in, seeking his nephew. He shoots Bullion dead but does not see King hide a gun behind his nephew's hat. She coldly shoots the Russian down, and he fires a gun concealed in his cane at Bond. King thinks he missed his target—but he was dead-on, cracking one of the shackles that held Bond. Zukovsky dies with a knowing smile, and 007 breaks free. He shoots Gabor down and takes after a fleeing King. Bond frees M and corners Elektra, who doesn't think Bond will kill her in cold blood. But she is wrong, and he shoots her dead.

As Renard takes off in the sub, Bond dives in to the water and sneaks in through a hatch. He finds Jones and starts to surface the sub. Gunfire ensues and destroys the sub's controls, sending it deep underwater. The sub begins to flood, as Renard prepares to load the reactor with the deadly fuel.

Bond swims outside the sub to reach Renard in the reactor room, while Jones nearly drowns in a waterlogged chamber. Bond pulls her to safety as he gets to Renard. Bond and Renard fight, and the villain locks Bond under a grate. The villain inserts the fuel rod into the reactor when a pressure line breaks loose. Bond quickly replaces it, forcing the rod into Renard's chest with deadly force. Bond and Jones escape through a torpedo tube as the sub breaks apart.

M and the MI6 crew locate Bond with thermal imaging, catching the agent and Jones in a warm embrace.

Die Another Day

(2002—British/METRO-GOLDWYN-MAYER/UNITED ARTISTS—133 MIN/
    COLOR) Based on an original screenplay by Neal Purvis and Robert Wade.
DIRECTOR: Lee Tamahori
ORIGINAL MUSIC: David Arnold
FILM EDITING: Andrew MacRitchie and Christian Wagner
PRODUCTION DESIGN: Peter Lamont
CAST: Pierce Brosnan (007/James Bond)
Halle Berry (Giacinta "Jinx" Johnson)
Toby Stephens (Gustav Graves)
Rick Yune (Zao)
Rosamund Pike (Miranda Frost)
Judi Dench (M)
Michael Madsen (Damian Falco)
Will Yun Lee (Colonel Moon)
Kenneth Tsang (General Moon)
John Cleese (Q)
Samantha Bond (Miss Moneypenny)

Along the North Korean coastline, Agent 007 surfs onto shore with two South Korean agents. Intercepting a helicopter, Bond takes the place of an arms dealer and makes his way onto a North Korean military installation, the headquarters of General Tan-Sun Moon. Meeting the general's son,

Colonel Moon, and his aide, Zao, Bond trades a briefcase full of diamonds for a large cache of weapons and vehicles. But he is quickly pegged as an imposter as the general arrives.

Bond detonates a load of C4 hidden in the case, embedding diamonds into the face of Zao, as Colonel Moon flees in an armed hovercraft. Bond follows in another, destroying the camp as he leaves. Amid gunfire, Bond hops onto Moon's vehicle, where the North Korean shows great skill in the martial arts. But Bond jumps to safety as the hovercraft tumbles over a waterfall, killing the colonel. The general captures 007 and will make him pay for killing his son.

After fourteen months of beatings and torture in captivity, Bond is exchanged for Zao, who was captured in the meantime. Sedated, hospitalized, and kept behind glass, Bond is suspected by M of revealing secret information during his imprisonment. He insists Colonel Moon had a Western ally, someone who betrayed Bond. M has his double-oh status removed.

Bond places himself into a state of cardiac arrest, then escapes when medics attempt to revive him. Entering a posh Hong Kong hotel in pajamas, long hair, and beard, Bond is quickly recognized and given the Presidential Suite, where he can clean up and collect himself. And make a deal with Chinese Intelligence, who are spying on him—Bond wants to get back into North Korea with their help. When he does, he'll eliminate Zao, who killed three Chinese agents.

But the Chinese find that Zao is in Havana, Cuba, and arrange for Bond to travel there instead. Zao has gone to the Isla Los Organos, where the Alvarez Clinic uses gene therapy to increase people's life spans. At the local hotel, Bond meets the beautiful Giacinta "Jinx" Johnson, and they spend the night together.

At the clinic, Jinx kills a doctor to get information on Zao, while Bond finds the actual Zao undergoing therapy to change his appearance. Jinx is trapped by local soldiers but dives into the water and takes off in a waiting speedboat. Zao escapes in a helicopter as Bond grabs a bullet-shaped pendant from him. Inside it are expensive diamonds—the same as those used in the failed arms exchange, and they bear the crest of the wealthy Gustav Graves.

Damian Falco, head of America's National Security Agency, is not pleased about Bond's escape and activities on the island. He informs M that MI6 had better get Bond under control, or the NSA will do it for them.

Graves makes a notable arrival to receive his knighthood at Buckingham Palace, parachuting in on a Union Jack silk. Later, Bond meets Verity, Graves' fencing coach, and watches as the billionaire spars with his personal assistant, Miranda Frost. Bond engages Graves in a fencing match, with one of the diamonds as the winner's prize. Bond defeats Graves after a fierce battle, and the industrialist graciously invites Bond to attend a demonstration of his Icarus solar satellite at his ice palace in Iceland. As Bond accepts, he receives an envelope from a server, containing a key.

The key opens the door to an abandoned London subway station, where M puts Bond back into service. Later, Bond cleans his weapon when he hears shots. He finds Moneypenny with a bullet in her head and M held hostage by terrorists. Bond wounds M, then kills the captors. Of course, everyone is fine—it's all a virtual game, hosted by Q Branch to sharpen Bond's skills. Q gives Bond a new Aston Martin, equipped with technology to make it invisible when necessary.

M briefs an MI6 agent before leaving for Iceland. It's Miranda Frost, who volunteered to infiltrate Graves' operation. But she's found nothing on him, even though Bond believes otherwise.

In Iceland, Graves arrives in a high-powered, jet-propelled ice racer to meet Bond. Jinx arrives, driving a new Ford Thunderbird. In a private room at the palace, Zao embraces Graves—who is really Colonel Moon, with facial features changed on Isla Los Organos. Graves greets his guests to demonstrate Icarus, capable of focusing laser-like rays on the Earth. The satellite will benefit agriculture around the world.

Secretly, Graves receives a glove-mounted controller for Icarus, while Bond is caught sneaking around. He breaks free, and Frost, who's been cold as ice to Bond, passionately kisses him to evade the guards. While Bond romances Frost, Jinx infiltrates Graves' solarium but is caught by Graves and Zao.

Bond cuts a hole in the ice and uses a miniature breathing unit to swim into the solarium, where he saves Jinx from being sliced in two by a laser. Bond fights with Mr. Kil, Graves' bodyguard, but a well-placed laser beam cuts him down. Jinx reveals she's with the NSA and is also on Zao's trail. The pair now realize that Graves is Moon.

Bond confronts Graves, along with Frost—who turns out to be a double agent. Frost was Moon's Western ally, the one who betrayed Bond to the North Koreans. As she prepares to kill Bond, he activates a sonic ring on his finger, shattering the glass floor and allowing him to escape in Graves' ice racer.

Graves powers up Icarus, focusing its beam on Bond's speeding vehicle. He heads over a sheer ice cliff, stopping the racer with its grappling hook brake. Graves cuts away a huge portion of the cliff, but 007 fashions a parasail surfboard from the racer and soars to safety. He grabs a snowmobile and heads for the ice castle.

Bond remotely controls his car and gets in as Zao follows in a weapon-laden Jaguar XKR. Meanwhile, Jinx is trapped in a room of the ice palace, and Graves and Frost board a cargo jet. He aims the Icarus beam on his palace, causing it to melt and threatening to drown the American agent.

Bond and Zao spin around inside the palace in their vehicles, crashing through ice walls as they melt. Bond fakes Zao into crashing his car into a pool, then kills him with a falling ice chandelier. Bond crashes into Jinx's room, but she's unconscious. He saves her with a kiss of life as the cargo jet takes off.

Bond and Jinx arrive at a US military base in South Korea. The North Koreans are mobilizing for an attack along the demilitarized zone. The sarcastic Falco insists that no one goes into the North, but M overrules him. Bond and Jinx ride personal stealth sky sleds into North Korea as Icarus blows up a US missile targeted to destroy it.

The pair sneak onto the cargo plane as it takes off, while Graves faces his deposed father, General Moon. The villain, now wearing a high-tech controller suit, uses Icarus to detonate the mines planted in the DMZ. Once cleared, his troops can pour into South Korea, Japan, and other countries. General Moon is not pleased with his son's plan, but Graves kills his father.

Jinx takes the plane's controls, as Bond's gun goes off in the cabin, which depressurizes. Soldiers are pulled into the sky, and Bond grapples with Graves. Frost corners Jinx with a sword, and she leaves the pilot seat, but not before secretly pointing the jet toward the Icarus ray. It begins to tear the plane apart, while Frost and Jinx engage in a sword fight. Johnson kills Frost with a knife to the heart, as Graves gets the upper hand on Bond. The villain dons a parachute, but Bond cleverly pulls his ripcord. The chute deploys, and Graves is pulled into one of the plane's engines. Using a helicopter stored in the cargo bay, Bond and Jinx fly away from the disintegrating plane.

Moneypenny has a romantic moment with 007, but it's only the Q Branch virtual simulator once again. Bond and Jinx share their own romantic moment—for real.

Casino Royale

(2006—British/METRO-GOLDWYN-MAYER/UNITED ARTISTS—144 MIN/ COLOR) Based on the Ian Fleming novel.
DIRECTOR: Martin Campbell
ORIGINAL MUSIC: David Arnold
FILM EDITING: Stuart Baird
PRODUCTION DESIGN: Peter Lamont

CAST: Daniel Craig (007/James Bond)
Eva Green (Vesper Lynd)
Mads Mikkelsen (Le Chiffre)
Judi Dench (M)
Jeffrey Wright (Felix Leiter)
Giancarlo Giannini (Rene Mathis)
Caterina Murino (Solange)
Simon Abkarian (Alex Dimitrios)
Jesper Christensen (Mr. White)
Ivana Milicevic (Valenka)

Prague, in the Czech Republic, and James Bond earns his double-oh status
with two kills. One is a nasty fight in a public restroom, resulting in the
drowning of an informer. The other is Dryden, an MI6 agent who's been
selling information to the other side.

In Uganda, the sinister Mr. White introduces a man named Le Chiffre,
a banker of questionable reputation, to a terrorist known as Obanno. The
terrorist gives Le Chiffre millions of dollars to invest, with a guaranteed
return, to finance Obanno's illegal activities. Le Chiffre uses the money
to short sell stock in a new airline venture known as Skyfleet, although the
move is contrary to market indications that Skyfleet will only increase in
value.

In Madagascar, Bond and Carter, a field agent, tail a bomber known
as Mollaka during a street match between a mongoose and cobra. Carter's
inexperience spooks Mollaka and he bolts, showing great athletic skill as a
free runner. Bond gives chase and keeps pace with the gymnastic terrorist.
They climb to the top of a building under construction, crossing to cranes
hundreds of feet in the air. Making their way back to ground level, Bond
grabs Mollaka at the Nambutu Embassy, where they're surrounded by local
troops. Bond shoots Mollaka dead and detonates a propane tank, escaping
in the confusion. Searching Mollaka's backpack, Bond finds a bomb and a
cell phone with a text message: ELLIPSIS.

In London, Bond makes his way into M's apartment, where he pulls the
SIM card from Mollaka's cell phone and traces the "ELLIPSIS" message to
the Ocean Club in the Bahamas. An angered M finds Bond and chides him
for killing Mollaka. She regrets giving Bond his double-oh status and tells
him to cool off somewhere for a few weeks. He figures the Bahamas are as
good a place as any to chill.

In Nassau, Bond finds the man who sent the message is Alex Dimitrios,
who is associated with Le Chiffre. Bond beats Dimitrios at poker, winning
his vintage Aston Martin and seducing his beautiful wife, Solange. Bond

Casino Royale (2006)—US advance one-sheet poster.

follows her husband to Miami and kills him after Dimitrios passes a bag to Carlos, a man he's hired to finish the job Mollaka started.

Bond tails Carlos to the Miami airport, where Carlos dons a security guard uniform from the bag and heads out to the tarmac. The new Skyfleet aircraft has been unveiled at the airport, and Carlos' plan is to destroy the plane with a small bomb attached to a fuel truck. Le Chiffre's short sale of Skyfleet stock will rake in millions and millions of dollars in the wake of the company's losses when the plane explodes.

Bond rides atop the truck as the terrorist drives wildly toward the plane. Jumping into the cab, Bond fights with Carlos. Bond brings the truck to a stop just short of the plane and is arrested by the police. Carlos detonates the bomb but finds it has been quietly attached to his belt by Bond. With the plane and Skyfleet safe, Le Chiffre has lost more than $101 million of Obanno's money. Solange is found dead as a result, with the assumption she tipped Bond to the bomb plot.

M has Bond implanted with a homing chip, telling him that Le Chiffre plans to recoup his losses by hosting—and winning—a major poker tournament at the Casino Royale in Montenegro. As MI6's best player, Bond will be entered into the game to beat Le Chiffre.

En route to Montenegro, Bond meets Vesper Lynd, a financial expert with MI6 assigned to watch Bond and the money being played. She shows a fair amount of contempt for her travel partner and intends on keeping everything on a strict business level.

In Montenegro, Bond picks up a new Aston Martin DBS and meets Rene Mathis, his local contact. To keep the local police out of the way, Mathis has framed the chief of police. Bond and Lynd pose as a couple and slightly warm to each other as they prepare for their evening at the casino.

At the poker table, the game is Texas Hold'em. Each player has bought in for $10 million; an additional buy-in of $5 million is available should the player lose his or her original money. The money has been placed in escrow, with a password chosen by each player. Play begins and Bond picks up on Le Chiffre's tic when he bluffs: a slight twitch in his eye. Bond places a homing device in Le Chiffre's inhaler during a break in the action.

Returning to his room, Le Chiffre finds Obanno waiting for him, and he wants his money. When the terrorist threatens to sever the hand of Le Chiffre's girlfriend, Valenka, the banker makes no protest but promises to deliver the money tomorrow. Using the planted homing device, Bond catches Obanno and a henchman in a stairwell, viciously killing them both while Lynd watches, horrified. Later, Bond finds Lynd sitting stunned in the shower. He sits with her and soothes her shock at the violence she witnessed.

Mathis has the two dead men placed in the trunk of one of Le Chiffre's men in a frame-up. Back at the gaming table, Bond loses everything to Le Chiffre, misreading his bluff. Lynd refuses to back his reentry with another $5 million, but an ally—Felix Leiter from the CIA—will back Bond as long as the CIA can take the collar on Le Chiffre.

Le Chiffre's girlfriend slips a deadly poison into Bond's martini, and he quickly leaves the table. Disoriented, Bond makes his way to his car and contacts MI6. Personnel at headquarters instruct the dying Bond on the use of a portable defibrillator, but it doesn't work, and he passes out. Lynd finds Bond and, noting a loose wire on the device, reconnects it and shocks 007 back to life.

Bond surprises Le Chiffre by returning to the table, ready to play. With more than $100 million on the table, Bond goes all in. Le Chiffre calls and is beaten by Bond with a straight flush.

Bond and Lynd dine in celebration, and the woman is called away by Mathis. Bond is suspicious and sees Vesper kidnapped by Le Chiffre's men. He climbs into the Aston Martin and races off in pursuit. But Lynd has been bound and left in the road. Bond quickly swerves to avoid her, flipping the car a number of times and coming to rest, with Bond unconscious.

Bond and Lynd are taken to a rusting cargo boat. The British agent wakes to find himself stripped and bound to a seatless chair. Using a large knotted rope, Le Chiffre punishes Bond, demanding the money he lost. Preparing to castrate Bond, Le Chiffre is shot in the head by Mr. White, who bursts in.

Convalescing, Bond believes Mathis was responsible for Vesper's and his capture. MI6 agents taze Mathis and drag him away. Vesper sits with Bond, and they are visited by the casino's banker, who needs their passwords to release Bond's gambling winnings. Bond enters "vesper" as his password, and the funds are released.

Bond pledges his love to Vesper and tenders his resignation to MI6 while they boat through the canals of Venice. They plan to take a long trip; Lynd will get the money and Bond will stock up on supplies. When M calls to discuss when Bond plans on depositing the money he won, he realizes Vesper has set him up by placing the money in her own account. And now she is out, collecting it.

Bond frantically searches for Lynd, finding her as she gives the money to someone named Gettler. He and his henchman grab Lynd and flee to an old building under renovation. Lynd is locked into an elevator cage and Bond shoots several flotation bags keeping the building above water. It begins to slowly sink, while Bond kills Gettler and his men. But Lynd kills herself by locking the cage from Bond and sinking into the water, drowning. And Mr. White, quietly watching from afar, leaves with the money.

Bond hears from M that Lynd had a boyfriend kidnapped by Le Chiffre's organization and she was blackmailed into cooperating with the villain. Bond will rejoin MI6 after a short rest, but there is no clue as to who is behind everything, as the trail has gone cold. But Lynd left a text for Bond on her cell phone before she died—a phone number for Mr. White.

On the edge of a seaside estate, Mr. White receives a call—and a sniper bullet to his leg. The man responsible? Bond—James Bond.

Quantum of Solace

(2008—British/METRO-GOLDWYN-MAYER/UNITED ARTISTS—106 MIN/
   COLOR) Based on the Ian Fleming short story title.
DIRECTOR: Marc Forster
ORIGINAL MUSIC: David Arnold
FILM EDITING: Matt Chesse and Richard Pearson
PRODUCTION DESIGN: Dennis Gassner
CAST: Daniel Craig (007/James Bond)
Olga Kurylenko (Camille)
Mathieu Amalric (Dominic Greene)
Judi Dench (M)
Giancarlo Giannini (Rene Mathis)
Gemma Arterton (Strawberry Fields)
Jeffrey Wright (Felix Leiter)
David Harbour (Gregg Beam)
Jesper Christensen (Mr. White)
Joaquin Cosio (General Medrano)
Fernando Guillen Cuervo (Chief of Police)
Glenn Foster (Mitchell)
Simon Kassianides (Yusef Kabira)
Stana Katic (Corrine)
Neil Jackson (Slate)

Cutting his way through crowded traffic on a mountain road, James Bond is pursued by machine-gunning thugs. Barely escaping them, Bond arrives at a Siena, Italy, palazzo. In the Aston Martin's trunk is a bound and battered Mr. White.

The palazzo is a field office for MI6, where M reveals to Bond that Vesper Lynd's boyfriend—Yusef Kabira—was supposedly found dead, but DNA proved it wasn't Kabira. Interrogated about his criminal organization, a smug White claims their people are everywhere.

Proving him correct, M's aide, Mitchell, pulls a gun and shoots an MI6 agent and Mr. White. Bond chases Mitchell, who flees through a large

Quantum of Solace—US advance one-sheet poster.

throng of horse-racing fans and onto the rooftops. Fighting hand-to-hand in a renovation site, Bond kills Mitchell. When 007 returns to the site of the ambush, he finds White is gone.

In London, MI6 traces money found on Mitchell to a man named Slate, who is in Haiti. Once there, Bond kills the knife-wielding Slate in his hotel room and assumes his identity, retrieving a briefcase from the front desk.

As Slate, Bond is picked up by the dark and beautiful Camille Montes. When it's discovered in the briefcase that Slate was supposed to kill Camille, Bond hops out of her car, and she speeds off. He follows in a stolen motorcycle to the dockside warehouse of Dominic Greene, Camille's former lover and the man who ordered Slate to kill her.

Greene welcomes Bolivian general Medrano, who seeks Greene's help to overthrow his country's government. In exchange, Greene will receive a parcel of desert property, possibly rich in oil. Greene offers Camille to the general—who killed her family—but Bond rescues her in a thrilling boat chase.

Dropping the girl on shore, Bond contacts M. Greene is an industrialist and philanthropist, running an ecological company called Greene Planet. M checks with Gregory Beam of the CIA, who claims to have no interest in Greene. But M knows otherwise.

Greene boards a private plane bound for Austria with Beam and Felix Leiter. A deal is struck, where the US will not stop the Bolivian coup, and in return, America will receive the lease rights for any oil found in the region. Greene notes that Bond is tailing them and needs him killed. Beam agrees, but Leiter pretends not to recognize 007's photo.

In Austria, Greene attends the opera, which also doubles as a secret meeting of his organization, known as Quantum, which includes Mr. White. Bond steals one of the private earphones, interrupting the conversation with a suggestion that they should hold their meeting somewhere else. As the guilty members start to quietly leave, Bond snaps their pictures for MI6.

Leaving the theater, Bond gets into a gunfight, and a bodyguard to an advisor for the British prime minister is shot by Greene's men. Bond is framed for the killing, and M restricts all of 007's credit cards and his passport.

Bond travels to Talamone, Italy, where Rene Mathis—exonerated of any involvement with Le Chiffre—has retired. Bond convinces Mathis to fly with him to La Paz, Bolivia. Once there, Bond is intercepted by Strawberry Fields, a pretty member of the British Consulate, who has orders to get Bond back to London on the next plane in the morning.

Bond does not approve of Fields' choice of hotel and insists on upgrading to something finer. He romances the girl in a luxurious suite, then they attend a fund-raiser held by Greene Planet, while Mathis meets with his old friend, the national chief of police. Greene appeals to the crowd to financially support his Tierra Project, which will rejuvenate the world's vegetation. Camille attempts to sabotage Greene's fund-raiser, and he prepares to kill her, but Bond intervenes.

He leaves with Camille in a van, tailed by the national police. When they pull him over, the police discover a beaten Rene Mathis in the trunk—whom they obviously planted there themselves. They quickly shoot Mathis, and Bond kills them both. Mathis urges Bond to forgive Vesper Lynd, as well as himself, and he stays with his old friend until Rene passes away. Coldly, Bond leaves Mathis in a garbage bin, and he is blamed for killing Mathis.

Bond and Camille fly to Greene's desert property, but are shot out of the sky by a jet and a helicopter. The pair parachute to safety into a sinkhole, although they are hard-pressed to make their way out. Bond and Camille find they are both after Greene to get to someone else—Camille wants Medrano for killing her family, and Bond wants White for the death of Lynd. Climbing to the surface, they discover that Greene has dammed an underground river—Quantum wants water, not oil. By creating a drought in Bolivia, Quantum will hold control over the much-needed water.

Back at the hotel, Bond finds M waiting. Fields has been killed by Greene, drowned in oil, with her body left in Bond's bed. Considering him to be a loose cannon and not to be trusted, M has Bond taken away, pending an investigation. But he escapes, telling M that Fields showed real bravery and that should be noted in the final report. M now knows Bond can be trusted.

Bond and Camille drive away, and Bond connects with Leiter in a dingy bar. They both believe their governments are on the wrong trail. With Greene in delivering money to Medrano in a hotel called La Perla de las Dunas out in the desert, Bond has to move quickly.

At the empty hotel, Medrano and the police chief wait for Greene, while Bond and Camille prepare to attack. Greene forces Medrano to sign a contract that will gouge the new government for water pricing, reminding him that Quantum is very powerful.

Bond kills the police chief as he leaves and runs after Greene. Medrano assaults a hotel worker in his room, but Camille stops him and shoots him dead. A crashed car has set off a chain reaction of explosions in the resort, and Bond pulls the frightened Camille to safety amid the flames. Catching Greene, Bond gets him to talk, then leaves him in the middle of the desert with a can of motor oil to drink if he gets thirsty.

Bond and Camille kiss and part company, with 007 taking off for Kazan, Russia. He finds Lynd's former boyfriend, Kabira, with Corrine, a female Canadian agent. She's wearing a knotted necklace, just like Lynd had. Bond lets the agent go, revealing what a villain Kabira is and suggesting she and her agency check their system for security leaks. Against his rage and desire for vengeance, Bond leaves Kabira in one piece and turns him over to MI6.

Greene was found dead in the desert, two bullets in his head and motor oil in his stomach. Felix Leiter was promoted into Beam's vacated position. Bond leaves Vesper's necklace in the snow, and M needs 007 back with MI6, but then—he never left.

The gun barrel sequence closes the film.

Skyfall

(2012—British/METRO-GOLDWYN-MAYER/SONY—143 MIN/COLOR) Based on an original screenplay by John Logan, Neal Purvis, and Robert Wade.
DIRECTOR: Sam Mendes
ORIGINAL MUSIC: Thomas Newman
FILM EDITING: Stuart Baird
PRODUCTION DESIGN: Dennis Gassner
CAST: Daniel Craig (007/James Bond)
Ralph Fiennes (Gareth Mallory)
Judi Dench (M)
Javier Bardem (Raoul Silva)
Helen McCrory (Clair Dowar)
Naomie Harris (Eve)
Bérénice Marlohe (Séverine)
Albert Finney (Kincade)
Ben Whishaw (Q)
Ola Rapace (Patrice)

James Bond finds himself in Istanbul, Turkey, hot on the trail of Patrice, a hired gunslinger who has grabbed a secret hard drive from an MI6 operative, loaded with the facts and figures of all the agents on Her Majesty's secret service—and more. The chase, first by car and then by motorcycle, leads to the top of a speeding train. MI6 field agent Eve shoulders her weapon and—with the remote order from M—fires at Patrice. But Bond is hit instead and falls into the water below. At MI6 headquarters, M begins to write 007's obituary.

A group of cyberterrorists begins releasing the names of the agents online—five each week. And their lifeless bodies quickly begin to add up. Meanwhile, 007 remains alive, but barely. He hides out near the Mediterranean, drinking, gambling, swimming in self-pity; with an unshaven face and red-rimmed eyes, he hardly resembles the suave and able agent he once was.

An attack on MI6 headquarters in London leaves M's office in ruins. Bond resurfaces as MI6 relocates underground and M is in fear for her job and her life. Bond is believed to be unfit for duty—from age and inactivity—so he's forced to resubmit to the physical and psychological tests all agents undergo. Gareth Mallory, the bureaucratic head of England's Intelligence and Security Committee, raises doubts about M's ability to lead and Bond's ability to still be effective. But M defends herself and assigns 007

Skyfall—British quad teaser poster.

the task of tracking the villain down, declaring that the agent has passed the battery of tests. This is a lie—he flunked them all.

At the National Gallery in London, he meets the young, computer-savvy quartermaster—Q—who sets Bond up with a tiny radio homing device and a new Walther PPK, equipped with a signature grip that allows only 007 to use it. Arriving in Shanghai, China, Bond catches up with Patrice, but the hit man dies before Bond can find out who hired him. A poker chip belonging to Patrice leads 007 to Macau, where he receives a huge payout—the casino cashier has mistaken Bond for the mercenary.

Bond is then approached by Séverine, a beautiful and mysterious woman who says she was waiting to see who redeemed the chip. Bond identifies her from a tattoo as a former sex slave who escaped the trade into the arms of a possessive lover, whom 007 takes to be the man he is looking for. Séverine offers to help him if he will kill her "employer," and warns him of an impending attempt on his life. Sure enough, her bodyguards attack him as he tries to leave. After one assailant unsuccessfully tries to use Bond's own PPK against him, a Komodo dragon slinks into the fray. Fortunately, the lizard doesn't care for an English meal and chooses to chew on Bond's opponent instead.

After a quick shower and dalliance with the girl on her yacht, the two are captured and taken to a deserted island, where 007 connects with Séverine's employer; the man identifies himself as ex-MI6-agent Raoul Silva and binds Bond to a chair amid a bank of computer servers. The villain makes a forward pass at 007, who deftly drops it without fumbling. Silva claims infinite reign over the Internet, being able to hack anyone, anywhere, anytime. In a cruel game of target practice, he then shoots Séverine dead for her betrayal.

But thanks to Bond's homing device, the villain is quickly captured and confined to a glass cage back at MI6's covert headquarters. He reveals part of his anger toward M and MI6, relating to his capture when still an agent in the Far East. As an act of loyalty, Silva took a cyanide suicide capsule, but he didn't die. Instead, he wound up grotesquely maimed—toothless and disfigured—choosing to wear a prosthetic piece to cover the injury. When Q tries to open Silva's computer, the hacking disables MI6 security, allowing the villain to escape.

Bond tracks Silva to London's Tube (its subway system). Disguised as a police officer, Silva derails a train and slips away once again. With his thugs also wearing police garb, Silva breaks into a governmental meeting where M is under scrutiny. Bond quickly drives off with his boss, zooming away in his trusty Aston Martin DB5 and hoping Silva will take the bait. Q fabricates a digital trail for the villain to follow.

Bond and M escape to Scotland and the Skyfall estate—007's childhood home—as Silva and his band of thugs give chase. Skyfall's gamekeeper, Kincade, helps defend the land. Bond holds off the villain's gunmen as Silva chases M into a local chapel. She's been mortally wounded with a gunshot by one of his men. Bond stabs Silva in the back and kills him, but M dies from her wound and 007 can only cradle her in his arms.

With MI6 rebuilding itself, field agent Eve Moneypenny is now assigned to a desk job, assisting the new M—Gareth Mallory—as 007 reports for duty.

9

Tomorrow Never . . . Heard of These

The "Unofficial" James Bond Projects

Thee's no doubt about it—everybody likes to get in on a good thing. Which, of course, was the case with James Bond. The name itself is golden, and for every "official" 007 entry, there is at least one "unofficial" attempt to cash in on the goodies. As this book's focus is essentially on the visual media of James Bond, we will forego the instances of music, merchandising, and other such arenas and look at several attempts to jump on the James Bond bandwagon, with or without the blessings of the owners of the rights to 007.

1954—Climax!

As soon as author Ian Fleming had penned his first James Bond novel, it became apparent that his hero was a natural for a visual medium, as well as in written form. The action, adventure, danger, romance, and exotic settings were all perfect for the new form of daily entertainment that was sweeping America in the early 1950s. It was the mesmerizing glowing glass tube known as television.

Fleming first published *Casino Royale* in the UK in April 1953. Within a year and a half, the American television network CBS produced a one-hour program of the title for a drama anthology series called *Climax!*

In the same vein as many of the anthology programs of the day, such as NBC's *Kraft Television Theatre* and *Philco Television Playhouse*, CBS's *Playhouse 90,* and others, *Climax!* presented a video dramatization of a written work, sometimes well known and sometimes not. For example, one week might feature a Gore Vidal adaptation of Ernest Hemingway's *A Farewell to Arms,* while another week would offer Vidal's take on Robert Louis Stevenson's *Dr. Jekyll and Mr. Hyde.* Or Rod Serling might take a swing at Ring Lardner's boxing story "Champion." The series ran for four seasons, 1954 to 1958.

Sensing an exciting one hour of TV at hand, CBS producer Bretaigne Windust paid Ian Fleming $1,000 for the rights to produce *Casino Royale* as an episode of *Climax!* Presented on October 21, 1954, it would be the third episode of the new series. Of course, Hollywood likes to have its way with certain aspects of a production. For CBS's *Casino Royale,* British secret agent James Bond would become CIA agent (and card sharp) Jimmy Bond, while CIA operative Felix Leiter would become a British agent named Clarence Leiter. History records the first James Bond as being played on the screen by American actor Barry Nelson.

Nelson had a solid, albeit unspectacular, career on television, the live stage, and in films. His first appearance found him supporting William Powell and Myrna Loy in 1941's *Shadow of the Thin Man.* By the 1950s, he was splitting his time between TV anthologies and live theater. In the 1960s, Nelson found himself as a semiregular panelist on TV game shows like *To Tell the Truth* and *I've Got a Secret.* He received a Tony Award nomination in 1978 for Best Actor in *The Act.* Retiring in 1990, Nelson passed away in 2007.

As sure-handed as the character of James Bond was, Nelson admits he was not. He told an interviewer in a 2004 issue of *Cinema Retro* magazine, "No one had ever heard of James Bond . . . I was scratching my head wondering how to play it." The fact that the live production would only be one hour in length also left the actor frustrated. He said, "I was very conscious of the fact that there wasn't much to go on. It was too superficial."

Facing off against Nelson's Jimmy Bond would be legendary Hungarian character actor Peter Lorre as the sadistic Le Chiffre. Lorre's résumé as an actor was certainly diverse: He was riveting as the psychopathic child stalker in Fritz Lang's 1931 German-language thriller *M,* demure as the sissified Joel Cairo in John Huston's 1941 classic *The Maltese Falcon,* and downright hilarious as the demented and drunken Dr. Einstein in Frank Capra's 1945 comedy *Arsenic and Old Lace.* With his pop eyes and European demeanor, he was perfect for the role of baccarat expert Le Chiffre. Not quite sixty years of age, Lorre died in 1964.

Climax! Casino Royale

(1954—American/CBS TELEVSION—52 MIN/BLACK AND WHITE) Based on
the Ian Fleming novel.
PRODUCER: Bretaigne Windust
DIRECTOR: William H. Brown
ART DIRECTION: Robert Tyler Lee and James D. Vance
CAST: William Lundigan (Host)
Barry Nelson (Jimmy Bond)

Peter Lorre (Le Chiffre)
Linda Christian (Valerie Mathis)
Michael Pate (Felix Leiter)
Eugene Borden (Chef De Partie)
Jean Del Val (Croupier)
Gene Roth (Basil)
Kurt Katch (Zoltan)

ACT I—As the program opens, Jimmy Bond stands outside the Casino Royale. Gunshots, aimed at the tuxedo-clad man, miss their mark. At the baccarat table, "card sense" Jimmy Bond quickly wins an enormous sum of money and attracts the attention of Brit Clarence Leiter. Bond has also attracted the attention of a "toad-like" man named Le Chiffre and an old flame, Valerie Mathis. Over scotch and water, Bond—an operative for the Combined Intelligence Agency (CIA)—finds that Leiter is a member of British Secret Service. Bond's assignment is to take on Le Chiffre in baccarat. A Soviet spy, Le Chiffre has been gambling with (and losing) his country's funds. If Bond can defeat Le Chiffre in the card game, the Soviets will cut their losses and eliminate the embezzling Le Chiffre. Bond and Valerie renew their acquaintance in his hotel room as the evening draws to a close. Bond knows Le Chiffre is behind Mathis' arrival at the Casino Royale, and while Le Chiffre and his men eavesdrop with a listening device planted in Bond's room, Valerie pleads with James to not play Le Chiffre and to leave town. He refuses. As the game begins the next evening, Bond receives a mysterious phone call, warning him that if he beats Le Chiffre, Valerie will lose her life.

ACT II—The game commences, with Le Chiffre dealing from the shoe. Le Chiffre quickly cleans out Bond's stake, but Leiter advances another F35 million to his associate, and play continues. The tables turn, and Bond now cleans out Le Chiffre, winning a total of

Barry Nelson as Jimmy Bond in *Casino Royale* (1954).

F87 million. While collecting his winnings, Bond discovers the advance of F35 million came not from Leiter, but from Valerie. But Mathis has now disappeared, and a frantic search begins. Bond stashes his winnings check behind the number plate on his hotel room door. Valerie, with Le Chiffre and his thugs, catch up with Bond in his room. It's revealed that she has been acting as a double agent, for both the Soviets and the French Secret Service.

ACT III—Le Chiffre tortures Bond in an attempt to locate the missing check. When he refuses to talk, Le Chiffre and his gang search the room, leaving Bond and Valerie tied up in the bathroom. But, using a razor blade Le Chiffre keeps hidden in his cigarette case, Bond cuts himself free. He subdues one of Le Chiffre's thugs, taking his gun and mortally wounding Le Chiffre. With his last breaths, Le Chiffre tries to escape with Valerie, but Bond finishes off the evil spy. Bond and Valerie embrace.

What Followed *Climax!*

It was an exciting time for television, where, unlike movies, the programs were presented live. Much like a stage play, there was no stopping, videotape editing, or going back to correct a flubbed line or missed cue. As such, *Climax!* was a live production, at least for its first few seasons. However, an often-told piece of Hollywood legend has been erroneously hung upon *Casino Royale*. As the story goes, Barry Nelson as Bond kills Peter Lorre as Le Chiffre. The actor, supposedly dead, lies still on the studio floor. But, forgetting he is in a live television production, Lorre supposedly stands up within camera range and walks off the shot, creating an unexpected and hilarious moment of television history.

In actuality, the myth has the correct series but the wrong episode. On Thursday, October 7, 1954, the very first episode of *Climax!* premiered on CBS. The show that week was one of Raymond Chandler's Philip Marlowe detective stories, *The Long Goodbye*. Actor Tristram Coffin was playing an author who is murdered (rather convenient having someone named "Coffin" playing someone dead). With his character sufficiently dead and believing he was not in the camera shot, Coffin got up and moved into the darkness behind the set. Newspaper accounts from across the country took note of the gaffe, while still praising the series as a whole.

To say that CBS's *Casino Royale* is a curiosity is an understatement. Produced live on a soundstage at Television City in Hollywood, it was a good choice (albeit the *only* one, since Fleming had only written the one novel up to that point). The interior sets of the casino floor, hotel hallway, along with Bond's and Le Chiffre's hotel rooms are understandably cramped and stage-play-like. Yet the camera work is inventive and first-rate, snaking its way among casino guests to keep up with the movement of the principals. The acting is quite good, especially knowing after the fact that Barry Nelson was clueless as to how he should play Bond.

It seems that CBS was not sure 1950s America was ready for a heroic spy from "across the pond," as evidenced by the fact that Bond is portrayed as an American agent (working for the not-well-disguised CIA—the Combined Intelligence Agency). His recurring CIA cohort in the future film series—Felix Leiter—was first depicted as a British Secret Service agent named Clarence Leiter in CBS' *Casino Royale.*

The show follows the novel relatively closely (understanding, of course, that much needed to be excised due to the TV time constraint of one hour; Nelson has said that scene and line cuts were taking place right up to the last minute before airtime). Even so, the nascent world of television had to make some adjustments for fear of offending the masses (and the FCC). In the novel, Le Chiffre tortures Bond using a carpet beater on the hero's most sensitive of areas while he is tied naked to a bottomless chair (if you haven't read the book, you can use your imagination). It's also a scene that is presented, more or less as written, in Daniel Craig's 2006 feature film version. In its place, the 1954 *Casino Royale* finds Bond trussed up and barefoot in his hotel room bathtub. Le Chiffre, seeking the whereabouts of the ₣87 million check, uses a pair of pliers to give Bond a nasty and painful pedicure. Pretty brutal stuff for 1954 American television.

1967—Casino Royale

Think of this as "the Bond film that *wasn't* a Bond film."

Let's set up the scenario. By the mid-1960s, the James Bond film franchise was thundering along like a runaway locomotive. The first films had brought in millions of dollars at the box office, while merchandising—in the form of plastic model kits, trading cards, action figures of all sizes, high quality die-cast metal cars, mocked-up weaponry of all sorts, and more—was selling like crazy at every department, variety, and five-and-ten-cent store around. Bond-like film and TV knockoffs—serious and spoofs—were being prepared by every major studio and more. (For starters, consider Dean Martin as Matt Helm, James Coburn as Derek Flint, Michael Caine as Harry Palmer, Don Adams as Maxwell Smart, Robert Vaughn as Napoleon Solo, Patrick Macnee as John Steed, Robert Conrad as James West, and Anne Francis as Honey West—no relation.) Basically, anything "Bond" was big business.

An agent and producer named Charles K. Feldman happened to own the movie rights to *Casino Royale.* How? Back in the mid-'50s, Ian Fleming had sold the TV rights for the book—as previously outlined—to CBS. But the film rights were sold in 1956 to actor/director/producer Gregory Ratoff, who died before his plans to bring Bond to the big screen could come true. Ratoff's widow sold the film rights to Feldman, who wanted to bring *Casino Royale* to theaters as a serious Bond film, much like the Broccoli/Saltzman series. He even wished to cast Connery as Bond and approached the two producers in an effort to work out a deal. When that failed, Feldman got together with Columbia Pictures and decided to make the biggest Bond spoof he could.

And he did.

Casino Royale (1967)—US one-sheet poster.

It was a production with an estimated budget of $12 million—25 percent *over* what Broccoli and Saltzman were spending at the time to make a Bond film. It was a film with some of Hollywood's biggest names—David Niven, Peter Sellers, Orson Welles, George Raft, Woody Allen, Ursula Andress, Peter O'Toole, William Holden, and foreign star Jean-Paul Belmondo. It had five directors, including Oscar winner John Huston. It was over two hours long.

It was exactly what it sounds like—one big mess.

Although a synopsis is usually a requisite in this book, suffice it to say that a retelling of the 1967 *Casino Royale* would be a waste of my time trying to explain it, your time reading it, and the publisher's ink printing it. While it does have a small cult following today, the film is almost unanimously considered unwatchable—an opinion initially voiced by various film critics at the time of its release. *Variety* magazine said *Casino Royale* was "lacking discipline and cohesion." Roger Ebert, writing for the *Chicago Sun-Times,* said it was "a definitive example of what can happen when everybody working on a film goes simultaneously berserk." Similarly, Bosley Crowther dismissed *Casino Royale* in the *New York Times* as "reckless, disconnected nonsense."

The film took a few things from Fleming's novel—mostly names like James Bond, Le Chiffre, and Vesper Lynd. Those, along with the film's title and a game of baccarat, were basically the only connections to the real world of Bond.

No matter, the Bond touch remained golden, as *Casino Royale* grossed more than $22 million in the United States and doubled that around the world. The soundtrack featured two Top Forty hit tunes—Herb Alpert and the Tijuana Brass' instrumental title theme and Dusty Springfield's "Look of Love," written by Burt Bacharach. Costar Orson Welles suggested that the film's success could be partially credited to an ad campaign with posters that featured the nude and psychedelically tattooed backside of a comely young lady.

1983—Never Say Never Again

Let's see if we can get this story straight (better pack a lunch—this may take a while).

In 1958, Irish filmmaker Kevin McClory began working with Ian Fleming to turn several of Fleming's Bond novels into movies. Along with screenwriter Jack Whittingham, McClory and Fleming wrote a screenplay called *Thunderball,* an exciting adventure that took James Bond underwater in a search for hijacked nuclear weapons, ending in a battle with villain Emilio Largo and SPECTRE.

Fleming published the novel of *Thunderball* in 1961, based on the screenplay by McClory and Whittingham, with one small problem. He neglected to mention the book (or credit the story) to McClory and Whittingham. A subsequent lawsuit resulted in proper credits for any future publications of *Thunderball* and film rights, along with the entities of SPECTRE and Ernst Stavro Blofeld, being awarded to McClory.

Wait—it gets worse.

At the very same time the lawsuit was taking place—and with absolutely *no* connection to Fleming or the other principles—film producers Harry Saltzman and Albert Broccoli, along with United Artists, asked Richard Maibaum to write a screenplay based on the *Thunderball* novel. When word of the lawsuit reached Saltzman and Broccoli, they changed course to steer clear of the mess and made *Dr. No* the first Bond film.

By 1965, the duo of Saltzman and Broccoli, with their company called Eon Productions, had made Bond a household name and wanted to film the Maibaum script, while McClory was itching to make *Thunderball* on his own. To avoid any ongoing legal hassles, McClory made a deal with Eon Productions that titled McClory as "producer" of *Thunderball*, while Saltzman and Broccoli were credited as "presenters." An additional provision of the truce kept McClory from making any film version of *Thunderball* for the next ten years.

In 1976, McClory collaborated with Sean Connery and Len Deighton to write an original screenplay for a Bond film called *Warhead*. Based on *James Bond of the Secret Service,* by Ian Fleming, McClory, and Jack Whittingham, the story involved a SPECTRE plan to blow up New York's financial district with robotic sharks (really!). Described as "*Star Wars* underwater," the film's plans were sunk by ensuing legal objections from Eon Productions. The unproduced movie script for *Warhead* came up for auction at Christie's in 2008, selling for nearly $70,000.

While it took nearly twenty years, Kevin McClory made his *Thunderball* in 1983, although his agreement prohibited him from using "James Bond," "007," or "Secret Service" in the title. No matter—*Never Say Never Again* is *Thunderball*.

Never Say Never Again

(1983—British/WARNER BROTHERS—134 MIN/COLOR) Based on the Ian Fleming novel *Thunderball*.
DIRECTOR: Irvin Kershner
ORIGINAL MUSIC: Michel LeGrand
FILM EDITING: Ian Crafford

PRODUCTION DESIGN: Steven Grimes and Philip Harrison
CAST: Sean Connery (007/James Bond)
Kim Basinger (Domino Petachi)
Klaus Maria Brandauer (Maximillian Largo)
Barbara Carrera (Fatima Blush)
Max Von Sydow (Ernst Stavro Blofeld)
Bernie Casey (Felix Leiter)
Edward Fox (M)
Alec McCowen (Q)
Pamela Salem (Miss Moneypenny)
Rowan Atkinson (Nigel Small-Fawcett)

A new M is in command at MI6, Britain's Secret Service. It seems he has little use for the licensed-to-kill members of the "00" department, as aging secret agent James Bond has been relegated to teaching and participating in war games. Sensing 007 may have lost his competitive edge, M sends him to the health spa known as Shrublands to clear his mind . . . and body.

Another guest at the spa is US Air Force pilot Jack Petachi, who is under the control of the beautiful and dangerous Fatima Blush. She is a high-ranking member of the evil organization known as SPECTRE, which plans to hijack two nuclear weapons with Petachi's help. The evil plan, called "The Tears of Allah," is masterminded by SPECTRE agent Maximillian

Kim Basinger as Domino Petachi and Sean Connery as Bond in *Never Say Never Again*.

Largo. The charming and soft-spoken Largo poses as a wealthy business-man, traveling the world in his yacht—the *Flying Saucer*—with his beautiful, blonde mistress, Domino.

Using an eye implant to fool security systems, Petachi loads real atomic warheads into Cruise missiles during a military exercise. No longer needed, Petachi is ruthlessly killed by Blush. Blofeld, SPECTRE's fearless leader, informs the world of the weapons theft. SPECTRE plans to extort 25 percent of every country's oil purchases as the price for not detonating the bombs. They have seven days to agree. M activates the "00" section and puts Bond on the case.

First stop, the Bahamas, where Bond hooks up with Fatima Blush. While scuba diving, she tries to kill him with trained sharks, but he eludes the man-eaters and escapes with the help of a beautiful woman who is deep-sea fishing. Bond eludes a second attempt on his life by Blush and tracks Largo to the South of France. Once there, 007 connects with local operative Nicole and CIA agent, and old friend, Felix Leiter. Posing as a masseur, Bond makes first-hand contact with Domino—who happens to be the sister of the murdered Air Force officer, Jack Petachi. That evening, Bond makes his way into a gala charity ball hosted by Largo. The two face off in an elaborate video game called Domination. Largo nearly dies while losing the game, and it's obvious to Bond and Domino that he is insane. Bond accepts a tango with Domino as his prize, where he informs her of her brother's demise at the hands of Largo. Nicole is discovered dead in 007's villa, and he chases after the murderous Blush in a sleek, jet-powered motorcycle. But the cunning villainess corners Bond and prepares to shoot the secret agent dead. Bond turns the tables, blowing Blush to smithereens with a missile-firing fountain pen.

Aboard the *Flying Saucer,* Bond enlists Domino's help as the ship heads toward Largo's retreat in North Africa. Once there, the game is over, as Bond is imprisoned and Largo offers his former girlfriend for sale to seedy Bedouins in a bleak courtyard. Bond breaks his shackles and rescues Domino on horseback, while Largo escapes with one of the nuclear weap-ons. Bond, Domino, and the horse jump to safety in the Mediterranean Sea, as a Navy submarine bombards the stronghold. Onboard the sub, word arrives that one A-bomb has been found in Washington, D.C., and safely disarmed. Largo moves the second bomb to an underwater grotto called The Tears of Allah, where it is armed and dangerous. While Leiter and his men subdue Largo's soldiers, the villain takes the bomb in an underwater sled toward its designated site. In full scuba gear, Bond fights Largo and is about to succumb to the evildoer, when Domino finishes off Largo with a speargun. Bond defuses the warhead, and SPECTRE has been defeated.

Now in retirement, Bond relaxes with Domino while M pleads with his former employee to return to active service, fearing for the security of the "civilized world." "Never again" is Bond's reply—punctuated with a reassuring wink.

The Aftermath?

Much excitement surrounded the release of this film, the least of which was the return of Sean Connery as 007 following a twelve-year absence. The film's title, the first not to be based on a Fleming story or novel, actually came from Connery's wife. After making *Diamonds Are Forever* in 1971, the actor flatly stated he would *never* play Bond again. As he prepared to begin filming the 1983 picture, she reminded him, "Never say 'never' again." Connery was convinced to go back on his word by producer Jack Schwartzman, who offered him a huge sum of money and a great deal of creative control to reprise his most famous role.

Director Irvin Kershner—an American television and film director who had worked with Connery in 1966 on *A Fine Madness* and had directed 1980's *Star Wars: Episode V—The Empire Strikes Back*—was chosen to helm the picture. Kershner stated in a DVD commentary that actress Kim Basinger was having a difficult time giving him a good performance. It seems that her husband, a hairdresser on the film, was standing off camera, approving or disapproving each of his wife's takes. Kershner had him thrown off the picture.

Although there aren't as many underwater sequences as found in the 1965 *Thunderball,* the ones in *Never Say Never Again* are still quite exciting. They were directed by Ricou Browning, who had some experience in working underwater. He had made his name in the 1950s playing the Creature in *Creature from the Black Lagoon.*

10

Licence to Thrill

All the Little Folks Who Make This Possible

The big names—the names before the titles—are the ones we are most familiar with. Actors and actresses are the faces we associate with Bond—Connery, Moore, Craig, Fröbe, Walken, Blackman, Seymour, Green. Those are the folks we connect with when our favorite 007 film hits the screen.

But is that all there is, my friend?

Across the last fifty years, hundreds and hundreds of people have contributed to the success of our favorite secret agent. Many names are recognizable, but most are not. Nonetheless, without these people—the producers, directors, technical wizards—Bond and his entourage would never have existed—at least, in the way we know them today.

While it would be difficult to address all the folks behind the camera (especially since many of those people do not receive credit in the films), there are some whose major input and contributions helped to shape the James Bond films.

The Producer

Male or female, the producer is the person who is ultimately responsible for the success or failure of a film. The producer acquires the rights for the property being made into a film (books or plays or TV shows are "adapted," while original stories are written directly for the screen). The producer develops a budget and secures the financing needed (as well as the insurance to protect the investment if something goes wrong). The producer chooses a director, a screenwriter (or screenwriters), and very often, has direct input to the stars in the project. The producer, as needed, can also influence the selection of technical experts—set design and construction, costumes, makeup, special effects, camera, lighting, editing, even the caterer—essentially, every aspect of a film.

In some cases, the producer can be the director, and/or the writer and/or . . . obviously, there can be many permutations of these roles. And when shooting the film is completed, the producer will oversee the editing, music scoring, sound mixing, and other postproduction needs. And when that's all done, the producer works with studios and other companies to distribute the finished product all over the world. Then there's Blu-Ray and DVDs, cable television and video-on-demand, not to mention marketing and advertising and merchandising.

If this job sounds like a lot, watch the credits of your next James Bond film closely. Take note of how many "executive producers," "producers," and "associate producers" there are—now you know why.

Albert Broccoli

Albert Broccoli knew the job of producer well.

Born in New York City in 1909, film wasn't always in his blood. Actually, his family in Italy had a background in horticulture, and some claimed to have crossed cauliflower and Italian rabe vegetables, resulting in . . . well, broccoli.

A cousin and school chums noted that young Albert bore a strong resemblance to a popular comic strip character of the time known as Abie Kabibble. They hung the nickname of "Little Kabibble" on him; later it was shortened to "Cubby."

The young man did spend time in the veggie farming business, but wanted something else. After selling coffins, cosmetics, and Christmas trees, Broccoli found himself in the mailroom of Twentieth Century-Fox. Becoming friends with reclusive aviation and movie mogul Howard Hughes, Broccoli became an assistant director on films like *The Outlaw* in 1943.

After several years with the US Navy in World War II, Broccoli returned to Hollywood to become an agent with the Famous Artists Agency. With several years of that under his belt, he wanted to produce films as an independent. With old friend Irwin Allen (later to be the master of the disaster film), Broccoli moved to England, where the pair started Warwick Pictures.

Arranging a contract with old acquaintance Alan Ladd, Broccoli and Allen's first film was *The Red Beret* (known in America as *Paratrooper*). The production crew for the picture reads like a "Who's Who" of James Bond films—director was Terence Young, writer was Richard Maibaum, cameraman was Ted Moore, actors like Peter Burton, special-effects folks like Cliff Richardson (father of John Richardson). Ladd followed with two more films at Warwick in a three-picture deal—all were box-office successes. In

America, Columbia Pictures handled most of the distribution for Broccoli and Allen.

Warwick Pictures released a variety of films through the 1950s—jungle pictures like *Safari,* sci-fi/horror pictures like *The Gamma People,* war films like *Tank Force.* During those years, Broccoli tapped the talents of young and upcoming production people like Ken Adam, Syd Cain, and others who would eventually join the Bond crowd.

A quick fan of Ian Fleming's spy novels, Broccoli arranged a meeting with the author in 1958 with the intention of acquiring the film rights. But with Broccoli's wife ill, he entrusted the appointment to partner Irwin Allen. It was a bad move, as Allen insulted the author and his books, considering them to be useless as even TV properties.

Never recovering from his partner's lack of vision, Broccoli bought Allen out in 1960. But the thought of producing a James Bond film had never left Cubby, so he started researching the rights for the books in 1961. Imagine his disappointment when he found they were no longer available. But Broccoli's determination led him to partner with the man who owned them.

Cubby Broccoli (far left) and Harry Saltzman (far right), the first producers of James Bond films on the big screen, with Sean Connery and Ian Fleming.

Harry Saltzman

Harry Saltzman was born in Canada in 1915 but grew up in New York. Family issues forced the young man to run away to Paris at the age of sixteen, where he joined a traveling circus. He soon found himself managing a circus, before the war broke out. Accounts of his service vary, with his children citing that Saltzman joined the British Royal Air Force and was a member of the American Office of Strategic Services. Other sources suggest he was an interpreter for the Allies.

After the war, Saltzman became involved in television production, supervising *Robert Montgomery Presents* and producing NBC's *Captain Gallant of the Foreign Legion,* starring Buster Crabbe, Flash Gordon from the 1930s serials. Like his future Bond producing partner, Saltzman moved to England to produce movies.

His first production in 1956 was a remake of *Ninotchka* called *The Iron Petticoat,* with Bob Hope and Katharine Hepburn. He started Woodfall Productions with English director Tony Richardson, releasing *Look Back in Anger* with Richard Burton in 1959, *The Entertainer* with Laurence Olivier in 1960, and the award-winning *Saturday Night and Sunday Morning,* also in 1960.

But Woodfall folded, and, always a big-thinking entrepreneur, Harry Saltzman arranged a short-term movie option in late 1960 on the James Bond novels (excepting *Casino Royale*) with Ian Fleming. Shortly after, Cubby Broccoli started looking into doing the same thing.

Introduced through a mutual acquaintance, screenwriter Wolf Mankowitz, Broccoli sought to purchase the options from Saltzman. Cubby had no desire to partner up with anyone anytime soon, but Saltzman would not give up the ownership. In 1961, Broccoli and Saltzman bought an existing company—Eon Productions—to produce the films, and began shopping the properties to major film studios. (A year later, taking the first names of their wives—Dana and Jacqueline—the pair formed Danjaq S.A., a Swiss company, for tax purposes. Danjaq was a holding company that would oversee the rights use and trademarks of James Bond, as they related to the films. Danjaq became Danjaq LLC, a California-based corporation, in 1988.)

Eon first approached Columbia Pictures, who would offer no more than $400,000 as a production budget. Knowing that would never work, the pair then approached David Picker, a top executive at United Artists. In a meeting that took less than an hour, a six-picture deal was agreed to, with a $1 million budget assigned for the first Bond feature.

Although *Thunderball* had been everyone's target (even Picker had looked to get the film rights a month before the Eon meeting), questions about ownership led to the decision to make *Dr. No* as the first James Bond movie. From his days with Warwick Pictures, Broccoli brought in a familiar production team—Young, Maibaum, and Adam, among others, to shoot the film.

With production complete, the first executive screening had everyone questioning the decision to make *Dr. No*. United Artists execs looked upon this yet-to-be-released film as "B" grade and weren't happy to be $40,000 over budget. The ever-ebullient Saltzman convinced the studio to support the film—with record-setting results in England theaters, as *Dr. No* showed consistently, twenty-four hours a day.

With a fifty-fifty partnership, Broccoli and Saltzman quickly became rich and influential members of the cinema world, although they were total opposites. Cubby was everyone's pal, while Harry was often a very difficult person to work with. While Broccoli liked to stay focused on a current project, Saltzman would keep six different irons in the fire. Cubby Broccoli kept his calm on most occasions, whereas Harry Saltzman was famous for a rough and fiery temper.

Even with different dispositions, one thing the team agreed upon was keeping Bond fresh through the first part of the 1960s. Not content to just be the "money men," Broccoli and Saltzman supplied their writers, directors, and production specialists with wild and exciting ideas all the time. As an example, Cubby Broccoli referred to the Aston Martin in *Goldfinger* as "that ridiculous car."

With a short attention span, Saltzman wanted to move on to other film projects, while Cubby was happy to remain busy with Bond. Broccoli did take a break to produce a film in 1968 based on an Ian Fleming children's novel, *Chitty Chitty Bang Bang*. As might be expected, the producer tapped Bond people, including writer Richard Maibaum, production designer Ken Adam, and actors Gert Fröbe and Desmond Llewelyn.

With the relationship in the late 1960s strained, not shattered, Saltzman alone produced a three-picture series with Michael Caine as Cold War spy Harry Palmer—*The Ipcress File, Funeral in Berlin,* and *Billion Dollar Brain*.

Still, he maintained his partnership in Eon Productions and was active in the Bond films until the end of 1975. With wife Jacqueline dying from cancer, Saltzman sold his interests in the Bond franchise to United Artists (why he didn't consult his partner first is not known). When Jacqueline died a year later, Harry Saltzman essentially retired from the movies, with the exception of producing *Nijinsky* in 1980 and *Time of the Gypsies* in 1988.

Aged seventy-eight, he died in Paris of a heart attack in 1994.

Michael G. Wilson

After Saltzman left the franchise in 1975, Cubby Broccoli forged ahead as solo producer for the Bond films. The last team effort, *The Man with the Golden Gun,* had not been to his satisfaction. Now, with Saltzman gone, Broccoli could focus on Bond without distractions.

After his first wife passed in 1956, Broccoli had met and married Dana Wilson. She had been formerly wed to Lewis Wilson—the movie serials' first Batman in the 1940s. Her son, Michael, was born in New York in 1942. With the marriage to Broccoli, Wilson became Broccoli's stepson.

Degreed in electrical engineering and law, Wilson joined Eon Productions in 1972 as part of the legal department to address some company tax issues. Cubby asked him to lend a hand when the producer went solo, starting with *The Spy Who Loved Me* in 1977.

His unique skill set and natural creativity suited Wilson well, as he became executive producer for the next Bond film, *Moonraker,* in 1979. With the following film, *For Your Eyes Only,* in 1981, Wilson began a five-picture collaboration as cowriter with longtime Bond screenwriter Richard Maibaum. When a writers' strike blocked Maibaum from working on *Licence to Kill,* Wilson finished the script on his own.

Michael Wilson was also involved with the taxing issues surrounding the replacement of Roger Moore as Bond. The actor passed fifty years of age when making *The Spy Who Loved Me,* so each film following raised the question of which would be his last. Along with Broccoli, Wilson worked through the "on-again, off-again" situation with Pierce Brosnan, finally selecting Timothy Dalton for two Bond films in the late 1980s.

As Cubby had taken Michael Wilson under his wing and schooled him in all things Bond, he slowly relinquished the day-to-day tasks of Danjaq and Eon to others. Yet Broccoli remained at the center of the situation when United Artists—still holding a portion of the Bond business—merged with Metro-Goldwyn-Mayer in 1981, becoming MGM/UA. In turn, Ted Turner purchased MGM/UA in 1986, splitting it into many entities and reselling much of it.

Then in 1990, a shady character named Giancarlo Parretti bought MGM/UA. But, lying about his financial status, he quickly was forced to forfeit the purchase. The resulting lawsuits—some involving Danjaq and Eon Productions—essentially kept Broccoli and Wilson busy for six years, while no Bond films were able to be made.

Cubby Broccoli underwent triple-bypass surgery in 1994, never fully recovering from the ordeal. Two years later, in 1996, he passed away at the age of eighty-seven.

Michael G. Wilson (left) and Barbara Broccoli, stepson and daughter of Cubby Broccoli, who carried on his legacy as Bond producers.

Although busy with producing and writing for the Bond films, Wilson still found time to make cameo appearances in every picture since *The Spy Who Loved Me* in 1977. Usually posing as a tourist or worker, he actually had made his first appearance as a soldier in *Goldfinger*.

Michael G. Wilson remains at the head of the Bond franchise to this day, more than forty years after joining Eon, now sharing the production tasks with another Broccoli.

Barbara Broccoli

Daughter of Cubby and Dana Broccoli, Barbara was born in 1960 and, of course, grew up in a home filled with (and built by) James Bond. As a child, she watched the filming of *You Only Live Twice* in Japan and considered her visits to London's Pinewood Studios "like going to Grandma's house."

Barbara began working with the Bond films during summer breaks in the late 1970s. She worked with the publicity department for *The Spy Who Loved Me* in 1977, writing captions for press stills. With a degree in film communications from a California college, she became an executive assistant for *Octopussy* in 1983.

Learning on the job from father Cubby and stepbrother Michael, Barbara worked hard and continued to make substantial contributions to the Bond films in the 1980s. She was one of a team of assistant associate directors for *A View to a Kill*, then became an associate director for Timothy Dalton's turn as Bond in the late 1980s.

When the smoke cleared from the MGM/UA-Parretti debacle, Barbara Broccoli joined her stepbrother as a producer for Pierce Brosnan's *GoldenEye* in 1995. The filming delay was not enjoyed by Broccoli, as constant questions about why another Bond film wasn't being made were difficult to answer.

Much like the ending scenes in Francis Ford Coppola's *The Godfather*, semiretirement for Barbara's father found him spending time with his grandchildren, including her daughter. After his passing, Barbara continued to produce Bond films alongside Michael Wilson.

Legacy and Honors

The legacy of the Broccolis and Wilson, along with Saltzman, did not go unnoticed over the years. Their efforts in pioneering and progressing a new genre of action film with the James Bond series earned them many accolades.

Harry Saltzman, along with partner Albert Broccoli, received the Golden Laurel in 1967, given to honor top members of the film industry. The two were nominated again in 1968 and 1970.

Cubby Broccoli received the Irving G. Thalberg Memorial Award in 1982 from the Academy of Motion Picture Arts and Sciences (as part of the Academy Awards ceremony). Presented by Roger Moore, Broccoli was honored as a producer who consistently delivered the highest quality of entertainment. With the award, Broccoli joined former winners like Walt Disney, Cecil B. DeMille, and Alfred Hitchcock, among others.

When the famed 007 Stage at Pinewood Studios, built in 1976, burned down in 1984, it was rebuilt and christened the Albert R. Broccoli 007 Stage. The honor was in recognition of the major contribution Cubby had made to the British film industry. (The facility burned again in 2006 and was once more rebuilt to serve film productions at Pinewood. As of this writing, it has not yet burned for a third time.)

In 1987, Cubby received the Officer of the Order of the British Empire (OBE) from Queen Elizabeth II for his service to the film industry (Michael G. Wilson and Barbara Broccoli received similar honors in 2008). In 1989, Cubby Broccoli received BAFTA's first Britannia Award, given to honor worldwide contributions to film entertainment. Even better, the award was renamed in 2011 for Broccoli himself.

The Director

While many producers are able to work in relative obscurity (unless your name is Broccoli), the film director is the person on whom the focus lands. He or she is responsible for turning the script into a movie and visualizing the written words for millions to see on the big screen. And everybody knows it.

The director works closely with the screenwriter (or writers, or is part of the writing team, or does it alone, or . . .), making sure the right words will convey the right images. The director works with the actors and actresses (despite some wild demands for money, percentage of the gross, trailers, and other perks that real working stiffs could never even imagine) to give them motivation and reason to be someone other than who they really are. The director works closely with the technical crew heads, such as the director of photography (affectionately, or not, known as the DP), art and production designers, costume and makeup designers, and visual-effects creatives. The director may use storyboard artists (or draw the panels him- or herself) to help illustrate the various scenes in a script. The director may or may not work directly with the film editor in postproduction, at the very least providing copious notes and guidance as to the tempo, pace, and rhythm of the final product.

Above all, more than wearing the perfunctory down jacket and baseball cap, directors must be incredibly prepared. They should be spending hours and hours before the first frame of film is exposed in the camera. They are obliged to have a handle on all creative and technical aspects of the property to which they will attach their name as "Directed by."

The eleven men who have directed the Eon-produced Bond films have made great contributions toward what has been seen on screens around the world for the past fifty years. Each has brought his vision of what Ian Fleming had in his mind when he first created the good commander in 1952. There's a reason the director's name is last thing you see before the James Bond film gets underway—he knows where you're about to go, because he's the one taking you there.

Terence Young

As the director of three of the first four Bond films, Terence Young may be the director most responsible for establishing the parameters for the franchise. Young shaped the character to become the cool, yet cold, secret agent.

Terence Young with Ursula Andress and Sean Connery on set of *Dr. No.*

Young was born in China in 1915, the son of a Shanghai police official. His family returned to their English roots, where Young attended St. Catharine's College in Cambridge. Completing his schooling, he wanted a career in film.

Starting as a young screenwriter, he worked with a team to script *The Fugitive,* a British crime drama, in 1939. He continued to write war films like *Suicide Squadron* before joining the prestigious Irish Guards of the British Army. After the war, Young returned to the cinema but wasn't interested in continuing as a writer.

His first directing job was an English mystery called *Corridor of Mirrors* in 1948. Although a relatively unremarkable film, it did feature a brand-new actor named Christopher Lee and, in a small part, a very pre-Moneypenny Lois Maxwell. He continued to direct a variety of pictures, including the comedy *Woman Hater* in 1948 and the adventure *Valley of the Eagles* in 1951 (which he also wrote).

In 1953, Young joined a new British production company called Warwick Films, started by Cubby Broccoli and Irwin Allen. He directed four films with Warwick during the 1950s, including war films like *Paratrooper* and *Tank Force,* a jungle picture called *Safari,* and an action film set in Afghanistan, *Zarak.*

When Broccoli and Saltzman set out to make *Dr. No* in 1962, they presented the directing job to Guy Green, Guy Hamilton, and Ken Hughes—all of whom refused. Remembering the director from his days at Warwick, Broccoli finally locked in Young for the film.

Immediately, it was clear that Terence Young would deliver the distinct and edgy style needed for this new genre, Yet by his own admission, the director had no idea of the success that would follow this first film, and the ones to follow. Much of that success can be pinned on Young himself, who poured his own personality into the Bond persona from the start. He also championed the idea of working closely with writer Richard Maibaum to dictate who this new film persona would be and how he would behave.

Even though Sean Connery was a young and capable actor, it was Terence Young who worked closely with the performer to mold the Bond character into a smooth and sophisticated man of action. Not so much the workmanlike Bond that Ian Fleming had written about, but using the rich and flamboyant style with which he wrote the stories.

The director became a mentor to Connery, fifteen years his junior. They dined out together, and Young offered advice on how to carry himself, which fork to use, and how to hold it. Young even took the tall and brawny Connery to his suit maker on swanky Savile Row. But many were still convinced the first Bond film would be the only Bond film.

The collaborative efforts of all involved proved the naysayers wrong—by millions. With *Dr. No* budgeted at just around $1 million, people like writer Wolf Mankowitz—who had worked on an early draft of the screenplay—were convinced the film would tank. Mankowitz was so sure of it, he asked that his name be removed from the credits. (If you listen closely, you can still hear his ghost softly kicking himself in the seat of his pants, fifty years later.) Director Young had been given estimates of $8 or $10 million in gross receipts. He figured with results like those, there would likely be another Bond film to follow.

Dr. No grossed over $16 million in American ticket sales—nearly $60 million worldwide—so yes, there would be another Bond film. And yes, Terence Young would direct it.

From Russia with Love began shooting in spring of 1963, with a cast largely chosen by the knowledgeable Terence Young. The director tapped the world's most beautiful women, like former Miss Israel Aliza Gur, Jamaica-born Brit Martine Beswick, and Miss Universe runner-up Daniela Bianchi. He chose star of German theater Lotte Lenya to play the unpleasant Rosa Klebb, deftly dancing around the character's lesbian tendencies, while still allowing her intentions with the lovely Tatiana Romanova to be clear.

While shooting *From Russia with Love*, several situations presented themselves that show just what a clever and resourceful director Young was. In one case, while shooting a scene at an Istanbul train station, the director found the sight of cameras, lights, and international movie stars attracted thousands of unwanted—and unsightly—bystanders. Young quietly asked one of his stuntmen to create a suitable distraction. Moving to a high balcony a short distance away, the stuntman hung over its side and yelled frantically for help. As the crowd rushed to see what was happening, Young called "Action!" and got what he needed.

In staging the fight scenes between gypsy women, played by Gur and Beswick, Young had the two rehearse every day for three weeks, perfecting their moves. Then, when shooting began, seeking the ultimate in realism,

Young did everything he could to encourage the ladies to kill each other during the catfight.

In an amazing demonstration of unflappability, Young took off one morning with the art director and a pilot in a helicopter over the waters of western Scotland to scout locations for the climactic boat chase. Although the copter had been showing signs of trouble, the crew took off. They rose slowly, stopped, then crashed into the water, sinking about fifty feet to the bottom. Quick thinking by members of the production on shore allowed them to dive in and save the three from drowning. To everyone's amazement, Young was back behind the camera, calling for the next shot, within a half-hour of the crash—acting as though nothing had happened.

Terence Young's sharp direction resulted in another success for the nascent Bond series. This time, with a budget of $2 million, *From Russia with Love* returned almost $25 million in domestic gross receipts, with nearly $79 million worldwide. No one could doubt the fighting—and staying power—of James Bond at the movies.

But Young was ready to move on, feeling he had nothing left to give the character he'd taken and nurtured into an international entertainment phenomenon. So he passed when *Goldfinger* came around, choosing to direct the bawdy period comedy *The Amorous Adventures of Moll Flanders,* starring Kim Novak and George Sanders. He also directed an international spy thriller with Henry Fonda and Robert Ryan called *The Secret Agents.*

Ready to take one more ride with the Bond series, Terence Young accepted the opportunity to direct *Thunderball* in 1965. With the success of the first three films, there was no doubt in Young's mind that the sky would be the limit—and it was, just barely.

Casting like he had before, Young chose a former Miss France, Claudine Auger, as female lead Domino—after passing on dozens of actresses, including Raquel Welch, Julie Christie, Faye Dunaway, and Luciana Paluzzi, who at least got the part of sexy killer Fiona Volpe. Once again, he put his trust in old partners like writer Richard Maibaum and production designer Ken Adam.

Even with the logistical nightmare of more than one hundred actors and crew members and more than twelve tons of production gear in the Bahamas, Young brought *Thunderball* in under schedule, thanks to the great organization and skill of the technical teams.

With a release date of Christmastime in 1965, *Thunderball* shattered box-office records of the time. Budgeted at a blustery $9 million (no wonder shooting on Nassau beaches included champagne during breaks), the film grossed over $63 million in America and more than $140 million worldwide.

Young would continue to maintain his reputation as a top-notch director with films like the terse thriller *Wait Until Dark* with Audrey Hepburn and crime drama *The Valachi Papers* with Charles Bronson. Young did have to endure the Korean War fiasco known as *Inchon* in 1981, which starred Sir Laurence Olivier as General Douglas MacArthur. With a reported budget of $46 million, the flop grossed a total of just over $5 million.

Retiring in the late 1980s, Terence Young died of a heart attack in Cannes, France, in 1994.

Guy Hamilton

With Bond still in its infancy—so to speak—after the first two films, Guy Hamilton stepped in to deliver what many fans and critics feel is the best Bond of them all, *Goldfinger*. To direct it, Guy Hamilton used plain old common sense. One part wonderful scenery, one part beautiful women, one part awesome gadgets, one part suspense, one part amusing humor—nothing high-brow, nothing low-class—just everything fun.

Hamilton was born in Paris to English parents in 1922. Up to age thirteen, he had dreamed of being a deep-sea diver but suddenly fell in love with the cinema and decided he would be a director. He moved between England and France, becoming a tea server for French filmmakers until the war broke out, when he joined the Royal Navy.

With his release after the war, Hamilton pursued his career in cinema, becoming an assistant director with London Film Productions. He worked and learned under director Carol Reed, including assisting on *The Third Man,* which featured Orson Welles and Joseph Cotten. Hamilton also worked with director John Huston on *The African Queen* in 1951.

Ready to move up to directing, Hamilton's first film in the chair was *The Ringer* in 1952. An assortment of films followed, with crime dramas, war stories, comedies, and even a musical. During the 1950s, he directed future Bond stars like Shirley Eaton in *Charley Moon* and Donald Pleasence and Pedro Armendariz in *Stowaway Girl.*

Although he had turned down *Dr. No,* Hamilton was ready for *Goldfinger* when Broccoli and Saltzman came calling in 1964. The decision was an easy one, as Hamilton was a longtime friend of star Sean Connery.

The director knew immediately how to let the audience know what they would be in for. Even though *From Russia with Love* had somewhat established the format of a precredit sequence to open the film, it was Hamilton who decided to make the sequence an all-out, over-the-top "bit of nonsense" that would have nothing to do with the story about to unfold. Using cinematic visual devices like a decoy seagull mounted to the top of a scuba mask, removing the wet suit to reveal a white dinner jacket and tuxedo pants, and spying an advancing attacker with the reflection in a lover's eye, Hamilton was like the carnival guy who cinches the seat belt, pulls the safety bar tight, and lets you know that you're about to take a fun ride on a roller coaster.

Like Terence Young before him, Guy Hamilton guided the performers to develop their characters that would last throughout the series. When actor Desmond Llewelyn wanted to address Bond with respect, it was the director who reminded him that his character of Q was never shown any respect by the secret agent and, therefore, should be constantly perturbed with 007's shenanigans.

Hamilton's direction made *Goldfinger* an instant classic. He took the opportunity to direct two of Harry Saltzman's projects outside the Bond world in the 1960s—*Funeral in Berlin* in 1966 and *Battle of Britain* in 1969.

When Sean Connery opted to do *Diamonds Are Forever* in 1971, Hamilton signed on to direct the Bond picture as well. Being away for three pictures, the director felt there were new avenues to follow, in terms of characters, locations, stories, and other facets that made Bond unique. He worked closely with new screenwriter Tom Mankiewicz to craft a new script from an original draft written by Richard Maibaum.

Like all good directors, Hamilton enjoyed a challenge. One of the many from *Diamonds Are Forever* involved the famous scene in Las Vegas where Bond and Case escape the police by putting their smoking-hot red Mustang up on two wheels to slip down a narrow alley. The original scene going up on two wheels was shot at Universal Studios in Los Angeles, with the car up on the passenger side wheels. Coming down on two wheels was done in Las Vegas but had to be reshot due to technical issues. The reshoot was a problem for the stunt drivers this time, and they were unable to get the Mustang to do its thing on two wheels. When another team was brought in, they got the job done—but on the driver's side wheels, opposite from the first shot, creating an enormous gaffe in continuity.

Unfazed, Hamilton filmed an additional shot during the car's interior close-ups, where actors Connery and St. John leaned from one side to the other. Edited between the two exteriors, the car—now logically—entered on two wheels, was tipped by its occupants, and exited on its other two wheels.

Hamilton was instrumental in helping newcomer Roger Moore slip into the role of James Bond for *Live and Let Die* in 1973, although American star Burt Reynolds had been under consideration for a while. The director maintained a calm demeanor as shooting got underway in New Orleans—not an easy task, as speedboats, attempting to cross land during the wedding scene, continually crashed into trees, and new Bond Moore weathered a painful attack of kidney stones. With locations there, as well as Jamaica and England, Hamilton delivered a new Bond picture with a new 007 for the summer of 1973.

Guy Hamilton returned to direct Roger Moore in *The Man with the Golden Gun* the next year, then left his Bond legacy to direct other films. Although he was set to head the new *Superman* film with Christopher Reeve in 1977, English tax laws prevented Hamilton from staying in Britain for more than thirty days, and he had to pull out.

Hamilton directed a sequel to *The Guns of Navarone* in 1978 called *Force 10 from Navarone,* featuring Bond performers Robert Shaw, Barbara Bach, and Richard Kiel. He also directed Fred Ward in the title role of *Remo Williams: The Adventure Begins* in 1985. The action-packed tongue-in-cheek spy film, based on *The Destroyer* novel series, felt like a Bond movie at times and was intended to be the first of a number of Remo Williams films (in the style of the 007 pictures). But a poor showing at the box office left this film as the only one made.

Guy Hamilton made his last picture in 1989, spending a relaxed retirement while responding to many requests for comments on his days of Bond.

Lewis Gilbert

Noted for directing three James Bond films, Lewis Gilbert never strayed very far from the spotlight of performing and performers. As a writer, producer, and director, Gilbert's body of work spanned more than fifty years.

Born in London in 1920 to parents who were music hall performers, Lewis Gilbert quickly made his way to the stage as a performer himself. By the age of thirteen, he was acting in British films like *Dick Turpin,* starring hulking actor Victor McLaglen. Gilbert passed on the opportunity to attend the RADA, choosing to study directing. By nineteen years of age, he was assisting Alfred Hitchcock on *Jamaica Inn,* with Charles Laughton and Maureen O'Hara.

As a member of the RAF during the war, Gilbert was assigned to the US Air Corps Film Unit, where he wrote and directed documentary shorts for the troops. He continued in this field after the war for the Gaumont-British film company. Gilbert's first experience in directing a feature film came in 1948 with the low-budget ballet drama *The Little Ballerina.* He continued with comedies, crime dramas, and war pictures, writing many as well as directing.

In 1959, Gilbert wrote and directed *Ferry to Hong Kong,* an action film starring Orson Welles and Curt Jurgens (who would again join the director nearly twenty years later as the villain in *The Spy Who Loved Me*). Into the 1960s, Gilbert directed films like the sea adventure *Damn the Defiant!*, with Alec Guinness and Dirk Bogarde. Lewis Gilbert was chosen in 1966 to direct the multiple-Oscar-nominated (including Gilbert himself for Best Director) hit dramedy *Alfie*, with Michael Caine and Shelley Winters.

Following *Alfie*, Gilbert took the directing job for *You Only Live Twice*, after turning down Cubby Broccoli's initial offer. The director immediately began to question his decision when scouting locations in Japan. Initially terrified as he had never flown in a helicopter before, Gilbert's anxiety rose when he found the pilot was an ex-kamikaze pilot from World War II. But the pilot turned out to be one of the best anyone could have asked for.

The director put his innovative spin into the Bond film in many ways, including the fight scene on the Kobe docks. While many struggles are filmed in close-up, Gilbert switched that out to one continuous tracking shot that followed 007 across the rooftops of the buildings, watching from above as he defeated one attacker after another.

After directing a number of films in the early and mid-1970s, Gilbert returned to 007 with *The Spy Who Loved Me* in 1977 when Guy Hamilton could not commit to directing. While much had changed in the ten years since Gilbert last headed a Bond film, the biggest change was Bond himself. The director had to rethink his vision of 007, as it was now Roger Moore and not Sean Connery in front of the camera. This Bond would be less rugged, smoother, have more humor than Gilbert's first.

Lewis Gilbert also looked at dozens of women auditioning for the role of Russian spy Anya Amasova. The task of interviewing beautiful ladies was tough, but someone had to do it. The director had clear criteria for his search: they had to be stunning visually, they had to able to act, and he preferred to work with up-and-coming performers. When he saw Barbara Bach at the last moment, he knew he had Agent XXX.

Gilbert worked closely with editor (and future Bond director) John Glen to assemble a film with maximum impact. He finished his troika of Bond pictures with the following entry, *Moonraker*, in 1979.

Gilbert entered the 1980s by hooking up with *Alfie* actor Michael Caine once more, directing him with Julie Walters in the Oscar-nominated *Educating Rita* in 1983. Among other films, he directed *Shirley Valentine* in 1989, *Stepping Out* with Liza Minnelli in 1991, and, connecting with Julie Walters again in the director's final film, *Before You Go*, in 2002.

In 2010, at age ninety, Gilbert published his autobiography, *All My Flashbacks*.

Peter Hunt

Another founding member of the Bond franchise, Peter R. Hunt left his mark on the first six films—as editor on *Dr. No, From Russia with Love,* and *Goldfinger*; as supervising editor and second unit director on *Thunderball* and *You Only Live Twice*; and as director of *On Her Majesty's Secret Service.*

Born in London in 1925, Peter Hunt's first interest was music, as he studied piano and violin. When he was old enough, Hunt enlisted in the Royal Army in 1942, serving in Italy and other areas of the European Theater. Reaching the rank of staff sergeant, he was discharged in 1947. Hunt stayed in Italy, studying art history at the University of Rome.

But with an uncle in the film business, the young man returned to England before finishing his degree, becoming a clapper holder at Denham Studios. Once the largest film facility in the UK, Denham would soon close down, and Hunt would become an associate editor at other studios, working on educational and industrial films as well as features. In the 1950s, he worked on sci-fi films like *Immediate Disaster,* war pics like *Hell in Korea,* and comedies like *Paradise Lagoon* (directed by future Bond associate Lewis Gilbert). Hunt would continue his connection with Gilbert, as he cut the director's films into the 1960s: *Ferry to Hong Kong, Sink the Bismarck!, Loss of Innocence,* and *Damn the Defiant!*

As the team for the first Bond film was being assembled, producer Harry Saltzman had always wanted to work with Hunt, whose reputation as a great editor had preceded him. It seemed that one thing or another always prevented the occasion, but this time Hunt was available, so he was assigned the task of editing *Dr. No.*

To set a fast tempo for the film, Hunt went against a tradition in the film world: never cut a scene during camera movement. Thumbing his nose at that notion, his quick-cut editing style established a dynamic form of storytelling, not seen on movie screens in the past. The style would become a standard, not only for Bond films, but many action films in the future.

Brought back for *From Russia with Love,* Hunt created an amazing highlight that has become timeless: the climactic fight scene on the Orient Express between Red Grant and 007. Shot with three cameras on a train car mock-up in Pinewood Studios, the final scene was comprised of sixty-seven cuts in just under two and a half minutes. The editor found himself waking in the middle of the night with an idea concerning the sequence, dressing and running down to Pinewood to work on it.

Hunt's innovations went beyond cutting style. With director Terence Young's agreement, Hunt put the opening sequence before the opening titles in *From Russia with Love,* establishing one of the many long-standing traditions in Bond films. Hunt also clarified the film's early story points by rearranging the order of shots that included Rosa Klebb's visit to SPECTRE Island, her recruitment of Tatiana Romanova, Kronsteen's chess match, and the meeting with Blofeld on his yacht.

Working under Guy Hamilton for *Goldfinger,* Hunt was a bit unhappy, feeling the theme of the films was changing. He also found that he wasn't in agreement with the way the director was shooting some of the scenes in the script, for example, the car chase outside Goldfinger's plant in Switzerland. Fortunately, with the support of Broccoli and Saltzman, Hunt was able to rearrange some of the sequences to better tell the story.

Moving up to second-unit director (essentially, the second unit is a production team that shoots scenes that don't need the director or principal performers) and supervising editor for *Thunderball,* Hunt was challenged by the many scenes shot underwater. With the physical motion slowed down, he found the task of keeping the pace brisk a tough one. Just as challenging was Hunt's role as editor on *The Ipcress File,* a film starring Michael Caine as spy Harry Palmer and produced by Harry Saltzman, at the same time as *Thunderball.*

The next film planned in the Bond series was *On Her Majesty's Secret Service,* with Hunt scheduled to direct. But the producers had contracted several directors for future films, and a huge mix-up resulted. Out of the confusion, *You Only Live Twice* became the next film, and Hunt was squeezed out—for the time being.

Filling the same roles of second-unit director and supervising editor on *You Only Live Twice,* Hunt found satisfaction in the change of scenery by shooting in Japan. He also avoided the quickly clichéd car chase by putting it up in the air with helicopters. Overall, Hunt felt the picture was disjointed, torn between the beauty and reality of scenes like the Japanese wedding and the fantasy aspects of grabbing a car with a big magnet and dropping it into Tokyo Bay.

After working on another Ian Fleming novel, *Chitty Chitty Bang Bang,* in 1968, Hunt took the directorial reins for *On Her Majesty's Secret Service,* bringing along many of the production crew from the children's picture he'd just finished. He also made a bold decision to veer away from the gadgets that had begun to overrun the Bond films. Hunt went back to the original novel and stuck to it, as the first few films had done.

Still, Hunt didn't have Sean Connery as Bond. Looking at hundreds of potential 007s, Hunt worked with Broccoli and Saltzman to make George Lazenby the new James Bond. Despite rumors to the contrary (sometimes from the actor himself), Hunt did actually direct and speak with the young and inexperienced Lazenby. Hunt also selected experienced actress Diana

Rigg to balance against the neophyte, as well as support and coach him where needed.

Although the script called for the character of Tracy to propose marriage to Bond, it was Hunt who chose to keep 007 in the controlling position when the scene was shot. When the wedding scene came, it was Hunt who wanted Bond to throw his hat to Moneypenny (usually reserved for the office coatrack) and leave her with a tear in her eye.

The director also showed real intuition in how to get a great performance, even from someone as inexperienced as Lazenby. The scene where Tracy is killed was set to start shooting at eight in the morning. Hunt intentionally took all day, rehearsing and rehearsing over and over. By five in the afternoon, Lazenby was exhausted, and Hunt was ready to use that for the underlying effect. The result was one of Lazenby's best scenes in the film. Many critics and fans believe that Hunt's direction make *On Her Majesty's Secret Service* one of the best of the Bond films.

However, the film would be the last Bond picture on which Hunt would work. Although invited back to direct *Diamonds Are Forever*, the delays between the two films lead to him being committed to another project by then. He directed other films, such as *Shout at the Devil* with Lee Marvin and Roger Moore, *Death Hunt* with Marvin again and Charles Bronson, and *Assassination* with Bronson and Jill Ireland.

Retiring in the early 1990s, Hunt suffered a massive heart attack and died in 2002.

John Glen

With the rare opportunity to work on eight Bond films, John Glen's roles as editor, second-unit director, and director allowed him to leave a large mark on the legacy. Spending twenty years with the 007 team, Glen worked with George Lazenby, Roger Moore, and Timothy Dalton.

Born in 1932 in Sunbury-on-Thames, a town not far from London, Glen started his film career at the tender age of fourteen. Hired as a messenger boy for Shepperton Studios, the job took the teen to every department in the facility for a solid introduction to the world of filmmaking.

Glen found the editing room the most interesting, and when the chance to work there came up in 1948, the sixteen-year-old settled right in. It was a fortuitous move, as his first editing job was helping to cut sound for *The Third Man*, starring Orson Welles and Joseph Cotten. He continued to edit film, sound, and dubbing tracks through the 1950s and 1960s, working on movies as well as TV shows like *The Avengers* and *Secret Agent*.

When Peter Hunt got the job of directing *On Her Majesty's Secret Service*, he brought his old friend—John Glen—in to edit, as well as direct the second unit, specifically the bobsled run fight between Bond and Blofeld. With doubles for Lazenby and Telly Savalas, Glen worked closely with Willy Bogner, a camera operator highly skilled in shooting from skis and sleds.

Continuing to cut film through the 1970s, Glen rejoined the Bond team to edit and direct second-unit scenes for *The Spy Who Loved Me* in 1977. It was Glen who directed the breathtaking precredit sequence of stunt skier Rick Sylvester gliding off a mountaintop, skydiving into the gap, and deploying a parachute emblazoned with the Union Jack. The sequence was budgeted at an amazing figure of nearly $300,000, which seemed to pay off. The scene is considered by many to be the best of the precredit scenes.

Assuming the same roles for the next Bond film, *Moonraker*, Glen once again accepted the challenge of directing the exciting precredit sequence. This one would feature a parachuteless 007 tossed from an airplane by Jaws. Bond then skydives to the parachuted pilot, relieves him of the pack, and floats safely to the opening credits. Shooting in California, Glen filmed more than eighty-eight jumps to get the final scene that ran just over two minutes.

Cubby Broccoli had taken notice of Glen's work since *On Her Majesty's Secret Service* and offered him the director job on *For Your Eyes Only* in 1981. Assembling a team of creative and technical pros, Glen tackled the task of refocusing the franchise toward a harder-edged Bond with a more serious tone. Gone would be the absurd bits like a hovercraft gondola zipping across St. Mark's Square.

Still, the director was able to introduce his own stamp—a "trademark" scene that would identify the film as a "John Glen film." Waiting for a suspenseful moment, Glen would make the audience jump by having pigeons suddenly fly onto the screen and away. In *For Your Eyes Only*, it occurred when Bond was climbing the mountain and reached into a crevice for a better grip. Out the pigeons flew, startling 007 and the folks in the theater.

Directing *Octopussy* in 1983, John Glen's precredit sequence was inspired by a Japanese TV commercial that featured a mini-jet flying through an airplane hangar. The mini-jet was flown by J. W. "Corkey" Fornof, and Glen had the stunt pilot recreate the bit, this time with Bond at the controls. Glen also had to work some persuasive magic in convincing a reluctant Roger Moore to wear the clown outfit and makeup in the film's conclusion.

After directing Moore's final appearance as Bond in *A View to a Kill*, John Glen undertook the task of finding a new 007. Following the Pierce Brosnan debacle, Timothy Dalton holstered the Walther for *The Living Daylights* in 1987. A consummate professional, Dalton found himself in a

bit of hot water with director Glen at one point during
the production.

Directors will always
review the scenes shot at the
end of the day, referred to
as "dailies" or "daily rushes."
Glen had always kept an
open-door policy when it
came to these, allowing
anyone on the crew to join
him in the screening room.
During production of *The
Living Daylights,* Dalton sat
in one day with other mem-

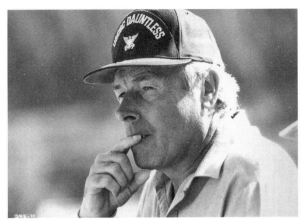

John Glen directing *Licence to Kill.*

bers of the crew and invited any comments that might be offered. He later
approached the director, as one of the clerical staff had criticized the way
Dalton was kissing Maryam d'Abo. Glen was not at all pleased with the input
and changed his policy: the previously opened door to the screening room
would now be closed to the crew.

With *The Living Daylights* becoming another hit in the Bond series, Glen
proceeded to start filming *Licence to Kill*—originally titled *Licence Revoked.* In
their infinite wisdom, the marketing department at MGM/UA had decided
that American audiences would not understand what "revoked" meant and
insisted the film's title be changed.

After an unsuccessful attempt to stage part of the action in China,
the script was changed to a fictitious Latin American country. With tax
problems in the UK, Mexico City became the studio location for the production. Shooting the scene where a rocket launcher was fired at 007's semi
truck gave Glen a real headache, as the rocket-powered missile prop was
launched, traveled two miles, and struck an unsuspecting telephone line-
man working at the top of a pole. Although not seriously injured, the poor
fellow had to be taken to the local hospital.

Legal issues would hold up the production of the next Bond film for six
years after the release of *Licence to Kill.* John Glen was informed by Cubby
Broccoli that whenever the next film would begin, there would be another
director in control. Glen was fine with that, having spent twenty years working on Bond pictures. However, he wondered what life after Bond would
be like.

He quickly found out, directing the second sequel to the popular *Iron
Eagle* series—*Aces: Iron Eagle III*—with Lou Gossett Jr. in 1992 and the

massive bust *Christopher Columbus: The Discovery*. With performances by Marlon Brando, Tom Selleck, and *Licence to Kill* alums Robert Davi and Benicio Del Toro, the $45 million film grossed a bit more than a mere $8 million in America.

Glen would direct the quirky sci-fi series for British TV *Space Precinct*, created by the father of Supermarionation—used in shows like *Fireball XL5*, *Thunderbirds Are GO*, and *Stingray*—Gerry Anderson. Glen's last film was *The Point Men* in 2001, starring Christopher Lambert and featuring *The Living Daylights*' Maryam d'Abo.

John Glen enjoys retirement, happy and proud for his time and contributions to the Bond series. As the director of five 007 films, no one has directed more.

Martin Campbell

Directing two Bond films, Martin Campbell holds a unique position in the history of the franchise—directing Pierce Brosnan in his first 007 film and Daniel Craig in his inaugural turn as Bond. Two different actors, two different production crews, two different centuries—and two different results.

The New Zealand native was born in 1940 (although some sources state 1943), and tried to start his career as a television cameraman there. Told that everyone wanted those jobs only made Campbell more resolved to break into the industry. He toiled in New Zealand slaughterhouses for about a year, then moved to London in 1965—where the competition would be twice as thick.

Campbell convinced folks at the BBC to take him on as an apprentice cameraman. Within ten years, he moved into directing—soft-core adult films like *The Sex Thief*

Martin Campbell, who directed the debut Bond films of Pierce Brosnan and Daniel Craig.

and *Eskimo Nell.* He then started directing British television programs like *The Professionals,* a series about agents from CI5—Criminal Intelligence—fighting terrorists.

The director made his first big impact when he took the reins of *Reilly: Ace of Spies,* a series starring Sam Neill, once considered as heir to the role of James Bond. The show gained nominations for BAFTA, Emmy, and Golden Globe awards. In 1985, Campbell directed the BBC miniseries *Edge of Darkness,* destined to become a fan favorite. (He would return to direct Mel Gibson in a 2010 feature film version of the show.) By the late 1980s, Campbell started directing action thrillers like *Criminal Law* with Gary Oldman and Kevin Bacon and the futuristic drama *No Escape,* starring Ray Liotta.

With the legal wranglings that held up the Bond films for six years out of the way, producers chose Martin Campbell to get things started again, with Pierce Brosnan as 007 in 1995's *GoldenEye.* Campbell regarded the opportunity as risky but also realized that doing a decent job as director would kick-start the film series. He was right, as the new Bond film grossed more than $350 million worldwide.

The success of *GoldenEye* opened bigger doors for Campbell, as he then directed action films like *The Mask of Zorro* (as well as its sequel, *The Legend of Zorro*) and *Vertical Limit.* When Daniel Craig was chosen to star as the new Bond in *Casino Royale* in 2006, producers turned to Campbell once more. The director insisted on returning to the books as the focal point of the film.

Recognizing that Ian Fleming had created a complex, flawed character—someone who drank too much, smoked too much, doesn't like to kill but has to for the sake of his job—Campbell embraced the chance to do an origin story with *Casino Royale*—the first book, the introduction (as it were) of the character for the first time. With Craig in the seminal role, Campbell chose to make Bond darker, more messed up, than he'd ever been in the past. The result was a very successful reboot, as *Casino Royale* brought in nearly $600 million worldwide.

The director headed into the second decade of the 2000s by visualizing the DC comic book superhero Green Lantern for the big screen in 2011.

Roger Spottiswoode

Experienced as a writer, producer, and director, Roger Spottiswoode brought a well-rounded résumé to *Tomorrow Never Dies* in 1997. Born in Ottawa, Canada, in 1945, he broke into the film world working with British film editor John Bloom.

At first, Spottiswoode was literally sweeping floors and making coffee for Bloom, but the editor shared a great deal of practical knowledge with his assistant. Cutting television commercials and documentaries, Bloom got the editing job on *Georgy Girl* in 1966, with Spottiswoode assisting with the cutting. Later, Spottiswoode was working in the editing booth on other features like *Funeral in Berlin* and *The Lion in Winter*.

Moody but brilliant director Sam Peckinpah had trouble in 1971 when editing *Straw Dogs*. Firing one cutter after another, he gave the twenty-seven-year-old Spottiswoode a chance to work on the film. Pleased with his work, Peckinpah kept Spottiswoode to edit *The Getaway* in 1972 and *Pat Garrett & Billy the Kid* in 1973. He also worked with Walter Hill in 1975 on *Hard Times*.

Many editors desire to move into directing, and Spottiswoode was no exception. He jumped at the chance to direct a low-budget slasher film called *Terror Train*, starring Jamie Lee Curtis, in 1980. He followed up as director of *The Pursuit of D. B. Cooper* the next year, an adventure story based on the true events of a plane hijacker and his disappearance with $200,000 in ransom money. Spottiswoode directed *Under Fire* with Nick Nolte, then penned the script for the action comedy-buddy film *48 Hrs.*, starring Nolte and Eddie Murphy. He also wrote the sequel, *Another 48 Hrs.*, in 1990.

Spottiswoode directed a wide range of films in the 1990s, including the dog-and-detective comedy *Turner and Hooch*, starring Tom Hanks; action film *Air America*, starring Mel Gibson and Robert Downey Jr.; and the embarrassing comedy *Stop! Or My Mom Will Shoot*, starring Sly Stallone and Estelle Getty. He also directed the award-winning HBO movie *And the Band Played On*, the compelling story of the start of the AIDS epidemic.

Although he had discussions with the Broccolis about directing one of the Timothy Dalton/Bond films, he passed. However, when *Tomorrow Never Dies* came along in 1997, Spottiswoode took the gig.

In helping to develop the script, Spottiswoode was insistent on having a new type of Bond Girl—someone strong, physical, independent, an equal to 007. From that concept, Wai Lin was created, with Michelle Yeoh chosen for her extensive experience in martial arts and action films.

Noting the impact of the tank chase in *GoldenEye*, Spottiswoode wondered what he could do as a topper in *Tomorrow Never Dies*. A larger vehicle wasn't practical, so he decided to put Bond and Wai Lin in the most open, vulnerable position he could conceive—handcuffed together on a speeding motorcycle. To increase the danger, Spottiswoode placed the pursuers into a low-flying helicopter. The result was action-packed and one of the film's highlights.

With the film being another big hit, producers approached Spottiswoode to direct the next Bond entry, *The World Is Not Enough*. But he had to beg off, saying he was too tired from the film he'd just completed. Taking some time off, he returned in 2000 to direct Arnold Schwarzenegger in the sci-fi action film *The 6th Day*.

Into the 2000s, Spottiswoode told the award-winning true story about the murder of an openly gay college student in NBC-TV's *The Matthew Shepard Story*. Among other films, he directed the 2008 war drama *The Children of Huang Shi*, teaming once more with Michelle Yeoh.

Michael Apted

A veteran director of more than fifty films of all sorts—features, short subjects, documentaries, television—when chosen to helm *The World Is Not Enough* in 1999, Michael Apted relished the opportunity to do a big-time action film.

Born in 1941 in England, Apted received a scholarship to study law and history at Cambridge University—attending with future R and Monty Pythoner John Cleese. His interests turned to television, and he served six months as an apprentice with Granada TV, a branch of the British independent broadcast outlet ITV. Soon after, he began his association with one of the most compelling documentary series ever created.

In 1964, Apted was a researcher for *Seven Up*, a TV documentary that highlighted the lives of a group of seven-year-old British children. Directed by Canadian Paul Almond, the show could be considered one of the forerunners of modern-day "reality television." Although the program was intended to be a one-shot effort, Apted came back seven years later to interview the same group of now-teenaged Brits with *7 Plus Seven*. He continued to revisit the group every seven years and update their situations, with the latest program broadcast in 2012—*56 Up*.

Unlike many directors who prefer to stay in documentary films, Apted easily made the transition to commercial projects, directing television plays

Michael Apted, who helmed *The World Is Not Enough*.

and movies for the BBC and ITV in the early 1970s. His first feature, *Stardust*, in 1974, told the fictional story of a 1960s rock star.

Apted directed Sissy Spacek to a Best Actress Oscar in 1980 in *Coal Miner's Daughter*, the film bio of country singer Loretta Lynn. He also directed films like *Continental Divide* in 1981, a romantic comedy starring John Belushi and Blair Brown; *Gorky Park* in 1983, a crime story set in Moscow; *Bring on the Night* in 1985, a musical documentary on Sting's first solo tour; and *Gorillas in the Mist* in 1988, nominated for five Academy Awards and starring Sigourney Weaver as gorilla specialist Dian Fossey.

In the 1990s, Apted directed films like legal drama *Class Action* with Gene Hackman; *Thunderheart*, a Native American murder story with Val Kilmer; *Nell*, which earned Jodie Foster an Oscar nomination; and *Extreme Measures*, with Hugh Grant and Gene Hackman.

When producers approached Apted about having any interest in directing *The World Is Not Enough*, he thought they were joking. They weren't, and he took the job, knowing that—unlike most documentaries—the film had a rabid audience waiting to see the final product. Apted knew he had to deliver a great action film.

The first thing Apted noticed about doing a Bond film was whatever he wanted, he got—something he wasn't accustomed to as a documentary director. Steadicam systems and cranes were easily at his disposal. Shooting for nearly four months, Apted really worked to make the characters interesting and—a recurring trait for Apted's feature films—created a strong, independent female in Elektra King. He also gave Bond a harder edge, which the studio folks didn't necessarily want.

With the success of *The World Is Not Enough*, Apted switched among documentaries, episodic television, and features in the 2000s, like the drama *Enigma*, starring Kate Winslet; *Enough*, with Jennifer Lopez; and *Amazing Grace*, with Ioan Gruffudd and Albert Finney. He also delivered another entry in the *Up* series with *49 Up* in 2005. Michael Apted directed the third episode in the *Chronicles of Narnia* fantasy films in 2010: *The Voyage of the Dawn Treader*.

Lee Tamahori

With the task of tackling the fortieth anniversary of James Bond in *Die Another Day*, the twentieth film in the series, Lee Tamahori decided to reflect on the previous 007 films and pay homage. The resulting film allowed the director to craft a new story while referencing the movies that preceded it.

Tamahori was born in New Zealand in 1950, with his mother from Britain and his father a native Maori—the Polynesian people who are indigenous to New Zealand. Seeking a career as a commercial artist after high school, Tamahori soon changed his mind and focused on photography.

In the mid-1970s, New Zealand began a big push into developing its own film industry, and the young man took a job as a boom operator. Thinking it had something to do with explosives in films, Tamahori was a bit disappointed to find he would be handling a microphone on a crane. Nevertheless, he was in the movie business and happy to be there.

He quickly moved to assistant directing, working on films like the war picture *Merry Christmas Mr. Lawrence* in 1983, starring David Bowie. Wanting to direct, Tamahori started by making television commercials in the mid-1980s. It was good experience, as he was working directly with actors and dialogue—all the elements that would easily translate to feature films.

His chance came in 1994, when he directed the highly acclaimed, award-winning *Once Were Warriors,* the gritty story of an urban family in New Zealand with Maori roots. Several films followed, critically praised if not box-office successes: *Mulholland Falls,* a solid film-noir detective drama starring Nick Nolte, Melanie Griffith, and John Malkovich; *The Edge,* a story of plane crash survivors, written by David Mamet and starring Anthony Hopkins and Alec Baldwin; and *Along Came a Spider,* a thrilling crime story with Morgan Freeman. Tamahori even directed an episode of the smash HBO series *The Sopranos.*

Tamahori's introduction to directing a Bond flick seemed to be something right out of . . . a Bond flick. Producers flew him to London's Heathrow Airport. Getting into the back of an Eon Productions Rolls-Royce, he was handed the highly secret script for *Die Another Day* to read on his way to meet Barbara Broccoli and Michael G. Wilson.

Once chosen and on-set, Tamahori found the producers were very agreeable to anything he thought would make the film better. Looking at the ice palace set at Pinewood Studios, Tamahori wondered what a car chase would be like staged there. Production designer Peter Lamont informed him the cost would double the set's original estimate to a figure of $3 million. Tamahori went to producers, and they "didn't even blink." Later, the entire experience of directing a Bond film hit Tamahori, and he burst out laughing in the middle of a take, with Pierce Brosnan hanging upside-down from a glacier.

After Bond, Lee Tamahori directed the sequel of the action film *xXx,* called *xXx: State of the Union,* starring Willem Dafoe, Samuel L. Jackson, and Ice Cube. He also directed the sci-fi thriller *Next* in 2007, starring Nicolas

Cage and Julianne Moore, as well as the true story of the Iraqi man who was forced to become the double for Saddam Hussein's son, *The Devil's Double*, in 2011.

Marc Forster

Even as a successful feature film director, Marc Forster had no interest in directing a James Bond film. Only the persuasive efforts of his agent got Forster to attend a meeting with producers Wilson and Broccoli. The result? *Quantum of Solace.*

Born in 1969 in Germany, Marc Forster grew up in Switzerland, where he attended an exclusive boarding school. At the age of twelve, he saw Francis Ford Coppola's *Apocalypse Now,* and he was hooked on the world of film.

Forster came to New York in 1990, enrolling in the prestigious New York University Film School. As his parents couldn't afford the tuition, he polled his family and friends to find a benefactor. He found one and focused on making short-form documentaries there.

His first feature film—writing and directing—was the ultra-low-budgeted *Loungers* in 1995. The story of aspiring lounge singers won a Slamdance Audience Award and got Forster an agent and an introduction to Hollywood.

Marc Forster, who directed *Quantum of Solace.*

His second film, *Everything Put Together* in 2000, earned a Sundance Film Festival nomination for the Grand Jury Prize and more respect for Forster. Which led to the chance to direct Halle Berry in her Oscar-winning performance in *Monster's Ball* in 2001. Forster continued to work with top performers like Johnny Depp in *Finding Neverland,* Ewan McGregor in *Stay,* and Will Ferrell in *Stranger Than Fiction.* In 2007, he directed the highly acclaimed *The Kite Runner,* set in Afghanistan.

Forster's meeting with Michael G. Wilson and Barbara Broccoli found the director trying to talk the producers out of wanting him, since he felt he wasn't an action-film director. But they persisted, and Forster was given the okay to use his creative team for *Quantum of Solace.* He could explore the complexity of a man like Bond, while featuring plenty of conflict. Still, he had little knowledge of what he'd gotten himself into.

What it was was a franchise film budgeted at $230 million, destined to bring in nearly $600 million worldwide. And Forster had a clear idea as to what he wanted. The film would be a sequel to *Casino Royale,* picking up within an hour of its ending. He also shook up the forty-six-year-old film series by opting to put the signature gun barrel sequence at the film's end, rather than the traditional opening position. And heaven forbid! He chose not to include the classic "Bond. James Bond" introduction, although he did shoot the scene. Forster set his action scenes in the four elements of air, fire, water, and earth, exploring the differences.

With the success of *Quantum of Solace,* producers offered the next Bond film to Marc Forster, but he declined. The director has enjoyed switching genres and chose to tell the true story of a drug-dealing gang member who found religion and built a children's orphanage in Africa. Starring Gerard Butler, *Machine Gun Preacher* won critical acclaim when it was released in 2011, but Forster wasn't standing pat. His next film, *World War Z* starring Brad Pitt, featured a worldwide zombie invasion.

Sam Mendes

Born in Berkshire, England, in 1965, Sam Mendes originally enrolled at Cambridge University to study art history. But he found directing a student play was incredibly satisfying and turned his sights toward theater.

Upon graduation, Mendes was brought in as director for the Chichester Festival Theater, then moved to the West End. At age twenty-five, he was directing Judi Dench in Anton Chekhov's *The Cherry Orchard.* He also began directing productions for the Royal Shakespeare Company. In the mid-1990s, Mendes directed successful revivals of the musicals *Cabaret* and *Company,* both of which were shown on British television.

Sam Mendes, tapped to direct *Skyfall.*

His first shot at directing film, 1999's *American Beauty,* resulted in winning five Oscars, including one for Mendes as Best Director. The film also garnered Best Director awards for Mendes in the BAFTAs, Golden Globes, and numerous film critic polls.

Mendes continued directing in theater, in England and on Broadway, as well as films. He helmed the Oscar-nominated *Road to Perdition* (with future Bond Daniel Craig), the Middle Eastern war film *Jarhead,* the Oscar-nominated *Revolutionary Road* with Leonardo DiCaprio and Mendes' then-wife Kate Winslet, and the comedy *Away We Go.*

Chosen to direct *Skyfall,* Mendes found the financial woes of MGM that delayed the filming actually helped the production. The extra time allowed for better screenplay revisions and discussions with villain Javier Bardem to develop a Bond baddie in the classic vein. The director also worked with screenwriters and Bond actor Daniel Craig to bring more humor to the spy, without compromising the direction of the series since its reboot in 2006.

Mendes' vision for *Skyfall* obviously struck the right tone with fans all over the world. Released in Europe at the end of October 2012 and in the US in early November, the film earned nearly $800 million in worldwide box-office sales from just its first few weeks in theaters—numbers that easily make it the most successful James Bond film to date.

The success of the twenty-third Eon Productions–produced Bond film ensured the franchise would continue beyond its first fifty years. Writer John Logan worked with producers Wilson and Broccoli to create a two-film story outline, even as *Skyfall* was opening around the world. With Daniel Craig signed to continue his role of 007, the untitled films—known simply as *Bond 24* and *Bond 25* for the present—are scheduled for tentative release in 2014 and 2016, respectively.

Selected Bibliography

007 Magazine Online. "Joe Robinson." Web. Accessed April 18, 2012. http://www.007magazine.co.uk/joe_robinson.htm

All the World's Rotorcraft website. "Wallis WA-116." Accessed February 7, 2012. Web. http://www.aviastar.org/helicopters_eng/wallis_nelly.php

Armanac, Alden P. "Seagoing Hydrofoils Fly over Waves at 60 Knots." *Popular Science,* July 1961, 56–61. Print.

Associated Press. "James Bond's Aston Martin from *Goldfinger* Nets $4.1M at Auction." *New York Daily News,* October 28, 2010. Web.

Barry, John. Interview by Terry Gross. *Fresh Air,* National Public Radio, March 23, 1999. Web. http://www.npr.org/2004/08/25/3870891/bond-theme-composer-john-barry

Bean, Sean. Interview by Andrew Duncan. *Radio Times* (London), May 11, 1996. Web. http://www.compleatseanbean.com/mainfeatures-77.html

Berger, Bob. "Aquapolis: City in the Sea." *Popular Mechanics,* June 1975, 77. Print.

Bish, Tommy. "Rockets from a Handgun." *Gun World,* September 1965. Print.

Blackman, Honor. "Pussy Galore Meets George Hook." Interview by George Hook. *The Right Hook.* NewsTalk 106-108 FM, May 3, 2012. Web. http://www.newstalk.ie/2012/programmes/all-programmes/the-right-hook/pussy-galore-meets-george-hook/

Bragg, Melvyn. "James Bond Special." *The South Bank Show.* ITV, October 22, 2008. Web.

Broccoli, Barbara, and Michael G. Wilson. Interview by Jason Solomons. Film Weekly podcast. *Guardian,* April 9, 2009. Web. http://www.guardian.co.uk/film/audio/2009/apr/09/film-weekly-podcast-james-bond-zac-efron

Brooks, Tim, and Earle Marsh. *The Complete Directory to Prime Time Network and Cable TV Shows: 1946–Present,* 9th ed. New York: Ballantine Books, 2007. Print.

Burlingame, Jon. "Bonding with the Score." *Los Angeles Times,* December 18, 1997. Web.

Connery, Sean. Interview. *Playboy,* November 1965, 75–84. Print.

Celi, Adolfo. "The Adolfo Celi Interview." By Piero Corsini. *Bondage*, 1984, 17–19. Print.

Chartrand, Harvey F. "Curtis Harrington: Living in Dangerous Houses." *DVD Drive-In*, May 17, 2005. Web. Accessed May 3, 2012. www.dvddrive-in.com/features/curtisharrington.htm

Chutkow, Paul. "Brosnan. Pierce Brosnan." *Cigar Aficionado*, December 1997. Web.

Connery, Sean. "When *GQ* Met Sean Connery." Interview by Andy Morris. *British Gentlemen's Quarterly* (London), October 2008. Web.

Cork, John. "The Life of Albert R. Broccoli." *Goldeneye* (Burbank, CA), Fall 1996, 3–17. Print.

Craig, Daniel. Interview by David Sheff. *Playboy* (UK Edition), November 2008, 57–60, 62, 64. Print.

Crist, Judith. "Hello, Barbra—After a Fashion." Movies, *New York*, January 20, 1970, 54. Print.

Crowther, Bosley. Review of *Casino Royale*. *New York Times*, April 29, 1967. Web.

D'Abo, Maryam, and John Cork. *Bond Girls Are Forever*. New York: Abrams Publishing, 2003. Print.

Dalton, Timothy. "Timothy Dalton Talks *Chuck, The Tourist*, and, of Course, Bond." Interview by Christian Blauvelt. *Entertainment Weekly*, November 1, 2010. Web.

Dorman, Nick. "Daniel Craig Set to Become Longest Serving James Bond." *The People* (London), December 18, 2011. Web. http://www.people.co.uk/news/uk-world-news/2011/12/18/daniel-craig-set-to-become-longest-serving-james-bond-102039-23642989/

Ebert, Roger. Review of *Casino Royale*. *Chicago Sun-Times*, May 1, 1967. Web.

———. Review of *GoldenEye*. *Chicago Sun-Times*, November 17, 1995. Web.

Fleming, Ian. Interview. *Playboy*, December 1964, 97–106. Print.

Flick, Vic. "Vic Flick 007 Guitarman." Interview by Pete Prown. *Vintage Guitar*, April 2012, 28–30. Print.

———. *Vic Flick Guitarman: From James Bond to the Beatles and Beyond*. Albany, GA: Bear Manor Media, 2008. Print.

Gilbert, Lewis. Interview by Francine Stock. *Film Progamme*. BBC4, March 26, 2010. Web. http://www.bbc.co.uk/programmes/b00rfl5w#p0073pgp

Glen, John. *For My Eyes Only*. Dulles, VA: Brassey's, Inc., 2001. Print.

Godwin, Robert. *Space Shuttle Fact Archive*. Burlington, Ontario: Apogee Books, 2007. Print.

Gordon, Bryony. "Roger Moore: I'm the Worst Bond, Apparently." *Telegraph* (London), September 23, 2008. Web.

Gordon, Chris. "Lazenby's Goulburn Bond." *Goulburn Post* (Goulburn, New South Wales, Australia), November 3, 2010. Web.

Gray, Marianne. "Painting 007." *Big Screen* (Cornwall, UK), June 1995. Web. http://pbfiles.cixx6.com/interviews/Inter057-Big_Screen-Painting007_1995%20.html

Gresh, Lois H., and Robert Weinberg. *The Science of James Bond.* Hoboken, NJ: John Wiley and Sons Books, 2006. Print.

Henry Repeating Arms website. "U.S. Survival AR-7." Web. Accessed January 25, 2012.

Hunt, Peter R. Interview. *Retro Vision* (Los Angeles), 1998. Web.

Ian Fleming's official website. Ian Fleming Publications. Web. Accessed February 14, 2012. http://www.ianfleming.com

"Inside *A View to a Kill.*" Disc 2. *A View to a Kill,* Two-Disc Ultimate Edition. Directed by John Glen. Santa Monica, CA: MGM Home Entertainment, 2000. DVD.

"Inside *Diamonds Are Forever.*" (Includes interview with Guy Hamilton.) Disc 2. *Diamonds Are Forever,* Two-Disc Ultimate Edition. Directed by Guy Hamilton. Santa Monica, CA: MGM Home Entertainment, 2000. DVD.

"Inside *Die Another Day.*" (Includes interview with Rosamund Pike.) Disc 2. *Die Another Day,* Two-Disc Ultimate Edition. Directed by Lee Tamahori. Santa Monica, CA: MGM Home Entertainment, 2003. DVD.

"Inside *For Your Eyes Only.*" (Includes interviews with Julian Glover and Michael Wilson.) Disc 2. *For Your Eyes Only,* Two-Disc Ultimate Edition. Directed by John Glen. Santa Monica, CA: MGM Home Entertainment, 2000. DVD.

"Inside *From Russia with Love.*" (Includes interviews with Daniela Bianchi, Walter Gotell, and Peter R. Hunt.) Disc 2. *From Russia with Love,* Two-Disc Ultimate Edition. Directed by Terence Young. Santa Monica, CA: MGM Home Entertainment, 2000. DVD.

"Inside *Octopussy.*" (Includes interviews with Maud Adams, Kabir Bedi, and Lois Maxwell.) Disc 2. *Octopussy,* Two-Disc Ultimate Edition. Directed by John Glen. Santa Monica, CA: MGM Home Entertainment, 2000. DVD.

"Inside *The Living Daylights.*" (Includes interviews with Timothy Dalton and Joe Don Baker.) Disc 2. *The Living Daylights,* Two-Disc Ultimate Edition. Directed by John Glen. Santa Monica, CA: MGM Home Entertainment, 2000. DVD.

"Inside *You Only Live Twice.*" (Includes interviews with Ken Adam, Karin Dor, and Lewis Gilbert.) Disc 2. *You Only Live Twice,* Two-Disc Ultimate Edition. Directed by Lewis Gilbert. Santa Monica, CA: MGM Home Entertainment, 2000. DVD.

Invention of the Laser—Bell Labs. "Schawlow and Townes Invent the Laser." Web. Accessed January 27, 2012. http://www.bell-labs.com/about /history/laser/

James Bond Car Collection (London). "Parahawk." July 5, 2010, 4–5. Print.

———. "Q Boat." February 3, 2010, 4–7. Print.

James Bond's Greatest Hits. BBC4, November 18, 2006. Web.

Jeffries, Dean. "Interview: Dean Jeffries, Hollywood Legend." By Arthur St. Antoine. *Motor Trend,* March 2006. Web.

Jet. "Tina Turner Performs Theme Song to New James Bond Movie, *GoldenEye.*" November 20, 1995, 60–64. Print.

Katz, Ephraim. *Film Encyclopedia,* 6th ed. New York: Harper Collins, 2008. Print.

Kelner, Simon. "On Her Majesty's Silver Service." *British Gentlemen's Quarterly* (London), November 2008. Web.

Krause, William. *Hollywood TV and Movie Cars.* St. Paul, MN: MBI Publishing Company, 2001. Print.

Lamont, Peter. "The *Thunderball* Phenomenon." Disc 2. *Thunderball,* Two-Disc Ultimate Edition. Directed by Terence Young. Santa Monica, CA: MGM Home Entertainment, 1995. DVD.

Lazenby, George. Interview by Wesley Britton. *Dave White Presents* podcast, January 7, 2009. Web. http://www.audioentertainment.org /ArchivePage.html

Lee, Christopher. Interview by Chris Tilly. February 10, 2009. IGN.com. Web. http://www.ign.com/articles/2009/02/10/christopher-lee-interview

Lisanti, Tom, and Louis Paul. *Film Fatales: Women in Espionage Films and Television, 1962–1973.* Jefferson, NC: McFarland, 2002. Print.

Macintyre, Ben. *For Your Eyes Only: Ian Fleming and James Bond.* London: Bloomsbury, 2008. Print.

———. "Was Ian Fleming the Real 007?" *Times* (London), April 5, 2008. Print.

Madonna. Interview by Larry King. *Larry King Live.* CNN, October 10, 2002. Web. http://transcripts.cnn.com/TRANSCRIPTS/0210/10/lkl.00.html

Maibaum, Richard. Interview by Lee Goldberg. *Starlog,* March 1983, 24–27. Print.

Malcolm, Derek. "Off-the-Peg Bond." *Guardian* (Manchester), December 16, 1969. Print.

Maronie, Sam. "Some Gentle Evil." *Starlog,* June 1995. Web. http://www .pleasence.com/articles/STAR-6-95.HTML

McLellan, Dennis. "Joseph Wiseman Dies at 91; Actor Played Villain in First Bond Film Starring Sean Connery." *Los Angeles Times,* October 21, 2009. Web.

Melton, H. Keith. *The Ultimate Spy Book*. New York: Dorling Kindersley, 1996. Print.

MI6 (unofficial James Bond website). "Jesper Christensen Will Not Return as Mr. White—'James Bond Movies Are Sh*t.'" February 18, 2010. Web. http://www.mi6-hq.com/news/index.php?itemid=8330

Monty Norman's official website. "The James Bond Theme Story." Web. Accessed March 30, 2012. http://www.montynorman.com/jamesbond /default.asp

Moore, Sir Roger. Interview by Ernie Manouse. *InnerVIEWS with Ernie Manouse*. Houston PBS, July 15, 2005. Web. http://www.youtube.com /watch?v=XOS8sRrd_Oc

Motor News Florida (blog). "The Mystery of the Missing *Goldfinger* Aston." December 15, 2009. Web. Accessed January 27, 2012.

Nashawaty, Chris. "The Greats: Christopher Walken." *Entertainment Weekly*, March 17, 2000. Web. http://www.ew.com/ew/article/0,,275687,00.html

Naughton, John. "Spy Harder." *British Gentlemen's Quarterly* (London), November 2008. Web.

Nelson, Barry. Interview by Lee Pfeiffer. *Cinema Retro* (Dorset, England), September 2006, 23. Print.

New York Times. "Desmond Llewelyn, Actor in Bond Films, Dies at 85." December 20, 1999. Web.

Norman, Monty. Interview by Graham Seaman. BBC Radio Swindon, November 2006. Web. http://www.bbc.co.uk/wiltshire/realmedia /monty_norman.ram

Parker, Barry. *Death Rays, Jet Packs, Stunts and Supercars: The Fantastic Physics of Film's Most Celebrated Secret Agent*. Baltimore: Johns Hopkins University Press, 2005. Print.

Paton, Maureen. "Shaking Off the Bonds of 007." *Telegraph* (London), April 24, 2006. Web.

Paul, Louis. *Tales from the Cult Film Trenches: Interviews with 36 Actors from Horror, Science Fiction and Exploitation Cinema*. Jefferson, NC: McFarland, 2007. See esp. "Gloria Hendry," 90–97. Print.

Pearson, John. "Rough Rise of a Dream Hero: Part II." *Life*, October 14, 1966, 113, 126. Print.

———. *The Life of Ian Fleming*. Kent, UK: Hodder and Stoughton, 1989. Print.

Pesce, Nicole Lyn. "Eva Green and Ewan McGregor Make *Perfect Sense*." *New York Daily News*, February 1, 2012. Web.

Prigge, Steven. *Movie Moguls Speak: Interviews with Top Film Producers*. Jefferson, NC: McFarland, 2004. Print.

Redenius, Doug. "James Bond Gadgets." *Modern Marvels.* History Channel. Directed by Tom Jennings. New York: A&E Television Networks, 2007. DVD.

Rigg, Diana. Interview by Mark Lawson. *Mark Lawson Talks To . . .* BBC4, September 27, 2011. Web.

Russell, Mark, and James Edward Young. *Film Music.* Waltham, MA: Focal Press, 2000. Print.

Scorupco, Izabella. "Scorupco Rising." Interview by Graham Rye. *007 Magazine* Online, 1996. Web.

Scott, David. "James Bond's Amazing Autogyro." *Popular Science,* June 1967, 66–69. Print.

Sessums, David. "Daniel Craig on James Bond: The Man Who Loves Being Bad." *Parade,* October 26, 2008, 4–5. Print.

Shuldiner, Herbert. "James Bond's Weird World of Inventions." *Popular Science,* January 1966. Web.

Siler, Steve. "Double-O Slow? *Car and Driver* Tests James Bond's Rides." *Car and Driver,* November 2008. Web. Accessed March 15, 2012.

Spencer, Kristopher. *Film and Television Scores, 1950–1979: A Critical Survey by Genre.* Jefferson, NC: McFarland, 2008. Print.

Swaine Adeney Brigg website. "SAB Bond." Web. Accessed January 25, 2012. http://www.swaineadeney.co.uk/products/bond_a/index.html

Swanson, Tim. "License to Chill." *Premiere,* November 2005. Web. http://pbfiles.cixx6.com/interviews/Inter034-License_To_Chill.html

Turner, Adrian. *Adrian Turner on "Goldfinger."* New York: Bloomsbury, 1998. Print.

USA Today. "BMW Roadster Meets Bond, James Bond." September 9, 1997. Print.

Variety. Review of *Casino Royale.* December 31, 1966. Web.

Walken, Christopher. Interview by Lawrence Grobel. *Playboy,* September 1997, 51–64. Print.

Wallace, David. "Friends Say It's Love: Long-Time Friend Jill St. John Is the New Woman in Robert Wagner's Life." *People,* August 30, 1982. Web.

Warburton, Nigel. *Erno Goldfinger: The Life of an Architect.* New York: Routledge, 2003. Print.

Weiler, A. H. "Screen: New James Bond." *New York Times,* December 19, 1969, 68. Print.

Zec, Donald. "Big Film . . . Small Fry." *Daily Mirror* (London), December 16, 1969. Print.

Index

The dates in parentheses each refer to a film's initial release. Character names are drawn only from James Bond films, not from the books or short stories.

THE FAQ SERIES

Lucille Ball FAQ
by James Sheridan and Barry Monush
Applause Books
978-1-61774-082-4
$19.99

The Beach Boys FAQ
by Jon Stebbins
Backbeat Books
978-0-87930-987-9
$19.99

Black Sabbath FAQ
by Martin Popoff
Backbeat Books
978-0-87930-957-2
$19.99

James Bond FAQ
by Tom DeMichael
Applause Books
978-1-55783-856-8
$22.99

The Doors FAQ
by Rich Weidman
Backbeat Books
978-1-61713-017-5
$19.99

Fab Four FAQ
by Stuart Shea and Robert Rodriguez
Hal Leonard Books
978-1-4234-2138-2
$19.99

Fab Four FAQ 2.0
by Robert Rodriguez
Hal Leonard Books
978-0-87930-968-8
$19.99

KISS FAQ
by Dale Sherman
Backbeat Books
978-1-61713-091-5
$22.99

Led Zeppelin FAQ
by George Case
Backbeat Books
978-1-61713-025-0
$19.99

Pink Floyd FAQ
by Stuart Shea
Backbeat Books
978-0-87930-950-3
$19.99

Bruce Springsteen FAQ
by John D. Luerssen
Backbeat Books
978-1-61713-093-9
$22.99

Star Trek FAQ
by Mark Clark
Applause Books
978-1-55783-792-9
$19.99

Three Stooges FAQ
by David J. Hogan
Applause Books
978-1-55783-788-2
$19.99

U2 FAQ
by John D. Luerssen
Backbeat Books
978-0-87930-997-8
$19.99

Neil Young FAQ
by Glen Boyd
Backbeat Books
978-1-61713-037-3
$19.99

HAL•LEONARD®
PERFORMING ARTS
PUBLISHING GROUP

31192020343487

Price: ~~...~~ notice.